NATIONAL
WRESTLING ALLIANCE

NATIONAL WRESTLING ALLIANCE

The Untold Story of the Monopoly That Strangled Pro Wrestling

TIM HORNBAKER

ECW Press

Published by ECW PRESS
2120 Queen Street East, Suite 200, Toronto, Ontario, Canada M4E 1E2

LIBRARY AND ARCHIVES CANADA CATALOGUING IN PUBLICATION

Hornbaker, Tim
National Wrestling Alliance : the untold story of the
monopoly that strangled pro wrestling / Tim Hornbaker

ISBN-13: 978-1-55022-741-3
ISBN-10: 1-55022-741-6

1. National Wrestling Alliance — History. 2. National Wrestling
Alliance — Corrupt practices. 3. Wrestling promoters — United States.
4. Wrestling — United States — History — 20th century. 5. Wrestling —
Corrupt practices — United States. I. Title.

GV1195.H67 2006   796.8120973   C2006-904102-4

Editor: Michael Holmes
Production: Mary Bowness
Printing: Transcontinental

This book is set in Adobe Garamond and Trajan

DISTRIBUTION
CANADA: Jaguar Book Group, 100 Armstrong Ave., Georgetown, ON L7G 5S4
UNITED STATES: Independent Publishers Group, 814 North Franklin St.,
Chicago, IL 60610

PRINTED AND BOUND IN CANADA

ECW PRESS
ecwpress.com

TABLE OF CONTENTS

Introduction

Crystallized in the annals of professional wrestling are the glory days of the National Wrestling Alliance, once standing as the most powerful organization in the sport's history. Formed several years after the end of World War II, the NWA bloomed from a modest Midwestern trade agreement into an exclusive syndicate, and its members demonstrated a newfangled methodology and foresight in the hopes of enhancing the industry. Cooperating to define a layered doctrine, regional circuits or "territories," and the streamlining of titleholders, NWA members improved all aspects of grappling. The group appeared to be an honest collection of people serving wrestling's best interests, which, in turn, left the NWA with few detractors.

Over the course of several years, the NWA morphed from a well-intentioned, localized union of promoters into an international conglomerate with an estimated 500 affiliates. Effectively pulling the strings of wrestling's biggest superstars, while providing exceptional entertainment for legions of fans worldwide, the Alliance soon controlled wrestling and its $25 million-a-year revenue. On the surface, there didn't appear to be anything wrong with the NWA's practices.

But by allowing their imaginations to spiral recklessly out of control, NWA members created complex fortresses that steadily punctured holes in the law. Persistent complaints about an illegal monopoly eventually attracted the attention of the Department of Justice, and set the table for a Federal Court case that was supposed to have ended the NWA's exclusive reign. The coalition was shaken to its very foundations, but found a way to survive. Through the hard work of the organization's major supporters, and the dedication of the thousands of wrestlers who traveled the world to meet the astronomical demand for pro wrestling, the Alliance endured.

Loyal fans today acknowledge the NWA's vast tradition, and respect the men and women who were committed to the institution and the sport as a whole. Wrestlers like Lou Thesz, Buddy Rogers, "Whipper" Billy Watson, Danny Hodge, Pat O'Connor, Gene Kiniski, Jack Brisco, the Funk Brothers, Harley Race, and Ric Flair were the heroes who built the National Wrestling Alliance, and for more than four decades, symbolized professional wrestling excellence.

CHAPTER ONE

THE ORIGINS OF
A WRESTLING MONOPOLY

During the 1940s, professional wrestling was predominantly controlled by two shrewd promoters: Tom Packs of St. Louis and Paul Bowser of Boston. Driven by the prospects of making money and increasing their share of the market in the United States and Canada, they presided over a jagged period in the sport's history. Their influence was amplified due to their personal management of the National Wrestling Association (NWA) and American Wrestling Association (AWA) champions, and it was widely accepted that Packs's Bill Longson and Bowser's Frank Sexton were the top two heavyweights in the business.

In many regards, Bowser's status was secondary to Packs's because of the latter's connections to the leaders of the NWA, an impressive gallery of state athletic commission members. The NWA authorized Packs to supervise the direction of their prized championship, which dated back to 1930, and the St. Louis promoter happily seized all of the power that came with such an endorsement. Having officially booked the champion since 1939, he was the catalyst behind the title reigns of acclaimed wrestlers Lou Thesz, Bronko Nagurski, Ray Steele, and Sandor Szabo.

Known as an assertive capitalist, Packs was respected for turning St. Louis into one of the finest wrestling cities in the world. His amazing success, coupled with a czar-like attitude, infuriated many of his fellow Midwestern promoters, and by the early 1940s, a rival movement began to take hold in the region. The outsiders each may have been slow in devising an effective cohesion, but their passion to sustain their operations without having to rely on Packs to send talent or his champion Longson was truly a motivating factor.

Orville Brown was the first major player to declare his independence. A hardworking family man and up-and-coming wrestler, he took a job in Kansas City as a booking agent for promoter George Simpson in 1940. Although he had a farm in the Columbus, Ohio, area and worked regularly for Al Haft, Brown was eager to return to his home state. He wanted in on the business end of wrestling in addition to holding a claim to the heavyweight championship, and on June 13, 1940, he beat Bobby Bruns at the Memorial Hall to capture the Midwest Wrestling Association "world" title. As the territory's principal fan-favorite for the decade to follow, Brown drew great crowds for his matches against dynamic opponents.

Soon thereafter, Brown's booking enterprises expanded to St. Joseph, Topeka, and Wichita. Wichita, incidentally, was the headquarters of Billy Sandow and Maxwell Baumann, a brother tandem who fronted the second group to stray from Packs's syndicate. While Sandow and Baumann had ill feelings toward Brown for running opposition in their town, it was their dislike of Packs's tyranny that spurred their actions in January 1941. Using a colorless derivative of the National Wrestling Association name, the siblings started the National Wrestling "Alliance," a sanctioning body under the control of a handful of businessmen.

To give their immature promotion footing, they gave Packs's champion Ray Steele until February 9 to consent to a match with Roy Dunn, the superstar of their faction, or be stripped of his title. The threat, limited to clubs in Kansas, wasn't overwhelming. Dunn's credentials were respectable, but he had had a tough time making his mark in professional wrestling, and lacked the flamboyance and connections to rise to the top. An AAU heavyweight champion out of Oklahoma A&M, and member of the 1936 U.S. Olympic team, he was impressed by the will of Sandow and Baumann to determine their own course, away from the glitz and glamour of the big shots of grappling.

Possessing an exceptional reputation as a shooter, Steele's nerve and skill could not be questioned. His time was constrained by the National Wrestling Association circuit, and he couldn't afford to squeeze in a ridiculous legitimate match with a former Olympian, especially when it wouldn't have benefited him in the slightest. When Steele failed to sign, the National Wrestling Alliance gave Dunn the title, and Roy was furnished a yellow-and-white-gold championship belt with 200 small diamonds encased in platinum.

It was true that the substantial figures being put up by Bill Longson were enough to create some level of harmony among promoters once separated by their champions. Primarily a heel, Longson drew better than 570,000 fans over his first 58 appearances in St. Louis between 1941 and 1944, was traveling at least 80,000 miles a year, and reportedly earning $50,000 annually. He matched up perfectly with any of the sport's leading grapplers, and shined in bouts against Bobby Managoff, Yvon Robert, Lou Thesz, and "Whipper" Billy Watson.

Despite the achievements of Longson, Sandow and Baumann were still reluctant to kowtow to Packs, even with their audience down because of the war. On April 28, 1942, they had Dunn lose the Alliance title to Ede Virag (Ede Ebner), who, in turn, traded the belt with John Grandovich on August 12 in Topeka, and on October 26 in Wichita. In June 1943, Virag took a booking into virgin territory, Des Moines, for wise entrepreneur Paul "Pinkie" George.

For several years, George had sought a stable moneymaker. He'd enticed AWA champion Maurice "The Angel" Tillet and NWA champion Sandor Szabo to do a handful of sporadic appearances. He imported Brown from Kansas City and Orville exceeded all expectations. Nevertheless, Brown's title claim in Des Moines was ultimately eclipsed by a more valuable piece of hardware, the NWA belt carried by Longson. On July 22, 1942, Brown put Longson over, ending his own reign in Iowa, though Orville returned to Kansas still holding his MWA crown.

Drafted into the United States Army, George served as a lieutenant for five months at Camp Dodge in the quartermaster corps, but an old injury suffered in a car accident kept him from combat. Still in the spirit to promote, Pinkie opened Riverview Park for wrestling in June 1943, and lined up wrestlers from the surrounding area. Jim Londos, a grappling idol, performed in his June 9, 1943, feature against Tom Zaharias.

The following week, Virag toured through with his National Wrestling Alliance title, the first of three showings in Des Moines that summer. But significantly more notable than what took place in the ring was the imprint left on Pinkie by the specialized name of the title he wore. The "Alliance" label was brought to his attention for the first time.

George was persuaded by rumors that wrestling was drawing upwards of 10,000 spectators per event in St. Louis, and immediately tried to obtain topflight athletes from Packs. After all, he'd known Packs for years, and Des Moines was only 270 miles from St. Louis. It made complete sense to share wrestlers. He was optimistic that he could lure Longson back into town, and cognizant that Longson was where the cash was, not Virag.

In the September 1, 1943, edition of his arena program, *The Iowa Sportscaster*, Pinkie announced that Virag was dethroned in St. Louis by Longson, and that it was the second time "Wild" Bill had won the championship. The article mentioned that Longson won the title from Brown in Des Moines "two years ago" (it had really occurred on July 22, 1942) and stated that "Virag held the title less than five months." In reality, he had been champion since October 1942, and was sponsored by Sandow and Baumann for the remainder of World War II. The Virag-Longson match in St. Louis was pure fiction. Pinkie wanted to establish Longson as the champion in his territory, accomplished that, and waited to hear from Packs.

But Packs didn't send Longson to Des Moines. He was busy booking the champion to Houston, Montreal, Toronto, and a network of towns that were essentially making himself and his grappler rich. Dismayed, but not crushed, George was prompted to adopt his own strategies, unperturbed by the happenings elsewhere. He formed yet another major Midwestern troupe working on the periphery of the St. Louis empire.

On November 3, 1943, Pinkie advertised Ray Steele as the National Wrestling "Alliance" World Champion, a mysterious development that likely shocked many of his well-informed customers. Steele's emergence as titleholder came out of left field, and to make matters even more confusing, the previous night in Minneapolis, Ray had been acknowledged as the "former NWA titleholder." No clear understanding of where Steele gained the "NWA" belt was provided, but it was quite obvious that a promoter could appoint anyone he wanted champion.

Seemingly influenced by Virag's tour, George adopted the signature words "National Wrestling Alliance" for his promotion without the direct consent of the name's originators, Sandow and Baumann. At the time, there didn't appear to be much of a backlash, and all parties forged ahead trying, first and foremost, to please their local audiences.

Des Moines was dark to wrestling until January 12, 1944, when Steele was again billed as the Alliance champion. Steele's matches away from Pinkie's territory had no effect on his standing in Iowa. He could conceivably lose every engagement not promoted by George, and still be recognized as a titleholder in the "Hawkeye

State." On May 10, 1944, Steele's reign came to an end when he was defeated by Dave Levin in Des Moines. Six days later, Steele won a rematch in Minneapolis, but, needless to say, didn't regain the title.

Levin was a popular grappler, but he was always on tour with Jack Pfefer and lived in California. What Pinkie needed was a regionally based heavyweight star who could attract crowds to the Coliseum on a regular basis. That's where Orville Brown came back into the picture. George had used Brown sparingly after Orville dropped the unification match to Longson in July 1942. In Kansas City, Levin lost the NWA and MWA titles to Lee Wykoff, and Wykoff was then conquered by Brown. When Brown made his return to Des Moines on November 8, 1944, George booked him as the National Wrestling Alliance champion.

With a humble background, sound wrestling ability, and an entertaining personality, Brown was an ideal fit in George's territory, and Iowa fans embraced his championship claim. A diverse list of challengers ventured through the area and Orville performed and delivered week in and week out. Among his most outstanding opponents were the Swedish Angel, Ras Samara, Bobby Bruns, Kola Kwariani, Ray Eckert, and Ed "Strangler" Lewis. Excitement was generated with Orville on the marquee, and Brown and George became close acquaintances.

Fostered by a need to share talent, George created an elaborate partnership with Brown and neighbors Tony Stecher in Minneapolis and Max Clayton of Omaha. Their arrangement enhanced the caliber of wrestlers for more than eight cities in the Midwest, and formed the foundation for the global National Wrestling Alliance. The quartet remained in the shadows of the nation's leading manipulators, but their fusion served to strengthen their roles in the marketplace.

Of the four men, Stecher was the most experienced. Born Anton Charles Stecher on February 7, 1889, near Dodge, Nebraska, Tony obtained a substandard education, and went to work at a young age on a farm. In January 1912, famous wrestler Dr. Benjamin F. Roller stopped in nearby Fremont and, as he was accustomed to doing, challenged all comers. Tony and his brother Joe, always up for a competition, opted to test the esteemed physician on the mat. Roller tossed them both, but was struck by Joe's — the larger of the two siblings — raw abilities.

Tony turned pro as a middleweight and began logging victories against foes from across the central states. He grappled John Solomon, Peter Fromm, John Svoboda, S.P. Morgenson, Jud Thompson, and Frank Coleman, and by 1914, he had claimed to be the middleweight champion of Nebraska. On October 15 of that year, he added to his laurels with a two-straight fall win over Tom Doctor in Dodge for the Kansas State middleweight title. Similar to the bout Joe would have with

Ed "Strangler" Lewis in 1916, Tony engaged in a five hour and 18 minute contest with Wesley Cobb in Stuart, Nebraska, on April 22, 1914. No falls were secured and newspaper reports stated that Tony led the match.

Although he showed his skills in matches against Clarence Eklund, a distinguished wrestler, Tony's true mission was not on the mat, but at the side of his undefeated brother. Joe, who was four years younger, battled demons off and on throughout his career, and needed a strong-minded second to protect him. Without Tony at his side, he could easily have been abused by devious promoters looking for a profitable mule to kick. Instead, he rose to the top of matdom, becoming one of history's most important pro wrestlers.

The siblings were also best friends. They traveled from coast to coast, with Tony brokering scores of consequential matches from 1917 to 1934. Joe won four claims to the World Heavyweight Title in that period, and dominated rivals using his famed "scissors leghold." A more critical and personal task lay ahead for Tony. At the age of 43, after several failed investments in Nebraska and California, a dejected Joe suffered a nervous breakdown and was hospitalized. Tony arranged for him to be moved to a VA hospital in St. Cloud, Minnesota, where he would attend to his brother's wellbeing until his own death.

Wealthy from his two decades of involvement in wrestling, Tony opened up shop as a promoter in Minneapolis. His inaugural program on February 21, 1933, marked the professional wrestling debut of football hero Bronko Nagurski. Nagurski, trained by Stecher, became a member of the Chicago Bears football team after a fine collegiate career at the University of Minnesota. Remarkably tough, Bronko built a mat routine upon the methods taught by his mentor, but lacked the colorful approach that many of his peers exploited. The populace, nonetheless, reacted positively to Stecher's shows and Nagurski's appearances boosted attendance.

Nagurski shot to the forefront of the Mondt-Fabiani syndicate with Stecher's help, and became world champion with a victory over Dean Detton on June 29, 1937, in Minneapolis. In Los Angeles and Chicago, he drew good houses, and had a second stint as titleholder under the sponsorship of the National Wrestling Association in the early 1940s. Wrestling in some parts of the country was hampered by the general indifference of fans, but Stecher and Nagurski still found a way to earn a bundle of money.

After a number of years as an associate of Tom Packs, Stecher severed his ties in 1943 and recognized numerous heavyweight champions, including Jim Londos, Bobby Managoff, and Bill Kuusisto. In November 1946, Sandor Szabo entered the territory with his "National Wrestling Association" title. The championship did not have a pedigree, but it effectively set up a local crown that held the interest of spectators. In December 1946, the title went to Dr. Len Hall, then returned to Szabo a week later in Minneapolis. Between April and June 1947, he traded the belt with former amateur champion Cliff Gustafson, and with Nagurski in 1948.

Stecher's decisions in Minnesota never conflicted with his talent agreement or hurt the promotions of his allies in Omaha, Des Moines, or Kansas City. The same was true for Clayton, George, and Brown. None of the quartet was undone by their egos or wanted to inflate their individual reputations beyond their respective territories. The group shared an enthusiasm for making money and protecting their businesses, and enjoyed the fruit of their collaboration. Stecher's experience, when combined with Clayton's personality, Brown's wrestling and booking abilities, and George's vision, presented a unique combination, one that stood out from the rest.

Maxwell McKinley Clayton was the third son of Samuel Thomas and Sophia Anna Elmer Clayton, born on April 30, 1896, in Hamilton County, Nebraska. Shortly after his birth, the family settled south of Central City in Merrick, where the Claytons owned a farm. In 1910, when Max was only 14 years old, his father was killed in a farming accident, and he and his brothers picked up much of the labor end of the family farm. At Central City High School, Clayton was a lauded quarterback in 1912–13, and played semi-professional football after attending a couple of semesters at the University of Nebraska.

Nicknamed "Squire," Clayton took a position as the boxing matchmaker for the Grand Island Elks Club and began building his resumé as a fight promoter. He soon hooked up with Omaha boxing maestro Jake Isaacson, and tended to the town's need for stable wrestling as early as 1926. Succeeding a long procession of superb promoters in the city, from Gene Melady to the famed Farmer Burns, Clayton ran the Auditorium on Monday nights and frequently featured the Duseks, John Pesek, Ed Lewis, and women's champion Mildred Burke. The public welcomed his endeavors and Clayton soon expanded to booking throughout Nebraska and up into the Dakotas.

The fifth midwestern wrestling promotion to blossom independently of Packs was started by Packs's former matchmaker, Sam Muchnick. Initially rebuffed in his attempts to secure a license, Muchnick proved that persistence paid off, and in December 1945 he opened up his small-time operation, instigating a fiery battle for St. Louis. In the months that followed, Muchnick received critical support from bookers Stecher, Billy Sandow, Al Haft, and Jack Pfefer, and repeatedly demonstrated his resolve. With the help of grapplers such as Gorgeous George, Frankie Talabler, and Frank Sexton, his crowds grew steadily, and by 1948, he had Packs irritated beyond belief.

Stecher was impressed with Muchnick's drive, and sent Nagurski and Joe

Pazandak from Minneapolis to help pummel Packs. With his boxing ventures on his mind, Tony joined Clayton and Pinkie George to fashion an innovating boxing cartel with the intent of luring prestigious fights to America's heartland. The unnamed guild, which prevented cities east of the Mississippi River from being affiliated, was formed during a meeting in Des Moines on January 18, 1948, where the three men were joined by promoters Bill Colbert (St. Paul), Max Yeargain (Topeka), and Tom McHugh (Kansas City). Clayton was selected chairman.

A comparable wrestling agreement was next on their agenda. That noteworthy symposium was called by Pinkie to the Gold Room of the Hotel President in Waterloo, Iowa, on July 18, 1948. Participating in the conference were George, Clayton, Brown, Muchnick, and Minneapolis matchmaker Wally Karbo, representing Stecher. Staged in conjunction with an evening program of "national importance" at Electric Park, headlined by Brown and Joe Dusek, the meeting created a new version of the National Wrestling Alliance and changed the course of professional wrestling forever.

Launching their coalition under the same designation as George's territorial regulatory body may have been more a matter of convenience than anything else, and surely baffled some devotees. It was clear that the two entities were vastly different. Pinkie was, essentially, the sole booker of the "Alliance" in Iowa. The new fraternity created delegates in an array of states, acting on behalf of dozens of promoters.

The novel statutes were simple in their description, but the directive was crucial. According to the meeting minutes, the following commandments were approved by both those in attendance and Chicago's Fred Kohler, who didn't make the pilgrimage, but consented to the nine principles of the NWA via telegram:

> 1. That this organization be a cooperative group in wrestling, with each member to be free to run his existing territory as he sees fit without the interference of any other member of this group, and at no time to be forced to pay any booking fee to any member of this group or to anyone else.
> 2. That all existing territories run by members of this group be respected and protected by the organization as a whole from any outside invasion of rights. Members of this group to do all in their power to help each other with talent.
> 3. This organization to recognise only one heavyweight, and only one junior heavyweight champion, and champions of and recognized by this group shall at no time demand or get a fee for wrestling bouts acceeding (sic) the usual 10%. It is further agreed: that said champions so recognized shall post a substantial amount of money in escrow to be held as forfeit by the Chairman-President. The amounts to be decided on by vote of this membership.

$5,000 — Amount by Heavyweight Champion — Orville Brown

$1,000 — Amount by Junior Heavy Champ — Billy Goelz

(This forfeit is insurance for this group that said champions will not run out or refuse to defend their title.)

4. All decisions of this group or organization will be by majority vote. Majority decisions will be final and accepted by all.

5. Said recognized champions will not at any time have to pay any member of this group or anyone else any part of the 10% they received from any matches.

6. That both champions have temporary managers, without pay.

a. Temporary manager for heavyweight champion — Merle Christy

b. Temporary manager for junior heavy champion — Fred Kohler

7. The managers must be fair in seeing to it that said champions are equally alloted (sic) in the different territories so that each member receive equal benefit in showing said champions.

8. That this group select a temporary Chairman-President and at the next meeting elect a permanent Chairman-President to preside for a term decided by this group.

Temporary Chairman-President selected — Pinkie George

9. The organization act as their own commission to police wrestling, and any wrestler who does anything detrimental to wrestling, or if any club of this group should suspend a wrestler, the suspension will be accepted by the whole group.

Professing his recognition by the NWA as the "happiest moment of my life," Brown was a crucial element in the union's formation. His promotion in Kansas City immediately acknowledged his claim to the Alliance championship and what was left of the Midwest Wrestling Association, whose "world" title he held at least ten times, merged into the NWA. Brown's influence was vital to the budding syndicate, and his connections to wrestlers from coast to coast constantly brought in fresh talent.

With their intentions down on paper, the parties affixed their signatures as a symbol of their commitment. As Pinkie recounted in a letter to NWA members dated September 9, 1949, he took "unusual pride in the original document." The agreement was special to him personally, and his missive mentioned that when the Coliseum burned down, he risked his life "to rescue the only thing — the document and papers of our group." His remarkable statement was substantiated to some degree in the August 14, 1949, *Waterloo Courier* when the newspaper reported that Pinkie was the last man in the building before it was destroyed, and had saved only "one file."

George's pride as "father" of the National Wrestling Alliance was well known.

In the last fifty years, his importance in the design of the NWA has been downplayed by people who believe the Alliance was an idea spawned out of a St. Louis office. There has also been a continuous string of falsehoods attached to the organization's fabled conception. Among them were that it was conceived on July 14, 1948, and the original meeting was attended by George, Muchnick, Stecher, Brown, Clayton, Al Haft, and Fred Kohler.

Max Clayton lived and worked at the Castle Hotel in Omaha for 17 years. Although he contributed to the meetings in Waterloo and Minneapolis, and was considered one of the Alliance's founders, he was not an official member in 1948–49 because of his bond to the Duseks. The Dusek Brothers were tied into Omaha and the Thesz faction in St. Louis, in competition with the new troupe. Clayton formally enrolled in July 1949 and remained a constituent until his death of a heart attack on July 1, 1957, at age 61.

Unable to make the trip to Waterloo due to prior obligations, Stecher sent his right-hand man, Wally Karbo, and hosted the September convention. His local "National Wrestling Association" championship went from Szabo to Cliff Gustafson on June 22, 1948. In addition to marketing the former University of Minnesota product as champion, Stecher properly mentioned Alliance titleholder Brown in publicity pieces. His loyalty to the NWA was never doubted by any of his peers, despite his refusal to give up Gustafson's claim, and he allowed Cliff to retire as champion on May 21, 1949. From that point, Brown became the one and only heavyweight titleholder in Minneapolis.

In 1952, Tony sold one third of his interest to Wally and his son Dennis Stecher, and began to slowly distribute more and more responsibility to both. On Saturday, October 9, 1954, he traveled to St. Paul with his partners to see a wrestling program, but on the journey back, he lectured Wally and Dennis. "Tony talked a great deal about future plans, telling us how he wanted things to work out. It seems now almost as if he was leaving final instructions," Karbo explained in a report to the *Minneapolis Morning Tribune*, printed on October 11, 1954. Feeling ill, Stecher called his son at three o'clock in the morning on Sunday, and died shortly after Dennis's arrival.

On October 13, 1954, Stecher's funeral occurred at the Wesley Church. The pall-bearers were protégés Nagurski, Kuusisto, Verne Gagne, Butch Levy, Stanley Myslajek, and Pat O'Connor. Promoters Muchnick, George, Kohler, Clayton, Alec Turk, and Ed Don George were also present. Four months after his passing, the Minneapolis business was restructured, with Dennis, his mother Leona, and Karbo splitting dividends three ways.

Stecher was a generous man. The wrestlers he booked were always given a fair shake and his kindness was renowned. He was pals with Jack Dempsey and Joe Louis, and had an excellent rapport with the news outlets in Minneapolis. As a result of his status in the city and his friendship with George Barton, a prominent sports writer for the *Minneapolis Morning Tribune*, notice of his death was printed on the front page of the paper. Few wrestling promoters have been afforded that measure of respect.

After Tony's death, his son Dennis was an active participant both in Minneapolis and the Alliance. Along with Karbo, he maintained the territory's pulse, and drew thousands of enthusiasts by bringing in the biggest names in wrestling. He autographed the Consent Decree, endorsed Dick Hutton over Edouard Carpentier as titleholder, and was a member of the NWA Board of Directors prior to dropping his stock when the tandem of Karbo and Gagne purchased the Minneapolis Boxing and Wrestling Club in 1959. The Stecher family bridged a gap between the era of Frank Gotch and the AWA, and Tony was instrumental in providing the tools Karbo and Gagne needed to run their own operations.

Tom Packs, the source of much of wrestling's angst, fell by the wayside only six weeks before the NWA's creation. Handicapped by financial problems brought on by poor investments, he sold his interests in professional wrestling and his office in the Arcade Building to Lou Thesz, Bill Longson, Frank Tunney, and Eddie Quinn. Thesz listed the purchase price as $360,000 in his 1995 autobiography, *Hooker: An Authentic Wrestler's Adventures Inside the Bizarre World of Professional Wrestling*. However, in two separate letters to Stecher and Morris Sigel, written on August 5, 1949, Sam Muchnick suggested a distinctly different amount. In the correspondence to Sigel, he wrote, "I can't figure how a man will give Packs $35,500 for a promotion and not (have) a piece of paper to show for it."

The transition in St. Louis from Packs to Thesz was seamless, and the heated war with Muchnick didn't miss a beat. A newcomer to the George-Stecher-Clayton partnership, Muchnick was as optimistic about the NWA's prospects as anyone. Still with much to learn, he was eager to dedicate himself to the coalition's growth, and felt more at ease knowing that his association would ensure top grapplers would appear for his company. Add to that the fact that a heavyweight champion of Brown's reputation was also going to make steady appearances, and Muchnick was convinced he could compete with Thesz in terms of popularity.

The National Wrestling Alliance was in its purest form, but was still generally inconsequential in the grand scheme of things. The midwestern pact was important to the individuals involved, but their decisions had little ripple effect beyond their territories. Veteran promoters were more apt to laugh at attempts to interlock franchises into a monopoly than be fascinated by the notion. The ideas were unrealistic, and many expected the NWA to disintegrate within its first year of existence.

In 1948, the Alliance had more going against it than for it, but firm management and the determination of those involved kept the dream alive. The standard agreement was strengthened in September, and the number of members increased significantly. The perks of the organization were becoming clear, and the adoption and application of some of the shadier aspects of the business were attracting all sorts of animated characters. The innocence of the NWA was eventually lost, but no one could have imagined what the Alliance would evolve into, or how it would strangle professional wrestling.

CHAPTER TWO

INTERNATIONAL EXPANSION

The concepts embraced by the officials attending the Waterloo meeting were revolutionary, yet some imagination was required to share the vision. Their idealistic strategy to systematically connect promotions under the banner of one sanctioning body was going to require a concentrated effort. The alliance needed time to establish itself and assure each member that they were all acting on behalf of their federation, and not just for themselves. The members of the National Wrestling Alliance were obvious believers, and their indomitable unit couldn't be shaken from its course. Further unification was in the plans.

Lou Thesz's investment in the St. Louis promotion maintained the same rapport with the National Wrestling Association that Tom Packs enjoyed. That meant he booked the championship and derived cash from gates beyond St. Louis as he, or whoever was titleholder, traveled the country with the prominent belt. The formation of the National Wrestling Alliance had the potential to affect Thesz's earning capabilities by giving safe harbor to promoters looking for an agreement that insulated their territories. The Alliance had an impressive sales pitch, exposing the hazards of operating unilaterally, or without a voice among state athletic commission appointees. If promoters were lured into the sphere of the NWA, accepting their champion, Thesz's title could become irrelevant.

Following the July 1948 gathering, the freshly launched Alliance was represented by members in Des Moines (Pinkie George), Omaha (Max Clayton), Minneapolis (Tony Stecher), Kansas City (Orville Brown), Chicago (Fred Kohler), and St. Louis (Sam Muchnick). Brown's job was to meet expectations in their capital cities, and strengthen their case for potential additions. The difference between Brown and Thesz had to be made clear to the public, especially in St. Louis, where fans traditionally supported the Packs-led Association championship. The confusion of two "NWA" champions not only roaming the Midwest, but appearing monthly in St. Louis, was enough to dishearten an audience who, surprisingly, demanded some level of sanity from wrestling.

The National Wrestling Alliance began to make their intentions public, touting the basic principles behind the cartel. Promoter Jim Downing of Salt Lake City, in early September 1948, announced that the guild was putting a mythical $25,000 behind Brown as titleholder. An article in the September 3, 1948, edition of the *Waterloo Daily Courier* erroneously reported that the "Midwest" Wrestling Alliance was striving toward the betterment of the entire industry, and that members met recently in Wichita to select Brown as their heavyweight envoy.

Downing's imposing endorsement was cited in the November 1948 edition of *The Ring* magazine, but misspelled their champion's name as "Orval" Brown. A puff piece on Brown circulated with an in-depth background story and a list of his achievements. Putting over his attributes and drawing ability, and using every trick of ballyhoo in the book, the leaders of the Alliance promoted Brown as the superior heavyweight champion. Their propaganda was being heard, and Thesz's confirmed advantage in the ratings diminished greatly.

Still laying the foundations of their fellowship, Alliance members met for a second time in Minneapolis at the Dyckman Hotel, which would, essentially, amount to their first annual convention. On Saturday, September 25, 1948, Stecher hosted George, Clayton, Brown, Muchnick, Frankie Talaber (for Al Haft of Columbus), and Bert Ruby (representing Harry Light of Detroit), and changes were made to the NWA statutes.

The minutes of the Minneapolis proceedings stated:

BE IT AGREED

1. That this organization be a cooperative group in wrestling with each member to be free to run his existing territory as he sees fit without the interference of any other member of this group, and at no time be forced to pay any booking fee to any member of this group or to anyone else.

2. That all existing territories run by members of this group be respected and protected by the organization as a whole from any outside invasion of rights. Members of this group to do all in their power to help each other with talent.

3. This organization to recognize only one heavyweight and one junior-heavyweight champion and champions of any kind recognized by this group shall at no time demand or get a fee for wrestling bouts acceeding (sic) the usual 10%. IT IS FURTHER AGREED: that said champions so recognized shall post a substantial amount of money in escrow to be held as forfeit by the Secretary-Treasurer, the amounts to be decided on by vote of this membership. It is further agreed that the Secretary-Treasurer be bonded for the sum of $10,000, the cost of the bond to be paid from the National Wrestling Alliance treasury.

4. This organization, by unanimous vote, decided to recognize Orville Brown as the world's heavyweight champion. It was also decided to hold recognition of a junior heavyweight champion in abeyance until the next meeting of the Alliance members.

5. Orville Brown, the recognized champion of this Alliance, agrees to post $2,500 cash with the Secretary-Treasurer on or before November 1, 1948, and $2,500 each additional time he should defeat a recognized claimant of the title, the money posted not to exceed $10,000 (ten thousand dollars).

6. All decisions of this group or organization will be by majority vote. Majority decisions will be final and accepted by all.

7. Said recognized champions will not at any time have to pay any member of this group or anyone else any part of the ten percent (10%) he received from any matches.

8. It has been approved by this group that the president of the organization act as manager and booker for the heavyweight champion.

9. This organization will act as its own governing body insofar as the conduct and actions of its wrestlers. If any wrestler does anything detrimental to the sport of wrestling, or detrimental to the interests of a promoter, he shall be

suspended by that promoter immediately after he completes his bookings. That promoter shall immediately notify all of the members of the Alliance, and those members shall also bar this wrestler from their territories. The only way he may be reinstated as a wrestler in good standing with the organization is by clearing himself with the promoter whom he injured. When he does so and this promoter notifies the Alliance, this wrestler becomes eligible for further bookings. Notification of reinstatement should be made to the Secretary-Treasurer.

10. A meeting of the National Wrestling Alliance shall be held at least once a year or at any time at the discretion of the President.

11. Upon signing this agreement each charter member will post $100 (one hundred dollars) and $50 (fifty dollars) each succeeding year. Any new members must pay $150 (one hundred and fifty dollars), plus $50 (fifty dollars) each succeeding year. This money to be posted with the Secretary-Treasurer to be used for the operating expenses of the organization.

This agreement signed and agreed upon this twenty-fifth day of September, Nineteen Hundred and Forty-Eight.

Signed by:

P.L. George, Tony Stecher, Max. M. Clayton, George Simpson (by Orville Brown), Harry Light (by Bert Ruby), Sam Muchnick, Al Haft (By Frankie Talaber).

All rules subject to amendment by majority vote of NWA membership.

AMENDMENTS:

Agreement #3 Amended to: Champions to receive 10% of 100% after taxes or 12½ % of 80% after taxes.

Agreement #5 Amended to: Champion to post $10,000 to be held in escrow and the parties to hold escrow money to be picked from the next general meeting, November 1949.

Agreement #8 Amended to: Sam Muchnick of St. Louis to act as booker for the heavyweight champion. Sam Avey book junior-heavy champ.

The charter members of the Alliance were listed as Stecher, Haft, Simpson, Light, Muchnick, and George. Kohler, who consented to the original contract in July, was erased from the register. Simpson was a comember with Brown, basically the "front" and Kansas City promoter, until being replaced by the latter's brother-in-law, Pearl Christy.

There was a definite separation between a genuine NWA "member" and an affiliated "promoter," and the factors that divided them were pivotal. The label "member" signified a dues-paying Alliance booking agent, a broker who controlled the heart of a specific territory. The NWA booker sent wrestlers to promoters within his territory, and earned percentages from house gates. The booker-member was often also a promoter, operating his territory's largest city. In some cases, local athletic commissions prevented promoters from holding a duel responsibility as a booker, and such situations were usually rectified with a subordinate of the Alliance member acting as a licensed promoter or matchmaker. The particulars were resolved in one way or another.

The objectives of the NWA were abundantly clear. The members wanted to eliminate multiple champions and frame guidelines that would cleanse the sport of practices that hindered their success. Their promises were bold, and the weight of the members' collective reputations couldn't make the words stand by themselves. Action needed to be taken, but it seemed, at the time, that more promoters than wrestling fans were electrified by the NWA's oath. Perhaps promoters felt they would have a say in the decision-making, where, previously, they were overlooked by arrogant dictators. Perhaps it was the social connotations, the harmonious attitude that appeared to be flowing through the club. Maybe it was just the finesse of the salesmen pushing the refined diatribe.

On the other side of the fence, Thesz was failing to rally promoters. His full schedule as titleholder made it hard for him to address the clash in St. Louis. Lou couldn't match the NWA's hoopla and back up his stake as champion, or stage meetings building on an innovative system of talent-sharing. The inspirational plotting of the Alliance was being done to shape the business. Still, in its infancy, the NWA was less than intimidating. Thesz wasn't overly concerned.

In fact, the ideas of the NWA were quite preposterous to most veteran outsiders. If a regional cluster of promoters could be dragged down by old school double-crosses and selfishness, how could one believe in a national institution with numerous thriving elements? Monopolies were always the goal of tyrannical forces in wrestling, and one by one, they had tumbled to the mat with devastating results. Independent promoters Billy Sandow and Jack Pfefer were constantly seeking to slice into a syndicate, and the National Wrestling Alliance painted a huge bull's-eye on itself.

In his October 22, 1948, program, Muchnick wrote regarding the Alliance in his column, "In the Ring with Sam Muchnick."

> Many people have asked me about the National Wrestling Alliance, of which group I am a member, and by which organization I was recently honored in being named Secretary and Treasurer. In order to clarify the rumors and stories in circulation about this governing body of wrestling, I will give you the complete outline.
>
> The Alliance was formed with the express purpose of some day having an undisputed heavyweight champion, just like in the days of Stanislaus Zbyszko, Joe Stecher, and Ed Lewis. It was also organized as a cooperative organization so that the promoters in it could help each other in the signing of major talent and to see that the wrestlers are in good condition, and keep the sport on a high plane, both on and off the mat.
>
> The National Wrestling Alliance, by unanimous vote, decided to recognize Orville Brown, of Wallace, Kansas, as the World Heavyweight Champion. Brown's record of the past ten years, his lineal claim, and his willingness to meet all recognized challengers was considered. Standing before the Alliance members, Brown also agreed to post a substantial cash forfeit, making it mandatory for him to meet any outstanding challenger when ordered to do so by a majority of the members.
>
> Personally, I was dubious about voting for Brown because I feel that there are any number of men to be considered for the honor. Tony Stecher leaned towards Cliff Gustafson; Al Haft favored "Ruffy" Silverstein. However, Harry Light, of Detroit, George Simpson, of Kansas City, and "Pinkie" George, of Des Moines, were staunch supporters of Brown.
>
> The Alliance, with affiliations in approximately 20 states and parts of Canada, has really started the ball rolling towards unification of the much-claimed wrestling title, and now has the applications of about six other promoters who wanted to become members of the body.
>
> One important thing about this Alliance is that no wrestler is barred from wrestling in its territory or out of it. No wrestler is told: 'If you wrestle for any promoters other than ours you will be barred.' We feel that the wrestlers are not chattels and may perform for whomsoever they choose. Some of our competitors are using the bludgeon and telling certain wrestlers that if they show for us, they are barred in their respective cities. While those methods are cheap

and petty, we will just go along and mind our own business and two thirds of the nation's mat stars have already agreed to wrestle in the more than 150 cities in the territories of the Alliance members.

Muchnick commented on Pinkie George, Al Haft, Tony Stecher, George Simpson, and Harry Light, finishing with: "I am the newest and youngest promoter in the group and hope with your continued support to succeed as my colleagues in the National Wrestling Alliance have done."

The "In the Ring" testimony embraced an approach that stood in stark contrast to the standard practice of blacklisting, but the compact signed in Waterloo and bolstered in Minneapolis also granted members the authority to suspend wrestlers for acts "detrimental to the sport of wrestling or detrimental to the interests of a promoter."

Alliance members preserved for themselves the maximum power available in their field, the ability to bar a noncompliant wrestler. The so-called blacklist was frequently confused for this general regulation of protocol. Missing a match, or ducking a contractual commitment were infractions that warranted suspensions, and the members of NWA reserved a measure of punishment as a recourse. Their formula wasn't unlike the practices of a state athletic commission or the National Wrestling Association. It should be noted that at the time, banishment by a private entity was considered illegal, while state-run blacklists were routinely tolerated.

Unimpressed by the goals of what he labeled the "Midwest Wrestling Alliance" in his column in the October 25, 1948, edition of *Sports Week Digest-Review-Forecast*, writer Marty Berg ripped the coalition. He suggested the $25,000 forfeit behind Brown was "fictional" and that "participants in this fraud established a set of rules governing their conduct, as well as the pachyderms under their control, which created a monopoly in their territory." Berg deduced that the members of the Alliance would be alienated, short of talent, and that "Orville Brown [would] have to wrestle himself every other night in 'defense' of his title."

Muchnick wrote the following to Jack Pfefer in a letter dated October 26, 1948:

> As I told you, I believe that the National Wrestling Alliance is solid and will work hand in hand. It's a good bunch of fellows and can do big things. I don't want peace, but I don't like war either. I think this country is big enough for all of us and for all of us to make money.

The struggle between Thesz and the NWA was a large obstacle on the road to widespread peace within wrestling. It was known that Lou's allies north of the border in Montreal and Toronto presided over major moneymakers, and would be crucial additions to the Alliance if a pact could be reached. The importance of ending the aggression encouraged a meeting in Chicago in October 1948. There, in an attempt to settle the rivalry, Thesz and his cohorts, Eddie Quinn and Frank Tunney, haggled with Muchnick, Haft, and Brown.

In a November 3, 1948, letter from Muchnick to Pfefer, Sam explained what had occurred in Chicago:

> I guess Wallace [Orville Brown] told you about the pushing around they tried to give me in Chicago — but Tony, Al, Pinkie, and Wallace stuck with me all the way through. The other fellows threw their weight around pretty much. Al just closed a deal which will prove a tremendous benefit to me and all of us. I would rather have him tell you about it himself. They got the old man mad, and he is working. Mr. Thesz popped off a little too much and so did his partners from Canada.
>
> It would be a great thing if Hugh Nichols would come into the Alliance. He is a great fellow. Sam Avey would also be a fine man for it, as he is very honorable. I was surprised that Thesz got up at the meeting and said that he was representing the Texas and Oklahoma territory. I have a denial from Morris' [Sigel] office on this, but I haven't contacted Sam [Avey]. I don't believe Thesz had that right. I feel that in due time, Morris will be with us. Had a nice visit here last week with Doc Sarpolis, and he wouldn't come to the meeting because he told me they prefer to remain neutral insofar as I am concerned.

The Chicago confab didn't produce a resolution to the hostilities, but it did energize the outfit in opposition to Thesz. In St. Louis, Buddy Rogers jumped from the Thesz group to Muchnick, and on November 26, 1948, he gave Muchnick his largest crowd to date — 9,176 people. Thesz had lost one of his best wrestlers to his adversary and the tides were turning.

In the publicity war, Pinkie George discredited the merits of Thesz's championship in the December 24, 1948, edition of the *Waterloo Courier*, saying: "His title claim is the most ridiculous of all. I remember Lou when he used to wrestle for me in Waterloo and was my chauffeur from town to town. Thesz is a nice kid. We even used him in Des Moines in a preliminary or two. He has no basis for a title claim."

Thesz was becoming more and more aware of the promoters leaving his syndicate to join the NWA. A myriad of entrepreneurs were connecting to the faction, and Lou fought fire with fire in Kansas City, Dubuque, Des Moines, and Wichita. Trying to keep his main hamlets — Houston, Dallas, Indianapolis, Memphis, and of course, St. Louis — in line, he was on a brutal schedule and was losing ground each day. The maneuvering of Alliance members was slowly taking a dominant share of the market, and some of Thesz's reliable American partners were considering membership themselves. There was no stopping the momentum of the NWA.

Brown was a credible and popular champion. In the St. Louis press, he candidly challenged Thesz, even putting $10,000 up with broadcaster Harry Caray as proof of his seriousness. He accepted dates in Minneapolis, where he held an opposing claim to that of Cliff Gustafson, the local titleholder. In newspaper interviews, NWA President Pinkie George speculated that the confusion in that town could be settled, probably with a title vs. title match. Meanwhile, Stecher knew Gustafson was planning to retire, and allowed him to do so on May 21, 1949, without compelling him to drop the championship. The Alliance belt took center stage from there.

Negotiations for Brown to expand his traveling circuit beyond his customary stops were underway. In the meantime, Thesz was ready to talk with Muchnick about uniting their promotions. On July 29, George, Brown, Haft, Talaber, Karbo, Muchnick, and Thesz met at the Deshler-Wallick Hotel in Columbus, where it was formally announced that the St. Louis conflict had been settled. To unscramble the title mess, Thesz agreed to wrestle Brown on November 25 in St. Louis, and Haft planned to discuss the prospects of claimant Frank Sexton challenging the winner with Paul Bowser. The Alliance extended membership invitations to Clayton, Kohler, Avey, Tunney, Quinn, Bowser, Sigel, and Joe "Toots" Mondt.

In September 1949, Avey and Kohler joined, and the NWA had nine members. Morris Sigel was the tenth and Clayton the eleventh, after difficulties between the Duseks and Pinkie George were mended. In conjunction with the Brown-Thesz contest in St. Louis, the Alliance's second convention would be convened with promoters from all over the country making arrangements to fly in. The NWA was making remarkable headway.

The month of November 1949 would see the conglomerate achieve great heights, but also face immense tragedy. Founder and heavyweight champion Orville Brown's career as an active wrestler ended in an automobile accident in northwestern Missouri on November 1, 1949. The demoralizing catastrophe shocked the industry and cancelled the unification bout.

In the aftermath of the loss of their heavyweight titleholder, the NWA went into its vital meetings with an even tougher task. In excess of 40 individuals from across the globe attended the open St. Louis convention at the Claridge Hotel during the weekend of November 25–27, 1949. Ed "Strangler" Lewis was named chairman of the assembly, and stressed early on in the proceedings that they would need to select a single champion.

A special championship committee was created, made up of Avey, Bowser, Haft, Quinn, Stecher, Tunney, Johnny Doyle, Bobby Bruns, Joe Malcewicz, and Karl Sarpolis. Ironically, Bowser, who continued to recognize a local "world" champion in New England until 1952, proposed that Thesz represent the Alliance as titleholder in light of Brown's accident. The board agreed unanimously. Thesz was asked for a $2,500 forfeit, retained by Stecher and Haft, and would be booked by Muchnick.

Ten new members were also inducted into the Alliance. Willing to autograph the fundamental pledge of the organization, and responsible for a $150 initiation fee, Bowser, Doyle, Malcewicz, Quinn, Tunney, Paul Jones, Al Karasick, Jerry Meeker, Hugh Nichols, and Roy Welch were admitted into the NWA. George and Haft were reelected, and Muchnick was granted his second stint as secretary-treasurer.

Leroy McGuirk was assigned to the Junior Heavyweight throne, booked by Avey, and liable for a $1,000 performance bond. The membership approved a $25 per member assessment for the Ed Lewis Fund that financed his travels as the good-will ambassador. Delegates from the National Wrestling Association were on hand and merged their ambitions with that of the Alliance. Association constituents, consisting of athletic commissioners, held annual meetings, often at the same time as their counterpart, the National Boxing Association, and picked officers.

Of the recruits to join the NWA, several stood out. Doyle, Malcewicz, and Nichols were veteran California bookers, well established in their territories as promotional kings. Quinn and Tunney furnished a gateway to Canada's top wrestling cities, and Karasick of Honolulu gave the group more of an international flavor. Lewis stood as a chief politician amid the various entities, and the addition of some of wrestling's most prosperous figures gave the Alliance credibility.

Between December 1949 and May 1950, Billy Wolfe, the agent for women grapplers, Ed Don George of Buffalo, and Dave Reynolds of Orem, Utah, were written into the directory. Tunney satisfied his obligations in May 1950, but Quinn failed to remit his introductory payment and endorse the bylaws until late in the year. Bowser was given a pass on signing the NWA agreement due to his continuing recognition of Sexton as champion. And because of various issues, Meeker and Karasick were removed from the index, leaving the Alliance 21 associates in total.

The NWA was now configured to include virtually every major promoter and wrestler from coast to coast. Joe "Toots" Mondt, Ray Fabiani, Jack Pfefer, and Jim Londos were among the notable holdouts. In 1950, Mondt, Fabiani, and Londos banded together in opposition to Kohler in Chicago, along with Leonard Schwartz, who had applied for NWA membership in November 1949 and been refused. Sterling "Dizzy" Davis was also denied membership because of a territorial war with Morris Sigel.

Muchnick was elected to his first term as president at the third annual convention at Dallas's Baker Hotel, from September 7–9, 1950. Sigel succeeded Haft as vice president and Avey was named treasurer. McGuirk became the inaugural NWA "second" vice president, an honor bestowed six months after his wrestling career ended in an automobile collision. New members were Cowboy Luttrall of Tampa, Mike London of El Paso and Albuquerque, and Joe Gunther of Birmingham. The Dallas caucus gave the society 24 members.

A tournament was recommended by the junior heavyweight championship committee to fill the vacancy, and it would be staged in Tulsa. The heavyweight cabinet was impressed with Thesz, and debated whether or not "Strangler" Lewis should accompany the titleholder on a more regular basis. Pinkie appointed a rules committee, and Kohler made a motion in protest that blocked NWA members from working with non-members, which was defeated eight to one. The problems in Chicago were being monitored by the Alliance, and a meeting in Columbus would be convened to try to resolve the feud.

Despite vocal gripes from Kohler, Toots Mondt, commander of Antonino Rocca, was inducted into the Alliance in October 1950. The contributions Mondt and other members were giving his enemy in Chicago showed the cracks in their supposed union, and Kohler felt he had no alternative but to resign. But in January 1951, following a peace accord that satisfied both sides, Kohler and Schwartz were both allowed into the Alliance. Membership increased to 30 with Karasick's readmittance three months later, and with the additions of Rudy Dusek from New York, Sam Menacker of El Paso, and Amarillo's Dory Detton.

The fourth convention was observed September 7–9, 1951, at the Mayo Hotel in Tulsa, and Muchnick, McGuirk, and Avey reprised their positions subsequent to a vote. Ed Don George was nominated first vice president. Six more promoters were approved to membership — Tex Hager (Boise), Don Owen (Eugene), Jim Crockett (Charlotte), Bill Lewis (Richmond), Cliff Maupin (Toledo), and Larry Tillman (Calgary) — giving the Alliance 36 distinct bookers. The applications of Harry Newman, Ted Thye, Al Mayer, and a pair of Cuban promoters, were rejected. Thesz and Verne Gagne, heavyweight and junior champions respectively, were lauded by the individual councils, and Stecher boasted about up-and-coming young grapplers Leo Nomellini, Mike DiBiase, Pat O'Connor, and Ray Gunkel.

Prior to the next annual colloquy, important substitutions in the roster took place. Orville Brown stepped into a member spot, replacing Pearl Christy. Pedro Martinez, based on his purchase of the Manhattan Booking Agency, swapped standing with Toots Mondt in March 1952.

Six committees (heavyweight championship, junior heavyweight championship, membership, rules, grievance, and an "Ed Lewis" committee) were set up by the NWA to handle specific tasks. The panels each had a chairman and meetings could be called at any point, usually at airport hotels to make the best of tight time constraints. In light of the important agendas, the president randomly scheduled assemblies for the main body of the Alliance, and associates made every effort to attend and participate.

Four months after he had attracted the largest gate in wrestling history, Johnny Doyle hosted the fifth conference in Santa Monica at the Miramar Hotel September 5–7, 1952. Muchnick was appointed to his third stretch as president, and Kohler became vice president. McGuirk and Avey were reelected. The membership committee accepted the applications of Bob Murray and Tex Porter of Seattle, Stu Hart in Calgary, and Salvador Lutteroth of Mexico City.

A number of remarkable decisions were made at the Santa Monica convention. Article #3 of the bylaws was modified to insert the recognition of a world light heavyweight champion. Article #14 was changed to include "Mexico," and the annual dues were increased to $100. Stecher, chairman of the heavyweight committee, suggested that a minimum one-dollar ticket fee for heavyweight title affairs be adopted. The members discussed the Leader Dogs for the Blind Fund, and attended a lecture by James Dow regarding an authorized NWA calendar.

The growth of the Alliance was staggering, from 20 members in November 1949 to nearly 40 in September 1952. Every segment of the United States was controlled by a member, and bookers governed all corners of Canada. Lutteroth's admission accommodated Mexican clubs, and full-time operations in Japan were being considered by Karasick, working from the Hawaiian Islands. The metropolitan areas of Chicago, Los Angeles, and New York would be administered by two members apiece, establishing a nucleus for vital telecasts seen across the country.

By 1952, the interconnected booking agencies were frequently demonstrating their cold approach to outsiders, and the NWA deemed any promoter not affiliated to the organization to be, basically, a hostile enemy. Depending on their dispositions, members coped with the arrival of an "outlaw" in their territory with a potent barrage of phone calls to peers and allies up and down the political structure.

In a perfect world, any promoter possessing an inborn spirit and the right mindset for pro wrestling would have been sanctioned by the Alliance, and aided in their pursuit of financial success. Name wrestlers would be made available by the region's lead agency, and everyone would celebrate their collective accomplishments on a daily basis.

But in reality, the NWA was evolving into a system that blocked anyone who didn't abide by the rules they created or fit into their overall scheme. Associates used strong-arm tactics in some instances to get what they wanted, and the formulas for their abuse of power were crafted in stone on a national level. Any outside promoters wanting to use Alliance talent were forced to send ten percent, typically, to their local NWA agent for every show they held, and those terms were not debatable. If a promoter refused to pay, he was isolated, and forced to hire grapplers from the indie pool.

The NWA used a multi-pronged system to restrain outsiders from gaining ground. Controlling the best talent in the business was the key in shutting down independents. Members used contracts to tie up wrestlers and the threat of suspension by state athletic commissions to keep their athletes in check. Their political leverage within those same athletic commissions limited the number of licenses issued to prospective bookers or promoters. Additionally, they locked in venues for pro wrestling in their major towns to exclusive deals.

In the event an opposition troupe was to land a license, arena, and talent, members united and sent their top grapplers to the promoter engaged in the conflict. Muchnick cleared the calendar and gave priority dates for the NWA heavyweight champion in a territory under threat, and often the local booker would schedule shows with premier wrestlers for the same evening an outlaw program was held. Members went as far as sending employees out to tear down posters promoting the opposition's show, or disparaging their product in newspapers.

Verbal and physical threats were not unheard of. The Alliance, while constantly defending its good intentions, included a number of unsavory characters who were not afraid to use malicious tactics to stomp out a rival. Intimidation was regularly used in promotional wars, but some promoters still defied the massive conglomerate and made their way without the NWA's support. Others resorted to lawsuits or retirement.

During the Santa Monica conference, the Alliance celebrated like royalty, and were unfazed by squandering $1,800 on food. They joked and ribbed their comrades, but when it came time for business, discussion turned incredibly serious. A resolution was introduced that suspended (blacklisted) any grappler who failed to adhere to their guidelines, appeared for a non-Alliance booker, or who specifically antagonized a member. No matter what the circumstances were, the ban was respected throughout the NWA.

Johnny Doyle later spoke with Justice Department investigator Stanley Disney about the Santa Monica decree. According to Disney's summary to his superiors on March 8, 1955, Doyle claimed the blacklist was created to discipline "wrestlers who get in bad with one member." Even after being told that it was illegal, members decided to go forward with the initiative. They notified each other covertly, sending postcards with the names of wrestlers they wanted suspended written in red ink. Doyle reported that he had gotten "about 25 to 30 such cards," and alleged that Muchnick was the mastermind behind the list. Interestingly, Muchnick later made the same claim of Doyle.

By March of the ensuing year, the statute was quietly pulled to safeguard the union. In reality, the blacklist proved to be illogical because bookers were always going to use the wrestlers who sold tickets. More often, it was a measure used to bully or coerce the talent and keep them in line. Promoters sought total control and the NWA seemed to be the ideal way to attain every conceivable measure of power.

Despite the negative implications of the NWA's growing dominance and the goings-on behind the scenes, fans were overjoyed with the Alliance product. It was estimated that the business was now making greater than $25 million annually worldwide, and the upsurge was expected to continue. Fans could see the improvements at arenas, and with the growth of the television medium, people of all ages were being entertained by wrestling spectacles nightly.

All members wanted to capitalize on the TV boom to highlight the colorful grapplers they featured in local arenas, but some sophisticated bookers were also able to manipulate their television interests to gain an outstanding advantage outside of their territory, thus increasing their individual influence overall. That, in itself, worked against the balanced union the NWA was striving for. Kohler's Marigold Arena program, for instance, was shown across the DuMont Network's array of affiliated channels from Seattle to New York City, and drew many complaints from fellow members that his TV offerings were hurting local promotions. Semi-national shows were also emanating from Chicago (ABC), Southern California (ABC), and Texas (CBS).

To settle the TV issues, 19 members met in St. Louis and selected a television committee on January 11, 1953. Dave Reynolds vehemently argued that the DuMont feed was hurting his business in Salt Lake City, and the NWA defused the situation with a series of accommodating stipulations. The light heavyweight championship committee named Gypsy Joe titleholder, and gave Pinkie George the job of booking him. Thesz and Danny McShain were applauded for their work as heavyweight and junior heavyweight champions.

Toots Mondt reemerged in Martinez's position months before the sixth annual NWA forum in the Hubbard Room of the Blackstone Hotel in Chicago, September 4–6, 1953. Each of the previously elected officers returned and Muchnick was quoted in the September 7, 1953, *Chicago Daily Tribune*, saying, "this has been the most successful convention in the history of the Alliance." Kohler, chairman of the heavyweight committee, reported on Thesz's labor as champion, stating that he'd appeared in 32 NWA territories. Advisors wanted to restrict Thesz's schedule to three matches a week unless there was special permission from both Lou and Muchnick — in case of an "emergency."

Members also carefully appraised the status of women's wrestling, and continued to stress that female grapplers were not to be booked on the same shows Thesz wrestled. Expressing their dismay with the bad blood between the former husband-and-wife duo of Billy Wolfe and Mildred Burke, members declined to make a judgment in the matter. The membership unanimously ratified a proposal that eliminated any official supervision of women's pro grappling.

The Health and Welfare committee, Kohler, Pinkie, and Ed Don George, presented a report advocating a three-dollar per man, per show premium for insurance benefits for wrestlers, bookers, and promoters. The progressive concept was originally brought up in April during a meeting in Hot Springs, Arkansas, as a way to "make men want to work for Alliance members because of the advantage of the insurance," according to the meeting minutes. The proposal would offer wrestlers protection if they were ill or injured, plus the added advantage of life insurance up to $10,000. Kohler recommended that the NWA evaluate the system for a year, but by a secret ballot, the membership rejected the idea twenty-five to five, evidence that members had no real concern for the well being of their talent.

Japan was a market the Alliance yearned to exploit. Karasick, between 1951 and 1954, invested capital in developing a fervent Japanese audience for wrestling, and crowed about having developed Rikidozan into a wrestling celebrity. He dispatched Bobby Bruns to Tokyo for a show on October 28, 1951, and his group concentrated on helping Asian wrestlers adapt to an "American" style. The Karasick-Bruns-Malcewicz inner-Alliance troupe cooperated with a distinguished theatrical company, Yoshimoto Kogyo Co., Ltd., and intermediary H. Hyashi.

Karasick disclosed, by way of Muchnick, that he was the talent coordinator for grapplers in Japan, and after drawing $68,000 for three programs (February 19–21, 1954), affirmed that "wrestling is there to stay" in his March 3, 1954, letter to the NWA president. Muchnick followed up with a correspondence to Hyashi, notifying him that Karasick was the point of contact, and that "no other booking office has the authority or backing of the National Wrestling Alliance to book matches in Japan at any future time."

With the Sharpe Brothers, Oki Shikina, Lou Newman, and Hans Schnabel, Karasick promoted Japan through 1954, and facilitated, along with Bruns, the creation of the Japan Pro-Wrestling Association (JWA). Directed to a degree by Rikidozan (until 1963) and figurehead president Count Yakeda, the JWA would be the National Wrestling Alliance's Asia affiliate for 20 years. Hundreds of thousands greeted international superstars, and wrestling's popularity in Japan set standards for arena turnout and television ratings. The seeds planted by American emissaries created an entertainment brand that has provided Japanese fans decades of thrilling action.

The rumor mill hit the Civic Auditorium headquarters of Karasick later in 1954, suggesting a Ted Thye and Jim Londos plot to invade Japan with competition. He also believed a contingent led by Mildred Burke was going to undermine what he'd achieved in Japan, perhaps kill wrestling entirely. The NWA was obliged to answer Karasick's plea for assistance, and denied Londos's request for wrestlers. Thesz made 14 dates in Honolulu for Karasick from August 1952 to October 1955, and bucked claims by Londos that he was the heavyweight champion. Lou also wrestled in Mexico City, Guadalajara, and Havana, doing much to spread the credibility of the NWA.

The 1954 annual gathering, held from September 3–5 at the Claridge Hotel in St. Louis, was attended by Muchnick, Brown, Avey, Clayton, Crockett, Wolfe, Welch, Mondt, London, Jones, Hart, Hager, Lutteroth, Reynolds, Quinn, Nichols, Tunney, Murray, Menacker, Karasick, Owen, Gunther, Haft, Pinkie, Don George, London, Dusek, Malcewicz, Detton, Maupin, Jim Barnett (for Kohler), Jack Britton (for Light), Wally Karbo (for Stecher), Frank Burke (for Sigel), and George Linnegan (for Bowser).

Chairman of the membership committee, Clayton tendered the applications of Cal Eaton and Rod Fenton, which were accepted unanimously. The submissions of Nick Gulas, Gorilla Ramos, Ed Contos, Ray Fabiani, and Pedro Martinez were rejected. Members were against any filming of matches, and banned it after existing contracts ended. There was a brief conversation about changing the organization's name to the International Wrestling Alliance, but the idea was discarded.

Thesz was praised by the heavyweight committee, led by Tunney, and it was determined that when a new champion was recognized, he would have to post more money in escrow than Lou had. Members wanted Thesz to wrestle four times a week, and agreed that the territory he was arriving in should always pay his expenses. Titleholders Baron Leone and Frank Stojack were congratulated for their accomplishments and for meeting all requirements. Officer rank went to Tunney as first vice president, McGuirk second, Avey treasurer, with Muchnick reelected as president and secretary. Barnett acted as the recording secretary.

By this time, the traditional territories of the Alliance were, for the most part, well established, but members still found reasons to bicker. There were disputes over the ownership of certain towns, leaving Muchnick and the grievance committee to arbitrate dozens of minor skirmishes. These tedious episodes included a northeastern clash for Lancaster and Camden between Quinn, Dusek, and Mondt; a hassle in Lawton, Oklahoma, between McGuirk and Detton, and the booking of Antonino Rocca by Mondt into Iowa for a rival of Pinkie George. Complaints streamed in like clockwork to the NWA headquarters, and each situation was addressed on a case-by-case basis.

The eighth annual NWA conference was held September 2–4, 1955, at the Claridge in St. Louis. After the resignations of Ed Don George, Bob Murray, and Dory Detton, the outfit dropped to 35, and eight members (Avey, Dusek, Lewis, Sigel, Malcewicz, Owen, Menacker, and Karasick) were not available to participate in the convention. In memory of Tony Stecher, who passed away in October 1954, the membership observed a moment of silence.

Martinez, Billy Watson, and Karl Sarpolis were admitted to the NWA, but Henry Irslinger, Pat O'Dowdy, and Joe Marshall were not. As per to previous years, the heavyweight committee lauded Thesz for his work as champion, but Muchnick acknowledged recent criticisms of Lou, specifically because he'd booked himself during an off week. Pinkie George led a motion to reelect the same executives and the body agreed. Furthermore, he recommended the naming of a third vice president, and Lutteroth was unanimously selected to the position.

Much of the discussion during the seminar revolved around a justice department investigation into the NWA for antitrust violations, a problem two years in the making. Spurred by rampant accusations of monopoly, the inquiry was expanding quickly and a crucial decision had to be made as to whether or not the Alliance should disband completely. An open vote took place, and there was a unanimous verdict to continue. Members received detailed advice from NWA attorney Harry Soffer, and recommendations from Muchnick on how they could proceed without blatantly breaking the law. The organization had peaked, and the Alliance was looking over a cliff with no where to go but down.

CHAPTER THREE

THE UNDISPUTED CHAMP

Lou Thesz

The goals of the National Wrestling Alliance would have been incredibly difficult to reach if one man hadn't stepped up to carry the heavyweight championship with the clear credibility Aloysius Martin "Lou" Thesz did beginning in November 1949. The idea of a national syndicate was almost laughable in the world of wrestling. Promoters knew that it had been tried previously, and always crumbled under the weight of greed. The core of the Alliance understood that they needed to reestablish faith in a single titleholder among the wrestling fan base. Thesz ascended to the throne, and from the moment the membership endorsed him as champion, until the day he lost the strap to Billy Watson in March 1956, he brought honor to the title.

Thesz led the NWA over innumerable hurdles with his hard work and dedication. He wasn't a huge crowd favorite, but he easily set a high standard for a touring world champion. In a universe governed by gimmicks and scoundrels, Thesz was a principled man playing a dirty game. He faced them all on the mat and in the dressing room, exposed the weaknesses of those trying to test him, and protected the coveted championship internationally. He raised the NWA world heavyweight title onto a distinguished plateau and was admired by peers, promoters, and fans.

Martin Thesz (1888–1970), Lou's father, arrived in the United States on March 16, 1907, when the *Carpathia* docked at Ellis Island from Carnaro, Triest, Austria. The 18-year-old shoemaker of Hungarian and German descent put down roots in St. Louis, and married Austrian-born Katherine Schultz (1892–1989). They had two daughters before migrating to Michigan's Upper Peninsula and Menominee County, near the boyhood home of Gus Sonnenberg. They settled in an Austrian community, Holmes, in 1915, where Martin labored on a farm. On April 24, 1916, a third child was born, a son named Aloysius, and they had a daughter a year later.

During the early 1920s, Martin and his family moved back to St. Louis. He opened a shoe repair shop, and his children went to area schools. Martin intrigued his young son with his Greco-Roman wrestling experience. That, combined with the abundance of competitive wrestling taking place along the banks of the Mississippi in Missouri and Illinois, heavily influenced Lou. For those who didn't attend wrestling programs regularly, the sports pages of newspapers provided thorough accounts of the wrestlers and matches taking place. Martin would take his son to shows, where Lou's vision of wrestling changed and a deep interest seized his soul. His path was set and he began to learn from the bottom up.

The St. Louis Arena, or the Coliseum, wasn't the place for a neophyte to make his reputation. Thesz, at age 17 and weighing 180 pounds, first grappled at the Ardison Hall with Eddie Piantanida on April 5, 1934, in Collinsville, just over the Illinois border. After ten minutes and fifteen seconds, he was pinned. The referee was Joe Sanderson, a veteran who became one of Thesz's earliest ring tutors. Lou returned to Collinsville, from his parents' home off Virginia Avenue in St. Louis, on April 24 and beat Ben Bailey in 8:15. The *East St. Louis Daily Journal* listed him as "Louis Phesz." On June 27, he debuted at the Social Center on Summit Avenue in East St. Louis for Raymond M. Gunn, a reverend for the Episcopal Church. That night, he fought to a 30-minute draw with William "Billy" Scharbert, Gunn's regional hero. Scharbert trained with Ray Steele (Peter Sauer) and Gino Garibaldi (Sam Curcuru) at the Rock Springs Athletic Club, and was also a student of Sanderson.

Earl Brady, who'd seen hundreds of wrestlers as a timekeeper in St. Louis, was a sports writer for the *East St. Louis Journal* at the time, and was impressed by the size and strength of Thesz. There was already an obvious difference between Lou and the others competing at the Social Center, and if anyone was going to break out as a star, it would be him. His second showing at Gunn's facility on July 11 was in the main event, and he was victorious over Walter McMillan in 28:57. Two weeks later, he beat Piantanida. Thesz was in the midst of his first push, but undeniably unprepared. Sanderson had provided the essential tools of the trade, but there was another man in St. Louis who would take Lou to the next level.

Wrestling in St. Louis during the mid-1930s was exceptionally vibrant and all the top heavyweights made a fortune appearing for promoter Tom Packs. In the midst of the prosperity, there was a well-known, but publicly unheralded wrestler employed by Packs noted for grinding and stretching opponents on the mat. He was George Tragos, a genuine shooter. Tragos lurked in St. Louis gyms, and as a light heavyweight, failed to shine amidst the colorful antics of his peers. Like many disciplined athletes, Tragos wouldn't modify his style to fit the needs of promoters.

Born on March 14, 1897, in Katsarou, Greece, Tragos ventured to the U.S. to join his father Bill (Vasili), brother Christ, uncle George, and cousin James in Chicago. He arrived at Ellis Island on the *Martha Washington* on March 28, 1910, and took work as a packer in a factory. Tragos was a fan of conventional wrestling, and widened his repertoire of Greco-Roman and catch-as-catch-can grappling while studying under Gary, Indiana, YMCA physical director George Pinneo. During the amateur wrestling season, he toiled in the Illinois Steel plant as a machinist, participating in meets at night. Tragos won both the AAU and YMCA championships in March 1919 at 158 pounds. He reportedly sailed abroad, and was a member of the 1920 Greek Olympic wrestling team in Belgium.

Tragos went pro and coached wrestling at the University of Missouri. Basing operations in St. Louis, he trained with a host of wrestling headliners including Ed "Strangler" Lewis, Joe "Toots" Mondt, Joe Stecher, and Jim Londos. Packs recommended him to Thesz, and the harsh instruction commenced almost immediately. Nothing came easy to Lou, and Tragos wasn't about to coddle his green protégé. The workouts were intense and drew out the best from the budding St. Louis wrestler. Thesz began to tour as a professional and quickly earned respect as an up-and-comer. A novice to the road, Lou did his time as a rookie, met some trustworthy people like Ray Steele, who would foster his growth, and learned the good and bad about promoters.

The good was Pinkie George and Tony Stecher in Iowa and Minnesota. The bad was Toots Mondt in Southern California. Thesz's stay in Los Angeles started in May 1936, and after a little more than a month, he found the conditions unbearable. He vacated the territory for San Francisco, his opinion of Mondt forever tainted. It was in the Bay Area that Thesz met legendary hooker Ad Santel (Adolph Ernst, 1887–1966). Santel had been involved in wrestling for 30 years, and was promoting in Oakland when he encountered the eager Thesz.

Santel spoke about Thesz during a phone interview with a wrestling-smart columnist for the *San Francisco Chronicle*, Will Connolly, for a February 24, 1953, column: "I tried him out in the Athens Club gym before I booked him. There wasn't much I could teach him. He followed the old style of catch-as-catch-can of my day. He was fast, strong and shifty. What I liked about him then was his ability to 'tear away.' I couldn't keep a hold on him, and I wasn't so old."

Thesz humbly became a student of wrestling, and took pride in his gymnasium sessions with Tragos, Steele, and Santel. He was the quintessential athlete, striving to be the best he could be. With mounting confidence, Thesz returned to St. Louis and figured into Packs's system as an undercard performer. The hometown boy was given an opportunity to win the hearts of local fans, and was successful after months of buildup. Smelling higher profits with the talented fan-favorite, Packs negotiated with Billy Sandow, boss of Missouri Athletic Commission heavyweight kingpin Everette Marshall, and sold the idea of giving the championship to Thesz.

On December 29, 1937, at the Municipal Auditorium in St. Louis, Thesz beat Marshall by countout in 53:48 and won his first "world" heavyweight title. Lou's father watched from ringside as his son won the crown before a throng of 7,534. Needless to say, Thesz wasn't an undisputed champion. Bronko Nagurski, the football luminary, held a version of the championship, and when Thesz won the crown, promoters in Chicago and Denver shunned the Marshall-to-Thesz lineage, and recognized Nagurski. But there was a reason.

The *St. Louis Globe-Democrat* referred to Lou's tilt as being for the "AWA" title, referencing the only current organization of that name, the sanctioning body of Paul Bowser of Boston. Bowser stripped Yvon Robert of the belt in his territory on January 25, 1938, and Thesz journeyed into New England as champion. The move saved Robert from having to job the title, but Thesz wouldn't have the same luxury.

In the eyes of Bowser, the brains of the unit, Thesz was nothing more than an interim titleholder. He had an Irishman in the wings who, he hoped, would whip his territory into a frenzy and generate buckets of loot. Bowser's purchase of the title left the promoters who supported Marshall out in the cold. On February 11, 1938, in Boston, Lou dropped two-of-three-falls to "Crusher" Steve Casey at the Garden, and lost the title. Thesz felt the sting of political maneuvering, and was not pleased.

Looking less and less like a pawn, and more like a knowledgeable player, Thesz coped with the ugly side of promoters trying to capitalize on his inexperience. That side of wrestling bothered him, and he longed for a day when he called more of the shots. The fact that he was so committed to learning how to actually wrestle, and absorbed the advice of Tragos, Santel, Steele, and Ed "Strangler" Lewis, gave him the knowledge and acumen to rise above the pack. As a shooter and hooker, Thesz's standing as an authentic grappler built to the point where he was a feared opponent.

At six-foot-two and weighing as much as 230 pounds, he was very agile, and willing to leave a mark on an opponent if necessary. In a field where reputations preceded you in dressing rooms far and wide, Thesz was a polished warrior who could break a man in two if pushed the wrong way. By 1939, universal acceptance of Thesz as a leading draw was being negotiated, and publicity in St. Louis sold him as a wrestler with few equals. His ethics, passion, and ability would prove that to be true.

The opponent conquered in Thesz's second world title victory was again the man from La Junta, Colorado, Everette Marshall, and the bout took place on February 23, 1939, in St. Louis. Within months, Packs and Tony Stecher arranged to transfer the strap to Nagurski, and Thesz did as he was directed.

Deals were brokered, and in board rooms, not legitimate contests, promoters decided champions. In a straight competition, Thesz would have administered a sound beating to NFL Hall of Famer Nagurski, but on June 23, 1939, at the Houston Coliseum, Lou made Bronko appear the master. Unfortunately, during the second fall, Thesz fell from the ring and suffered a fractured kneecap. Possessing the guts to tough it out, he trudged his way through the finish and passed the belt to Nagurski. Early examinations suggested he would be incapacitated for three months. Those predictions were accurate, and he returned to wrestling on a semi-regular schedule by the middle of September.

Thesz broadened his horizons to Toronto and Montreal. In Eddie Quinn's realm, he captured the regional "world" title on June 12, 1940, with a victory over Leo Numa. He lost the belt to Yvon Robert on October 23. Unfit for military service due to his weakened knee, Thesz worked as a superintendent for the Todd-Houston Shipbuilding Corporation at Bend Island in Houston, acting in aid of the war effort. The need for soldiers in the defense of the country continued to deplete the wrestling ranks, and in 1945, Thesz's physical condition met the standards of the U.S. Army, and he was drafted.

After taking of the oath at the San Antonio Reception Center, Lou was sent to Fort Lewis, south of Tacoma, Washington, for his initial instruction. Identified as a wrestler, Thesz's medic training morphed into a role as a coach of hand-to-hand combat, a position many wrestlers assumed, and he barely escaped a tour of duty in Japan. Although he wrestled when he had the occasion in the Northwest, or on furlough, Thesz didn't return to the professional ranks full-time until his discharge in July 1946.

The marketplace was ruled by the championship of the National Wrestling Association and the reign of "Wild" Bill Longson during the war. Longson, a dominant box-office heel, was at the top of a short list of principal headliners that also included Whipper Watson, Yvon Robert, and Bobby Managoff. Thesz reemerged into the wrestling limelight in 1946, and was part of the exclusive collection of grapplers that the NWA and Montreal world titles revolved around.

The departure of Packs in June 1948 gave Lou the chance to monopolize the NWA championship. He pooled his resources with Tunney, Quinn, and Longson to acquire the lucrative St. Louis business and control the booking of the heavyweight title. The title was the valuable ingredient in the transaction and the consortium netted a percentage of the champ's income wherever he wrestled. Since they dictated the course of the title, it could easily be manipulated to suit their interests.

On the books, Lou's father Martin owned 90 percent of the newly incorporated Mississippi Valley Sports Club, while Tunney and Quinn held 5 shares each. The documents were signed before a notary on June 15, 1948, in St. Louis by Thesz, Tunney, and Quinn, and were filed with the Missouri Secretary of State under a fictitious name on December 23, 1948. The factual financial summary had Fredda Thesz, Lou's wife, holding 55 percent of the company's shares, the spouse of Longson, Althea, owning 35, with ten divided between the two Canadian promoters.

Eager for improved numbers in St. Louis in the promotional war against Packs's former assistant Sam Muchnick, Thesz won the association title from Longson on July 20, 1948, in Indianapolis. Just days prior to the title switch, Muchnick met with key Midwestern organizers and formed the National Wrestling Alliance, a private fraternity that was projected to grow. The potential expansion of the Alliance was distressing to Thesz, especially if promoters in cities he relied on jumped sides. In St. Louis, he brought in wrestlers from all major booking offices, including Primo Carnera, Antonino Rocca, the Duseks, Sandor Szabo, and Enrique Torres.

Thesz was an acquaintance of two of the Alliance's founders, George and Stecher, and was fond of them, but his desire to maintain his St. Louis office overruled a potential merger. He reached out to friends and assured himself that he could endure a hostile fight. Harsh words were exchanged and it was apparent that the St. Louis conflict would split the sport into halves. Muchnick knew a unification of their promotions was best for the wrestling business, but was content in how things were progressing.

The National Wrestling Alliance recognized Orville Brown as world heavy-weight champion. Brown was comfortable with his wrestling proficiency, but Thesz believed he could beat Orville in a straight match. The St. Louis press began investigating their respective title claims, and sparked a debate as to who would prevail.

Morris Sigel, a Houston promoter with loyalty to Thesz, was being solicited for membership in the NWA. Sigel saw the advantages of the Alliance, and heard propositions from both groups. That July, by coincidence, Thesz and Muchnick were in Houston at the same time. The Houston-Dallas charter was crucial to Thesz, and Muchnick's touting of the Alliance was making headway from coast to coast. Exhausted by the latest round of critical diplomacy, Lou asked for a meeting with Muchnick, and the walls came down.

Specific terms were approved, and the divide in St. Louis was healed. Shareholders were compensated by the monetary success of two separate wrestling promotions, the Mississippi Valley Sports Club and Muchnick's enterprises, as well as a valuable booking agency. The deal was finalized by mid-August 1949, and benched Bill Nelson, Thesz's matchmaker.

Heavy consideration was given to whether Thesz or Brown should go over in the planned unification contest. Before the championship match could be staged, Brown was nearly killed in a car accident and subsequently retired. The National Wrestling Alliance met in St. Louis, and on November 27, Thesz was declared world champion by a unanimous vote. From 1949 to 1953, the coalition grew to more than 30 associates in the United States, Canada, and Mexico, representing hundreds of promoters. This gave Thesz an expansive wrestling circuit in which to defend his belt, and the prominence of the Alliance strap grew more than any wrestling championship in decades.

Thesz's stamina as a traveling champion surpassed expectations, and booked by Muchnick, he went into cities of all sizes. Thesz was able to produce an engrossing match with an array of diverse opponents, and carried himself like an elite dignitary, wearing suits to and from the dressing room. Adhering to a high standard of professionalism, he had the skill and integrity of a champion who measured up against contemporaries in other sports.

As American families began to bring televisions into their homes in the late 1940s and early '50s, station managers discovered wrestling was a popular weekly series. The appeal of wrestling on TV helped spread Thesz's fame. Gates grew in many cities, especially in the three major markets: Chicago, New York City, and Los Angeles. Thesz, in his journeys, visited arenas throughout North America, Hawaii, Mexico, and even Cuba. Walking the line between face and heel, Lou marched forward and tried not to disappoint the paying public.

A highlight of his six-plus year run as NWA champion was his May 21, 1952, bout with Baron Michele Leone at Gilmore Field in Hollywood. Thesz and Leone, after months and months of aggressive advertising, drew 25,256 fans, paying a record $103,277.75. The match lasted three falls, Thesz taking the first and third, unifying the Pacific Coast title with the NWA strap. For the 42 minutes of grappling, Lou earned $9,000. Thesz and Leone did good business in several towns, but a growing animosity silenced a long and profitable feud.

Santel gave his estimation of Thesz and his drawing power in Connolly's column in the February 24, 1953, edition of the *San Francisco Chronicle:* "Most promoters would rather have somebody else the champion," Santel admitted. "Thesz is dull. I can think of 20 others who are better showmen, and not bad wrestlers either. But they can't beat him. He is a throwback to the days when wrestling was on the mat, not on the feet."

Regardless of some opinions, Thesz was appreciated by the heavyweight championship committee of the National Wrestling Alliance, which scrutinized gate figures annually. There were always naysayers who complained under any circumstances. Particularly if they felt money was being lost, or that business could be boosted with someone else in the spot. Opinions among NWA members differed, but where it counted most, the leadership of the organization believed in Thesz and his sportsmanship. They loved his dedication to their title.

In early 1955, future National Football League Hall of Famer Leo Nomellini was the beneficiary of a slick move that diced the title in an attempt to enhance attendance. This was two years before the Edouard Carpentier calamity blew up in the NWA's collective mug, and the first time Alliance members adopted a gimmick that called into question the purity of their precious championship. At the time, Nomellini was a noted football player for the San Francisco 49ers and a star grappler. His March 1955 match with Thesz was a carefully crafted ploy, and not a random shoot ending in confusion.

Leo Joseph Nomellini was the oldest child born to Paul (1888–1943) and Julia P. (1901–1990) in Lucca, Italy, on June 19, 1924. Around 1927, Paul and Julia returned to the United States, settling in Douglas, Illinois, where Paul worked in a candy store to provide for his family. Paul had been a citizen of the U.S. since 1905, and patriotically served in World War I. In 1934, the Nomellini clan migrated to Chicago, but Leo ignored football at Crane Technical High School.

Like his father, Nomellini went off to serve his country, and while in the Marine Corps at Cherry Point, North Carolina during World War II, the six-foot-three-inch accomplished piano player was courted by coaches to play college football.

Bill Hopp, on behalf of the University of Minnesota, recruited him, and after spending 19 months in the South Pacific, Leo reported for duty to Bernie Bierman on the football fields of the North Star State. Nomellini was a tackle or guard and became a two-time all-American, unanimously selected in 1949. He earned a long list of football achievements and was selected eleventh overall by the San Francisco 49ers in 1950 — the new team's very first draft pick.

The athletic capabilities of "Leo the Lion" were not limited to the gridiron, as Nomellini demonstrated an aptitude for wrestling while at Minnesota. In 1950, he placed second to Ohio's Bill Miller with a loss by referee's decision in the heavyweight finals of the Big Ten Tournament. Trained by Verne Gagne and Tony Stecher, Nomellini debuted as a pro wrestler, and his jaunt to San Francisco put him in the backyard of one of wrestling's most sincere promoters, Joe Malcewicz. To hone the skills of his grappler, Malcewicz brought in Bronko Nagurski to mentor Leo, and the Bay Area fans responded in droves to Nomellini's ring exploits.

Prior to the 1955 match, Malcewicz staged two Thesz-Nomellini title bouts, drawing 7,200 and a gate of $25,509 to the Winterland on February 24, 1953, and on June 16, 1953, bringing in a record 16,487 fans with a gate of $52,000. Both exhibitions were well advertised and gave wrestling a great boost on the West Coast. Thesz won the initial match in two-of-three-falls while Nomellini held the titleholder to a one-hour draw in the second.

The public was eating up the hype going into a third contest, and another five-digit gate was anticipated. Three years earlier, some Alliance members believed the NWA had missed an opportunity by not maximizing the potential of the Thesz-Leone feud. Hollywood, of course, drew wrestling's first $100,000 gate, and several other cities did ample numbers with the bout, but a minority opinion in the Alliance wanted Leone to beat Thesz at Gilmore Stadium, setting up a series of rematches nationwide. While Thesz wasn't going to consent to such an idea in 1952 with Leone, he was a little bit more open to the Alliance's unconventional strategies in 1955, and when a plan to manipulate the finish of his match with Nomellini was concocted, he was all ears.

Thesz wasn't going to be pinned by Nomellini. Nor would he even lose his championship. The arrangement would be handled in such a way that both men would leave the San Francisco ring with a claim to the title, leaving the door open for matches anywhere in the Alliance. The scheme was hatched well in advance by Malcewicz, chairman of the championship committee, Thesz, Nomellini, and NWA president Sam Muchnick, and circumvented the official rules to make a few extra bucks. Or so they hoped.

As expected, San Francisco fans responded in droves with 12,253 customers paying $41,607.53 to see the Cow Palace program on March 22, 1955. Thesz won the opening stanza in a little less than a half-hour, and Leo captured the second by countout in 10:30. The third fall saw Lou repeatedly kick Nomellini from the ring apron to the floor, while the irate patrons yelled riotously, and the referee gave warnings. Enough was enough, and Thesz's actions warranted a disqualification at the 11:16 mark.

Referee Mike Mazurki named Nomellini winner and proclaimed him the new champion. The California Athletic Commission concurred, endorsing the football great despite the vehement protesting of Thesz and his manager Ed "Strangler" Lewis. The angle sold terrifically in the area, and local newspapers provided top-to-bottom coverage of all the hysteria, including a formal decree from NWA member Malcewicz that he was claiming the championship on behalf of Nomellini no matter what the Alliance officially decided.

The National Wrestling Alliance concluded that Thesz was still the rightful champion, because the belt couldn't be lost on a disqualification. Nevertheless, word of Thesz's defeat shot across the wires, and was written about in newspapers large and small. Stories suggested that it was Lou's first loss in 937 matches.

Breaking the monotony was also a key factor in the decision to run Nomellini as a secondary heavyweight titleholder on the Alliance circuit, and many envisioned Leo generating a wealth of excitement. The day following the controversial San Francisco bout, since, technically, the championship hadn't officially changed hands, Muchnick resumed booking Thesz as the legitimate titleholder. At the same time, Muchnick commenced scheduling dates for Nomellini, the new, disputed champion.

For every show in which he appeared, Nomellini earned 12½ percent of the net and kept seven. Muchnick and Malcewicz got two percent each, while the remaining one and a half went to expenses. Nomellini traveled through a number of territories: Texas, the central states, and upper Midwest among them, and the friction between conflicting champions was evident in press reports. But the projected boost in crowds across the board was missing and Muchnick quickly voiced his dismay at the lack of interest among members in booking Leo.

Given its so-called commandments and the stunning amount of effort and time it took to create undisputed champions, there was an assumption that the Alliance was going to protect the honor of its titles first and foremost. While people might not have seen it at the time, the NWA clearly demonstrated in the Nomellini affair that their heavyweight championship was nothing but a prop — a revelation that showed the organization's hypocrisy. The title's integrity had been compromised as members tried to make a fortune off the angle, but instead did little but undermine Thesz's standing with the public.

Thesz-Nomellini was apparently a feud that wasn't going to sell outside of San Francisco, and there was never really a return payoff. The idea was ultimately scrapped. Muchnick announced in his NWA Bulletin #10, dated July 19, 1955, that "Lou Thesz defeated Leo Nomellini in St. Louis on Friday, July 15, thus erasing any taint that might have been connected to the heavyweight title as recognized by the NWA."

From 1950 until January 1, 1956, "Strangler" Lewis was employed as Thesz's manager, and the two traveled together constantly. Handling numerous functions as Lou's second, mostly as a publicity hound, Lewis advised the titleholder and still had an obvious love for wrestling after 40 years in the business. He earned 2½ percent of the proceeds of every match the champion participated in, a tidy sum he depended on.

Lou and his father Martin sold their stock in the St. Louis office to a combination of individuals in December 1955, and their interest concluded on December 30 with a show at the Kiel Auditorium. Wrestling "Nature Boy" Buddy Rogers on that occasion, Thesz won by disqualification when his challenger refused to break a hold. For an average of 175 dates a year, Thesz's income had been $50–60,000, far less than typical reports that put him in the six figure category. His percentage of St. Louis business had supplemented his earnings since 1948.

Promoters that obtained bookings for Thesz paid him 15 percent of the gate after taxes, for which he personally collected ten percent (increased to 11 in 1956). The outstanding five points went to the president's office and Lewis. Thesz dealt only in cash, and demanded a statement from all programs with complete analysis of house numbers and deductions. Beginning in September 1955, the bookers themselves sent checks, made out to the National Wrestling Alliance and covering the extra five percent, to St. Louis. Muchnick relayed the money to treasurer Sam Avey in Tulsa, who deposited the funds into the Alliance account. Avey was then responsible for paying both Muchnick and Lewis.

The $2,500 performance bond Lou initially posted with the Alliance treasury as collateral was upped to $10,000 by the middle of the decade. When he won the title again in 1963, the forfeit was $25,000.

On March 15, 1956, Thesz, hobbled by a fractured ankle, surrendered his belt to Whipper Watson. Thesz regained the title on November 9, 1956 in St. Louis, beating Watson by countout. In a letter to Muchnick dated November 13, 1956, and reprinted in NWA Bulletin #3 (November 16, 1956), Thesz wrote: "I cannot tell you how happy I was and am to have regained the championship. It was always my dream to have held the title five distinct times, as my old friend the Strangler did."

In the letter, Thesz also outlined several recommendations he felt were vitally important going forward, starting with the need for first-class transportation, as "a champion representing a sport should certainly do it properly." He also felt the title holder should have the right to veto opponents if he thought a deserving wrestler was sitting out because "some Johnny-come-lately" maneuvered his way into a title match.

Additionally, Thesz stressed that he wanted to "work under humane conditions," wrestling two weeks, five days per week, followed by a week off. It was more common for the champion to work three weeks on, and one off, heightening the tension between Thesz and his booker. Subsequent champions were saddled with the same schedule. Complaints were louder when the titleholder was compelled to wrestle on his off week, though Muchnick said he would only arrange such a match if it was crucial. With promoters hungry for income, their appeals to Muchnick during the wrestler's break were frequent, and decisions on a particular match's importance were subject to debate.

The Alliance placated Thesz by establishing a system of payments to Strangler Lewis starting after the 1956 convention, and continuing off and on through 1960. Even with proactive measures designed to keep the peace, Thesz's next year as king would not be a happy one. He was becoming increasingly bitter toward the promoters he was making rich, and felt the NWA's values were obscured underneath the obvious selfishness of its members.

Planning a tour overseas in 1957, Thesz gave his blessing to a proposal that, like the Nomellini situation, split the NWA championship into two pieces. On June 14, 1957, in Chicago, Edouard Carpentier took a win over Thesz by disqualification, thus walking away with a tainted claim to the title. The unexpected wrangling between Eddie Quinn and Muchnick at the annual convention in August ended with the former pulling out of the organization. In response, Muchnick claimed that the NWA had never sanctioned Carpentier as titleholder, and that Thesz remained the champ.

Almost four years after their first match in Honolulu, Thesz wrestled Japanese legend, Rikidozan (Mitsuhiro Momota, 1924–1963), in his homeland, on October 7, 1957. Their Tokyo contest at Korakuen Stadium ended in a draw and received a television rating of better than 87.0. Rikidozan's legacy in Japan was comparable to that of Frank Gotch in the United States, and his matches with Thesz were the ultimate competitive spectacle for fans in the Far East.

Any enthusiasm for the NWA dissolved while he was overseas, and Thesz, from Australia, notified Muchnick by mail that he wanted to drop the strap. He was, however, very selective about who he would put over, and potential candidates

Buddy Rogers and Verne Gagne were seemingly out of contention. Thesz finally agreed on Dick Hutton, a wrestler known for his exceptional skills. Thesz knew Hutton would hold the championship he treasured in the same high esteem, and did the job on November 14, 1957, in Toronto.

On the suggestion of Lewis, Thesz and his wife toured Europe, and Lou took on a handful of wrestling dates. He claimed the International Title and solidified his status in England and France. Beginning in February 1958, he worked as an independent in the U.S., and often wrestled Hutton, putting him over in Toronto, St. Louis, and Houston. In 1959, he joined Quinn's movement in opposition to Fred Kohler in Chicago, and the Eaton-LeBell group in Los Angeles. Thesz was quoted in an article written by Jeane Hoffman, printed in the May 24, 1960, edition of the *Los Angeles Times,* stating:

> I won't retire. I've tried it, and it doesn't work. I get bored. I try to keep busy waterskiing in Mexico, skin diving, sailing, swimming, skiing from Mammoth to St. Moritz and I was even an akc judge for Doberman pinschers. But it isn't like being active. So, I've worked out a happy medium where I'm on the road only 175 days a year. Ed Lewis and I once figured that our game was worth a "dollar a mile," and we traveled 250,000 miles a year. I just cut down on miles. Sure, I cut a few dollars, too, but so far as net take, I make out nearly as well. This way, I can go surfing at La Paz with my wife Fredda, and eight-year-old son Jeffrey, or take an attractive mat engagement in Singapore.
>
> The wonderful thing about wrestling is that age is no detriment. It's an asset. So long as you keep in top condition, you can keep on by using your knowledge and experience, relying on body leverage and a foolproof bag of tricks. I'll challenge any of these young kids. I haven't even been hurt, except for a broken kneecap and broken ribs.

Thesz was further pushed away from the Alliance and what it stood for when the brass approved the switch of the title to Buddy Rogers, a shrewd operator. Thesz's prediction that Rogers, via Capitol Wrestling owners Toots Mondt and Vincent McMahon, would flip the NWA onto its head came true, and Thesz felt a sense of vindication when Muchnick asked him to reprise his role as champion in late 1962.

Could Thesz, at 46 years of age, still meet the demands of NWA champion? Could he bring stability to the members of the Alliance in the wake of the Rogers debacle? Muchnick and the NWA believed so. On January 24, 1963, in Toronto, he won a one-fall bout over the Nature Boy and took the belt. The title change failed to deter McMahon and Mondt from their chosen path, and the World Wide Wrestling Federation was formed. Other NWA promoters, Doc Sarpolis in Amarillo and Stu Hart in Alberta, recognized a separate champion, but eventually Thesz tied up loose ends.

When asked why he was still wrestling by *Toronto Daily Star* columnist Jim Proudfoot on February 2, 1963, Thesz said: "Ego, that's all. You're retired and enjoying yourself clipping coupons and then one day you tell yourself, heck, you're just as good as you ever were. So you have to prove it to yourself. The legs are the problem. It took me six weeks to get them back in condition, running through soft sand on the beach."

The untarnished reputation of Lou as a hooker was once again at the forefront of many rogue promoters' minds, and considered by bold grapplers. One instance, on May 2, 1964, in Detroit, he met a lethal shooter with some of the same qualities. Karl Gotch was a veteran from Europe, trained in the legendary "Snake Pit" by Billy Riley in Wigan, Lancashire, England. An accomplished amateur, Gotch had the skills to test Thesz in a legit bout, and their Detroit struggle added a level of intensity and realness that most matches lacked. Thesz kept his championship, but suffered several broken ribs in the process. Thesz and Gotch were rivals inside the ring and out, and because of their mutual respect, each had to be constantly aware of a potential shoot. They found some time between actual wrestling holds to perform, but their feud didn't translate at the box office.

As champion from 1963 to 1966, Thesz did well financially, and succeeded in returning a measure of unity to the NWA. He met every requirement and faced all contenders. A proposed unification match with the WWWF "world" champion Bruno Sammartino was contemplated across party lines, but dismissed when certain criteria weren't met. There were a number of competing attractions throughout North America, but no one wore the badge of heavyweight wrestling champion like Lou. Retaining his astonishing reflexes and tremendous skill, Thesz worked exceedingly hard to make opponents look good in the ring.

Thesz's last stint as NWA champion ended on January 7, 1966, in St. Louis. Defeated in three falls by Gene Kiniski at the Kiel, he concluded a stretch of 1,079 days as titleholder. His reign had been a success, and the Alliance was stronger than it was before he took on the job. In the years that followed, Thesz wrestled on shows for friendly promoters, and was not only willing to sell for opponents, but put countless performers over. He wrestled all the greats: Verne Gagne, Shohei Baba, Danny Hodge, Dara Singh, Jack Brisco, Dory Funk Jr., Nick Bockwinkel, and Johnny Valentine. Between 1966 and '68, he made two trips to Japan, before seemingly calling it quits in January, 1970.

Bored with inactivity, Thesz returned and cruised the southeast from March to October 1973, then ventured to Tokyo for a tag match with Gotch versus Seiji Sakaguchi and Antonio Inoki on October 14, 1973. Maintaining his astonishing shape, he wrestled off and on as the years passed, appearing in as many as 30 bouts annually. Lou teamed with promoters Buddy Lee (1932–1998) and Danny Davis to run adjacent to NWA members Lee Fields, Roy Welch, and Nick Gulas under the Universal Wrestling Association banner in 1976.

In a shocker confirming his distate for the NWA, he went into Toronto in opposition to his old crony Frank Tunney. Thesz was allied with Can-Am Promotions (Milt Avruskin and George Cannon), another independent faction, on June 6, 1976, but the head-to-head conflict put them on the wrong end of a 7,000/600 ratio. Finding himself in need of money after a divorce, Thesz, shortly before his 62nd birthday, returned to the ring full-time for Gulas in 1978.

Three years later, he wrestled in Leroy McGuirk's territory for two months, and had an extended tour of Japan in 1982, going undefeated. On November 16, 1987, he participated in an "old-timers" battle royal sponsored by the World Wrestling Federation outside New York City with ex-world champs O'Connor, Kiniski, Carpentier, Pedro Morales, Killer Kowalski, Nick Bockwinkel, and Bobo Brazil. Thesz eliminated O'Connor to win the special event in front of an astonishingly small crowd of less than 5,000. Lou's final match occurred on December 26, 1990, at the age of 74 in Hamamatsu against a former protégé named Masahiro Chono. Using an STF (Step-over Toe-hold Facelock), Chono won by submission in 5:10. Thesz's courageous effort capped a career that saw him wrestle in seven different decades.

As Lou got older, he became more accessible to the wrestling audience, corresponding with disciples on two internet message boards. His wisdom gave people an inside track to wrestling's history and he fascinated pundits with his point of view. He served as the Cauliflower Alley Club President from 1992–2000, and was honored in May 1993 by World Championship Wrestling in Atlanta with an in-ring ceremony. The WWF had a ceremony of their own for Thesz, Muchnick, Kiniski, Brisco, the Funks, and Harley Race on October 5, 1997, at the Kiel Center in St. Louis.

In September 1998, Thesz was inducted into the Professional Wrestling Hall of Fame at the International Wrestling Institute and Museum in Newton, Iowa, and into the Missouri Sports Hall of Fame on February 17, 2002.

Thesz passed away on April 28, 2002, in Orlando. The legendary wrestler, who won his first world title at 21 years of age and his last at 62, was 86 when he died. He held the National Wrestling Alliance title for more than ten years altogether, and never rested on his laurels. As a dog lover and trainer, he groomed 52 dogs for Dogs for Defense, Inc. during World War II, and served as a selfless soldier in the army. He was mentored by the likes of Ed "Strangler" Lewis and Ray Steele, and counseled grapplers himself throughout his career.

Despite only a freshman-level high school education, Lou was extremely intelligent, classy, and well versed in international culture. Always in the company of celebrities, he took enormous pleasure in his VIP treatment at restaurants and clubs, yet he was as charitable as he was talented. In his estimated ten million miles of globetrotting, he exhibited his love for wrestling to the public, and the high regard he had for the sport never diminished. Despite the ever-changing dynamics of wrestling as a form of entertainment, his straightlaced image remained an anomaly of the ring. Thesz was a perennial champion in the minds of his fans, and left his mark deeply in the heart of wrestling.

CHAPTER FOUR

THE BACKBONE
OF THE ALLIANCE

Sam Muchnick

SAM MUCHNICK

While Pinkie George was, in essence, the "father" of the National Wrestling Alliance, Sam Muchnick was the man who nurtured the organization from its inception. In his 22 years as president, Muchnick took the NWA to its greatest heights, and successfully navigated his role as chief wrestling politician amidst an array of desperados. His cordial attitude, even-toned manner, and unassuming authority flattened the walls put up by cynics trying to impede the Alliance's progress.

As the ultimate arbitrator, Muchnick solved many complex disputes, and won countless friends among wrestlers and his fellow promoters. The business was tough, and a thin-skinned promoter wouldn't have survived in a small town, let alone at the top of the ladder. As the leader of the NWA, Muchnick did what was best for the Alliance, and at the same time, continued to run a stable St. Louis corporation.

Arriving two months prematurely during his parent's trip to see family in the Ukraine, thirty miles outside Kiev in the town Novograd-Volinsk, Sam was born Jeshua Muchnick on August 22, 1905, to Saul (1872–1952) and Rebecca "Bela" Salob (1883–1980). His parents had met and married in St. Louis the year before, and in the interests of their newborn, decided that it was safest for Jeshua to remain in the Ukraine rather than risk an unforgiving trip across the ocean by boat. Saul returned to their home in St. Louis alone, and to his job as a presser in a clothing factory. The young family was reunited in 1911, and with Jeshua's half-sister Bessie, made the voyage back to America, through the Port of Baltimore. His father would change his son's name from Jeshua to Sam.

Sam and his brothers Harry and Simon were reared in a blue-collar community on Franklin Avenue in St. Louis. Graduating from Central High School in June 1924, he was working as a postal clerk when a twist of fate landed him a gig as a sportswriter for the *St. Louis Times*. As the rookie in the office, Muchnick reported on Municipal League baseball and basketball, college athletics, and greyhound and horse racing. Mentored by sports editor Sid C. Keener, and writers George Henger and Charles "Kid" Regan, Sam worked his way up to primary correspondent covering the St. Louis Cardinals. Accompanying the team on the road, he sent an inning-by-inning chronicle back to the *Times* staff, and not only became friendly with the players and coaches of the Cardinals, but knew all the celebrities of baseball, including Babe Ruth.

By the summer of 1930, Muchnick's journalistic work spawned several articles about the local wrestling promotion of Tom Packs, and Sam was an unofficial adman for the promoter. Sam showed an unusual level of seriousness in his wrestling writings, holding the often-questioned sport to the highest standards, an approach that Packs appreciated. Occasionally, the *Times* printed a column, "In the Ring with Sam Muchnick," a piece dedicated to boxing and wrestling news. The effective advertising built a friendship with Packs, and when the *Times* and the *Star* merged, Muchnick accepted a P.R. position with the St. Louis promoter.

The enthusiastic Muchnick was well known and well connected throughout the sports world, and turned down more lucrative offers to enter wrestling. He did his research, spending hours at the various St. Louis gymnasiums, especially Harry Cook's joint at Sixth and Pine Avenue. He was very impressed by the culture of professional wrestling, and made many friends. Packs found good use for his educated prodigy, and Muchnick's job description evolved to managing grapplers, refereeing, acting as a road agent, and matchmaking.

Muchnick bonded with Lou Thesz, the young St. Louis heavyweight. They frequently traveled together, and Sam was in Lou's corner the night he dropped the NWA title to Bronko Nagurski in Houston in 1939. When Thesz suffered a legitimate fractured kneecap in the contest, it was Muchnick who drove him to St. Louis, and arranged for him to see a reputed orthopedic surgeon he knew from his days covering the Cardinals. Muchnick and Thesz started off on what would be a roller-coaster ride of a relationship, one that would both create resentment, and see great fortunes realized.

In September 1941, Muchnick's ties to Packs were severed, and any number of incidents could be considered the backbreaker. Sam applied for a license to conduct his own events in St. Louis, independent of his former boss. The Missouri Athletic Commission, ever protective of Packs, denied his submission. Muchnick objected openly to the ruling and filed again. Then he tendered a third request, but the result was the same. Not giving in, Muchnick planned for his first program on March 24, 1942, at the St. Louis Arena, and got talent from promoters Ed White, Jack Pfefer, and siblings Max Baumann and Billy Sandow. Commission members answered with a simple threat — if Muchnick tried to run without a license, those involved would be arrested.

Muchnick obtained a temporary injunction from a circuit court judge to stage his show, and went forward. Shortly thereafter, he appeared before a military draft board, and refused a potential deferment. His career as an Army Air Force soldier began on May 15, 1942, and he did his basic training at Jefferson Barracks, Missouri. Muchnick did two years on the Panama Canal, and in July 1944, returned to the continental United States. He was deployed to several locations prior to an eight-month stretch as a public relations sergeant at Scott Field. He was honorably discharged on September 18, 1945.

Reborn into sports promotions, Muchnick petitioned the Missouri Athletic Commission for a license on October 4, 1945, and after an intentional delay, was approved by Arthur Heyne. He had his initial exhibition on December 5 at the Kiel Auditorium, and imported Ed "Strangler" Lewis, his protégé Cliff Gustafson, Ede Virag, Roy Dunn, and Lee Wykoff. Everette Marshall, who was to wrestle Jack Conley, failed to show, and Sam dutifully drew up a letter to Heyne asking for his suspension. The request was denied.

Inside a five-day span in February 1946, Packs drew 10,000-plus fans featuring Bill Longson and Buddy Rogers, while Muchnick's turnout was around 3,500 with Virag, Gustafson, Don Eagle, and Frankie Talaber. Fighting the establishment was a daunting task, as Muchnick was well aware. His army increased with active and growing support from Al Haft, Paul Bowser, Tony Stecher, and Pfefer.

In 1947, Muchnick married Helen Wildefong at the home of friends in Galveston. His persistent efforts and quiet discipline helped expedite a steady increase in the popularity of his shows. Packs retired following his June 4, 1948, Kiel program and liquidated his grappling business. A strong consortium of wrestlers and promoters purchased the offices at the Arcade Building. At the head of the group was Sam's old buddy, Lou Thesz. Thesz's franchise had the advantage, but Muchnick's underdog status didn't deter him.

Muchnick realized he needed aid from his Midwestern neighbors. Receiving an invitation from Orville Brown, perhaps through Wally Karbo, during a July 1948 vacation in Michigan, he was encouraged to attend the meeting of promoters in Waterloo, Iowa, that expanded Pinkie George's National Wrestling Alliance to a host of new territories.

Members were invited to their first convention in September 1948 in Minneapolis, and Sam was appointed secretary-treasurer. Another meeting occurred at a Chicago hotel in late October, at which Muchnick, George, Haft, Brown, Chicago impresario Fred Kohler, and National Wrestling Association champion Thesz were present. Muchnick proposed a merger with Lou, hoping to end their battle in St. Louis. That compromise was declined, and Thesz continued his duel responsibilities as promoter and wrestler.

The edge in the promotional war went to Thesz, with Longson and Whipper Watson headlining, but Muchnick gained steam, peaking on February 4, 1949, when 10,651 witnessed a match featuring Buddy Rogers and Don Eagle. During a trip to Houston in July, he was surprised by a suggestion to merge from Thesz, and consented verbally. Muchnick and Thesz were in Columbus on July 29 for a conference that introduced the Alliance to their merger. It was decided there that Sam would be the booker for the unified NWA champion after Thesz wrestled Brown in November.

In August 1949, an accord was hammered out and formally signed by Muchnick and Thesz. The treaty was multifaceted, and kept secret from the public. The Mississippi Valley Sports Club, headquartered in the Arcade Building, and Muchnick's accommodations at the Claridge Hotel (Sam Muchnick Sports Attractions) remained open, running shows on different weeks. Together, the entities had interest in the St. Louis Wrestling Enterprises, the "front" booking office for both promotions. Profits from house gates were divided 50/50. For supervising the scheduling of wrestlers, Muchnick garnered a third of the revenue from the booking agency, counting programs in Evansville, Indianapolis, Louisville, Cape Girardeau, Hannibal, and Sedalia. The rest was carved up among the investors of the two promotions.

The Missouri Athletic Commission had full knowledge of the transaction. Charles Orchard, chairman of the commission, was adamant that certain stipulations were respected. He wanted everyone to maintain a low profile, and refrain from being seen in each other's offices. To the St. Louis audience, the wrestling competition in the city under the arch appeared to continue as usual.

The truce between Thesz and Muchnick was, essentially, consistent with the common interests of the notorious National Wrestling Association and the private membership of the National Wrestling Alliance. Having two "NWA" world heavyweight champions on the scene was illogical, and a unification bout was deliberated. It was determined that Thesz and Orville Brown would wrestle for the undisputed championship on November 25, 1949, in St. Louis. A car accident on November 1 ended Brown's career, and after the NWA declared Thesz champion on November 27, Sam worked out an itinerary for Lou's travels.

Muchnick encouraged the organization's progress, and followed the instructions of Pinkie George, the man he openly credited as the NWA's founder. He executed the president's directives, even when they were unpopular, and supported the administration's structure. In letters to promoters, Sam enthused about the prospects for the Alliance, and how he believed a cooperative could effect the wrestling industry.

In Dallas, during the weekend of September 8–10, 1950, Muchnick was voted to the helm of the NWA, and was forced to balance his regular operations in St. Louis with the demands of manager of the Alliance. Muchnick found the presidency had more disadvantages than perks. Trying to keep members in line was difficult, and he had to employ a range of diplomatic approaches to appease all parties. Muchnick used the Alliance's evolving bylaws to weed out problems. The elimination of all regional "world" champions was job one.

Muchnick exhibited a lot of patience with Haft, Tony Stecher, Paul Bowser, Eddie Quinn, and Johnny Doyle when it came to narrowing the heavyweight division down to a lone titleholder. Because of the undisciplined nature of the business prior to the Alliance's creation, it took three years to get affiliates in line. The NWA already had a reputable and competent grappler in the role, and Thesz was successfully traversing the landscape, making money for the entire group.

At the September 1951 convention in Tulsa, Muchnick called for a vote regarding a policy that would establish a solitary heavyweight and junior heavyweight champion by February 1, 1952. Bookers who flagrantly contravened that stipulation would be banished from the Alliance without a hearing. The plan was unanimously approved by the 25 attending delegates.

Muchnick also discussed his problems with being president. Members knew his importance, and decided to make it worthwhile, financially, for Muchnick to stay on. The initial offer called for an annual $500 fee, per associate, be paid to Sam for his duties. That plan was modified and endorsed unanimously, raising Thesz's per-match earnings to 15 percent, with 2½ percent going to Ed Lewis, and the other 2½ to Muchnick. The percentage was considered payment for booking the title-holder, a job Muchnick had done for free from November 1949 until September 10, 1951.

The top minds of the Alliance knew that if the syndicate was left in the hands of anyone else, it wouldn't work. Muchnick's positive outlook, reinforcement of the rules, and unselfishness allowed the coalition to flourish, swelling from 26 members in 1951 to nearly 40 in 1952. Most bookers were experienced enough to know the undesirable idiosyncrasies of the wrestling business, where double-crossing and backstabbing were commonplace. Their anxiety about the unscrupulous actions of their cohorts often led to brutal meetings behind the closed doors of conventions.

In dealing with veteran powerbrokers, Muchnick discovered that belligerence was the norm, but he aspired to see the good in all, even those in the membership with tarnished reputations. He devised novel formulas to pacify combatants, and often played all sides in his mediation.

The board of directors, heavyweight, and junior heavyweight committees converged in St. Louis on January 6, 1952, and the decree that called for a single heavyweight champion by February 1 was a primary point of discussion. Haft and Bowser both commented on the legacies of the Midwest Wrestling Association and American Wrestling Association, respectively. Haft explained that he was not billing his regional heavyweight kingpin as a world titleholder. In Boston, Bowser used Don Eagle as the Eastern champion, but was adamant that his champion didn't conflict with or, in any way harm, the official Alliance titleholder. The pair agreed to hype Thesz over area champions, and by the end of the conference, they had satisfied the membership.

Another dilemma faced Eddie Quinn in Montreal. A district champion had been featured in Quebec since the mid-1930s, and was, basically, the heart of Quinn's operation. Quinn was apprehensive about terminating his local champion, and received a special exemption in light of his circumstances. Doyle proposed an amendment to Article 4 of the bylaws that allowed Quinn to continue to sanction a provincial titleholder, and the faction agreed unanimously.

The process of diminishing rival claimants was a worthwhile undertaking. Promoters often tested the authority of the Alliance, and Muchnick, who monitored all aspects of wrestling, was quick to admonish potential violators in his memorandums. Sam's NWA Bulletin #11 on June 1, 1954, addressed the title situation:

While one of the main reasons for the formation of the Alliance was for the recognition of one champion in each division, and while some of us have not honestly abided by this pledge, I would say that this phase of the Alliance work is secondary to other important matters. I would recommend that, if every one of us cannot go along with this rule, that the Alliance could eliminate the recognition of champions, but could go on with its other good work, and still have a great organization. The protection of our territories, and the co-operation among each other, in my opinion, is more important than the recognition of champions, but, if we are going to recognize champions, let's all abide by the decision of the majority, and not make our own rules for selfish gain.

The members of the NWA may have hoped that independent promoters would be automatically stifled by the influence held by the combine, but that level of control was unrealistic. Ostracized "outlaws" were emerging daily. A strong force in the elimination of anti-NWA factions, Muchnick rallied talent in critical situations and bolstered morale. He kept a public face, and watched as the U.S. Government opened an investigation that threatened the Alliance's future.

Muchnick and the NWA donated 25 percent gross receipts for one show by an affiliated member to the Leader Dogs for the Blind, and raised almost $40,000 in the first year overall. On May 9, 1953, Sam and his partners at the Mississippi Valley Sports Club debuted wrestling from the St. Louis House Auditorium, broadcast on KSD-TV and sponsored by Stag Beer. The first main event was The Great Zorra vs. Bill Longson. Muchnick and the MVSC also established SAMAR Television Wrestling, a company that would coordinate between KSD and their St. Louis ventures. It was incorporated on May 8, 1953.

Hostilities broke out in Southern California in 1953, and Muchnick went west to referee between the four principals involved in the Los Angeles booking configuration. Sam brokered a peace accord agreed to by Cal Eaton, Mike Hirsch, Hugh Nichols, and Johnny Doyle, but in January 1954, Doyle sold his stock in the company. The enterprising side of Muchnick came to the forefront when he recommended to Nichols that the local agency be revamped, giving Hugh, Eaton, and Hirsch 25 percent each, Jules Strongbow 12½, Fredda Thesz (on behalf of her husband Lou) 6¼, and himself 6¼ percent. Muchnick and Thesz would put up $10,000, split down the middle, but negotiations stalled and the deal was never completed.

Muchnick and Thesz, booker and champion, were a formidable combination. They both brought unparalleled professionalism to their jobs, but with Muchnick entitled to a fee from every show the titleholder wrestled, there was a measure of friction. Thesz complained about bookings in obscure towns. Muchnick countered that those appointments were made by local members, and that he merely set up the visit into a specific territory. There was the belief that Sam had the clout to solve that problem with an Alliance-wide policy, but that edict was never made.

In an August 29, 1955, letter to Stanley Disney of the Department of Justice Antitrust Division, Muchnick wrote:

> Regarding myself. I am not a candidate for presidency, and never have been. I have been drafted each year. This year I intend, definitely, to step out, because I have never liked the idea of my salary being paid via 2½% from the champion's appearances. This method of paying has confused the issue, as some of the members feel that the 2½% is for booking the champion, when, in reality, it is a method of paying my salary as president. This goes whether Thesz is the champion, or whoever beats him. So, if they still feel they must have me, I may agree to stay on if another method is arrived at to pay me. Otherwise, I will let some one else have the headaches I have had for the past five years. I can then devote more time to the promotion in St. Louis.

Muchnick's grievances were addressed at the September 1955 convention in St. Louis, and again the membership made new concessions to keep Sam on as president. Muchnick told the assembly that he didn't want to rely on the champion having to wrestle to be paid, and agreed to continue as president only if he was assured a $15,000 annual salary. Members unanimously endorsed the proposal. Muchnick would collect a $1,250 check monthly, doled out by the treasury.

The fixed salary basically erased Sam's need to run a territory, and the booking he did for the six towns he controlled dwindled to just one, St. Louis. Arrangements with neighboring offices facilitated a high degree of talent for his territory, but as time went by, he no longer had to depend solely on adjacent bookers. Athletes from across the globe made special preparations to fly into St. Louis to grapple for what was judged to be the pinnacle of the business, an operation superior to all others. Muchnick had created an island all wrestlers wanted to travel to, and with promoters vigorously jockeying for position, a trip by their star to St. Louis could only strengthen a promoter's cause.

St. Louis did have levels of politics that increased acrimony among shareholders. Thesz's negative opinion of the office and its major players continued, and in December 1955, he sold his stake, transferring a majority percentage to Muchnick. Longson replaced Martin Thesz as the certified promoter of the Mississippi Valley Sports Club.

When Ed Lewis initially retired from managing Thesz in January 1956, the champion's portion of the 15 percent he generated from every title defense was increased to 11. The NWA got 4 percent, which paid Muchnick and the $2,500 yearly salary of his secretary. At the 1956 caucus in St. Louis, members reapproved a measure furnishing $625 a month to the Strangler for public relations, receiving 1½ of the 4 percent taken in by Muchnick. Sam retained his normal 2½, and his assistant earned a quarter of that revenue.

The growing inquiry by the FBI and Department of Justice soon reached the front door of Sam's office. He accommodated investigators by granting interviews and providing access to his records. As the confident voice of the Alliance, Muchnick admitted to no wrongdoing, and defended the NWA in very legal terms. He reached out to his friend, Congressman Mel Price, the buffer between the NWA and investigators, and went to Washington on several occasions to discuss a possible settlement. The Consent Decree, signed by the Alliance membership in 1956, was the product of his labor.

Despite Muchnick's hard work, the NWA was deteriorating. The organization's leadership attempted to placate dissenting members prior to Thesz's trip overseas by dividing the world championship in June 1957. The plan appeared, at least on paper, to be nothing short of ingenious. But a personal grudge proved that their strategy was, in fact, remarkably fragile. The negative slide that commenced when the Department of Justice brought down the hammer was exacerbated by disputes in the heavyweight division. The NWA had always relied on its world champion to create the bulk of the organization's credibility, but that confidence was now fractured.

A sequence of events that confused fans saw the formation of Alliance factions who explicitly violated bylaws by approving a world champion outside the official titleholder. In the 14 months prior to December 1957, the club lost eight members: Eddie Quinn, Paul Bowser, Paul Jones, Cal Eaton, Rod Fenton, Rudy Dusek, Max Clayton (deceased), and Hugh Nichols (deceased). Another handful would desert the fraternity before the August 1959 convention.

Needing Thesz to clean up the muddled heavyweight ranks, Muchnick got terrible news in a dispatch postmarked from Australia. Lou notified Sam that he was done representing the Alliance, and insisted that he drop the belt at the earliest possible date. As usual, Thesz would surrender the belt only to someone of his choosing.

Dick Hutton, a wrestler with four years pro and 15 years of amateur experience, was an immediate choice. Hutton had NCAA championships and Olympic participation in his background, and was a true grappler who could bring credibility to the NWA strap. Muchnick and Thesz were keen on his credentials and size, but the one component Hutton lacked was color. That minor detail wasn't enough to veto a stint as champion. On November 14, 1957, he defeated Thesz in Toronto for the championship.

Muchnick coordinated with the owner of the Chase Park Plaza Hotel, Harold Koplar, who started the network KPLR (channel 11) on April 28, 1959, to debut *Wrestling at the Chase*. Emanating from the Khorassan Room at the hotel (May 1959 to 1970), and KPLR Studios (1971 to 1983), the television show was classy and innovative. The program aired Saturday nights at 10:00 p.m. and was hosted by Joe Garagiola. Other commentators and play-by-play men were Don Cunningham, George Abel, John Curley, Eddie Gromacki, Larry Matysik, and Mickey Garagiola.

Over the course of Sam's tenure, assistant matchmakers Dick Patton, Frankie Talaber, Vic Holbrook, Bobby Bruns, Billy Darnell, and later, Pat O'Connor, gave St. Louis a vibrant blend of wrestling and histrionics. In September 1959, the branches of the Mississippi Valley Sports Club and Sam Muchnick Sports Attractions publicly merged, and shareholders agreed to the formation of the St. Louis Wrestling Club.

Attempts to get people energized about Hutton were soon exhausted. It wasn't that Dick wasn't valuable as a wrestler; the marketplace had changed. Integrity was a prized trait, but didn't automatically provide drawing power. The fact that Edouard Carpentier was being recognized in many important towns, and the disorder that followed, wasn't helping either. After 13 months, Hutton was replaced by Pat O'Connor, a New Zealander and former British Empire champion.

O'Connor exceeded the territorial limits that Hutton had run into, including getting over in Chicago. He was sanctioned by both the National Wrestling Alliance and the National Wrestling Association, which was returning to prominence as a regulatory body, with Muchnick as an associate member.

Disheartened by the waning NWA membership, the general apathy of his peers, and the renewal of the Justice Department's investigation, Muchnick vacated his Alliance post without rancour when an appeal to elect a new president was made in August 1960. The election of Frank Tunney to head the NWA, with Sam serving as the executive secretary, treasurer, and booker of the heavyweight champion, created what Muchnick later referred to as a "divided leadership."

Toots Mondt and Vince McMahon carried their agenda to Acapulco for the 1960 convention and loudly advocated Buddy Rogers replacing O'Connor as NWA champion. Their campaign to persuade their colleagues proved fruitful. Muchnick and the board of directors signed off on Rogers, and a crusade to whip enthusiasts into a frenzy in Chicago, the location chosen for the switch, was scripted. An outdoor show during the summer of 1961 would see the belt change hands.

Inherently controlled by the Capitol Wrestling Corporation, Buddy became one of the hardest working champions in history. His reign preserved the financial health of key personnel in the Alliance. But smaller territories, once the core of the fraternity, suffered. The NWA had taken their heavyweight champion into the "big time," and only the top tier enjoyed the grandstanding of Rogers. The Alliance as a whole felt the effects of the jagged booking, and desperate promoters were weathering the storm by any means necessary.

If Muchnick had a key antagonist in the wrestling world, it was Kohler, who was selected NWA President in August 1961. Their strained relationship worsened when Sam unilaterally approved the membership requests of Johnny Doyle and Jim Barnett. Nixing the decision, Kohler impeded the duo's efforts to join, and eventually halted the progress of their applications completely. The Kohler-Muchnick quarrel had roots going back to the 1953 recognition of Verne Gagne as U.S. champion, and continued when, in 1955, Kohler bought Indianapolis, a town Sam had booked previously. When Eddie Quinn invaded Chicago, Kohler believed Muchnick was supporting his competition, and in the period between 1955 and 1961, both men wrote gossipy memos to government officials complaining about the other.

In November 1961, Muchnick was hospitalized in St. Louis, and while the Alliance's principal loyalist was out of commission, Kohler called the board of directors to Chicago for the purpose of collapsing the NWA. Dissolving the organization had been a hotly debated topic for years, and there were always those in favor of doing so. In their estimation, the Alliance had lost its ability to function under the radar of government officials and with attendance down, any belief that it was helping everyone prosper was gone. Muchnick had undying faith in the coalition and what it symbolized to pro wrestling, and didn't want to see it pulled apart by any means other than a unanimous vote during a meeting of its members.

In the end, the renegades failed in their endeavors, and Muchnick recovered. He resumed booking Rogers on a smaller circuit that concentrated on priority towns. In August 1962, Doc Sarpolis of Amarillo was elected NWA president, and ironically, West Texas was a territory that recognized a champion other than Rogers. Sarpolis had Gene Kiniski as his world titleholder.

No one could have imagined that the president of the NWA would recognize a champion outside the official titleholder. But that's exactly what happened in 1962–63. However, any alleged animosity toward Capitol Wrestling was exaggerated, as NWA members picked Vince McMahon to be the second vice president at the August 1962 conference. Three months after the meetings in St. Louis, Rogers was injured in Montreal, and Killer Kowalski laid claim to the championship, further disrupting the NWA.

Looking for balance and a little stability, Muchnick and the board of directors decided the time had come for Rogers to step down from the throne. Sam knew McMahon had his own ideas about the future of his champion, and there was additional skepticism as to whether Rogers would just lay down and consent to have his belt taken away. Muchnick asked Lou Thesz if he would wrestle Buddy and capture the NWA title, returning the championship to a more secure environment. Thesz agreed, but locking the elusive champion into a bout proved to be tough.

Rogers dodged the first two matches on account of his injury, but fell into a third in Toronto that he couldn't avoid. Actually, it was a threat to his belt deposit that forced the contest on January 24, 1963. Muchnick was present to deliver the cash, and Buddy did the job for Thesz. The St. Louis office knew McMahon was going to form his own sanctioning body, and the World Wide Wrestling Federation was soon recognized as the new conglomerate in the Northeast. The WWWF declared Rogers world champion, asserting that he'd won a tournament in Brazil.

The lines of communication from Muchnick to McMahon were always open. Even the unwritten bylaws of the NWA, which included blacklisting independent operators, could not have stopped Capitol Wrestling. Muchnick believed it made sense to maintain bonds rather than start an unwinable war. A stubborn and more emotional leader might have viewed the creation of the WWWF a different way. McMahon and Mondt admired Muchnick, and kept talent trading-lines open with various NWA members, specifically Tunney in Toronto, and Luttrall-Graham in Florida.

The rampant chaos between 1956 and '63, kindled by the U.S. Government's investigation, the Thesz-Carpentier foolishness, and the Rogers debacle, had been costly. Muchnick was elected NWA president on August 24, 1963, at the convention in St. Louis, and a renaissance began that Sam hoped would reverse the slow decline of the organization.

NWA membership slipped from 38 in 1955 to just 16 in 1961. With Thesz back on top, Muchnick called for harmony among all groups for the common good of wrestling. The AWA and WWWF offered diversity in their individual markets, and their promoters were invited to participate in Alliance conferences.

Trustworthy and gracious, Muchnick earned admiration wherever he went. Known throughout the St. Louis community, he often participated in fundraisers, and was a fixture at the annual sports-businessmen's dinner. Sam was always in contention for the "Outstanding St. Louis Sports Figure" honor that was awarded every November, sponsored by the Elks' Sports Celebrity Committee (B.P.O. Elks No. 9), and voted on by broadcasters and writers. Two hundred and fifty of his friends surprised him with a party celebrating his 20th anniversary as a promoter, following his December 3, 1965, program at the Kiel Auditorium.

The connection of Muchnick to local writers gave wrestling a pass in St. Louis and preserved the illusion. That advantage also applied to the National Wrestling Alliance. Muchnick's status as president gave the NWA credibility that bucked speculation about grappling's authenticity, challenged the claims of whistleblowers, and slowed the momentum of the U.S. Government's antitrust case. Understanding that wrestling was a brand of entertainment, he booked with a mind to satisfying his paying crowds, and used psychology to his advantage. Most importantly, he had an exemplary record in giving his audience what was advertised. A "no-show" was one way for a wrestler to guarantee he'd never be booked in St. Louis again.

For athletes, wrestling in St. Louis for Muchnick was a privilege. Thesz, Rogers, O'Connor, Orville Brown, Bobby Managoff, Wladek Kowalski, Johnny Valentine, the Von Erichs, Harley Race, Jack Brisco, and Gene Kiniski were all successful in St. Louis, and knew that when it was all said and done, they'd be paid fairly.

Dick the Bruiser was quoted in the July 12, 1991, *St. Louis Post Dispatch* as saying: "I enjoyed the fans in St. Louis and wrestling at Kiel Auditorium and at the Arena. What I liked about St. Louis the most was the promoter, Sam Muchnick. Sam always gave you what he promised you. He said if you beat this guy or that guy, you will get this much money, and he always kept his word. Sam gave you the exact count of the house and the right cut of the gate. I got a kick out of how if he promised you $2,050.34 and he would have the 34 cents in the envelope for you."

Terry Funk said similar things in the January 4, 1999, *St. Louis Post Dispatch*. "Sam was the heart of professional wrestling for decades. He was the biggest thing that ever happened to me. I don't know anyone who didn't respect the man. He was a true patriarch. You didn't have to count the house when you worked for Sam. Back then, you got a percentage, from eight to ten percent, and Sam had the dignity to give it to you."

On top of his income at home, Sam grossed comfortable wages as booker of the NWA titleholder, and took the responsibilities that came with the Alliance presidency seriously. But his sacrifices were costly. Later, he admitted that the chore prevented him from running a bigger circuit and even had an impact on his health. Muchnick was constantly busy, on the phone acting as an umpire, mailing circulars or bulletins, attending big shows, and commanding the attention of Alliance members.

Additionally, he was the central influence on the NWA board of directors and the heavyweight championship committee. Wrestlers vying for the heavyweight title had to make an impression on him in St. Louis before they were given any real consideration, and promoters lobbied for his approval. It was basically accepted across the politically motivated wrestling landscape that Muchnick was the key person in deciding who would hold the NWA title.

Hoping to step down at the August 1972 gathering in Las Vegas, Muchnick was convinced to continue as president for another year, his 20th in the 25-year history of the Alliance. That single year became three. In August 1975, he turned the job over to Jack Adkisson, and the booking of the world heavyweight champion to recording secretary Jim Barnett. Muchnick remained an advisor and a member of the board of directors until his retirement in 1982.

As he edged into his mid-70s, he promoted a multitude of talented newcomers, and wasn't disappointed. Muchnick was a fan of Bob Backlund, the Von Erichs, Ted Dibiase, and the antics of Bruiser Brody (Frank Goodish). He was an avid speaker for the St. Louis Wrestling Club publicity department, providing interviews with Robert Burnes of radio station KMOX before shows at the Kiel. From his offices at the Claridge (suites 230–32) and later the Warwick, Lenox, and the Chase hotels, Sam coordinated his wrestling operations, advised his employees, and mentored his bright young prodigy, Larry Matysik.

On January 1, 1982, Muchnick staged his final wrestling program at the Checkerdome in St. Louis. The extravaganza, headlined by NWA champion Ric Flair and Dusty Rhodes, drew a sellout crowd of 19,918, and featured Pat O'Connor, Dick the Bruiser, Harley Race, Bulldog Bob Brown, Baron Von Raschke, David Von Erich, Greg Valentine, Ox Baker, and Rufus R. Jones. St. Louis mayor Vincent Schoemehl proclaimed it "Sam Muchnick Day." Sam's interest in the St. Louis Wrestling Club was sold to Bob Geigel and Harley Race, adding their names to the ownership roster that was also comprised of O'Connor, Matysik, and Verne Gagne.

The National Wrestling Alliance entered a new phase after Muchnick retired. NWA Presidents Adkisson, Eddie Graham, Bob Geigel, and Jim Crockett each had distinct visions for the group, and, in time, the core principles that had been set in concrete were slowly being chipped away. The collective effort was losing momentum in a dash for individual accomplishments and prosperity, and the presidency became a title that could be exploited to manipulate pieces of the puzzle in one's favor, rather than used to hold the cooperative together. An aggressive national sweep by a gifted third-generation promoter was sufficient enough to set an irreversible course for the Alliance that even Muchnick wouldn't have been able to prevent.

In support of World Championship Wrestling executive Jim Herd, a St. Louis businessman and longtime friend, Muchnick gave a promo for Starrcade 1990. The event at the Kiel Auditorium showcased a Pat O'Connor memorial tag-team tournament, and a spot for Dick the Bruiser as special referee. Sam was also a distinguished guest at a WWF pay-per-view on October 5, 1997, at the Kiel Center. He was honored by the Missouri Athletic Club with a meritorious award in 1988, was given the Bruce Campbell Memorial Award, and was inducted into the St. Louis Media Hall of Fame, the Missouri Sports Hall of Fame on April 20, 1992, the St. Louis Jewish Sports Hall of Fame on December 3, 1992, and the Professional Wrestling Hall of Fame on May 17, 2003.

The Muchnicks instilled an enthusiasm for education in their three children, Richard, Daniel, and Kathryn, and their offspring went into professional fields far away from the hubbub of wrestling. Sam's mother passed away in December 1980, preceding the sudden death of his wife by only weeks, and the combined loss devastated him.

Muchnick invested in assorted businesses and had one share, reportedly worth $25,000, of the Cahokia Land Trust, which owned the Cahokia Downs Race Track, one mile south of East St. Louis. He was an acquaintance of President Harry Truman and was invited to the inaugural galas for Presidents Eisenhower, Kennedy, Johnson, and Nixon.

While wrestling was Muchnick's livelihood, baseball was his passion. Astonishingly knowledgeable, he could hold his own with any of diamond's leading sports scribes, and regularly attended Cardinal games in St. Louis and during the spring in St. Petersburg. Possessing a razor-sharp memory, Sam recalled baseball players from decades past and, more often than not, knew their batting average.

Although rasslin' was bashed for its theatrics in newspapers, Sam brought irrefutable integrity to the sport and it was his intent to help wrestling gain in respect. For 33 years he was the glue of the National Wrestling Alliance, and was arguably the most powerful promoter in professional wrestling history. On the morning of Wednesday, December 30, 1998, Sam Muchnick died at the age of 93 at St. John's Mercy Medical Center.

CHAPTER FIVE

THE
NEKOOSA STRANGLER

Ed "Strangler" Lewis

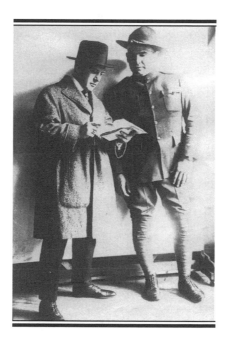

Ed "Strangler" Lewis wrestled 6,200 matches over his long career, and was defeated only 33 times. Yeah, it was the same Lewis who went dancing after a five-hour marathon in 1916 (his opponent, of course, was hospitalized).

Even ignoring the embellished stories of Billy Sandow, an examination of the facts reveals that Lewis was a celebrated professional wrestler on par with other sports luminaries of the 1920s. He brought the mantle of heavyweight wrestling champion into the mainstream, becoming the fascinating personality that wrestling needed. He defined a legacy in the shadow of Frank Gotch, an American grappling legend, and took over the tag of "Strangler" from its originator, Evan Lewis, and served the name well.

The parents of the Strangler began their lives on the European continent. His mother, Molla Gueldenzopf was born in Saxon-Wiemer, Germany on March 22, 1866, and moved with her parents to Sheboygan Falls, Wisconsin in 1882. Three years later, 27-year-old Jacob Friedrich, born on December 28, 1858, in Deinheim, Hessen, Germany, also immigrated to the United States and settled in central Wisconsin. The two were married on September 26, 1887, lived southwest of Nekossa in Port Edwards, and had their first child, Fred, in October. In July 1889, Minnie was born, followed by Robert Herman Julius on June 30, 1890. Jacob and Molla, of the Lutheran faith, had daughters Hattie in 1893 and Mary in 1894.

During the 1900s, Jacob became the marshal for the Village of Nekoosa, and was identified by natives as "Chief." Robert was employed as a delivery boy for Gutheil Grocery in his early teens. A natural athlete with great strength, he excelled in many sports. As a member of the Nekoosa youth baseball team, Robert once traveled to Pittsville for an important game. One story about his transition into professional wrestling ranks had the baseball team in dire need of funds to return home, so he stepped forward to challenge a local wrestler. If he was able to win, the team would have the money to get home. Robert was victorious and his pro career was launched, without any proper direction.

Leo Huber, owner of Huber's General Store in Nekoosa, remembered the event differently: "Bob Friedrich, that's Strangler Lewis' real name, you know, used to play baseball for the Nekoosa team. He wanted to raise money to take the team to Pittsville for a game, so to raise money, they put on a wrestling match. Bob wrestled a man named Brown. This was the beginning of his career."

Friedrich got his early coaching in wrestling from Fred Bentz, a Nekoosa neighbor. Soon he was battling men of all levels of experience, and finding that he was winning a lot more than he was losing. In early 1910, he caught the eye of Billy Potts, a Minneapolis fight manager, who recognized his potential. Potts helped get Friedrich into a special three-on-one handicap match versus Stanislaus Zbyszko on February 10, 1910, at the Dewey Theater in Minneapolis. Robert lasted 12:30 with the exalted Zbyszko, four minutes longer than all of the other competitors combined. Zbyszko commented on the young man's strength, saying that he was the strongest wrestler, of that age, that he'd ever seen.

The impressive showing gave Robert confidence to advance in his training, and it wasn't long before he was the most revered heavyweight in the region. On November 11, 1910, in Grand Rapids, Robert beat Jack Foley, a Canadian champion, winning the first and third falls. Eight days later in Rudolph, he went over Dave Sharkey, a grappler of sizeable reputation. Upset at the defeat, Sharkey demanded a rematch, and on November 29, he was tossed again, in straight falls at

Nekoosa's Brooks' Hall.

The most significant bout of his early career, outside of the Zbyszko affair, was against Marshfield's Fred Beell. Beell, who eclipsed Frank Gotch in 1906, was regarded as one of the country's best wrestlers. Outweighed by 40 pounds, Beell grappled with the nimble young lion on January 3, 1911, in Grand Rapids. After seven minutes, Beell took the opening fall, and then won the second in 22 minutes. Like Zbyszko, he praised Friedrich, emphasizing that he needed suitable coaching. Bob heeded the advice, made the pilgrimage to Beell's Marshfield farm, and learned from the wisdom of his master.

Friedrich relocated to Lansing, Iowa, just west of the Mississippi River. Between 1910 and 1912, Bob wrestled in Wisconsin, Iowa, Illinois, Minnesota, and the Dakotas. An early blemish on his record came on October 26, 1912, when he was defeated by James Souden in Sheboygan Falls. Friedrich won a rematch on October 31.

In January 1913, Robert arrived in Kentucky, a territory promoted by William Barton and Heywood Allen. Prior to a match with Bob Manoogian in Louisville on January 24, a decision was made that would change wrestling history. Friedrich would compete on the circuit under the guise, "Strangler Lewis," a nod to the distinguished Strangler from Wisconsin, Evan Lewis. Manoogian, known as Bob Managoff, would use the designation "Bob Fredericks." Barton later took credit for the discovery of Friedrich and both Allen and Managoff would both claim responsibility for giving him the name Ed "Strangler" Lewis.

Jerry Walls took over promotional duties at the Lexington Opera House and inked Lewis to a contract. Lewis, on September 18, 1913, beat Dr. B.F. Roller when the physician was unable to continue, winning a version of the American heavyweight title, a championship also being claimed by Charles Cutler of Chicago. William Demetral triumphed in Lexington on October 21, winning the title when Lewis was hurt after being pushed into the orchestra pit. Lewis went to Macon, Georgia, and wrestled all comers at the Georgia State Fair. His skipper negotiated with promoters in Chicago to get him dates in the Windy City, and Lewis debuted there on November 3.

Lewis's stellar resumé prompted Walls to issue a challenge to Chicago's leading heavyweight, Cutler. The *Chicago American* and *Chicago Daily Tribune* ran great press on the exploits of the promising Lewis, including a long article in the November 30 *Tribune*. Unimpressed, Cutler confronted Lewis in a Chicago restaurant on November 17, 1913, and vulgar words led to violence. The Strangler got the better of his rival, punching his adversary in the face. Cutler, and a table, went to the ground, and restaurant employees rapidly pulled the pair apart. Their formal match, however, on November 26, closed with a victory for Cutler at the Globe Athletic Club.

Successive losses by Lewis to Americus (August "Gus" Schoenlein) on December 29 in Chicago, and Roller on January 23, 1914, in Lexington, were followed up with Billy Sandow's request for a match against Yussif Hussane. Sandow had led the stampede of Billy Jenkins several weeks earlier in Lexington, but his optimism faded after two tough defeats. On February 5, 1914, Lewis appeared at the Ada Meade Theater in Lexington, prepared to wrestle anyone who accepted his invitation. For every minute his opponent was active, they'd receive a dollar, and $25 was the award for staying in with Lewis 15 minutes. Sandow answered the call himself, and lasted ten minutes.

Influenced by New York promoter William Brady, Sandow wrestled, but also managed and promoted alongside his brothers Julius and Maxwell Baumann. His stable of talent included Jenkins, Hussane, Roller, and later, Marin Plestina, in barnstorming tours. That Sandow and Lewis crossed paths in Lexington was significant for both men, but months would pass before they met again. In the meantime, the Walls-Barton connection got Lewis into Indianapolis, where Ed trained with veterans Charlie Olson and Billy Schober. Schober later claimed that it was during these sessions that Lewis learned the headlock.

Cutler was victorious over Lewis in an extension of their feud on April 27, 1914, in Lexington. Still searching for a talented protégé, Sandow signed the Strangler away from Walls, and focused on duels with title contenders. To tune up for his title defense against Joe Stecher on July 5, 1915, Cutler retained Lewis as a workout partner, and Ed was in the champion's corner the night of the match. Stecher won in straight falls, and Sandow immediately pursued a title bout for Lewis.

That opportunity offered itself in Evansville on October 20. After two hours, Lewis fell from the ring and declined to continue. Although the contest was profoundly criticized for its sluggish pace, with neither wrestler committing himself to actual competition, the bout put Lewis's name in the headlines. Sandow capitalized on the confusion, spewing a variety of stories that disparaged Stecher and made his grappler sound like a future champion.

An international tournament at the Manhattan Opera House in New York, commenced in November. The event was promoted by Jack Curley and Samuel Rachmann and would involve a mix of Greco-Roman and catch-as-catch-can wrestling. Lewis entered the fracas on November 22 and trounced Charles Christansen in one minute and ten seconds. Lewis was billed as being from Germany, following the global theme. Between November 30 and December 11 Lewis wrestled six draws with the finest the tourney had to offer. Three of the deadlocks were against Wladek Zbyszko, and two were with Alex Aberg, including a one hour and four minute match on December 9, which was stopped by police at 1:00 a.m. The sixth draw was a 20-minute exhibition with Cutler on December 7.

Lewis would dominate against the previously invincible Masked Marvel (Mort Henderson) on December 20, winning in 11:50. Two days later, Lewis and the Marvel fought to a one-hour-and-59-minute draw. On December 29, the Strangler wrestled Alex Aberg under Greco-Roman rules, and was defeated. It was his only loss at the Opera House.

On January 15, 1916, Lewis beat Roller and captured his American title. Sandow, proving that his verbal talent equaled Lewis's wrestling skills, boasted to newspapers about his man's championship and disputed any claim Stecher made to being the "real" titleholder. Sandow said that if Stecher wanted the rights to the title, he would have to go through Lewis first.

The Baumann Family rallied behind Sandow's discovery. Jules, his older brother, promoted hot spots in upstate New York, while Billy's younger sibling Max operated out of offices in the Savannah, Georgia, area. Another brother, Alexander, built the headlock machine the Strangler practiced his famed maneuver on. Despite Lewis's victories in the Northeast, it was Stecher who was the top grappler across the Midwest and deep into the heart of the wrestling community. It was a market Sandow and Lewis wanted to tap into, and a win over "Scissors Joe" was a surefire way to accomplish that feat.

Lewis wrestled Stecher on July 4, 1916, in Omaha at the Fairgrounds. The two wrangled in a tedious five-hour draw. Lewis's stalling was ripped by writers, and a match that should have been synonymous with everything good about pro grappling turned into a deplorable mess. There were an estimated 20,000 fans in attendance, and the gate was around $30,000. Afterwards, jaded spectators doubted the wrestlers had given their all, and instead of boosting his image, Lewis took the brunt of the blame for the debacle, while Stecher remained the local hero.

Lewis said the following about the match: "We wrestled five hours without either of us securing a fall. At the end of the bout, which was halted by the referee, Stecher appeared to be all in. His pulse was 125, and according to those who witnessed the encounter he could not have stood the strain ten minutes longer. I offered Stecher a return match, but he refused to accept it, saying he was through wrestling with me. I cannot account for his statement, as I always gave him a square deal in every one of our matches. I intend to rest up during the summer months, getting back into the game sometime in September. If Gotch retires, as he says he will, and Stecher makes good on his statement that he will not wrestle with me again, I will lay claim to the heavyweight wrestling title."

In 1920, Sandow remembered the contest this way:

> Three years ago, Stecher was hardly known outside of Omaha. He had, however, thrown every man he had met inside of 15 minutes. Out that way he was thought unbeatable, and they said the man didn't live who could stay half an hour with him. Albert (sic) Cutler, the American champion, had gone 25 minutes with him, and next to Joe, of course, he was called the second wonder of the world, in Omaha. I finally arranged a match between Lewis and Stecher. It was three years ago last summer.
>
> They met in the open air under a broiling Nebraska sun. The bout started at 1:30 and at 7:00, after five-and-one-half hours of wrestling, without either man being off his feet once, folks began to run automobiles up to the ring so that they could throw their headlights on the men, that they might see each other. At this late day they was just beginning to realize what a great match that was. Now, but they didn't then. They held Lewis's money up for four days on the grounds that there was something shady with the match. They couldn't believe that mortal man could stay beyond half an hour with their Joe. To show the stuff that the Strangler's made of, let me add that Lewis took a shower, had a light supper and danced until 4:30 the next morning. Ed Smith refereed the bout and he'll never forget it, or the heat either.

The propaganda machine created by Sandow shaped most, if not all, of the public opinion of the Strangler. Lewis was in the infancy of his career, but he already had an extraordinary reputation. Stecher, who was wrestling a formidable combination of mental and physical demons, dropped his title to Earl Caddock on April 9, 1917, in Omaha, giving Sandow a new target to home in on. But rather than putting a full-court press on Caddock, Lewis opted for a match with Finnish Olympic champion John Olin in Chicago on May 2 for Olin's version of the crown. Olin, months earlier, had thwarted Stecher in a contentious affair in Springfield, Massachusetts, and parlayed the tainted victory into a title run. Lewis won their match when Olin could not continue after two hours, 37 minutes, earning his first world title.

Sandow envisioned a unification match between Lewis and Caddock, but before that contest came to fruition, the Strangler traded his title with Curley's star, Wladek Zbyszko. On June 5, Zbyszko won a fall from Lewis in San Francisco, but Ed regained the championship in Boston on July 4. Their feud extended into the winter at a theatre in New York City, where Wladek trampled Lewis in the finals on December 22, 1917, in 1:47:37. Zbyszko's win earned him his own world title, meaning that Caddock, Lewis (who maintained a baseless claim), and Wladek each held "world" championships.

The limitations of Caddock, stuck in Iowa due to his military commitments as a member of the 88th Division, preparing for action in Europe, gave Des Moines a pair of crucial title bouts. On February 8, 1918, Caddock beat Zbyszko on points, and 7,000 fans paid a record of $26,000 to observe the festivities, at that time the fourth largest wrestling gate in American history. On June 21, Lewis and Caddock wrestled, and the bout again went to the Iowa athlete by decision.

Proving that a loss could not wipe his championship claim clean, the Strangler held his title until a March 21, 1919, Madison Square Garden loss to Zbyszko. Lewis's big matches between 1916 and 1919 included two bouts with Ad Santel in San Francisco, a draw against Stecher in New York City on April 26, 1918, and a rematch with Stecher on March 3, 1919, in Chicago, where he earned a single fall in 2:12:37. Caddock, in May, was ready to make his homecoming, on a leave granted to attend to his ill wife, and Sandow was making plans for a match for Lewis and the primary titleholder. No one, at the time, knew how the war had affected Caddock.

Lewis and Zbyszko wrestled on April 28, 1919, in Chicago, and the latter was victorious, earning a bout against Caddock. Less than a month later, Lewis vanquished Wladek in Chicago, and if Caddock never wrestled again, it was the Strangler who had the strongest claim to the title, with wins over Zbyszko and Stecher. None of the others could make that claim. That changed on July 4, 1919, in Omaha when Stecher routed Lewis in straight falls, three years after their infamous stalemate. Caddock served as special referee for the bout. As for his own war service, Ed served as a military instructor of hand-to-hand combat at Camp Grant in Rockford.

The "Man of a Thousand Holds," Caddock recovered enough to wrestle Stecher in New York City on January 30, 1920. Stecher went over and was decreed the undisputed champion. Twelve days before Christmas 1920, Curley promoted Lewis-Stecher at the 71st Regiment Armory, and the Strangler captured his first "main line" world title in 1:41:56. The title was passed to Stanislaus Zbyszko on May 6, 1921, in a short match that drew an estimated 10,000 fans to New York's 22nd Regiment Armory.

The tranquility of a national wrestling scene that operated as fairly as possible could only last so long. A power struggle was looming. It wasn't until after Lewis regained the title from Zbyszko on March 3, 1922 in Wichita that Ed and Sandow embarked on a mission to branch off and take control. Essentially, they confiscated all authority from Curley, the affluent Northeastern promoter, and went into business for themselves.

With important outlets in Kansas City, Tulsa, and Chicago, Sandow and Lewis protected their stake by hiring a full-time "policeman," Nebraska's John Pesek, and an innovative training partner, Joe "Toots" Mondt. The group introduced a wide assortment of manufactured challengers for the Strangler, some of whom were not suitable for preliminary bouts, but Lewis carried the matches with entertaining exhibitions.

The unconventional style of working, albeit not entirely modern, was more elaborate and absorbing than the usual fare. Lewis intentionally acquired heat, and wrestling audiences cried foul when he "crippled" opponents with his headlock. The inventive angles were driving people into complete hysterics, periodically pushing crowds to the verge of rioting. Midwestern fans were just a decade removed from watching the technical performances of Frank Gotch. Now they were seeing the current champion, Strangler Lewis, purposely maiming a ring rival. Lewis was perfect as an erratic and violent wrestler, and Sandow was brilliant in the way he spun the webs.

Sandow, the architect, compiled a stable of grapplers who followed his orders, and those "outlaws" wanting a shot at Lewis would have to tackle Jack Pesek beforehand. Pesek, a shooter beyond compare, simply could not be beaten. Legitimate matches with Stecher or the much heavier Zbyszko may have given him the most trouble, but Stanislaus was a member of the tribe. Stecher, at the time, was more interested in baseball. From 1922 to 1925, Sandow and Lewis dominated heavyweight wrestling in America, and all but bankrupted Curley. In early 1925, the champion and his manager decided to bring a newcomer into the picture, and it would be a move they would forever regret.

Wayne Munn, in 1896, was the first of five children born to Dr. Betheul and Retta Cordiella Fugate Munn in Colby, Kansas. Three brothers, Wade, Monte, and Glenn, and a sister, Elizabeth, followed. When Wayne was three, the family migrated to Fairbury, Nebraska, southwest of Lincoln. As a teen, he did a stint as a clown in the Campbell Brothers Circus while gaining notoriety on the football field at Fairbury High. Wayne enrolled at the University of Nebraska in 1916, and at six-foot-six and 230 pounds, he became an immediate superstar. Besides football, basketball and boxing, Munn wrestled as a heavyweight for coach Hugo Otoupalik and won a Missouri Valley conference championship.

After duty in the United States Army Reserves as a lieutenant during the war, Munn went on hiatus from athletics. He practiced law, sold insurance, and was an automobile vendor in Sioux City, before being convinced by promoter Gene Melady to become a professional boxer. Under the guidance of Mike Gibbons, Munn was said to have lost 40 pounds in training. Writers billed him as a boxer with the potential to be in the class of Jack Dempsey. His backers felt they might have the next champ in their midst.

But before they could start counting their cash and celebrating championships, Wayne had to weather his debut. The hype continued into the match, and with a size advantage over 195-pound Jack Clifford, it seemed obvious that Wayne had everything but experience. But on November 16, 1923, in Sioux City, Munn's opening bout ended when he was knocked out, no match for his opponent's skill. His second stab at pugilism also finished badly, with Munn losing to Charley Paulson in the third round.

Munn abandoned boxing and turned to wrestling. Courted by Sandow, Wayne joined the most powerful syndicate in wrestling, and began his schooling in Omaha. His premiere as a grappler was on February 12, 1924, in New York City, defeating Bill Beth, with his football maneuvers proving a unique addition to wrestling.

Sandow and Lewis set the table for Munn not only to challenge for the world title, but to win the championship. The bout would have some controversy, spark a lot of interest, and lead to a huge payday in a rematch. On January 8, 1925, in Kansas City, Munn "upset" Lewis in three falls and became the disputed champ. The drama intensified when Lewis refused to give up the diamond belt, and Munn's manager, Gabe Kaufman, rushed into court. At the same time, Sandow settled on a stadium in Michigan City, Indiana, for the rematch. Despite having solid thinkers plotting the course, the Lewis-Sandow corps were blinded by greed, and overlooked the fact that Munn was new to wrestling.

Those in charge felt comfortable with their new champion. They booked Munn into matches against carefully picked opponents, sheltering him, and would never let an outsider get their hands on him in the ring. On April 15, 1925, Munn was slated to grapple a key member of Sandow's group, Stanislaus Zbyszko, in Philadelphia. Zbyszko had done the job for Munn, a wrestler he could easily topple dozens of times in an hour, on February 11 in Kansas City, losing two straight falls. The second go was expected to be another noble performance by Zbyszko, and a bout that would further help Munn win the hearts of fans. The tilt in Philadelphia went two falls as planned, but unfortunately for Sandow, Lewis, and Munn, the winner was Zbyszko.

The double-cross of all double-crosses had occurred. Stanislaus tore into his green opponent, winning the first fall in 8:11 and the second in 4:53. Jack Curley reemerged from the shadows to push Zbyszko to win the title, and the deed was executed flawlessly. The three-year reign of Lewis and Sandow at the top was over. The spin master then went to work.

Sandow insisted that because Munn hadn't defeated Lewis in a fair match, the Strangler was still titleholder, no matter what happened in Philadelphia. The Decoration Day scrap in Michigan City was going ahead as scheduled. Curley's faction was also promoting a show on May 30, their program headlined by Zbyszko and Joe Stecher in St. Louis under the auspices of Tom Packs. Midwestern fans had a choice of championship matches that weekend.

The Sky Blue Arena played host to an estimated 14,000 fans that afternoon from Chicago, Detroit, and South Bend. Lewis gave up the initial fall, but procured the second, and then the third to successfully defend his title. Michigan City promoter Floyd Fitzsimmons proudly placed the gate at $50,000. In St. Louis, 15,000 enthusiasts watched Stecher dethrone Zbyszko at the University Athletic Field. Stecher won his match in straight falls.

Curley was now in a position to punish his enemies after his "blacklisting," and while past grievances were often resolved for the good of wrestling, he took great pleasure in his revenge. His methods relegated Lewis and Sandow to insignificance, and Curley wasn't going to rest until they were back counting pennies in their hometowns of Nekoosa and Cherryvale.

The Strangler and his camp tried their best to fight the quarantine, running opposition to established promoters in St. Louis, Los Angeles, and Chicago, but their shows were mediocre by comparison. Even worse, wrestlers in the troupe began to dive overboard, among them the renowned "policeman," John Pesek.

All parties eventually acknowledged that business needed a boost, and the feud between Stecher and Curley and Lewis and Sandow ended in late 1926. Weary of the constant demands of being titleholder, Stecher wanted to step away from the championship, and that paved the way for Lewis's return. In St. Louis on February 20, 1928, Ed took back the title before 8,000 fans at the Coliseum.

Lewis was now champion for a fifth time, but he still wasn't universally accepted. Curley, who attended the switch in St. Louis, was still bitter, and rejected his title ambitions. Lewis and Sandow, instead, courted Curley's most notable rival, a promoter who aspired to be the czar of the industry, Boston's Paul Bowser. It was Bowser who pushed the notion of football players invading pro wrestling post-Munn, and masterminded the rise of Gustave Adolph Sonnenberg (1898–1944) in 1928. Bowser wanted Lewis's title for Sonnenberg, and was willing to pay $50,000 for a January 4, 1929, match in Boston. The unseasoned Sonnenberg snapped up the title in two falls, and Lewis made Gus look like a wrestling prodigy.

Sonnenberg was a mat sensation. Swallowing his pride, Curley dealt with Bowser, and Lewis made his first New York City appearance in five years on January 21, 1929. Lewis, who had been married twice, to San Jose doctor Ada Scott

Morton and to Bessie McNear of Kansas City, took his third bride on May 8, 1929. He wed Elaine Tomaso in Riverside, California, and Sandow was his best man.

The Strangler did extensive traveling along the Bowser-affiliated circuit, and further helped turn Sonnenberg onto an icon. In 1930 in Los Angeles, Lewis put over Everette Marshall, showing his absolute willingness to lose bouts for the good of the business. A clause in the Bowser contract stipulated that if Sonnenberg lost the title, he would only lose it to Lewis, and a substantial amount of cash was allegedly posted in escrow as a forfeit, to ensure the Boston promoter held up his end of the bargain. Not surprisingly, Bowser reneged and Ed Don George beat Sonnenberg for the title on December 10, 1930.

Apparently Bowser didn't consider the possibility of a vengeful Strangler shooting on his champion. Perhaps he just assumed that the Olympic and collegiate credentials of George would prevent a double-cross. Either way, things turned out poorly for Bowser and his titleholder on April 13, 1931, in Los Angeles. Lewis won the opening fall in 1:10:26, and the second in 7:42 before 12,000 fans at Wrigley Field, capturing his sixth world title. Angry with this turn of events, Bowser plotted his revenge, but knew that a plain double-cross was impractical. No one was going to pin the Strangler without his approval. Bowser weighed his options, searching for a viable angle, and came up with a doozy for Lewis's May 4 match in Montreal.

Following the playbook, Lewis gave Henri DeGlane, another ex-Olympian, the first fall in 33 minutes. Expecting to win the last two falls to retain his championship, the Strangler was shocked when he was disqualified by referee Eugene Tremblay, who claimed he had bitten his opponent. Sandow soon realized what had happened and vehemently protested. Montreal Athletic Commission Chairman Dr. Gaston Demers said that Sandow didn't have a license and directed police to take the manager from the ring. DeGlane held his right arm in agony, and upon examination, teeth marks were found in his skin. DeGlane claimed Lewis had made the marks when he was securing a headlock.

The matter was beyond their control; Sandow and Lewis were bilked out of their title, and attempts to influence the Montreal commission proved futile. DeGlane had effectively pulled off a double-cross, and the world title was back in the clutches of Bowser.

Sandow made a statement, recorded in the May 6, 1931, edition of the *Montreal Gazette*: "Lewis never bit anyone. If DeGlane was bitten, and your physicians say he was, so we accept that statement, then he bit himself. That is an old, old circus wrestling trick, practiced in Europe for years and resorted to often by wrestlers to gain disqualification of an opponent when wrestlers are meeting all comers. Your police department could easily establish who did the biting by photographing the bite marks and having a cast made of the jaws of Lewis and DeGlane to see which fits the marks. Then it would be known."

Slowing down, Lewis went into semiretirement. Meanwhile, Sandow stepped up his scheming. He signed former Notre Dame footballer Joe Savoldi, hammering a stake between himself and Lewis. The 16-year association of Lewis and Sandow, amidst brewing animosity, expired in late December 1931. Billy would go on to employ the services of Colorado onion farmer Everette Marshall, a bright newcomer.

The Strangler continued to tour, and despite being pudgy and suffering from the consequences of an eye disease, trachoma, he could still put on a show. His fluctuating sight-loss left him in regular distress, but his amicable nature endured. In April 1932, Jim Londos, the star for Curley and Mondt, abandoned the cartel, leaving New York promoters without a champion. Mondt went to Wisconsin to rendezvous with Lewis, hoping to impress on his friend their critical need for his return. Mondt and Curley were desperate; they had to bury the hatchet with Lewis and Bowser to remain afloat.

Deals were made, and Bowser forces marched into New York City. Storming the territory, Lewis saw the New York Athletic Commission order Londos to consent to a match or be stripped of his title. Londos would not wrestle straight with Lewis, and the commission acted in late September. On October 10, 1932, Lewis took on Jack Sherry, a longtime indie wrestler thought of in certain circles as the uncrowned champion, for the vacant crown at the Garden. Lewis won in 1:24:15, nabbing his seventh title.

The local commission appointed Londos's "policeman" Ray Steele the number one contender, and on December 5, 1932, with no pact in place to work the match, Steele and Lewis were facing a dreadful shoot. Referee Eddie Forbes tried to protect the integrity of the commission, while allowing the necessary leeway for a night of entertainment. His restraint was commendable, but went for naught as Steele refused to stop fouling Lewis. After three warnings for illegal punches, Steele was disqualified at 32:55. Irate fans began to riot in protest, and Curley was a victim of the post-match carnage. The travesty might have been avoided had the commission followed the script imagined by promoters, and resisted trying to police a contrived sport.

Unfortunately for the New York outfit, Lewis, even on his best days, could not spark the interest of fans. People just weren't buying that the out-of-shape Strangler was leading the heavyweight, especially with Londos fresh in their minds. Bowser's prodigy Jim Browning, who Lewis respected very much, was chosen as his heir, and on February 20, 1933, Browning took the championship in 57:50 before 5,000 fans at the Garden. The loss represented the end of an era. He was increasingly receptive to putting wrestlers over in different areas of the country, losing to Savoldi, Earl McCready, Ed Don George, Nick Lutze, Sammy Stein, and Gus Sonnenberg.

The formation of the "Trust" several weeks later brought divided promoters and wrestlers onto the same page. That included Lewis, Steele, and his principal adversary, Londos. Londos, born sometime between 1894 and 1897, was just a little younger than Lewis, and where Lewis was on the down side of his career, Londos was peaking. The "Golden Greek" was the biggest draw in the business, and the two athletes were compared on many levels, with Lewis being the more imposing wrestler in terms of ability, size, and strength, while Londos was the better thespian. Divisions among bookers prevented them from matching up for years, but prior to 1930, the two had wrestled a reported 14 times. Lewis prevailed in a majority of their bouts, and Londos had never beaten the Strangler.

The barriers that had impeded a Lewis-Londos fantasy match were now worked out, and the brouhaha everyone was waiting for was scheduled for September 20, 1934 in Chicago. In publicity mode, Lewis appeared with Art Fields and Fred Hall, a radio comedy duo, to build the excitement. The bout was the talk of the city, and promoters and dignitaries were making arrangements to witness the historic event. Newspapers devoted extensive coverage to Lewis and Londos, unlike any clash since Gotch-Hackenschmidt, and the *Chicago Daily Tribune* even printed a photo of Ed and his parents dining at the Brevoort Hotel.

A record gate of $96,302 was paid by 35,265 fans to see the spectacular at Wrigley Field. Lewis's parents and sisters sat ringside to watch the 49 minute and 27 second match. Ed gave Londos the victory, collected his earnings, and sailed for Europe. Promoters were still eager to use him on their cards, and his agenda was full through the early part of 1935. In late July, the Strangler announced that he was going to hang up his boots to train Vincent Lopez, an up-and-comer for the Mondt-Daro conglomerate in Los Angeles. A complete retirement was out of the question.

The Strangler did not support some of the techniques being used by wrestlers, from dropkicks to, ironically, the elaborate angles his own managerial team originally inspired. He wanted honesty in wrestling, and his newfound sensibility was confirmed when he agreed to participate in one of wrestling's last noteworthy shoot contests, an August 13, 1936, bout against Lee Wykoff at the Hippodrome in New York City. The show marked the arena's first foray into athletics, and 3,000 fans were present to see a sincere effort from the headliners.

Lewis sustained a painful injury in the days leading up to the match, according to gossip revealed years later, and those who believed the match would be a brief encounter were flabbergasted when it went two hours, 14 minutes. Both wrestlers fell from the ring and were counted out, unable to continue. Wrestling fans in attendance that night may have concluded at that point that such dawdling, competitive pro bouts were no match for simulated tomfoolery.

Lewis was married a fourth time in January 1937, to Bobbie Lee West in Yuma, Arizona. Eleven months later, he again announced that he was quitting wrestling. There was speculation that the Wykoff tussle had demonstrated that he was no longer the wrestler he once was, but Lewis was a noble sportsman at heart. It wasn't long, however, before he was confidently hyping the possibility of losing 50 pounds for a battle with the unbeatable Great Gama of India. His dedication to wrestling remained, but Lewis could not turn the clock back to 1925.

Eager to invest his savings, Lewis opened cafés in Glendale (709 South Brand) and Long Beach (4300 Long Beach Blvd.). He also planned to build an arena in Glendale, and received licenses from the California Athletic Commission to promote boxing and wrestling. To make a few extra dollars, Lewis managed Hard Boiled Haggerty and Tarzan White in Southern California in 1939. He was also hired as an assistant matchmaker at the Legion Stadium in Hollywood, booking heavyweights, beginning on July 10, 1939.

The volume of his investments put a strain on the Strangler's accounts, and his arena venture disintegrated. He gave up his cafés by May 1941, and instead of sweating in a gymnasium and keeping fit, he enjoyed socializing at establishments like the Knickerbocker Bar. He was unreserved, wanton, and recklessly squandered his wealth. The sports community called upon him regularly, and Lewis attended innumerable charitable functions. Promoters were always looking to attach his name to their bill, and going into 1941, Lewis was regularly featured as a guest referee.

Lewis came out of retirement again in 1942, and shortly after the death of his father in April, he began to exercise intensely to regain his conditioning. He made appearances in Los Angeles for Ray Fabiani and injected spice into the latter's international tournament. The Strangler went to Philadelphia, booked by Jack Pfefer, and had a final push by Orville Brown in the central states. On November 5, 1942, he beat Brown in Kansas City for the MWA world title. The bout spawned a rematch on November 26 that Lewis won, passing him the MWA title belt, and a victory in Columbus on December 3 gave him a definitive claim. Over a two-week span in January 1943, he lost both the Kansas City and Columbus versions of the championship to Wykoff and John Pesek, respectively.

During World War II, Lewis visited military installations and entertained troops. He weighed more than 300 pounds at this point, the portliest he'd ever been, and wrestled only occasionally. He traveled with promising Cliff Gustafson, was accommodating to Sam Muchnick's campaign in St. Louis, and even went to Hawaii to scare off Jack Sherry for Al Karasick. The Los Angeles Athletic Club hired him in early November 1947 as a wrestling coach, and, in need of money, he worked as a greeter for the famous gym. A new organization, the bogus Wrestling Promoters' Association of America and Allied Countries, brought the Strangler aboard as commissioner, at $25,000 annually, in December 1948. The National Wrestling Alliance had a similar plan for Lewis, and it would actually make good on its promise to pay him.

At the November 1949 convention in St. Louis, Ed was named "ambassador of good will" for the NWA. The NWA membership roster was mostly made up of his friends, people he'd either influenced or made money for. It was payback time for promoters trying to help the ailing Strangler financially, and a system to compensate him with a $25 monthly payment from each member was approved. As a socially gifted spokesman for the developing coalition, he would handle any controversial issues, wandering from territory to territory ironing out snags. In 1950, Ed mentored Timothy Geohagen in Ontario, and late in the year, received authorization to join NWA champion Lou Thesz as his official second.

Some NWA members grudgingly contributed to the fund, whereas others refused, and, in 1951, the Alliance formed an "Ed Lewis Committee" to preside over all matters related to the wrestling luminary. The Thesz-Lewis combination was working out better than anticipated, freeing up the NWA titleholder from obligatory advertising sessions at radio stations or with newspaper writers. During the 1951 convention in Tulsa, the membership ratified a measure that raised Thesz's per match income to 15 percent, allocating 2½ percent to the NWA, and 2½ percent for Ed's wages.

Still contending with his vision problems, Lewis garnered cash from every show the champion wrestled, from rural Texas to Madison Square Garden. He traveled and taught Thesz, building on a treasured friendship, and Lou was privy to a side of the Strangler that only a few were exposed. The NWA again discussed the money going to Lewis at the 1955 convention in St. Louis, and frugal promoters swayed the vote, eliminating that additional percentage. Lewis remained on the payroll through January 1, 1956, when his run with Thesz ended.

Surprisingly, the membership renewed their pledge to Lewis with a $7,500 annual salary at the September 1956 conference, and in November, Thesz asked Muchnick if Ed could return to his side as an advisor. He did so in a limited capacity, and also touted Dory Funk Sr., Bob Ellis, and Pepper Gomez.

Late in 1957, Muchnick pleaded with his colleagues to hire Lewis to boost the credibility of NWA champion Dick Hutton. The request was ignored by some tight-fisted promoters, but where Lewis did appear, he did much more than assist in marketing. He lectured children about fair play and having compassion, expressing his own firm beliefs through August 1960.

Lewis went blind from trachoma. Destitute and struggling, he relied on his wife, acquaintances, and donations to survive. Living meagerly in the Tulsa area, the Strangler believed deeply in religion, and spoke with utter conviction. Just weeks before his death, while he was confined to a nursing home after several strokes, a special marker was dedicated to Ed and his legacy on Prospect Avenue in Nekoosa. The emblem was created by the South Wood County Historical Corporation, and the text was written by Marshall Buehler. On Sunday, August 7, 1966, Lewis passed away at a Veteran's Hospital in Muskogee. He was 76 years old.

There wasn't a more likeable guy in professional wrestling than Ed "Strangler" Lewis. He emerged from the era of Cutler, Stecher, Caddock, and Gotch to immortalize himself, independently. His charisma was palpable, giving him the upper hand in the ballyhoo department, and especially useful when writers were penning the muddled history of wrestling. A gentleman, Lewis was beloved by sports editors, promoters, and leaders of charities, and his kindness was almost mythical in proportion. Most importantly, Lewis was phenomenal with wrestlers. He offered guidance, and, in many ways, acted as a father figure.

Robert Friedrich embraced the moniker "Strangler" Lewis, and used psychology to expose the weaknesses of his opponents. Joe Stecher was one of his few legitimate rivals, an ideal adversary who could have Lewis running for safe harbor. Their 15 year rivalry sits in wrestling lore, as do Lewis's days charging across the United States with Billy Sandow, calling out challenges to Jack Dempsey, and busting out through raucous crowds under police protection.

Today, Lewis is enshrined in the Wisconsin Athletic Hall of Fame, the Tragos/Thesz Wrestling Hall of Fame at the International Wrestling Institute and Museum, and in the Professional Wrestling Hall of Fame.

CHAPTER SIX

CHICAGO'S CONSUMMATE ENTREPRENEUR

Fred Kohler

The patriarch of Chicago's wrestling scene was a bombastic and versatile character named Fred Kohler. Once described by noted broadcaster Jack Brickhouse as "the best wrestling promoter who ever lived," Kohler took his business from an annual revenue of $18,000 around the end of World War II to more than $100,000 per annum during the 1950s. With the success of his Saturday night television program on the DuMont Network, he arguably became the most powerful man in wrestling.

Fred Kohler was actually born "Fred Koch," with a twin sister, Mildred, on January 6, 1903 in Chicago. They were the second set of twins born to German immigrants Frederick "Fritz" (1874–1929) and Katherine "Katie" (1876–1952) Koch.

His father was the proprietor of Koch's Hall in Chicago at 1764 North Larrabee Street. Fred attended Manierre School and Lane Technical, where, as a football player, he excelled at three positions and captained the team. As a swimmer at the Larrabee YMCA, he trained with the future Tarzan, Johnny Weissmuller, and wrestled as an amateur.

As Fred grew into a teenager, the City of Chicago was overrun by crime, and his father's German social hall, a gathering place for cultural and political functions, was affected by the escalating corruption. Fritz had a dominant personality, resistant to the fresh ideas of his son. The two frequently clashed, leaving much ill feeling. Fred treasured the lessons he learned from his loving mother, however, and she had an enormous impact on shaping his life.

A hard-nosed battler, Fred fought throughout his childhood — anyone from neighborhood bullies to friends. Coaches nurtured his natural wrestling instincts, and Kohler demonstrated his grit in formal competitions. Representing the Hamlin Park squad, he placed second in the 175-pound division of the 1928 Central AAU Wrestling Tournament in Chicago. As an occupation, he worked as an assistant physical director at a Chicago YMCA and studied to become a die machinist.

The hall at 1764 Larrabee was open to professional wrestling, with the likes of Lou Talaber competing during the 1910s. According to legend, Fred promoted his first bouts there in 1925, and packed the hall with several hundred spectators. Using the aliases "Fred Kohler," given to him by Dubuque promoter Heinie Engel, and "Freddie King," Koch began to accept cash for wrestling engagements. Often appearing at small Chicago clubs, he held his own against many established middleweights.

At the same time, he continued to broker matches for even smaller venues, finally earning a spot managing affairs at the Marigold Gardens in 1934. He also staged shows at the Prudential Hall, Merry Gardens, Rainbo Fronton, and later at the Arcadia Gardens, featuring Jack "Bad Boy" Brown, Charles Fischer, Al Williams, Nanjo Singh, Rudy Kay, John Silvy, George Dusette, Whitey Walberg, Hans Schnabel, and Ivan Rasputin. Promoting events at local facilities did wonders both for Kohler's reputation and his wallet. Hoping to one day contend with the mighty promoters of the "Trust," he found a solid fan base who enjoyed his weekly mayhem.

The fact that Kohler was making money using a majority of non-heavyweights was astonishing, and by 1936, he was ready to expand his operations to compete with his adversaries. The businesses of Joe Coffey and Ed White suffered in the fallout of Dick Shikat's double-cross of Danno O'Mahoney in New York City. Kohler, on the other hand, had agreements with the "Little Trust," Billy Sandow,

Adam Weissmuller of Detroit, and Al Haft of Columbus, who held the contracts of Everette Marshall, Ali Baba, and Shikat, respectively.

The Chicago point man for the Haft-Sandow syndicate, Kohler received the blessing of the Illinois Athletic Commission to acknowledge the winner of the Baba-Marshall bout at the Stadium on November 20, 1936, as "world" champion. A noteworthy crowd of 9,736, paying $7,505, saw Marshall take the victory in 35:44, and gain recognition in Illinois. With those numbers, Kohler successfully moved into the big time. Seeing that the tides were turning, White met with his youthful competition at a downtown hotel in December, and united the two factions. Their joint interests commenced on January 5, 1937, with a Coliseum program headlined by Marshall and Jim McMillen.

For most of 1937, the pair endorsed Marshall as heavyweight champion. When Sandow dealt away Everette's title to the Packs-Bowser troupe, Kohler and White aligned themselves with Joe "Toots" Mondt and brought in ex-Chicago Bear Bronko Nagurski, a titleholder in Los Angeles, New York, Philadelphia, and Minneapolis. They promoted the Rainbo Fronton, White City Arena, Park Casino, and regular cards at the Coliseum. After a six-year hiatus, Fred revisited the Marigold Gardens on February 12, 1941, and Ruffy Silverstein and Paul Bozzell drew 1,700 spectators.

Coffey passed away on December 10, 1941, and White retired in September 1942, leaving the 39-year-old Kohler undisputed king of all Chicago's wrestling promotions. His dream had been realized. While employed as a machinist and consulting engineer, he had often labored on less than five hours of sleep so that he could continue to present matches. Pleasing his fans with well-rounded entertainment and colorful wrestlers, Kohler felt, would sustain his promotion, and despite a drop in popularity, Fred was in a position to call the Windy City his own, and wasn't about to let it go.

Kohler had a true gem in his wrestling combine. Walter Palmer (1912–1998) served an important role as Chicago's top heavyweight during the war and was Fred's "go-to" star. Palmer was a true workhorse, a talented shooter who once schooled for the 1936 Olympics. A product of the park athletic system, he was trained by Lou Talaber and maintained his amateur status by competing professionally under a false identity and a hood as the "Red Ace." Palmer toured the Southwestern U.S. and Mexico, returning to his hometown in early 1940 a more confident and proficient professional. Palmer built an impressive win streak, and by 1944, he was claiming a version of the world title, which newspapers referred to as the "Midwestern" championship.

Professional wrestling made its television debut in Chicago on July 10, 1946, on

WBKB (channel 4), and showcased a match between Palmer and Flash Gordon from the Rainbo Arena. Kohler's Wednesday night show was broadcast weekly at 8:15 for less than a month. Technical problems annoyed viewers, as glare from the lights at the Rainbo proved too strong for the station's cameras. WBKB briefly cancelled their relay from the Rainbo, but Russ Davis resumed his mat commentary once the glitch was fixed.

There were concerns that wrestling on television would cut into the size of the live audience, and some prognosticators believed that TV was going to kill grappling altogether. WBKB overlooked such fears, expanding to offer Kohler's Monday night events from the Midway Arena. Television was doing more to spotlight wrestling than anyone could have predicted. Given that so few shows were available, and that sports led all TV programming with 120½ hours per week, wrestling was also contributing to the medium's appeal. The wild and wooly performers that wrecked havoc in downtown venues were brought into the living rooms of America, and people from all walks of life were exposed to the grappling business for the first time.

Wrestling on TV helped turn around poor gates, but it didn't happen overnight. In fact, wrestling was suffering in many parts of the country in 1948. Kohler was first to notice the positive effect of television. He was quoted in the April 4, 1948, edition of the *Chicago Daily Tribune* as saying: "We've been televising about two years and find that after people see wrestling on the screen for a while, they want to see it in the Rainbo or Midway arenas. Our net receipts are about double what they were without television. We now have people call during telecasts to complain about the referee or one of the wrestlers. On nights when wrestling is not telecast because of hockey, our receipts are up $300 to $500, but we feel these are fans created by television. Wrestling is televised in Milwaukee, and it has helped the gate there."

The detractors remained, but when a second channel, WGN, premiered as a television station on April 5, 1948, on channel 9, wrestling was immediately part of its programming. On Thursdays at 8:30, the station broadcast wrestling from the Madison Athletic Club, a smaller facility, with Jack Brickhouse as commentator. The Rainbo series ended its stretch on WBKB on September 29, 1948, when Davis signed off, and restarted a week later on WENR (channel 7) with Wayne Griffin as the anchor. Television ratings soared and, by November 1949, Fred's three programs were receiving better than a 35.6 share of viewership on their respective evenings, with the Rainbo the most popular.

Kohler booked his own regional heavyweight champion, sanctioned by his own Illinois Wrestling Promoters Association. He wasn't a part of the Tom Packs or

Midwest Wrestling Association syndicates, but was intrigued by a July 1948 gathering in Waterloo, Iowa. Even though he was invited, and an area newspaper reported he would be present, Fred didn't make the trip for the summit that founded the National Wrestling Alliance. He sacrificed a second chance to hobnob with Tony Stecher and Max Clayton in Minneapolis in September, but did host a cluster of promoters at a Chicago hotel in October 1948.

Despite initially agreeing to join the pact, and being a supporter of the innovative cartel, Kohler maintained his sovereignty. On January 14, 1949, he promoted the International Amphitheater for the first time since 1938, and 9,486 people paid $17,864, the largest wrestling turnout in Chicago in more than a decade. His February 11 Amphitheater production was headlined by National Wrestling Association titleholder Lou Thesz.

Kohler's three live television programs gave him a tremendous advantage over any potential rivals. The triumphant January 14 Amphitheater program was broadcast on WENR, and that same day, the *Chicago Daily Tribune* printed a story announcing the ABC network's plans to send live wrestling from the Rainbo eastward via coaxial cable. Beginning on Wednesday, February 2, Kohler's grapplers would be seen in New York City on WJZ-TV (channel 7).

Amid problems with the management of the Rainbo, Kohler threatened to leave and launch from the Marigold Gardens on July 20, 1949. Concessions were made by Leonard Schwartz, the arena's owner, but the damage had been done. TV executives at the DuMont Network were impressed with Kohler's Rainbo offerings on ABC, especially the steady rise in ratings in New York.

Terms were approved for televised wrestling on WGN with feed across DuMont from a new show at the Marigold on Saturday nights at 9:00. The series debuted on September 17, 1949, with a main event of the Schanbels versus Rudy Kay and Benito Gardini. The premiere was broadcast in New York on WABD (channel 5) from 10:00 p.m. to midnight. On September 24, it debuted on Boston's WNAC (channel 7), and expanded throughout the eastern half of the country, from St. Louis to Buffalo.

With two semi-national programs, Kohler was now a hugely influential figure and welcomed into the National Wrestling Alliance in September 1949. Bringing a sturdy intellect, he offered novel concepts to the group, and was a strong backer of a collaborative system that benefited all members.

The tension between Kohler and Schwartz was not resolved, and Fred walked away from the Rainbo and the ABC-TV outlet to focus on his Marigold endeavors. When Schwartz obtained a promoter's license to run in opposition, their feud exploded, and the double-cross of Don Eagle was among the highlights of their battle. Fred used his membership in the Alliance to fend off his rival, opening up his arenas for appearances by heavyweight champion Thesz and NWA junior champion Leroy McGuirk.

Sixteen years after Jim Londos and Ed "Strangler" Lewis broke gate records at Wrigley Field, Kohler returned wrestling to the ballpark under the guise of a benefit for the Chicago Heart Association. With the Illinois Athletic Commission on board, and allowing him to bill the main event as being for the NWA "championship," Kohler invested money and time into his June 21, 1950, card at the northside stadium. Envisioning more than 10,000 fans and a gate of $40,000, the promoter was disappointed when Thesz and Buddy Rogers drew only 7,638 paying $30,265. A second Wrigley show, held on July 27 and highlighted by Thesz and Gorgeous George, attracted approximately the same amount of spectators, but only a gate of $19,229.

At the September 1950 convention in Dallas, Kohler brought up the idea of eliminating the assistance certain Alliance members were giving nonmembers, and wanted Haft and Bowser suspended for breaking Alliance rules. He was voted down, but the president nominated a special committee, consisting of Muchnick and Stecher, to attempt mediation. All sides were unhappy with the results, which left Kohler perplexed and wondering about the impartiality of the arbitrators. On November 22, 1950, he informed the NWA via mail that he was resigning.

Kohler's December 9, 1950 correspondence to Muchnick explained his point of view:

> I am herewith submitting a detailed explanation of the reasons I referred to in my resignation as "obvious reasons." Upon receipt of the bulletin from the National Wrestling Alliance which had officially notified NWA members that Chicago was considered an open city, and that Toots Mondt was accepted as a member of the National Wrestling Alliance, my first impulse was to resign immediately. However, I restrained that impulse and weighed the possibilities, results and reactions that might occur in the event that I did resign.
>
> I eventually decided that to maintain my respect and pride, resignation was the only logical thing that I could do. I have done more to establish the National Wrestling Alliance heavyweight champion on a national and international basis than any member in the Alliance.
>
> First of all, to declare Chicago an open city, which permits fellow members to book wrestlers in opposition to me, is ridiculous, considering the bylaws of the National Wrestling Alliance. Secondly, the NWA lost a lot of prestige by such a declaration.

To permit Paul Bowser, "Toots" Mondt, and Al Haft to book wrestlers in Chicago in opposition to me is bad enough, if they themselves were loyal members of the Alliance, but they are not. Not one of the three bookers have done anything to advertise Lou Thesz as the world's heavyweight champion. They have their own champions and are advertising them as such. This is a violation of the bylaws and actually subjects them to expulsion from the Alliance, but at no time was any action even considered to expel Paul Bowser and Al Haft. "Toots" Mondt should never have been permitted membership in the Alliance. He has ridiculed the Alliance, he has attempted to put the Alliance in ill repute, and he is advertising others than Lou Thesz as heavyweight champion in his territory.

Al Haft has been the least cooperative of all, although being one of the original members of the National Wrestling Alliance. At no time has he advertised Lou Thesz or Leroy McGuirk as world's heavyweight and junior heavyweight champions. Al Haft advertises Frankie Talaber as junior heavyweight champion and Don Eagle as heavyweight champion. Also, Al Haft has never contributed a cent to the commitment made by all members to retain Ed "Strangler" Lewis as goodwill ambassador for the NWA. Al Haft conspired with Paul Bowser to advertise and declare Don Eagle as world's heavyweight champion.

Al Haft has made claims that he has a just grievance with me. Ask him what his grievance is, and take the following things into consideration when he answers. He pleaded with me to advertise, publicize and develop Don Eagle as an attraction in Chicago and on television. After doing this, he tied up Don Eagle in a managerial contract with Paul Bowser, making it necessary for me to consult Chief War Eagle, Paul Bowser, and Al Haft for any match that I might want Don Eagle to participate in.

I had planned a big show at the International Amphitheater and had Buddy Rogers already advertised and publicized to participate in the wind-up. At that time I was using one or two of Jack Pfeffer's (sic) men. Mr. Haft called me and asked me as a brother Alliance member to discontinue using Rogers, as he was appearing in several cities in Ohio in opposition to Al Haft's promoters. Whereupon I phoned Mr. Pfeffer and notified him that I was now an Alliance member, and wanting to be loyal to the Alliance, I would have to take Buddy Rogers off my Amphitheater card, together with three other of Pfeffer's men.

I underwent tremendous expense in reprinting circulars and window cards in order to cooperate and abide by Al Haft's wishes. For this reason, I now feel justified in again doing business with Mr. Pfeffer, now that Al Haft is booking wrestlers in a joint promotional venture at the Rainbow (sic) Arena in the city of Chicago, represented by the partnership of Leonard Schwartz, "Toots" Mondt, Jim Londos and Ray Fabiani.

If Al Haft, "Toots" Mondt and Paul Bowser would make an effort to live up to the bylaws of the NWA, I would consider withdrawing my resignation or reapplying for membership in the Alliance.

Muchnick asked members if Kohler had a legitimate complaint in a letter ballot, then held a meeting in St. Louis in January 1951 that Fred ignored. During the weekend of February 3–4, 1951, Muchnick, Schwartz, Mondt, Bowser, Clayton, Brown, Pinkie George, Sam Avey, and Kohler assembled in Chicago to discuss their differences. A compromise was reached, and Kohler was reinstated into the fold. Schwartz's application was also approved, giving Chicago two member-bookers. Kohler, as the senior Alliance operator, was given exclusive rights to all official NWA champions.

While an amicable solution had been reached, Kohler's views of the National Wrestling Alliance had turned a corner. He witnessed the unscrupulous tactics of members firsthand and was no longer optimistic that the organization worked for their collective interests. Kohler concluded that he would pursue economic success by whatever means necessary, and if that meant contradicting formal edicts, so be it. Satisfying his customers and providing for his family were his top priorities, but, for the sake of harmony, he'd contribute to the Alliance like any other associate.

Known for his leadership, Kohler was frequently called upon by colleagues for advice, and his gregarious personality always kept his peers on their toes during the routinely profane NWA gatherings. When Fred wasn't devoting his time to the wrestling business, he was involved in the community, giving generously to charities and the underprivileged. With connections to politicians at all levels, Kohler was a close friend of influential Illinois Senator Everett Dirksen (1896–1969).

Former University of Minnesota standout Verne Gagne deserves a lot of the credit for resurrecting Chicago grappling. Proving to be a better draw in the city than Buddy Rogers, Gorgeous George, or other established wrestlers, Gagne took on a headliner role in late 1951 and helped Kohler forget the mediocre numbers of the previous year. He sold out the Marigold on December 8, 1951, then drew over 10,000 to the Amphitheater on January 25, 1952, against Thesz, accomplishing something none of the major names could do in Chicago in almost two years. His 60-minute stalemate with Thesz didn't hurt his reputation either.

Kohler was ultimately responsible for making Gagne a national superstar. There was no question that Gagne had turned heads during his stint as world junior champion, and had had an impressive amateur career. But becoming a pro grappling idol was another thing entirely, and it was Kohler's booking of Verne on WGN and the DuMont Network that made Gagne one of the most widely acclaimed wrestlers of the era. The day after Gagne wrestled Thesz, Fred stood as proud as a father when dignitaries from the *Police Gazette* gave the wrestler a sterling silver championship belt for "his contribution to clean and scientific wrestling in 1951."

In the summer of 1953, Kohler opted to introduce a regional championship, and heeded the advice of Billy Watson in labeling it the "United States" title. A week before the opening night of the NWA's fifth convention at the Blackstone Hotel in Chicago, September 4–6, 1953, Fred spoke with Muchnick regarding his new "sectional" belt. Muchnick said that if the championship was correctly described as a regional strap, and didn't conflict with official Alliance-sanctioned titles, there would be no problem.

On Saturday, September 5, Jack Brickhouse informed spectators at the Marigold and watching at home that Verne Gagne was, indeed, crowned U.S. champion. A delegation of NWA members were on hand to witness the affair. To make sure there was no confusion, Muchnick, in an article printed in the *Chicago Daily Tribune* on September 7, 1953, denied that the Alliance officially granted Gagne any unique recognition. The U.S. title was sanctioned by Kohler only, and Verne's title did not supercede that of Thesz.

Kohler, the NWA's reigning first vice president, and chairman of the heavyweight championship committee, presented Gagne with the new championship belt emblematic of the U.S. title, on September 12 at the WGN-TV studios. Despite Kohler's numerous attempts to unequivocally distinguish between the importance of the U.S. and world titles, there was still uncertainty about who exactly was the top heavyweight wrestler. In response to the confusion, Muchnick issued a press release affirming Thesz's status, and called for the National Wrestling Association to follow suit after its Milwaukee convention.

Additionally, the NWA sent Strangler Lewis to Chicago to personally discuss the situation with newspapers and a trendy sports-radio host. Lewis reportedly accused Kohler of trying to become the "czar" of wrestling, and of overstepping his bounds by naming a U.S. champion. Fred appeared on the same show a short time later, and reiterated what Lewis said: "Lou Thesz was still world's heavyweight champion recognized by the National Wrestling Alliance, that Verne Gagne was only the United States heavyweight champion, and only recognized by a few promoters in the middle west." In a letter to Muchnick dated October 2, 1953, he went further:

Members are permitted to have sectional champions. First of all, has the naming of Verne Gagne as United States heavyweight champion created a detrimental effect on fellow members of the Alliance? This can only be determined by the houses that are drawn by Thesz in those cities that were in range of the Saturday night shows from Marigold via the Dumont Network. It wasn't my intention to becloud the championship title held by Lou Thesz as I, through my facilities of newspapers, radio and television, plus films and magazines, have done more to get recognition of Lou Thesz's world heavyweight championship title than any other member in the National Wrestling Alliance.

It is true that some confusion has been created wherein some people are asking when did Verne Gagne beat Lou Thesz for the title, and is not Lou Thesz still champion of the world. This confusion which you may think or deem detrimental is, to the contrary, beneficial. An example of this is the results of the first match between Lou Thesz and Baron Leone out on the West Coast, which drew $100,000. There the same kind of confusion existed with Johnny Doyle advertising Baron Leone as the world's heavyweight champion and films that I had made here in Chicago of Lou Thesz wherein the commentary constantly referred to Lou Thesz as world's heavyweight champion. Was Lou Thesz ever able to draw those kind of houses on the West Coast as he did after those films went in there and created this confusion?

Muchnick was between a rock and a hard place, taking a great deal of criticism for letting Kohler get away with naming his champion. A lot of the scorn was coming from Thesz, who felt that his reputation was being tarnished. Working feverishly to appease all sides, but particularly Thesz, Muchnick retracted his previous authorization and demanded that Kohler pull his sponsorship.

Kohler, already somewhat alienated, scoffed at the request, and reminded himself that his loyalties were to his customers first and his peers second. He did what he believed was right, and continued to promote Gagne as the U.S. titleholder on his DuMont show. In response, and as a measure of punishment, Muchnick granted exclusive rights to Thesz to Chicago's other NWA member, Leonard Schwartz. Kohler pushed back, and had Brickhouse proclaim Gagne a "world" title claimant on TV.

The escalation of the inner Alliance tiff moved Muchnick to arrange a conference at the Morrison Hotel in Chicago on November 8. He appointed a committee composed of Avey, Stecher, Jim Crockett, and Morris Sigel, while Kohler insisted that four members be assigned who received the DuMont feed into their territory, to balance the panel. Mondt, Clayton, Ed Don George, and Pinkie George joined the fray, with Sigel acting as chairman. After some deliberation, Kohler met

Muchnick halfway, agreeing to bill Gagne as the "United States television champion," a move which satisfied those in attendance.

Encouraged by the rejuvenation in Chicago compared to the apathy of the Northeastern audience, Mondt and Charley Johnston, matchmaker and promoter respectively at Madison Square Garden, joined with Kohler. The new combine, known as Sports Promoters' Engineers, Inc., was an "efficiency outfit," according to Fred. They invested money in many towns, sent talent, and earned huge percentages of the gates. Kohler's booking agency was the main supplier of wrestlers, and he was getting the bulk of the cash because of it. Among the cities revitalized by this trust were Chicago, New York, Milwaukee, Buffalo, Newark, Minnea-polis, Denver, and Omaha.

Kohler was now generating a mint, and everything circled back to his Marigold series. The value of his telecast on the Dumont Network exceeded $50,000 a year. Fred's profits combined his television revenue, kinescopes to all 48 states, house-show gates in Chicago and the surrounding area, and booking fees covering approximately 100 grapplers. He was also earning a healthy cut of the gross at the Garden in New York City beginning in October 1953, and taking 20 percent of Antonino Rocca's $80,000 annual income. There wasn't a more successful individual in the business.

Kohler's prosperity peaked, and in March 1955, DuMont unexpectedly cancelled his semi-national program, eliminating more than half his overall power in one fell swoop. Executives cited "rising costs" for halting production, and not surprisingly, the network was inundated with complaints. Five months later, to pacify angry viewers, a Thursday evening studio show from the Telecentre in New York made its debut. This, obviously, did nothing for Kohler, whose influence in dozens of cities had been terminated.

Using a rash of newcomers, he kept Chicago's Amphitheater running with at least average attendance as wrestling's popularity began to wane. Dick the Bruiser, Reggie Lisowski, The Shiek, Angelo Poffo, Roy McClarity, and Don Leo Jonathan were added to cards also featuring Gagne, Thesz, and Hans Schmidt, and provided the chaos mat enthusiasts counted on. Talent-sharing deals with Mondt and Eddie Quinn of Montreal also helped, but the downward slide continued.

WGN silenced its Saturday Marigold offering on May 11, 1957, replacing it with "Theater Date" at 8:00 p.m. Wrestling fans were subjected to films such as *Woman in the Window* and *Footlight Serenade* instead of the hard-hitting grappling action they had watched since 1949. Jack Brickhouse, the attentive ringside analyst, was relieved of his mat responsibilities. Kohler spent $48,000 on his interests in 1958, and even though he was celebrating his 10,000th wrestling match on March 7, he was nearly bankrupt.

It was amazing how far Kohler's promotion had fallen in just a few years, and it demonstrated how much he relied on TV. He was a fighter, however, and to keep wrestling on Saturdays, Fred obtained a slot on channel 5 at 11:00 p.m. to broadcast vintage Chicago tapes. Although the program did put wrestling on TV that particular night, it did little to bolster his weekly arena shows. Kohler finally got back on WGN on Thursdays at 7:30, with Russ Davis doing grip-by-grip commentary. This, he hoped, would be the move that finally improved turnout and provided relief for his dying business. It didn't. On December 21, 1958, he was quoted by the *Chicago Daily Tribune* as saying, "I've got the sponsors but can't seem to get the TV time spots that I lost in June 1957. But I'm certain things will be different in 1959."

The great rift between Kohler and Sam Muchnick remained. Despite being a member of the board of directors, Kohler rarely followed the NWA handbook. Still, he felt betrayed when wasn't consulted about the Dick Hutton–Pat O'Connor title switch. Not once had he advertised Hutton as champion, nor did he invest money announcing that O'Connor, from suburban Glenview, had captured the championship. In February 1959, hostilities were taken to another level when Kohler suggested that O'Connor pay him $10,000 for dates in Chicago, and at less than the champion's standard 11 percent. O'Connor, frustrated by the demand, walked out on the meeting, and later asked Muchnick not to book him into any bouts in Chicago.

Months later, Kohler sent a scathing missive to Muchnick after Eddie Quinn sealed up a deal to sponsor wrestling from Chicago Stadium, launching a crosstown war for the city. He believed that since Quinn and Muchnick were partners in St. Louis, Sam had to have been in on the invasion. "Just prepare yourself for retaliatory measures as soon as it becomes evident that you are cooperating with the opposition," Kohler wrote. Muchnick denied any aid to Quinn, but the latter didn't need it. He had approval from the Illinois Athletic Commission to operate live from the WBBM (CBS) studios every Saturday afternoon, and Ben Bentley and Bobby Managoff handling the booking for a gaggle of well-known wrestlers.

Kohler's extreme reaction showed his anxiety. A second letter to the NWA president solicited dates on champion O'Connor, seeking to capitalize on his Alliance membership. In retrospect, Kohler may have regretted his financial ultimatum to the titleholder.

Marveling at Kohler's accusations and his appeal for O'Connor, Muchnick fired back on June 10. He reminded the Chicago booker of the unwarranted demands he'd made on the NWA champion, and O'Connor's resulting anger. To book O'Connor in Chicago, Muchnick now required Pat's permission, and he conveyed his dismay at Kohler's "veiled threats." He followed up with a memo to Roy Hunter of the Chicago branch of the Antitrust Division and attached copies of correspondence between himself, O'Connor, and Kohler.

Even without television, Kohler thought he could defend his territory with the usual cast headlining, publicizing the pandemonium in newspaper reports. The wrestlers had other ideas. Dejected by their decline in popularity, the lack of airtime, and slim paydays, Gagne and others packed up and left Kohler behind. Kohler's longtime protégé Jim Barnett, who was reinforcing his place as one of the nation's premier booking agents, joined the mutiny, straining a decade-long working relationship. Fred conceded that his loss of TV exposure dimmed the prospects of his stars, but he maintained his enthusiasm despite the slow deterioration of his empire.

Kohler's ingenuity in tough times underlined his brilliance as a promoter. Not only was he battling a well-prepared outsider on his own turf, but he had been deserted by his best wrestlers when he needed them most. What happened next was the melding of two powerhouse minds, and the rebirth of Chicago as the capital of the wrestling industry.

District of Columbia impresario Vincent McMahon smartly used TV to become matchmaker at Madison Square Garden. He made no efforts to conceal his ambitions, and his progressive Bridgeport telecast flushed out a timeslot in Chicago. Beginning at midnight on Saturday, September 19, 1959, his program debuted on WNBQ (channel 5) (NBC). Spending as much as $2,400 a month, Kohler bought commercial advertising during the broadcast and personally did the announcing. He promoted his future shows, did interviews, and renewed public awareness. While Bridgeport TV exposed the Chicago audience to the northeastern style of wrestling, Kohler and McMahon finalized a system that would supply the former with reliable talent.

To prove that he was not supporting Quinn's promotion, Muchnick was willing to book O'Connor on one of Kohler's shows, but only at the percentage the NWA champion was normally guaranteed. And that $10,000 deposit request was also, obviously, out the window. With gates in Chicago steadily improving, money was the deciding factor in summoning the NWA titleholder back to the Windy City. On February 19, 1960, a throng of 7,500 at the Amphitheater watched O'Connor, Rocca, the Fargos, Bearcat Wright, Johnny Valentine, and Bruno Sammartino. The gate was close to $19,400.

That summer, the cutthroat skirmish escalated, but the likelihood that Quinn would bounce Kohler from power became remote. Kohler's successes were accumulating. His desperation at the prospect of luring enough spectators to barely break even months before now give way to unbridled optimism. Kohler organized three outdoor programs at Comiskey Park and his stable of wrestlers were outselling Quinn's, which included Thesz, Killer Kowalski, and Edouard Carpentier.

A visionary, Kohler prepared for a crowd of 50,000 and a gate of $100,000 for his July 29, 1960, card, and sent out 30,000 mailers to potential audience members. He stacked newspapers with articles and promos, arranged for special posters to run on the sides of hundreds of city buses, and used the Bridgeport series to spread the word. The result saw 30,275 paying $89,675 to see O'Connor beat Yukon Eric, and Buddy Rogers pin Bearcat Wright.

The second Comiskey show drew 17,206 with a gate of $52,350.40, while the third had a paid admission of $81,549.40, from an audience of 26,731. Before the end of the year, Quinn threw in the towel, submitting to Kohler's toehold. For ten indoor shows at the Amphitheater, and three at Comiskey Park, Fred sold 156,543 tickets. Chicago fans were once again hooked.

After 1961, professional wrestling under the auspices of Fred Kohler would last only four more years, but they were an interesting forty-eight months. It is worthwhile to note that without the assistance of publicity mastermind Richard Theodore "Dick" Axman, things might have gone differently. Axman was there at the beginning, when Kohler outlasted Coffey and White, and established revolutionary periodicals *Wrestling As You Like It*, and later, *Wrestling Life*. Axman gave Kohler's wrestling some of the finest marketing anywhere in the country, and helped sell tickets through his unique ability to make wrestling seem important. Born in Port Huron, Michigan, on February 27, 1891, Dick was a full-time sports writer by 1930, and was teamed with Kohler as early as 1938.

When his elusive $100,000 gate was finally achieved during the summer of 1961, Kohler had a right to celebrate, but he also had to acknowledge the contributions of his top aide, Axman. Their collective efforts, combined with the excellent production of the Bridgeport show, built the Rogers-O'Connor extravaganza into a record-shattering house on June 30, 1961, at Comiskey Park. The estimated 38,000 fans set a new American gate record, depositing $125,000 into the till. Rogers won in three falls and captured the NWA world heavyweight title.

Kohler was the Alliance's first vice president when, on August 26, 1961, he was voted to replace Frank Tunney as NWA president at the convention in Toronto. He served a year in the unpaid position, and in August 1962, Karl Sarpolis was elected to the spot. For the period between June 1961 and June 1962, Fred pulled in nearly $400,000 for 12 events featuring superstars Rogers, Rocca, Carpentier, Valentine, Art Thomas, Shohei Baba, Bobo Brazil, and Billy Darnell. Wrestling in Chicago was back at the forefront of the American grappling landscape — but all good things had to come to an end.

Six days before Lou Thesz beat Buddy for the NWA Title in Toronto on January 24, 1963, Rogers was in Chicago for a match with Brazil, drawing over 9,800 people and earning a gate of $28,149. Instead of booking the Nature Boy as an ex-champion for two matches in February at the Coliseum, Kohler exercised the prerogative of Capitol Wrestling because of their talent agreement, and continued to recognize him as a titleholder — basically dismissing the tussle north of the border.

The two Coliseum programs were flops, and Kohler suspended operations in March. Something was clearly wrong. The billing of Rogers earned criticism from St. Louis, and essentially cut his links to the National Wrestling Alliance. Going a step further, Kohler formally withdrew from the NWA and founded the "International Wrestling Alliance." For more than a decade, he'd debated with himself about the value of the NWA and finally decided that enough was enough. In the advertising for his April 5, 1963, Coliseum show, which drew 3,140, Kohler cited Buddy as a former champion, and bragged about the title claims of "Golden" Moose Cholak. The Capitol talent deal went on, but fans continued to be indifferent toward the product being offered.

Reports came out in early April 1963 that the famous Marigold Arena had been sold by Kohler to Faith Tabernacle, Inc. for $200,000, for use as a nondenominational church. The 1,800-seat facility was constructed in 1896 and saw thousands of wrestling matches promoted by Kohler. All the greats wrestled there, from Ed "Strangler" Lewis to Thesz.

Rogers and Brazil headlined on May 24, 1963, luring 6,000 to the Amphitheater, but the match went a mere 64 seconds. Of course, there was a reason why Buddy could only wrestle a short match. He had been advised by his doctors after being stricken by a heart ailment only weeks before, that he take it easy in the ring. Still, the blindsided crowd was less than impressed. On June 14, 1963, Fred ran his last show under the auspices of the Kohler-McMahon syndicate, and drew 3,100. *Heavyweight Wrestling from Bridgeport* survived on WNBQ until September 7, but Kohler's sponsorship was gone. Without television, Fred found himself in a predicament very similar to the one he faced in the late 1950s.

The Chicago promoter was going to put his company behind matchmaker Jack Pfefer and the one leading grappler who would associate with his fumbling IWA, Johnny Valentine. The always effective Valentine could carry the mantle through sheer popularity, and on the night he beat Cholak for the IWA world title, July 12, 1963, 6,000 were present. The rest of the July 12 program highlighted Pfefer's creations, Bruno Nasartino, Slugger Kowalski, Texas Bruiser, and Jim Barrett, all colorful performers. Banking on Valentine to deliver, Kohler was heartbroken when Johnny bailed on the promotion entirely, giving in to the wishes of "New York."

The departure of his heavyweight champion didn't bode well, and Pfefer's innovations weren't working with the fans. After Valentine's exit came the idea for George Valentine (Edward Welch). This second "Valentine" also went to the head of the promotion, winning a 16-man tournament on October 4, 1963, for the vacant IWA world title, but unlike Johnny, he stayed in Chicago. Jackie Fargo, booked as the "world wide federation" champion, beat Valentine on November 15 in a unification match.

With a batch of Pfefer impersonators packing his cards, Kohler's business plummeted. Fred's third wife, Jacqueline, compelled him to hire her son Billie Jack Cude Kohler (1927–1998), who became the official secretary for Fred Kohler Enterprises, Inc. Fred funded his ventures in several Wisconsin clubs, including Green Bay, during the early part of the 1960s, but Billie took on more of a role in Chicago when things began to go awry. In early 1964, it was Billie who arranged to sell a percentage of the promotion to William Afflis (Dick the Bruiser) of Indianapolis. Afflis was expanding his interests, and Chicago seemed to be a natural stop for grapplers from Indiana to wheel through. What the deal accomplished, immediately, was to send name wrestlers back to the International Amphitheater.

In went O'Connor, Art Thomas, Hans Schmidt, Wilbur Snyder, Harley Race, Angelo Poffo, Bobby Managoff, and the perfidious runaway Johnny Valentine. Bruiser himself wrestled in Chicago on May 15, 1964, but no import wrestler could cure the ailing figures. Fred was losing money, but he held on until November 1965, when he sold the territory outright to Afflis and Snyder. Fred Kohler Enterprises was dissolved on November 12, 1965.

After leaving wrestling behind, Kohler was involved in two corporations, Kohler and Besser Electronics and Custom Rubber Molders, Inc. in Rolling Meadows, then formed Fred Kohler Associates, a consulting firm. In an ironic twist of fate, he was voted out of his position as president of Kohler and Besser Electronics by his partners, specifically his stepson Billie, in a real-world double-cross. In 1967, he acted as the athletic committee chairman for the Medinah Temple, and was on a five-man athletic board for the Illinois State Department of Registration and Education.

Living at 2 Stuart on Oxford in Rolling Meadows until the summer of 1968, Fred suddenly moved to Arizona, just outside Phoenix. The hardships of wrestling and business in general caught up with him, and he was ready for the serenity of retirement. The dry air of the Southwest was cleaner than the smoke-filled halls he had promoted. His third marriage had been tough on his family, especially his youngest daughters. Fred had been given a physical and a good bill of health shortly prior to his death in his sleep on August 24, 1969, at the age of 66.

Showing his astuteness extended beyond wrestling, Kohler invented an underground sleeve for the telephone company, and was a natural at any business. He was a member of the legendary Polar Bears, and had even grappled with a live bear in the 1930s. To protect kayfabe, he often spoke in the old carny lingo, and he enjoyed singing with his kids. Fred owned the Marigold, Lake County Stadium, and adjoining Sally's Ringside Inn in Round Lake Park, where his family often spent time. He loved Chicago and his loyal fans, but most importantly, his children. His dedication to pro wrestling for more than 30 years is proven by the attendance records he set and the affection he inspired in his audiences.

CHAPTER SEVEN

THE RED-HAIRED
SHOOTER

Joe "Toots" Mondt

Joseph "Toots" Mondt was a revered figure in the professional wrestling fraternity for nearly 60 years. The Colorado product evolved from schoolyard brawler to a master of the catch-as-catch-can form. An unconventional wrestler, Mondt was exceptional on the mat, able to match grips with the best in the business. He later transitioned smartly into the booking and promoting of matches, and had success everywhere he went. Contributing to the development of vaudeville-type dramatics in wrestling, Toots was instrumental in shattering the bubble that once protected the illusion that grappling was a legitimate sport. Although controversial, Mondt was almost always in the top tier of promoters and he will remain among the most unique sports personalities of all time.

To fully comprehend the saga of the Mondt Family, one has to go back to January 22, 1904, and the small town of Humeston, Iowa. That day, the famous Farmer Martin Burns, a champion wrestler, appeared at the opera house and delivered a ten-minute lecture about health and fitness. Burns then offered $25 to any man that he could not conquer in 15 minutes. The first to accept the challenge was a courageous 230-pound construction worker named Frank Mondt. Mondt's bravery exceeded his skills during the several-minute encounter, and was decisively defeated by the more experienced grappler.

Frank (1864–1916) was married to Lucilla "Lula" Mae Hutchins Mondt (1870–1953), and had nine children. James Ervin was the third child born, following Ralph and Arthur, at Garden Grove, Iowa, on January 18, 1894.

The Mondts moved to Weld County, Colorado, later in 1904, and settled just east of Ault. James, a terrific athlete, made his pro wrestling debut against a much older Fred Blumenthal in 1910, competing in a park, and earning a one-dollar purse. By 1915, he wrestled off and on to supplement his earnings while working as a laborer, before joining a vaudeville act under the guise of "Tudor" Mondt.

James occasionally competed at regional fairs and carnivals as the "Masked Marvel" and engaged locals for money. The difficult battles tested Mondt's mettle and were almost always on the level. He fought competitors big and small, and proved fearless. Stories of his father's duel with the celebrated Farmer Burns compelled James to go eastward to Omaha in hopes of studying under the great wrestler. Mondt made the journey, showed his worth, and became a member of the Burns troupe. The teachings of the Farmer etched the fundamental principals of catch grappling into his soul.

There was an abundance of wrestlers circulating in the Midwest, barnstorming, in the late 1910s, and Mondt, known as the "Colorado Cowboy," was increasingly active. Headquartered in northern Colorado, he combined the lessons he learned from Burns with the theatrical talents he picked up as a vaudeville performer, and found his niche. Well conditioned and determined, Mondt's real gift was his intellect, which gave him a resounding advantage on the mat. He would claim the Rocky Mountain light heavyweight title, and among the grapplers he faced were Ad Santel, Jack Taylor, Stanislaus Zbyszko, Tony Bernardi, Taro Myaki, and Henry Sorenson.

Before the end of the decade, James adopted the name "Joseph," and the sobriquet "Tudor" would spawn the lifelong moniker "Toots," as in Tootsie. Living with his family at 818 4th Street in Greeley, Mondt took a job in Fort Collins coaching the Colorado A&M (Aggies) wrestling squad from the program's inception. At a tournament in Denver in January 1921, with a 260-person field, five of Mondt's pupils walked away victors, including four wrestlers and one boxer. In March, his squad won an intercollegiate championship, taking 28 of 31 matches.

Toots went to San Francisco following the 1921–22 wrestling season and continued to build his reputation. A promoter there asked Mondt to show him his array of athletic stunts, and introduced him to some new moves. Mondt embraced the innovative approach and tested the market with the fresh ideas. Cultured in the behavior and lingo of pro grappling on a larger scale, he returned to Colorado inspired to strengthen his ring repertoire.

In 1922, Toots met heavyweight champion Ed "Strangler" Lewis for the first time. Lewis and his manager Billy Sandow were vacationing in the state, enjoying the weather around the Broadmoor area of Colorado Springs, when he took a match in Eaton versus Jatindra Gobar on October 10, 1922. Mondt was in attendance, and, in a meeting with Lewis and Sandow, astounded the duo with his views of wrestling. Mondt was a good talker, but he was also more than impressive in gym workouts that showed the full range of his talents.

It didn't take long for Sandow and Lewis to be utterly dazzled by the youngster, and they hired him into the fold. Mondt left his position as coach of the Aggies, and within weeks was a nationally recognized wrestling star. On November 10, 1922 in Boston, Toots won the first fall of a match with Lewis in 30:15, lost the second fall in 32:15, and then the third in 2:05. He traveled the Lewis-Sandow circuit, extending from coast to coast, and as the rivalries between syndicates intensified, Mondt was there to lend his expertise. By adding gimmicks to matches and pushing the right buttons of enthusiasts, Mondt's true worth shone through.

The Lewis-Sandow combination helped shape the future of wrestling, with an important assist from Mondt, who injected spice into what had previously been mostly tedious matches. Instead of playing to the segment of the audience who loved old school wrestling, the group enlarged the fan base with scripted mayhem and sensational storylines. With numbers at the box office declining post war, their approach shook the entire industry. From injury angles to the creation of actual heels, novel routines were drafted night after night by Lewis and the cast. The champion wrestled the same opponents regularly, and built up Tulsa, Kansas City, and Chicago.

Mondt and Lewis may not have been on par physically, but Toots could, amazingly, hold his own in a straight shoot with the Strangler. Legend has it that the two wrestled countless matches in the gym, including one grueling session that reportedly lasted 12 hours. Wrestling on equal terms with Lewis in a legitimate contest, and using the Strangler as a barometer, easily turned the Colorado grappler into one of wrestling's great warriors. Bold and hard-hitting, Mondt was as skilled as he was bright. In an era of pretenders, he was a standout on the mat.

The visionary approach of Sandow and Mondt generated mesmerizing new ways to make cash. Making up rules as they went along, they systematically eliminated their competition. Wrestlers and promoters who were not a part of the organization or benefiting from the profitable new approach were in despair. Among them were Jack Curley, the leading promoter from New York, and the Stecher Brothers. Mondt and Joe Stecher were matched in what deteriorated into a full-blown shoot on February 11, 1924, in Kansas City. After winning the first fall and dominating much of the bout, Mondt punched Stecher and knocked him out. Stecher, in turn, was declared the winner by decision. But Mondt had demonstrated what it meant to be a wrestling "policeman."

The double-cross of Wayne Munn in 1925 impeded Sandow and Mondt's progress greatly, and instead of holding the coveted championship, the title was now in the hands of rivals. Mondt proved to be a team player all the way. During Munn's tenure, he followed orders, losing falls to his inexperienced opponent, and mixing his moves into the scripted ploy. The crafting of unique angles was paramount to the success of Toots and his allies. Despite the loss of the championship, they used their smart promotions and spin to manipulate the audience. Preferring to stay independent from the Stecher-Curley combine, Mondt, Lewis, and Sandow marched ahead as if the dreadful betrayal had never happened.

Big business, however, was on the other side of the spectrum, and wrestlers were abandoning the Lewis clan for employment in the Stecher troupe. The distinction between the two entities disappeared and Mondt lost matches in New York City to Alex Garkawienko and Pat McGill for Curley. He was also defeated in several matches by Joe Malcewicz in 1927, and suffered a knee injury that would be the beginning of the end for his career on the mat. Mondt's protracted feud with Sandow's brother Max Baumann over their individual levels of influence led to a "him or me" ultimatum for Sandow. Sandow stuck with his blood, ending Joe's association with the faction. Toots eventually landed in New York with Curley.

Limiting his schedule, Mondt gave Curley the full extent of his knowledge, from wrestling and booking, to the management of an office. Toots stepped into a role as Curley's right-hand man, helping to rebuild grappling in New York. The decision to stop relying on Paul Bowser's champion, Gus Sonnenberg, led Mondt and Curley to search for an alternative. They pulled strings in the New York and Pennsylvania athletic commissions, stripping Sonnenberg of his claim, then planned a match to decide a new champion.

Toots mentored Dick Shikat (Richard Schikat, 1897–1968), a tough German grappler, and propelled him into the spotlight. The move proved excellent, as

Mondt took a relatively colorless performer to the top of the industry, getting fans excited about him in their two most important cities, New York and Philadelphia. When Shikat wrestled Jim Londos in Philly on August 23, 1929, he was the crowd favorite. Shikat won the title in front of an estimated 30,000 people, and was presented with an 18-karat gold belt studded with 19 diamonds.

Shikat's popularity hit a peak under the direction of Mondt, but he was soon eclipsed by Londos. An admired trailblazer, Londos was rebounding from a decade of steady headlining and regular defeats at the hands of name wrestlers, and was well established in many towns. He had a distinctive look, a colorful persona, and carried a solid and growing following. With backing from Philadelphia promoter Ray Fabiani and Tom Packs of St. Louis, Londos beat Shikat for the belt on June 6, 1930. While Shikat couldn't rise to the level of Sonnenberg's achievements, Londos could.

Besides his matchmaking duties, Mondt put wrestlers over in matches on the ladder leading to Londos. By early 1932, he was all but retired, and edging into Boston and Washington, D.C., as a booker on behalf of Curley and Fabiani. The incredible revenue being made with Londos headlining was steadily building bank accounts, and the Greek's ability to tour nationally was a major factor in their success.

For two years, Londos carried the syndicate on his back, and by April 1932, he was extremely weary. In an abrupt shift, he severed ties to the New York office, effectively cutting Curley and Mondt out of the fortunes that were still to be made. As a final sock in the eye, Jim signed on with the Johnstons and Rudy Dusek to keep up his appearances in New York City in opposition to their promotion.

Without a credible heavyweight champion, Mondt met with Strangler Lewis in Wisconsin, and convinced his old friend to return to the ring. A pact was made between Mondt, Curley, Jack Pfefer, Rudy Miller, and Shikat that, on paper, seemed to be powerful enough to neutralize Londos's northeastern audiences. Surprisingly, Curley and Mondt also repaired their relationship with Bowser.

An extravaganza at the recently constructed Madison Square Garden Bowl on June 9 was headlined by Lewis and Shikat, and drew approximately 25,000 fans. Lewis won, earning a future match with Londos. With the simmering anger between the rival conglomerates, there was no way Londos would agree to go head to head with the Strangler, and several months later, Lewis beat Jack Sherry for the vacant championship in New York City. Mondt had survived the departure of Londos, but something was about to happen that would alter the future of the famed Toots forever.

Driving an automobile to a vacation site in Collingwood, Ontario, on Nottawasaga Bay with his brother Ralph on August 21, 1932, Joe was involved in a deadly head-on automobile accident. Twenty-one-year-old Theressa Luccioni was killed instantly in a wreck three miles east of Collingwood on Highway 24, after Mondt's car smashed into a car driven by J. Edward Burnie. Toots, only slightly injured in the collision, was charged with manslaughter and released on $6,000 bond.

Coincidentally, a month later in New York City, Mondt broke his right wrist in a second car accident. That wreck, on September 23, was caused by another driver and saw wrestler Dick Shikat suffer a fractured arm, and Sandor Szabo and Jack McArthur both receive minor injuries. Mondt was eventually convicted and sentenced to a year in jail on November 10, but released the next day on $20,000 bail, pending an appeal. Toots was exonerated in the retrial which ended on February 6, 1933, but the painful events in Ontario proved costly.

Free of legal woes, Mondt was able to refocus on his business priorities, and arranged the slick double-cross of Londos in Chicago after a first attempt at the Greek in September 1932 failed to go through as anticipated. In attendance at the Stadium to see the April 7, 1933, Londos–Joe Savoldi match, Mondt watched the former win a single fall with the assistance of a crooked referee. Savoldi claimed the title, derailing the Londos phenomenon, and Toots had his revenge.

In New York, Mondt found the peace with Bowser to be a lot less aggravating. It was Bowser's superstar Jim Browning who went over the Strangler for the world title on February 20, 1933, at the Garden, with Bowser paying Mondt and Lewis a reported $42,000 for the switch. The exhausting war with the Londos tribe lasted until that November, when a meeting at the Pennsylvania Hotel in New York City shaped a national cartel that would control all major wrestling in North America. Mondt, Curley, Bowser, Fabiani, Packs, and Ed White inked a ten-year agreement that ended their hostilities and shared both talent and profits.

The Pfefer scandal and resulting storm gave Mondt reason to leave New York for a short stretch in Washington, and then move to Los Angeles in July 1934. Accepting a public position as the manager of wrestlers Browning and Chief Little Wolf, Toots became the matchmaker for the Daro Brothers, Lou and Jack. Los Angeles would be taking an entirely different road than that of the "Trust," and Mondt's position allowed him to once again knife the Greek champion in the back. On February 27, Londos missed a controversial bout with Little Wolf in Los Angeles, forcing the California State Athletic Commission to suspend him, and strip him of all recognition.

To determine a new kingpin, Mondt and the Daros brothers promoted an international tournament. On April 24, 1935, the series of matches began at the Olympic Auditorium in Los Angeles, with 15 bouts on the bill. Among the wrestlers participating were Vincent Lopez, Kimon Kudo, Ernie Dusek, Joe Savoldi, Hans Steinke,

Sandor Szabo, and Juan Humberto. Three months later, on July 24, Lopez beat Man Mountain Dean in the finals and captured the vacant title.

Mondt's leadership helped invigorate L.A. wrestling fans, and crowds improved measurably. He was the cornerstone of all booking in the region and the envoy between the Daros and eastern promoters. A second tournament was staged by Toots, this one in Philadelphia, to give credibility to the assent of Dean Henry Detton (1908–1958). Detton was a shooter strongly backed by Mondt, with a one-way ticket to the world championship. His tournament victory came on February 28 when he conquered Strangler Lewis.

Anxious to get the Trust's title away from Danno O'Mahoney, Toots wanted approval from Bowser for Danno to yield the belt to Detton, preferably on March 9, 1936, in Philadelphia. Other contenders for the championship were Yvon Robert and Ernie Dusek, but Mondt's influence was making headway. Joe's old prodigy Dick Shikat was booked to wrestle Danno at Madison Square Garden on March 2, and their match was expected to go according to the script, leaving O'Mahoney's title intact for the match with Detton.

The prerogative of managers and promoters to dictate the future of wrestling in a carefully constructed manner was threatened the minute the Garden bout between Shikat and O'Mahoney turned into a shoot. Needless to say, the finish didn't make Mondt happy, and one famous story had Shikat facing a pipe-wielding Mondt in the dressing room of the Garden after the betrayal. Shikat, ultimately, took the title away from the Trust, and settled for a relationship with a bunch of scheming independent promoters.

The Trust was angered by the double-cross, but willing to accept their losses to work with Shikat. Mondt offered him $50,000 to wrestle two matches in Los Angeles with Lopez, but was turned down. The ambitions of the Al Haft and Billy Sandow troupe, planning the future of Shikat, did not involve Mondt, Curley, Bowser, or Fabiani. Trying to protect business in Los Angeles, Mondt arranged a ceremony at the Biltmore Hotel on April 27, 1936, and honored Lopez with the "Lou Daro" Trophy, emblematic of the heavyweight title. Shikat, in turn, lost his championship to Ali Baba, silencing a court case pending in Columbus.

Cunning power plays were made in several cities, but of all towns, New York was hit the hardest. Curley was reeling, and he used the athletic commission to get a Shikat-Baba rematch on the local scene. Their May 5 match at the Garden drew a dismal 4,000 spectators. In an effort to regain footing, Mondt orchestrated an insidious double-cross of Baba, and Jack Pfefer, who had no allegiance to Baba, Haft, or Sandow, was ready to negotiate.

When it was all said and done, a deal was made to replace Hans Schnabel in the main event of a show against Baba at Meadowbrook Field in Newark with Dave Levin (George Wenzel) on June 12. In the first fall of the bout, Baba landed a drop-kick that Levin claimed was a low blow, falling to the mat. The move prevented Levin from continuing, and referee Frank Sinborn proclaimed him the champion by disqualification. Mondt assumed his contract at a cost of $17,000.

With support from commissions across the country, Levin entered Los Angeles using the premise that he was striving to earn recognition in California. Mondt, Fabiani, and the Daros finalized their preparations for a Levin-Lopez contest on August 19 at Los Angeles's Wrigley Field. In two of three falls, Levin won what was sold to the public as a full-blown shoot. Little did fans know that everyone was on the payroll, and Levin and Lopez had put on a brutal exhibition of worked violence while 15,321 paid $20,723 to see the match.

A little less than two months later, in Philadelphia, Levin dropped the championship to Detton. Mondt praised Detton's skills, and believed he had an authentic sensation on his hands. Inflated numbers printed in Los Angeles area newspapers suggested that was true, but it was the opposite in New York, where Detton, and wrestling in general, was suffering. The November 18, 1936, match between Detton and Levin drew only 2,500 devotees to the Garden. He did well elsewhere, but a huge turnaround in New York was not to be. At least not on Detton's watch.

His championship reign would end during the summer of 1937, and Toots was elated about the prospects of Dean's replacement, hoping football star Bronko Nagurski could draw the figures Gus Sonnenberg had. On June 29, 1937, in Minneapolis, Nagurski beat Detton in 46:37 and captured the world title.

As Mondt told NEA Service Sports Editor Harry Grayson in an article printed in a myriad of papers, including the Frederick, Maryland, *Daily News*, on August 16, 1937: "For years I've been waiting for a man who really can catch the popular fancy. Nagurski is the man. Such demonstrations as they give him in Minneapolis and Los Angeles reflect his ability to win popularity. The country will be mad about him. He has everything, a physique which makes you catch your breath when he peels off his robe. He's the strongest man I've ever seen on a mat. He's as fast as lightning, and has the earnest manner and the obvious love of rough competition that excites the crowd."

Jim Londos returned to the wrestling circuit, and won a claim to the championship on October 4, 1937, in Baltimore. Immediate box office comparisons to Nagurski were made, and a match against Bronko seemed to be the one people were clamoring for. Mondt and Fabiani signed Londos, and pit the competitors against each other in Philadelphia on November 18, 1938. Londos overcame his foe in 47:11 before 10,000 at the Convention Hall, and won Nagurski's title. The hostile relationship between two of wrestling's biggest personalities (Mondt and Londos) was stabilized by Fabiani, an impartial middleman who often reminded them that their main goal was making money.

Mondt's booking office faced a crisis when a special California State Assembly began investigating wrestling and boxing in April 1939 over a slew of alleged infractions. Attendance was down, and in their desperation to remain above water, the management of wrestling at the Olympic had reportedly neglected to pay their talent. Incited, primarily, by the doings of Toots and Jack Daro, a mutiny occurred, which spawned a second promotion in the area, governed by Nick Lutze and George Zaharias in July 1940.

A suspected war for the territory ended prematurely after Daro announced he had lost $70,000 over 17 weeks, and planned to retire from wrestling. Mondt relied on Daro's license at the Olympic, and told *Los Angeles Times* sports writer Al Wolf on September 3, 1940, that he was discontinuing booking in Los Angeles. He sold the remnants of his office to Lutze in September 1940 for $2,000, signalling a new era in wrestling promotions in Southern California.

With his options now open, Mondt rejected a solid proposition in the Pacific Northwest to return to the turbulent climate of New York. He joined a booking agency at the twelve-story brick Longacre Building (1476 Broadway) in Times Square with Alfred "Al" Mayer, reestablishing his presence locally. Their agency was initially in Pfefer's old space in room 416, four floors below the Johnston Brothers' office on the eighth floor. The Johnstons and Rudy Dusek ran wrestling in the city, ruling an 18-club circuit in the area with more than 15 shows per week.

The Al Mayer Booking Office was managed by Mondt for seven years. Unlike the Johnstons, who held licenses to promote at downtown venues, Mondt exploited his ability to direct talent, supplying grapplers to the Johnston-Dusek combine, and to numerous other promoters in the region. Mondt had links to promoters all over the country, especially Fabiani, his successor at the Olympic in Los Angeles.

Diminished by the authority of Tom Packs, Toots was no longer in charge of the dominant faction behind wrestling. Instead of leading the fold, dictating champions, and capturing percentages of high-priced gates throughout the nation, he was relegated to a role below many of the big shots he used to rub shoulders with. But Mondt's wrestlers were still imperative in northeastern cities.

The New York agency didn't have any trouble making money. Mondt's acquaintance with Los Angeles boxing manager Babe McCoy procured the rights to Primo Carnera, the former boxing champion. Carnera gave Mondt, Mayer, and McCoy a valuable wrestling asset, and Toots accompanied his cash cow as his second. All promoters wanted Primo on the bill, and the trio made a dominant percentage of their man's money for every match he wrestled. During the 1940s, Mondt and Mayer booked the likes of Babe Sharkey, Frank Sexton, Joe Savoldi, Man Mountain Dean, Chief Little Wolf, Martin "Blimp" Levy, Marvin Mercer, Ed Gardenia, Jack Steele, Ed White, and the Masked Panzers.

Mondt would follow a three-step process to reemerge as a leader in the wrestling industry. First, in 1948, Toots split from Mayer and founded the Manhattan Booking Agency, of which he served as president, with Paul Rudolph "Rudy" Miller (general manager) and Henry "Milo" Steinborn (matchmaker). Having run with Carnera for as long as possible, Mondt looked for another workhorse who could create and command a dominant following. Through crafty scheming, Mondt acquired the contract to the heavily touted Antonino "Argentina" Rocca by edging Rocca's personal manager, Kola Kwariani, out of the picture. Rocca succeeded at the box office, and Mondt's stock soared. Rocca, in fact, was soon even more of a draw than Carnera.

Finally, Toots arranged for the highly publicized return of wrestling to Madison Square Garden. Uniting the combines in the greater New York City area, Mondt and his partners made the announcement that the Garden would feature pro grapplers on the night of February 22, 1949, for the first time in 11 years. The imaginative Gorgeous George would be showcased with Ernie Dusek, while Emil Dusek, Angelo Savoldi, The Golden Superman, Wilbur Nead, Butch Levy, Howard Cantonwine, Ray Schwartz, and George Becker were on the undercard. A $40,000 house was expected. But the poor turnout put a damper on any post-event festivities, as the event drew only 4,197 fans, paying a pathetic $13,959.83. Three days later in Glendale, California, Mondt's brother Ralph died at the age of 58.

The second show from the Mondt-led group, ten months later, on December 12, 1949, was headlined by two of Toots's preeminent stars, Rocca and Carnera. Rocca wrestled and beat Gene Stanlee, while Primo took the measure of the Green Hornet. The audience was an encouraging four times larger than the February show, 17,854, and the gate was $50,639.28.

Mondt was proactive in his efforts, and his seizure of Rocca's managerial contract from Kwariani was one of the most astute and perceptive maneuvers in wrestling history. No one could be sure how Antonino would sell on a national scale, but Mondt's instincts caught him the biggest fish on the market, and he personally earned a huge percentage of the grappler's earnings. Rocca was a huge boost to Toots's New York office, and promoters across the globe wanted to hire him.

Strangely enough, the arrival of television as a premier promotional tool was the main reason Mondt couldn't grasp more control of the wrestling universe. It was the two TV programs out of Chicago, on the DuMont and ABC networks, that viewers in New York were soon captivated by. Toots needed the wrestlers from those telecasts filling dates in his territory, and paid bookers Fred Kohler and Al Haft well for talent. His 1950 inclusion in the National Wrestling Alliance, a strong trade agreement, was also vital in securing the necessary wrestlers.

Mondt, Miller, and Steinborn sold the Manhattan Booking Agency to Pedro Martinez, a wealthy former wrestler and promoter from Rochester, in January 1952 for a reported $100,000. Martinez, in turn, shifted 25 shares, worth $25,000, back to Toots and hired him as general manager to administer the day-to-day operations of the company. The entity was incorporated on January 30, 1952, by Mondt's accountant and friend, Richard Sackoff, who kept the books at 351 West 42nd Street (the Holland Hotel) in New York City. Mondt tendered his resignation from the NWA on February 20, 1952.

In June 1952, because of the instability in New York and a real concern about the health of his investment, Martinez liquidated 50 percent of his stock in the outfit. Twenty-five percent each went to Kwariani and Rocca, placed under the names of their respective spouses. On January 10, 1953, Martinez and Mondt endorsed a contract that transferred Pedro's last 25 shares of capital stock at $250 a week, plus interest, over a 100-week period. Mondt's membership in the Alliance was reinstated.

Martinez's economic venture into New York City depended on Garden numbers, and after two middling shows (November 18, 1952, and January 5, 1953), NWA champion Lou Thesz and Rocca flopped on March 24, 1953. After selling off his percentage, Pedro expected to collect the last $25,000 from Mondt, but after a year of broken promises and a payment of a mere $5,250, their relationship had become fiercely antagonistic, eventually ending in violence.

On February 15, 1954, Martinez waited in the dressing room of the Garden for Mondt, hoping to recover his $19,750. Rather than getting a check, Martinez decked Mondt, and the incident was made public by both Dan Parker in the *New York Daily Mirror* and by the *New York Post*. The altercation became legend in the mat world, and Mondt carried the embarrassment of that fateful evening for the rest of his life.

The brief regeneration of wrestling's popularity in the Northeast was fueled by a late-night phone call between Mondt and Kohler on September 14, 1953, which ended with the approval of the latter to furnish his top grapplers to New York clubs. Kohler would be compensated to the tune of one third of every show in which his talent appeared, from the St. Nicholas Arena to the Garden. The accord also covered venues that Mondt booked in Philadelphia, Washington, and

Baltimore, and initially extended from October 1953 until September 1954.

Nineteen-fifty-four was a trying year for Mondt. Excessively dependant on Kohler's TV and the availability of Chicago grapplers, Toots watched while his towns suffered. Despite a fairly profitable 1953–54 season, the Manhattan Booking Agency went bankrupt in April 1954, and on August 26, Martinez bought the company at public auction for $200, reportedly including the "exclusive services of" Rocca.

At different points, Mondt employed Jack Pfefer, Johnny Doyle, and Bobby Stewart, and had the brain power of Jim Barnett on his side, but his syndicate was crumbling. His power was significantly reduced, and a heated argument with the Pennsylvania and Maryland athletic commissions over his exclusive rights to book Baltimore and Philadelphia was the last thing he needed. Toots used his membership in the NWA to protect what he felt was rightfully his, and was always looking to gain the upper hand.

Toots created Manhattan Wrestling Enterprises, a progressive booking agency, and the Garden endeavors of the Kohler-Johnston-Mondt crew remained mediocre until their apparent self-destruction in May 1955. Wrestling spectators in New York City were notoriously fickle and the only thing that was a constant was the drawing capabilities of Rocca.

What the Northeast needed was an explosive and innovative weekly television show. Executives at the DuMont Network, tired of the apathetic studio productions of Haskell Cohen, gave Washington promoter Vincent McMahon the two-hour spot on Thursday nights in New York City beginning at 9:00 on channel 5 (WABD) on June 21, 1956. This would be the broadcast that revitalized New York wrestling, and Toots would use McMahon's programming to boost Garden attendance. It also cut Vince into the territory, and formed a partnership that would lead to the creation of Capitol Wrestling.

The partners retained their connection with Kohler, and struck an important deal with Eddie Quinn in Montreal. On February 4, 1957, Rocca and Gagne beat Schmidt and Karl Von Hess before approximately 19,300 people at the Garden, followed by Rocca-Schmidt in front of 19,995 on March 11. An amazing 20,125 were drawn to the Garden on March 30 to see Rocca and Miguel Perez defeat Don Stevens and Wildman Fargo.

The Mondt-McMahon arrangement was incorporated as the Capitol Wrestling Corporation on August 5, 1957, in Washington D.C., and in New York on March 10, 1961. McMahon was the corporation's president, and he and Mondt each owned 50 percent of the company until they sold 8 percent each to esteemed West Coast booker Johnny Doyle. In an article in the *Washington Post and Times Herald*,

Sunday, February 2, 1958, McMahon was quoted as saying the following about Mondt's responsibilities in the business: "[Mondt was the] contact man who oversees the entire operation, a sort of manipulator."

An FBI interview with McMahon on July 15, 1960, gave more insight into Mondt's position in Capitol Wrestling. McMahon told investigators Mondt was in "financial difficulties" when the corporation was established in 1957, and that his stock had been put in the name of Phil Zacko. By 1960, Mondt was an official shareholder and the vice president of the company. McMahon admitted that Mondt was semiretired and "used in an advisory capacity," and that "99 percent of all the business is conducted without consulting Mondt."

Another discussion on July 18 with Rudy Miller revealed that McMahon was the boss, and that Mondt acted only as an advisor, often away from the office for "weeks at a time." Mondt confirmed the statements, saying McMahon was the "individual who formulates and dictates the policy of the corporation."

Using TV as leverage to gain an advantage in critical regions, particularly New York City, Boston, and Philadelphia, Capitol Wrestling tilted the marketplace in their favor, edging out competitors and creating their own network. Deals with Quinn, Kohler, and others eased the trading of principal wrestlers, including Rocca, Dick the Bruiser, Edouard Carpentier, Kowalski, Schmidt, and O'Connor. Capitol's stable of wrestlers grew, and fans responded positively to the creative booking. Mondt and McMahon no longer had to rely on imported talent, and as their television interests expanded to Los Angeles in 1963, promoters began to phone them for dates.

Mondt's connections to writers, politicians, businessmen, and the New York and Maryland Athletic commissions helped the corporation dodge most controversy. Where doctrine could be bent, it was, and rather than focusing on the limits of their territory, the leaders of Capitol Wrestling examined the complete picture. They recognized the potential in unclaimed towns and adjusted their booking to bring new districts into the loop. Toots worked with promoters from various parts of the country, but the policies of Capitol rarely considered the needs of others. Mondt acknowledged he was only in wrestling for the money, and if that undercut fellow promoters or the grapplers themselves, so be it.

A quarrel with McMahon prompted Mondt to relocate his base of operations to Pittsburgh in 1960. He lost his officer status in Capitol and the dispute pushed McMahon to pursue his own membership in the NWA. Mondt and McMahon settled their grievances, and Toots preserved his interest in D.C. and New York City. A larger-than-life character, he was a gifted multi-tasker, and lived for the thrill of making cash in wrestling. The nightlife was also attractive, as were the horse tracks, where he was a regular. Toots enjoyed the spoils he earned in wrestling, and reveled in being an elder statesmen.

Well aware of the national wrestling scene, Toots wanted to know how towns were doing in comparison to New York, particularly what wrestlers were drawing. Buddy Rogers, a regional champion in Montreal in early 1960, was for years a consistent top earner, and was considered a natural fit for wrestling in the Northeast. After an October 1955 booking at the Garden and subsequent clash over money, Mondt had a beef with Rogers, vetoing a potential run under any other circumstances. But McMahon was planning to acquire Buddy's services, and Capitol was going to maximize his potential first in their territory, then in the faces of the entire NWA.

Mondt closely monitored the path of McMahon and Capitol Wrestling from his office in Pittsburgh, providing crucial advice along the way. He was a frequent traveler to northeastern cities, and attended assorted social gatherings and NWA conventions. Toots was a member of the Alliance from 1950–52 and 1953–63, and served on the board of directors, heavyweight championship committee, and as chairman of the membership committee.

In 1969, he quietly retired from the Capitol Wrestling board of directors and as vice president of the company. McMahon honored his partner's contributions by keeping Mondt on the payroll through the first half of the 1970s, and Toots was occasionally called in for counsel.

In the years that followed, Mondt sold his property in Jackson Heights, Long Island, spent some time in Albuquerque with his nephew Bill, a football coach at the University of New Mexico, and with promoter Mike London before settling in St. Louis with his wife Alda. They lived in the Lewis and Clark Towers at 9953 Lewis and Clark Boulevard, and Toots frequently had lunch with Sam Muchnick.

He was quoted in an article by Lou Sahadi, printed in the Winter 1974 edition of *Wrestling Sports Stars*, as saying: "Sure I quit while I was still young enough to continue wrestling. But as soon as I found out I wasn't in demand anymore, I quit wrestling and turned to promoting. Looking back, I have never regretted it. Wrestling has been good to me. I enjoyed being a wrestler and I enjoyed being a promoter even that much more. At least it gave me the opportunity to spend more time at home with my wife Alda."

Joseph "Toots" Mondt died of pneumonia on June 11, 1976, at the age of 82. His widow Alda died on June 1, 2003, in St. Louis.

Toots was raw, intelligent, and an often impressive man. His imposing size and forceful personality drew attention in any room. Possessing a quick wit and imaginative wrestling mind, he commanded the respect of others. He had many enduring friendships, and like his pal Ed "Strangler" Lewis, was a consummate publicist with unparalleled contacts in newspaper sports departments across the country. It didn't matter if he was quietly speaking with partners in a hotel office, or among a room full of dignitaries, he was articulate, yet skilled in the carny vernacular — and immensely persuasive. Mondt's demeanor left an indelible mark on the wrestlers he employed. His reputation varied depending on who was asked, and complaints from one corner were matched by favorable comments from others. His system of one dollar for the wrestler, and two (or three) for him didn't win him many fans, but it was the law of the land. And in New York City, where the lights of pro grappling shined bright, you either played ball or hit the road.

It may have been shocking for an outsider to learn that the balding, shoeless, cigar-smoking and portly gent ringside at the Garden had all the power, but it was true. Toots influenced what was written about the sport, the achievements of wrestlers, and the future of grappling. The man who once engaged in shoot matches against the sport's best ultimately used his mind to create superstars and earn capital. Addicted to the glory and the money, Toots Mondt was one of a kind and, frankly, wrestling was lucky to have him.

CHAPTER EIGHT

WRESTLING'S FIRST $100,000 GATE

Thesz v. Leone

Professional wrestling's popularity reached a peak during the Great Depression, when Ed "Strangler" Lewis challenged world champion Jim Londos at Wrigley Field in Chicago on September 20, 1934. The wrestlers drew an attendance of 35,265, and a gross of $96,302, both records at that time in the United States. The gate figure broke the 23-year-old standard established by Frank Gotch and George Hackenschmidt at Chicago's Comiskey Park in 1911. The Londos-Lewis sensation followed years of buildup and took the efforts of the "Trust," a collection of promoters who ran all aspects of major league matdom. The dramatic display satisfied the audience, everyone was well paid, and the gala made grappling history.

Seventeen years passed before a wrestling match even approached the level of anticipation that existed for Londos-Lewis. There was enormous interest in NWA world heavyweight champion Lou Thesz's bouts with challengers Buddy Rogers and Verne Gagne, but neither came close to the heat generated on the West Coast between the titleholder and "Baron" Michele Leone.

Born on June 8, 1909, in Pettorano sul Gizio, Aquila, Abruzzo, Italy, Michele Leone was the son of Giovanni and Anna Federico Leone. A clever athlete from a young age, he first became aware of the art of wrestling when his globe-trotting uncle, the original Michele Leone, brought back a fresh understanding of the sport learned in India and created a wrestling club. Fascinated with the ideas of his uncle, Michele immersed himself in grappling. He drank up the elder's wisdom, which recommended everything from exhaustive conditioning to strict dieting.

The authentic mat instruction gave Leone the confidence to leave his home for wrestling engagements in Rome in 1937, where his enthusiasm and charisma made up for his rawness. Using the shoot techniques taught to him, he reportedly won a tournament in Rome prior to traveling through Western Europe and South America. In 1938, he arrived in New York City, where he met up with resourceful promoter Jack Pfefer. Pfefer, who always had his eye out for international talent, booked Leone as the Italian champion, and gave him his start in the business. Leone used the name "Michael," or "Mike" Leone on occasion, and achieved modest success during the first decade of his American experience.

Leone was a pioneering wrestling villain, billed as the "Mighty Mouthpiece" for his scathing rants. In the 1940s, his shtick earned larger paychecks on the Northeastern booking trails of Rudy Dusek, from Bridgeport to Washington, D.C. Playing the part of an unruly heel, Leone suffered many disqualification losses, and was pinned in matches against recognized stars Babe Sharkey and Ernie Dusek. In the District of Columbia, where Joe Turner enjoyed Michele's act, Leone captured the beltless tag-team championship of the city twice with Jim Austeri and Al Norcus.

The theatrical moves of Leone were growing on fans, including his regular foolishness, snide remarks, and arrogant sauntering. In the end, it didn't matter if he lost every other match, or got himself disqualified. All that was important was that he was drawing numbers with his outstanding routine, and his rewriting of the rulebook was unimportant in the minds of fans who appreciated his comedy. It is possible that Michele was influenced in the molding of his character, but he manipulated the gimmick from the jump. Instead of running with a one-trick pony, he found new ways to sell his eccentric persona to the wrestling audience.

Johnny Doyle booked wrestlers in the Los Angeles area and held the rights to

Primo Carnera, Enrique Torres, and, incidentally, Gorgeous George. The unprecedented publicity machine behind George began in the office of Doyle, and it was in Los Angeles that he first became a leading attraction. Leone, in August 1949, was finishing up dates in the northeast and looking to California for future employment. Doyle was impressed with Leone's wrestling skills, inked him to a contract, and helped him adopt the nickname "Baron."

Under the new persona, with a renewed sense of purpose, Leone debuted in southern California in October 1949. One thing California wrestling had going for it was an abundance of television outlets, and Leone's unabashed slapstick proved to be a valuable asset. Seeing dollar signs in the antics of his new find, Doyle cleared a path for sustained exposure. The "Baron" was rolling.

Within his first week in Los Angeles, Leone was headlining at the Olympic Auditorium. On November 2, 1949, he won two of three falls from Terry McGinnis in front of 8,000 spectators. Leone's early feuds in the territory were with Leo Garibaldi, Jack Claybourne, and Kimon Kudo, and Michele participated in tag bouts with both Lord James Blears and Gorgeous George, two of wrestling's top performers.

Leone wrestled the sport's number one national superstar, Antonino Rocca, on March 8, 1950, at the Olympic, and their bout not only sold out (10,400), it turned away an estimated 6,000 aficionados. Rocca won the single-fall affair in 14:26. The $13,000 gate was nearly equaled for their rematch on August 16 at the Auditorium. This time, the two battled to a double countout in 34 minutes before another crowd of 10,000. Later in the month, Michele beat Leo Garibaldi for the local version of the world junior heavyweight title.

Doyle next built up the nobleman by pitting him with the reigning California "world" champion, Enrique Torres. Although beaten countless times by Thesz, Torres had held the distinction of California titleholder for almost four years. The contest with the Baron packed the Olympic to the rafters on November 22, 1950, and Leone won the second and third falls to become a dual champion.

In the ring, the Baron displayed his superior showmanship and intrigued audiences with his well-versed wrestling skills. He was exceptionally strong for his size, and during the day, the strutting aristocrat could be seen training on Muscle Beach. At night, Leone grappled on a circuit that sent him to the Pasadena Arena or Legion Stadium on Monday, the Valley Garden Arena or San Diego Coliseum on Tuesday, the Olympic on Wednesday, Long Beach on Thursday, the Ocean Park Arena in Santa Monica on Friday, and the San Bernardino Arena on Saturday. He was a sight to behold, and once the word got out and people caught him on TV, arenas were crammed with new fans.

Leone's balanced combination of heel heat and broad appeal carried the Olympic to new financial heights. He had lengthy jet-black hair, said to be a "family custom," and a painted scowl that infuriated the meekest of onlookers. Staying away from alcohol or nicotine, Leone focused on clean living. He was a healthy eater, and was dedicated to personal training. With appearances on television programs such as *Dennis Day, Charlie Aldridge*, and *Horace Heidt's Family Night Show*, the Baron raised his profile, and few other wrestlers, even on a national scale, were getting the exposure he was.

Wrestling was booming in the Los Angeles area, and there wasn't a bigger icon than Baron Leone. In 1951, he sold out the Olympic Auditorium with Gorgeous George, Billy Varga, Danny McShain, Ernie Dusek, and twice with Black Guzman. Thousands of fans were turned away. Thesz came into the territory in early July, and found himself standing in the shadow of the local champion, something that bothered him immensely. His concerns would be addressed at the annual NWA convention in Tulsa, where the matter of eliminating the California "world" title was at the top of the agenda. The press frequently compared Thesz to Leone, and harped on their differences when Lou returned in September.

Doyle knew Leone's staggering popularity was too much to ignore and that something eventually had to be done to remain in the good graces of Thesz and the NWA. As a member of the championship committee, he understood the goals of the organization to limit regional "world" heavyweight champions, and promised not to book Torres or Leone as a titleholder outside California. The tension was growing, nonetheless, and climaxed with a threat of suspension. When Doyle failed to act quickly enough, the NWA actually banned him, and while Johnny considered his newfound independence, two area matchmakers tried to grab his Alliance spot. Muchnick wanted to negotiate, and Doyle finally caved.

A unification match was the only solution. With a preliminary agreement from all parties, Doyle brokered a deal that would sort out the mess. According to the storyline, Thesz was eager to wrestle Leone, showing his intent by signing an open contract to grapple any time, any place. The Baron, on the other hand, declined the match, concerned that it would interfere with a $20,000 opportunity to wrestle in Europe. As Leone's decision played out in the press, a real dispute over payoffs loomed behind the scenes. Because he was NWA champion, Thesz was getting a set ten percent of the gross after taxes, but Leone wasn't protected by any such statute.

Still, Leone would be forced into a contest whether he liked it or not. That was the way things were done in southern California. The foremost grapplers were booked by John J. Doyle Enterprises, an outfit owned by Doyle, Eaton, and Mike Hirsch. The Baron had climbed to the apex of wrestling because of their push. His years of scuffling for a piece of the pie paid off in a true explosion in Los Angeles, and the question was whether he could afford to confront his "managers" about their unusually large cut of his paycheck? No, he had little recourse in that matter. But he could get a message across to them in another way.

Although the bout wasn't yet confirmed, Doyle began around-the-clock promotion in late January 1952, hyping the potential skirmish every chance he got. He spoke with journalists, placed advertisements, and fed the hype, setting a new standard for a single match. Smart promoters in advance of the Londos-Lewis bout in 1934 took comparable measures, and the payoff had been record-shattering. One major difference was that in 1934, they only had access to radio and newspapers, whereas Doyle and his mates had television to promote the affair.

TV commentator Dick Lane's magnificent propaganda whipped fans into a fury, and he could probably be credited for selling as many tickets for the clash as either of the wrestlers. On February 16, 1952, Doyle was joined by Leone to discuss the possible contest with Thesz on KNBH, channel 4 in Los Angeles, and the Baron sold their hostilities perfectly. The table was set for a showdown.

On April 21, 1952, Leone and Thesz formally signed a contract for a May 21 bout at an undetermined outdoor stadium, and Eaton engineered a photo op with the *Los Angeles Times* as he stood between the two participants. The terms were two of three falls with a two-hour limit. If the time expired, and if the falls were even, the referee and two judges would pick a winner. The bottom line was that Eaton and Doyle expected record attendance, and if they wished to achieve that, they needed more than 35,265 for the national wrestling record, or 23,765 (Londos-Dean from 1934) for the California record. Londos-Lewis's $96,302 remained tops for a single gate in U.S. grappling history, and the state record was $69,745.50 (Sonnenberg-Marshall, from 1930).

Eaton announced on April 28 that Gilmore Field in Hollywood would host the outdoor spectacle. Fundamentally a baseball diamond for minor league team, the Hollywood Stars, Gilmore Field would be primed to accommodate more than 20,000 fans for wrestling's biggest championship bout in years. The California State Athletic Commission gave the match "unofficial sanctioning," a blessing from Eaton's pals, and with the commission receiving five percent of the take, the chairman was likely to let it go ahead without any undue pressure. Tickets went on sale and wrestling fans, in their frenzy, paid as much as $10 for ringside seats (about $70 today).

With Thesz, Leone, the National Wrestling Alliance, and the California State Athletic Commission under standing orders, Doyle spun his promotional web. Promotion on the area's weekly telecasts increased, and when Thesz invaded the territory in the first week of May, an all-out blitz began. Televised training sessions on Sunday afternoons at 1:00 from the Wilmington Bowl were open to the masses, and on May 11, more than 4,000 people came to see Thesz and Leone prepare. The events were broadcast as *Wrestling Workouts* on KLAC (channel 13) for two hours. During the week, the wrestlers trained at the Olympic Auditorium beginning on Tuesday, May 13, with numerous guest wrestlers including Sandor Szabo, Hombre Montana, Ray Piret, the Christys, Rito Romero, Nichols, and even Ed "Strangler" Lewis.

Lewis triggered an additional level of interest in Thesz-Leone. Well known in the area, he hyped the approaching match to his many friends and contacts. Sports writers kept an open-door policy with the Strangler. They wanted to hear what he was doing, who he was backing, and what his views were. His assessment of the championship bout was heard by correspondents who respected his every word.

As Thesz's spokesperson, Lewis gave the champion the colorful voice some complained that he lacked. As a quiet, meticulous babyface, Thesz couldn't flaunt his talents or ballyhoo his accomplishments. Lewis could. He compared Lou to the champions of old, repeatedly criticizing modern-day theatrics. Two columns by *Los Angeles Times* sportswriters Paul Zimmerman and Al Wolf in the days before the match repeated Lewis's hype about the NWA champion exactly as its promoters wanted.

The National Wrestling Alliance world champion since November 1949, Thesz had crisscrossed North America dozens and dozens of times. He wrestled all of the era's greats, but outside "Whipper" Billy Watson in Toronto, had never faced a situation where a regional grappler held such sway. There wasn't a better matchup in the business, not in Chicago, New York City, or St. Louis. Los Angeles was prepared for Thesz and Leone, and now the wrestlers themselves had to deliver.

The training sessions proved very popular and Doyle made the most of their second and final televised *Wrestling Workouts* from the Wilmington Bowl on Sunday, May 18. Eaton went out of his way to announce that proceeds from the weekday sessions at the Auditorium would be donated to the U.S. Olympic Committee, and that all fans would receive free autographed photos of the wrestlers. The engineered marketing, no matter how basic, furthered the momentum, dramatically boosting ticket sales. People understood that the Gilmore Field extravaganza was something different from the casual weekly wrestling shows. It was a one-of-a-kind happening and the hip Hollywood crowd was not going to miss it.

The physical differences between Thesz and Leone were distinct. Thesz stood 6'2'' and weighed 222 pounds, down from his normal wrestling weight of 228–230. Standing five inches shorter, Leone carried his 208-pound frame like a bodybuilder. In the early edition of Los Angeles area newspapers on May 21, articles alerted readers to the size differential, their different wrestling philosophies, and details about the wrestlers' personal lives. After the last advertisements were printed, the last phone calls to radio stations had been dialed, and there was nothing left to say, the program went forward as planned. The date was Wednesday, May 21, 1952, and the show began promptly at 8:30 p.m. with four preliminary matches.

Ray Piret, a sparring partner for the Baron, was given a shot on the undercard, losing to Dr. Lee Grable in the initial match. An entertaining little-person feature saw Sky Low Low beat "Irish" Jack Cassidy, then longtime rivals "Wild" Red Berry and Billy Varga fought to a draw in 15 minutes. San Francisco area "world" tag team champions the Sharpe Brothers came to Hollywood and beat up Vic Christy and Sandor Szabo in 11:06, with Mike Sharpe pinning Vic. The semifinal was California "world" junior champion Rito Romero against NWA world junior champion Danny McShain in a winner-take-all match. Two locally booked titles could have been wiped off the map by the end of the night, but the junior heavyweights finished in a stalemate.

Leone entered the ring to mixed applause, wearing a Roman toga. It was obvious that Thesz was the crowd favorite. The NWA champion wore what the *Los Angeles Times* dubbed "special shoes" for the bout, created by his father, equipped with "neolite" on the bottom of his right shoe, and the left sole fitted with a rough rubber. The combination would allow him to spin to the mat more quickly, giving him an advantage. Eaton and Doyle had decided that the reliable Mike Mazurki (Michael Mazurkiewicz, 1907–1990), a 6′4″ product of the Ukraine, was the man to conduct officiating duties. Mazurki was a former wrestler, and by 1952, a true fixture in Hollywood, having acted in more than 50 films. Outside the ring ropes was Thesz's manager, Lewis. A contingent of gleeful officials sat in the front row.

The main event lasted a little less than 45 minutes, and held the crowd's undivided attention. They reacted to every facial tick and maneuver. Thesz looked to be the brighter of the two during the first fall, nimbly dodging the Baron's attempts to get a hold of him. Once Lou acquired the upper hand, he utilized an old move popularized by Londos and specifically sharpened in training — the airplane spin. Off balance and looking for relief, Leone was pummeled with an array of dropkicks. Finally, at the 31:20 mark, the California champion was pinned.

Stanza two saw the gladiator from Italy battle back to best Thesz, forcing Lou to submit to a neck hold in 6:30. By that point, the heavy lifting was over, and all they had to do was carry it the remaining 4:20 to a crisp finish. There was a difference between the two wrestlers in that Hollywood ring other than their size, and it sincerely bothered Thesz. Leone was lackadaisical with his side of the effort, sending a message to his commanders, but the Baron, even at 50 percent, still captivated the emotional crowd. The NWA champion used a backdrop to polish his opponent off, and scored the winning pinfall.

Gilmore Field was sold out, with 25,256 in attendance, and thousands were left outside the stadium, wishing they had tickets. The turnout set a record for wrestling in California, but even more important was the gross paid into the till. That amount was simply astonishing — $103,277.75, a new record for professional wrestling, eclipsing the 1934 bout featuring the Strangler and Londos. The show marked the first ever $100,000 gate, proving that the timing and promotional efforts had been perfect. Doyle, his many partners, and the wrestlers, split the net of $81,523.45.

The encounter was a work, and a prearranged finish was used to give the paying customers what they wanted: excitement. However, the match did provide a semblance of reality that may have only been obvious to the three men in the ring, any wrestlers who were watching, and to the eager promoters sitting in the audience. Thesz didn't hold back or pull his punches. At some points, he brutalized Leone, taking advantage of a lesser-skilled athlete.

The reasons behind his "stiff" ring work may have had several layers. It was later alleged that a pair of promoters involved in arranging the match went into Thesz's dressing room prior to the Gilmore affair and asked Lou to lose the NWA championship to Leone, a ploy that would set up a return bout. Lou, of course, rejected the idea, but went into the match, even with Mazurki officiating, concerned about a potential double-cross. The contest held too much importance for him to ignore the possibility, or the will of the unscrupulous people behind the scenes. Thesz pummeled Leone, making sure everyone understood his seriousness.

While many people weren't aware of the proposal made to Thesz, or the champion's general mindset, there was an understanding among wrestlers about why the Baron just went through the motions on that memorable night. He didn't appear to be a focused grappler striving to hook Thesz, nor was even he as animated as he usually was, which was surprising to those expecting his "A" game. Leone worked sloppily, gaining his revenge on his bookers in his own way, but Thesz believed that his dreary performance hurt prospective rematches. And he may have been right. Years later, when the night's genuine figures trickled out of a California athletic commission meeting, the reasoning behind Leone's actions were a little more clear.

Under oath, and testifying against his former allies on February 15, 1957, Doyle claimed that Leone made $6,650 for his night's labor. From that, he paid the booking agency an estimated $2,200. In addition to receiving healthy sums from the net, minus payments to the commission, Gilmore's owners, talent, and other dues, Eaton and Doyle were taking extra cash from the pay of their celebrated wrestler. Enough was obviously not enough.

When it was all said and done, Leone was paid 5.46 percent of the net, and according to Doyle's testimony, he wasn't the only one shafted that evening. Automatically paid ten percent of the net for being the NWA champion, it was agreed that Thesz would get 15 for the Leone match. But Doyle said that instead of receiving $12,228, Thesz settled for $9,000, the rest going to the booking office.

Sam Muchnick testified that day as a rebuttal witness and stated: "Doyle phoned me the day after the match. He told me that expenses had been considerable, and that if they took $15,000 off the top it would mean a $10,000 purse for Thesz instead of the customary 15 percent. I told Johnny that if it was okay with Thesz, it was okay with me, and that's how he was paid off."

A letter written by Thesz was read into the record at a meeting in April 1957, and claimed that he never wrangled over money with Eaton, only Doyle, and that he was "satisfied" with how he was paid.

The undercard talent were nickel-and-dimed. Despite the record figures, the preliminary grapplers got the California minimum of $15, according to hearsay. Semifinalists got no more than a few hundred dollars.

Jack Geyer, an influential sportswriter for the *Los Angeles Times*, was less than impressed by the event, and his scathing report on May 22 was riddled with sarcasm and disgust. The press gave the tussle extensive post-bout coverage, and a headline was printed at the top of the *Times* sports section. Organizers were happy with their profits, and Doyle was given credit for making it happen. His stock in the National Wrestling Alliance rose, and members would congratulate him wholeheartedly in September when he hosted the annual convention in Santa Monica.

Incidentally, a Thesz-Leone rematch was used by Doyle and Nichols against Eaton as the southern California wars began to tear apart the local syndicate in September 1953. Reduced to using independent talent for programs at the Olympic because of a falling out with the NWA bookers, Eaton sat idly by and watched the bout staged at the Legion Stadium in Hollywood on September 22, 1953. The affair was relatively unsuccessful compared to their first match, but still drew 5,000, paying $23,000. Part two was longer and more suspenseful than the initial bout, but the outcome was the same. Geyer even returned to add his notable commentary in the *Times* the next day, and it's very likely that more people read his mocking article than observed the bout live. Any hope of a $200,000 rematch was lost.

Thesz and Leone went on the road, and the two faced off in Indianapolis, Salt Lake City, Tampa, Miami Beach, El Paso, and Tulsa. Leone was rewarded for his contributions to wrestling by the NWA, and pushed to the top of the world junior heavyweight division. On August 17, 1953, he won the second and third falls over Danny McShain in Memphis to capture that championship.

Remaining under contract to John J. Doyle Enterprises, Leone was transferred to the agency of Leroy McGuirk of Tulsa. As was customary, Leone would pay his California managers 30 percent of his earnings over the first $200 a week, and as his official booker, McGuirk garnered 2½ from the 12½ percent revenue for every date, after taxes. Leone, like Thesz and light heavyweight champion Frank Stojack, was responsible for signing an exclusive pact with the NWA that, for one dollar, gave his "services as a wrestler in contests wherever the National Wrestling Alliance has promotional or matchmaking rights, or wherever the National Wrestling Alliance has a member or affiliates."

Doyle abandoned the California syndicate in January 1954, and his booking office, which held the contracts of numerous wrestlers, including the Baron, was closed. The withdrawal was limited to Doyle, and Eaton and Nichols made sure Leone knew that he was to continue sending money westward. Eaton and Nichols even had Muchnick speak with Leone personally, Doyle said in an interview with Stanley Disney in May 1955, and threatened an NWA-wide ban if he didn't follow through with those obligations, worth thousands of dollars.

The junior title brought a standard income of at least $35,000 a year (inflated in the press to $80,000 annually) and enhanced the national recognition Leone had gotten from the Thesz bout. He wrestled across the country, fulfilling the needs of NWA associates to a high standard. The one big issue that remained was the fact that Leone declined to sign the NWA contract that was required of the three sanctioned titleholders. A year after his victory over McShain, at the annual convention in St. Louis, after being lauded by the junior championship committee for his excellent work, a decision was made to put pressure on Leone to sign the binding agreement.

In a letter to Sam Avey, McGuirk's partner in Tulsa, in November 1954, Muchnick expressed his frustration with the Leone situation and suggested a possible remedy. The NWA President affirmed that "a lot of headaches [could be] eliminated" by sending a wrestler into the ring to shoot on Leone, and physically take the championship. Cyclone Anaya (Jesus Valencia) was proposed as a candidate to attempt the underhanded move, but ultimately, it proved unnecessary.

On March 21, 1955, Leone defended his junior championship against Gorgeous George in Tulsa. Leone and George were similar in many ways, especially in how they both had been transformed from journeymen to superstars in Los Angeles. They were gold at the box office, were physically similar, and could work a crowd with the best in history. Paying a large guarantee, with a percentage to the contestants, promoter Sam Avey locked up the match, only to be disappointed at the gate when bad weather kept fans home. Leone won the third fall by countout and retained his title before less than 1,000 devotees.

After nearly 20 months at the head of the junior division, Leone lost the belt to "Gentleman" Ed Francis on April 11, 1955, at the Fairgrounds Junior Arena in Tulsa. He won the opening fall in 19 minutes, lost the second in ten, then was pinned six minutes later after some controversy. Leone's loss to Francis was his first to someone other than Thesz in more than five years. Prior to their rematch two weeks later in Tulsa, the Baron spoke about his agenda in a mix of kayfabe and straight shooting. His comments were printed in the April 24, 1955 edition of the *Tulsa Daily World*: "If I can't beat this baby face from Chicago, I don't think I'll stay in this country. I may take off for Italy, if I can't beat guys like this. If I win, of course, I'll stay in the United States. The money's here. I've made good money in the U.S. But my mother's been wanting me to come home for a visit. If I'm not the champion, then there's no reason why I can't go."

Leone put Francis over a second time, losing the first and third falls. His plans to leave the U.S. came to fruition, and, with his wife, Billie, he traveled to Europe to spend time with family. The famed nobleman quietly went into semiretirement, and shortly thereafter, left the spotlight for good. He was financially stable, traveled often, and rarely appeared in public. On December 30, 1963, at Valhalla Memorial Park in North Hollywood, Michele acted as a pallbearer at Gorgeous George's funeral. Promoter Mike LeBell was later able to convince him to return to the Olympic Auditorium for a special ceremony that honored his career on April 14, 1965, but a mere 3,321 fans were on hand to pay tribute.

The magnetic Leone was struck by an automobile crossing a street in Santa Monica, suffered head trauma, and passed away on November 26, 1988, at UCLA Medical Center in Los Angeles. He was survived by his wife of 34 years, a brother in Argentina, and three sisters in Italy. The wrestling community mourned the loss of the famed Baron, but his decades on the mat, his ability to generate excitement, and the legend surrounding wrestling's first $100,000 gate will live forever.

CHAPTER NINE

UNITED STATES V.
THE NATIONAL
WRESTLING ALLIANCE

The monopolistic customs of the National Wrestling Alliance were more widely known by 1950, but most sportswriters were still confusing the Alliance with the National Wrestling Association, a rigid body of bureaucrats. Mistaking a band of morally challenged businessmen with a host of political appointees wasn't so far-fetched, the fact was that there were two NWAS with totally different mission statements.

Holding an edge over independents or "outlaws" by dominating principal wrestlers and television outlets, the members of the National Wrestling Alliance had few legitimate competitors. They were well organized, connected to politi-cians, and often went out of their way to eliminate a threat infringing on another member's sacred territory. Those involved with grappling were coping with the new system, but the marks, editors, and investigators were gradually learning things about the cartel in command of professional wrestling.

Just how much power did the NWA have? North America was broken up into more than 30 territories, each run by a select booking agent, and tied into the grand conspiracy to lock out opposition. Associates were responsible for inking deals with local TV stations, and a handful of national programs reached cities far and wide. Influential agents like Joe "Toots" Mondt and Fred Kohler managed hundreds of the most-recognized grapplers, having signed them to exclusive contracts that made it impossible for a nonmember to book them. Local promoters were required to pay hefty booking fees, and it was a situation where you either paid up the ladder or you didn't play ball.

In each state, the NWA's tactics trickled down into the heart of professional athletics: the regionally governed athletic commissions. By bonding with the movers and shakers in their particular areas, Alliance bookers reinforced their positions greatly. They donated money to causes, held political fundraisers, and made sure anyone who expected an envelope full of cash got it in a timely fashion. This system of compensation in return for safeguarding their promotional efforts was considered quite normal in most NWA territories.

The Indiana Athletic Commission demonstrated their favoritism towards the Alliance in August 1953 when they passed an ordinance governing the booking of pro wrestlers. They issued only four booking licenses — to Kohler, Sam Muchnick, Al Haft, and Cliff Maupin, all NWA members — and other promoters in the state who wanted to stage a program had to negotiate with them. There was no room allowed for competition.

Potential whistleblowers were being pushed to their limits, and it was clear to any independent-minded individual trying to make his way in the wrestling business that the Alliance held a distinct monopoly. The Sherman Antitrust Act, passed by the U.S. Congress on July 2, 1890, had been created to regulate big business and any restraint of trade in commerce. Although the monopolistic practices of the NWA were not yet on the radar of government officials, it was just a matter of time.

The collaboration of wrestling bookers did improve the standard of matches across the board. Talent moved freely, and the whittling of champions down to a single titleholder in every weight class was apparently very high on the NWA's list of priorities. The Alliance improved grappling on all levels, but their clandestine actions soon veered further and further away from what the government considered legal.

Drunk with power, Alliance members continued to attract negative attention.

Finally, on January 27, 1953, a mysterious figure stepped into the Boston office of the Federal Bureau of Investigation with accusations that he had been "discriminated against" by the NWA. The person "wished to complain that the National Wrestling Alliance was a monopoly which existed throughout the United States and Canada whose purpose is to control all wrestling matches." The charge was documented, but the matter was not pursued.

A second accuser, identified as Nick Lutze, a downtrodden Hungarian-born promoter with 30 years of mat experience, called the FBI in Los Angeles on April 14, 1953. Lutze asserted that the Alliance was operating in an unlawful fashion and controlled 90 percent of all wrestling talent. Several months earlier, Lutze had successfully negotiated a television contract with KNXT (channel 2) for Saturday night wrestling from the Valley Garden Arena in North Hollywood, which commenced on February 7, much to the dismay of Eaton and booking agent Johnny Doyle.

International Wrestling, as Lutze's series was known, forced Eaton and Doyle to run opposition on Saturday nights. Their show, originating from Pomona, was telecast on KLAC (channel 13) a half-hour earlier, and Doyle lined up his best wrestlers to grab the audience. When Lutze shifted to the Wilmington Bowl, Doyle moved into the Valley Garden Arena on Saturdays, again with top names.

The syndicate's alleged manipulation of wrestlers received the harshest criticism. Lutze claimed the NWA was blackballing athletes who appeared on his programs. Among the matmen that wrestled for him between February and April were Primo Carnera, Fred Atkins, Kay Bell, Myron Cox, Tom Renesto, Lord Carlton (Leo Whippern), Roy McClarity, and Frankie Murdock. Vic Holbrook, Lutze said, was threatened with a suspension if he wrestled a date for him. Lutze then provided the FBI with a list of people he believed would substantiate his claim. Maurice LaChappelle, Ed McLemore, Morris Cohen, and Billy Sandow were mentioned as individuals who had suffered similar treatment at the hands of the Alliance.

Two weeks before blabbing to the Justice Department, Lutze had traveled to Chicago for an NWA meeting to thrash out his problems with Doyle and Eaton. Lutze wanted to settle their differences and maybe even join the elite clique. Infuriated when things went horribly wrong, he left abruptly, and readied his remarks for the government. The FBI recommended a "preliminary inquiry at the local level." The file was passed on to superiors.

Muchnick got wind of the charges, and lectured the members of the NWA at the Labor Day weekend convention in Chicago. In a firm tone, he advised that the Alliance retain an attorney to "handle all Alliance business that may come up in the courts," and warned that "some outsiders are trying to create the impression that we are a monopoly." He was particularly worried about the actions of

McLemore, who was in Santa Monica the year before, and had heard the plan to blackball grapplers who wrestled for a nonmember. Little did he know that it was Lutze, and not McLemore, who had sparked the inquisition.

Because of staffing complications, the Los Angeles branch of the Department of Justice delayed the inquest until the first part of 1955. In the interim, cracks in the NWA system developed. Ed Contos of Baltimore went to the Maryland State Athletic Commission and squawked about his difficulties getting wrestlers from Toots Mondt in September 1953. Chairman John Marshall Boone contacted Muchnick to defuse the situation, but very little changed. Boone appealed to Muchnick a second time. He did not oppose the Alliance monopoly, he simply desired an improvement in the way Baltimore bouts were being handled. He said they had had no problems while Pedro Martinez was heading the New York office, but could never get together with Mondt to straighten out the mess. Muchnick did what he could, notifying the grievance committee, which scheduled a summit in Kansas City in an effort to end the feud. In Baltimore, however, Boone used the bankruptcy of the Manhattan Booking Agency as an excuse to declare the city "open," available for a booker other than Mondt, on April 27, 1954. Pennsylvania, shortly thereafter, followed suit.

Frank Wiener, Chairman of the Pennsylvania Athletic Commission, called the conditions in his state "deplorable" in a letter to Muchnick, and demanded a better class of wrestlers booked into his towns. It was so bad in Philadelphia promoter Ray Fabiani had to close his main venue for lack of wrestlers, and ended up losing nearly $15,000. The Pennsylvania governor warned that he'd suspend all wrestling if significant changes weren't made. Mondt was holding promoters hostage, and using his NWA membership and influence to stifle grappling in major metropolises based on his own whims.

To fulfill his talent needs, Contos brought in grapplers from Al Haft, which prompted Mondt to steal Charleston from the Columbus booker in retribution. Toots and fellow NWA member Rudy Dusek refused to give up rights to Baltimore or Philadelphia, and the applications of Contos and Fabiani, submitted prior to the September 1954 convention, were denied. Boone, in a telegram to Muchnick, strongly recommended that Contos be endorsed, and was furious when his suggestion was ignored. The NWA determined that Mondt and Dusek "owned" the two towns in question after a 25–11 vote, and informed both promoters that their previous understanding was still active.

On October 4, 1954, Boone became the first public official to openly lambaste the NWA for its monopolistic practices. He recommended the strengthening of existing rules to eradicate dictatorships. Several days later, Wiener echoed Boone's statements, and declared Pennsylvania was an "open" state, in defence of the Alliance's declaration.

A little more than three weeks after Boone's remarks, an irritated independent operator in Los Angeles named Frank Pasquale filed a $550,000 lawsuit against Cal Eaton, Robert Eaton, Mike Hirsch, and Hugh Nichols in Superior Court, alleging that there was a scheme to restrain trade in southern California.

On December 17, 1954, Pasquale sent a wire to U.S. Attorney General Herbert Brownell Jr. and according to the December 18, 1954, edition of the *Los Angeles Times*, a portion of the note read: "Sam Muchnick, president and secretary of the NWA, by long distance, called wrestler Charles Moto at Los Angeles and notified him he'd be blacklisted through the U.S. if he wrestled at South Gate Arena . . . this is the first time a national connection with local monopoly has exposed its hand."

The deposition of Lutze had been filed away, so it was the accusations of Pasquale in February 1955 that ruffled feathers in the FBI's Los Angeles bureau. Complainants also told agents that the NWA was violating antitrust laws and that there was a "nationwide conspiracy." Attorney James M. McGrath looked at the incoming evidence, and his dispatch was sent up the chain, landing on the desk of Stanley Nelson Barnes (1900–1990), a California superior court judge and reigning "trustbuster" as the Assistant Attorney General. Barnes approved further inquiries, and the Los Angeles den of hungry examiners went to work.

Investigator Stanley Disney was put in charge, and starting with Johnny Doyle, built a case for prosecution. Doyle knew a lot about the inner mechanisms of the Alliance and, on February 25, revealed numerous confidential facts about its members' practices. Having resigned from the NWA in January 1954, Doyle had personal knowledge of the southern California combine's plot to put Lutze out of the business.

Doyle mentioned the intimidation that kept Mr. Moto from wrestling for Pasquale, after an original objection by Hugh Nichols. Moto was told he'd be blackballed in all NWA territories if he agreed to the date. The booker also suggested that Disney talk to Lutze, Jack Pfefer, Lord Carlton, William Olivas, Ernie Steffen of the Wilmington Bowl, and Harold Gartner of the Valley Garden Arena. An internal memorandum and summary of the conference with Doyle, written by Disney, called Johnny an "impressive and open witness," but that "he undoubtedly engaged in a lot of hatchet activities for NWA himself until January 1954, and so might prove to be a somewhat embarrassing witness."

In the days that followed, Disney communicated with Gartner, Pasquale, and Carlton before revisiting Doyle on March 8. Their second discussion was more comprehensive. Johnny presented his own memoirs dating back to joining the Alliance, and provided a synopsis of wrestling's history in Los Angeles since the introduction of television. In his continuing efforts to aid in the probe, he furnished a laundry list of potential whistle-blowers, from Ted Thye to Mildred Burke.

Burke was interviewed in Reseda on March 23, 1955, and as Doyle suggested, was eager to vent. She said that women's wrestling had long suffered because of the conduct of its chief handler, Billy Wolfe, her ex-husband and most recent enemy. Her testimonial was particularly ugly and included stories of spousal abuse; death threats from Alliance members directed at Jack Pfefer; blackballing, adultery, corruption, and tax fraud; and an accusation that Wolfe's over-training of their adopted daughter Janet (Janet Boyer) was the reason she died in July 1951.

Benny Ginsberg, a retired wrestler and matchmaker for Toots Mondt, Muchnick, and Doyle, spoke with Disney on March 24, 1955, in Van Nuys. Among his memories from his "40 years" of grappling was the charge that Lou Thesz had paid Orville Brown "something" for the NWA title in late 1949. He explained the differences in the St. Louis offices, and what he knew about of the initial days of the Alliance. Ginsberg recounted the troubles in southern California, and reported that Pat Fraley, Rube Wright, and others had been blacklisted in the region.

Former world heavyweight champion Stanislaus Zbyszko wrote his inaugural letter to the Antitrust division in Los Angeles on March 24, 1955. Two years earlier, Zbyszko contributed an eight-page piece to *True — The Man's Magazine* (August 1953) that was a factor in the breaking of kayfabe. He evaluated modern wrestling and was acutely critical of Primo Carnera and Antonino Rocca. Although the periodical didn't mention the NWA by name, his disdain for the Alliance's methods were well known.

Zbyszko's March 24 memo compared the Alliance to the infamous Maybury Gang and steered detectives to McLemore, Pfefer, Max Baumann, Tony (sic) Harmon, Sterling Davis, and Al Bisignano. Zbyszko said Pfefer had been forced out of Fort Worth at gunpoint, and claimed the arsons at McLemore's building and Davis's home were "instigated by [the] Alliance." Joining him in the anti-NWA fight was his younger brother Wladek, and the siblings began a steady correspondence with the government. Barnes returned a note stating, "your cooperation in making this information available to us is appreciated."

Disney and Doyle got together again on April 26, and Johnny spoke about his chat with Fred Kohler. Doyle told Kohler about his new TV deal, and asked him for talent. In turn, Kohler inquired about whether the government's investigation was active. Doyle surmised from that query that Fred would consent, and almost be obligated to send wrestlers if Disney contacted him, knowing that they were delving into the behavior of the NWA.

If it was possible, Doyle was going to use the Justice Department's investigation of wrestling to regain his footing in Los Angeles. Chicago grapplers would certainly help in those endeavors. Also on April 26, the Antitrust Division prepared a letter for Kohler wanting to know which West Coast promoters he supplied with wrestlers.

On May 9, 1955, Disney got a phone call from Jack Pfefer, and in his office memorandum to James McGrath, he concluded that the diminutive, indie booker "seemed somewhat eager to dodge me." In a brief statement, Pfefer said that the Alliance had never bothered him: which was a complete fabrication.

During the morning of May 16, Assistant Chief General George Derr interviewed U.S. Senator Edward John Thye of Minneapolis, the sibling of promoter Ted Thye. Concerned with antitrust violations in sports, especially in boxing and wrestling, Thye clarified his brother's dissatisfaction with the National Wrestling Alliance, and how he had abstained from joining the syndicate. Ted, in his exclusive promotions of Australia, stopped relying on American wrestlers out of anxiety that they would be barred from future jobs. The senator suggested that they speak with his brother regarding his plight, and the two conferred about the option of federal intervention to supervise professional wrestling.

Doyle heard from Kohler by telephone on May 19, and Fred said that he would open all of his records to the government if need be. Confident that additional details could be uncovered by a trip to see Kohler in Chicago and Muchnick in St. Louis, Disney pressed his superiors for authorization. Between May 23 and June 10, he interviewed Ernie Steffen, Al Billings, Harry Rubin, Hardy Kruskamp, Ted Thye, and Joe Malcewicz.

Two sessions with Thye happened in Portland on June 8 and 9, and they proved to be very informative. Disney listened to wrestling tales going back to the mid-1910s, but focused on the promotional wars of the Pacific Northwest that had destroyed that territory. Thye described how his booking agency (Western Athletic Club) had been slowly pushed out by Jerry Meeker, Bob Murray, Hat Freeman, Don Owen, and the pressure of the NWA. Talking about Lou Thesz, he mentioned that there were a handful of grapplers in Australia and India who could potentially have beaten him in legit matches. He said that he'd teamed with Leo Leavett and Jim Londos to run Japan, invoking a battle with his old friend Al Karasick of Honolulu.

Malcewicz was the first active NWA member the government consulted, and Disney made the best of his jaunt to San Francisco on June 10. In examining the promoter's files, he found them to be limited; there was nothing there pertaining to the Alliance. His participation, Joe admitted, in the NWA conventions had been more social than serious, but he knew that Muchnick told the membership that they were not to show prejudice against wrestlers or nonaffiliated promoters in any way. In a memorandum dated June 13, 1955, Disney reported that "Malcewicz is a bluff, rough speaker who answers every question at length and to little purpose."

Permission came from Washington on June 15 for Disney's trip to important locales in the Midwest. Muchnick was notified in advance that a bloodhound was on his way, but Sam had been proactive. He'd already ventured to Washington and met with Derr at the Justice Building. Disney's legwork, however, was going to expedite the collection of documents, necessary if an outsider was really going to understand the NWA. Always cordial, Muchnick removed all the roadblocks to the government's study of wrestling, and focused instead on the positive core values of the Alliance.

A combination of Disney's reports and growing criticism forced McGrath to officially open an investigation. On June 17, 1955, with encouragement from Washington, McGrath publicly announced a probe of wrestling, stating that the results would be used for "possible improvements in procedure, and for legislative action if necessary."

In a June 23 "special" bulletin, Muchnick advised the membership that the NWA was being watched, confirming the reports that had been in the press. Any highly methodical scrutiny of NWA practices had dramatic implications Sam wanted to head off at the pass. Unfortunately, the inquiry, reported in all types of media, only brought out more complainants.

Disney spoke with Menacker on June 20 via telephone. The bulk of the conversation had to do with the Southwestern territory from El Paso to Phoenix. Menacker bought Andy Tremaine's stake in the El Paso booking agency for $5,700 in 1950, and was partnered with Mike London. Eager to expand, Menacker was given rights to Mesa and Tucson from his pal Johnny Doyle, and established Rod Fenton in Arizona as their representative. Fenton procured Phoenix from Jim Londos and Ed Contos, and joined the NWA in 1954.

Personal problems with London prompted their separation, Menacker explained, and he aligned temporarily with Amarillo's Dory Detton. They eventually reconciled, and the NWA determined that Menacker, because he had kept all receipts for El Paso during their hiatus, owed London $10,000, which was subsequently paid. Menacker's conflicts with Detton and London went on for several years, and he had recently bid $30,000 for Bob Murray's Seattle promotion. Disney, in his internal memo, classified Menacker as an "intelligent witness," but would also be "reluctant," and "undoubtedly serve as an apologist for the other NWA members if he could do so without lying."

Everything leading up to Wednesday, June 22, was a preview for the main event, a dialogue with the NWA's kingpin, Sam Muchnick, at the Claridge Hotel. Over the course of two days, Muchnick was grilled by Disney on such hot-button topics as blacklisting and the red-ink postcards, their alleged monopolies, and the general history of the union. Because the investigation involved associates in dozens of states and the puzzle pieces were scattered far and wide, Disney hoped his stint in St. Louis, where he had total access to NWA files, would provide much-needed answers.

Muchnick asked about the parameters of the inquiry, whether it was a criminal or civil case, and if he could be personally held accountable if he stayed on as president. He threw out the option of voluntary disbanding of the NWA, and whether they could still be prosecuted if that occurred. Disney told him such a move would have no bearing on the investigation. Candidly, the antitrust attorney clarified the motivations of the Justice Department and the assorted illegal infractions he had discovered. A consent decree was mentioned, but Disney refrained from characterizing it as a possible solution.

One thing Muchnick sought to avoid was a public proclamation, either by the Department of Justice or in a federal courtroom, that wrestling was a scripted sport. Kayfabe was still prevalent in the 1950s, and despite revelations by Dan Parker, Herman Hickman, Johnny Heim and others, most wrestling enthusiasts believed in what they were seeing at the arena and on television. Muchnick feared the circulation of guarded information would demoralize the fans entirely, sinking the industry.

In Chicago, Disney met with Kohler on June 24 and 25 at his Grace Street office. Kohler gave his version of the dispute with Leonard Schwartz, and deciphered a letter found in his records, stamped September 16, 1950, identifying 24 wrestlers who had performed for his rival. The Don Eagle-Gorgeous George fiasco was discussed, and Fred confessed to planning the double-cross. Kohler also discussed his booking company, Fred Kohler Enterprises, his promotional entity, Sports Promotions Engineers, Inc., and the International Wrestling Agency, a talent operation that held the contracts of three wrestlers, Antonino Rocca, Verne Gagne, and Pat O'Connor. Disney reviewed Muchnick's file cabinets, and did not believe they had been "cleaned" to remove incriminating papers.

The NWA's predicament was serious, and Disney's brief alerted Muchnick and Kohler to the scope and ramifications of the investigation. There was no escaping the government's wrath, and even dismantling the coalition wouldn't prevent prosecution. A memorandum from James McGrath to George Derr in Washington on July 5 clarified Disney's attitude after more than four months of strenuous analysis: "Mr. Disney feels rather strongly that criminal action should be taken against the NWA and certain of its principals."

On July 15, 1955, a 17-page memorandum was submitted by Disney to his Los Angeles boss with a recommendation for a grand jury investigation into the NWA and the wrestling business. He elaborated on a conspiracy of 38 bookers in controlling specific territories, browbeating promoters into dealing with Alliance associates, the sale of towns, discrimination, price fixing, and systematic blacklisting. The power of the NWA was evident, and Disney suggested that a civil case be brought against it in Los Angeles Federal Court.

Muchnick was cunning in his writings to the Antitrust Division, admitting that some members of the NWA had "deviated from the true purposes of the organization, and there is no question that some corrections should be made." His attitude was key, and he was always reaffirming his willingness to cooperate. The correspondence was consistent throughout 1955, but varied in context. One important factor, acknowledged by Stanley Barnes on July 19, was that Muchnick was eager for the chance to explain the NWA's side before a decision was reached about pursuing the case.

Barnes agreed to allow Muchnick and the NWA a hearing. Ironically, Muchnick named Johnny Doyle as the culprit behind the red ink blackballing postcards, an opportune jab at the man he believed had caused the hassle. He also denied ever discouraging Mr. Moto from wrestling for Frank Pasquale at the South Gate Arena, as claimed in December 1954. Unusually hands-on, Muchnick asked for constant updates and showed he was willing, at any time, to travel to Los Angeles or Washington.

Prior to the NWA caucus in St. Louis, Muchnick told officials he thought the Alliance was in a position to splinter because of "internal difficulties." Sonny Myers's antitrust suit in Des Moines Federal Court, filed on August 2, 1955, against Pinkie George and the National Wrestling Alliance added further credence to the argument that the NWA was truly a monopoly. Needless to say, the annual convention at the Claridge Hotel in St. Louis, held from September 3–5, 1955, was going to be critical.

Alliance attorney Harry Soffer was present when Disney was in St. Louis. He listened carefully to what was being said, knowing their game plan would have to be adjusted immediately after the session. At the NWA conference, Soffer discussed the mounting crisis, and proposed modifications to NWA statutes. He gave those in attendance assurances that were corroborated, surprisingly, by Cal Eaton. In August, Eaton had flown to Washington and reportedly met with unknown government representatives. He was confident that his efforts would thwart the inquiry, and boasted about his success to peers.

Soffer recommended dropping two bylaws, Article 3, Section 4, and Article 9, Section 1, and a motion was made by Pinkie George to do just that. Paul Jones of Atlanta seconded the proposition, and the motion passed unanimously. The latter regulation, having to do with the appropriation of territories and their protection, was the most worrying to the Justice Department. Its abolition was central if the NWA was going to convince the government of its willingness to reform, but regardless of the apparent change in attitude, the Antitrust Division had reason to believe the action was a sham.

The membership gave Soffer the job of revising their constitution from top to bottom, and accepted a measure that suspended all NWA directives until restructured policies were drafted. These commandments, "in no way would infringe on antitrust and restraint-of-trade rules," according to the meeting minutes.

With no choice but to accommodate snooping inspectors, members kept their cool, and were encouraged by their leaders' commitment to the true values of their guild. Alliance members became a little more optimistic that the NWA might withstand the growing catastrophe, and small-town promoters sat back and waited for peace. Muchnick, at the head of the table, was determined that his years of labor would not be undone by the recent rash of accusations.

The majority of discourse at the September powwow concerned the government's investigation and the numerous outstanding legal suits involving members. Hugh Nichols criticized Kohler's booking Las Vegas for Doyle, which was being broadcast in Los Angeles on KTTV. He threatened to invade Denver and Albuquerque (two of Kohler's towns) if Chicago wrestlers didn't stop making appearances in Vegas. Justice Department documents speculated that Eaton had financed Karl Sarpolis's purchase of Amarillo to assist in his planned Colorado and New Mexico incursions. The threats were enough to get Kohler to withdraw, and he promised the NWA he'd be out of Las Vegas by October 1.

Following up on an earlier offer to cooperate, the Antitrust Division contacted Eaton on September 13, 1955. They made a lengthy list of demands, and particularly wanted copies of any letters, including mail to and from Muchnick, Kohler, Doyle, Sarpolis and dozens of others. The events of the previous few weeks had spiked interest in the Eatons, but it wasn't restricted to the Department of Justice.

The opinions of those in exile were thrust into the spotlight during the California State Assembly subcommittee investigations of wrestling and boxing on October 17, 1955. Doyle came out of the gate swinging at all of his former partners, especially Eaton, and had some striking information for the shell-shocked members of the committee. Besides accusations that Eaton was acting as both a pro-moter and as a booker, illegal in the state, Doyle asserted that Eaton had frequently bragged of his power over the athletic commission.

The unrelenting testimony from credible witnesses at the State Building in Los Angeles fed the storm bearing down on NWA affiliate Cal Eaton. The day after Doyle and Pasquale hurled their dramatic indictment, referees Joe Woods and Al Billings fired rounds at the entire wrestling business, breaking kayfabe and publicly revealing that wrestling matches were "fixed." The men described under oath how they were given the results of contests they officiated beforehand. Billings said, "It's a known fact that bouts are decided in advance. I used to work for Cal Eaton in his booking office. I used to tell the referees who was to win the bouts."

Billings, an ex-wrestler nicknamed "Sledgehammer," continued his tirade, lev-eling off with a focused critique of the local Alliance member: "He's (Eaton) often boasted to me that he had the athletic commission in his hand. When I worked for Eaton, I heard him say, 'I'll put that damn Pasquale out of business.' Eaton also said, 'When Goodie (California Governor Goodwin Knight) gets in we'll have things our own way.'" Notably, other licensed referees wanting to keep their jobs with the Eatons refused to admit that they, too, had been given the outcome of bouts.

On October 19, the Eatons were afforded the opportunity to defend themselves and came prepared to fight fire with fire. Cal, denying all allegations, called the words of Pasquale and Doyle "in the nature of character assassination," and any thought of his ruling the athletic commission was "unthinkable." He denied that there had ever been a monopoly in the region, stating that he'd "never considered Pasquale as competition."

Cal's wife Aileen added that Pasquale had been a milkman prior to becoming a promoter, investing in grappling only after winning a theater jackpot. She also said that Mike Hirsch and Cal had acquired Doyle's stake in their booking office because "they couldn't trust him." Promoters affiliated with Eaton in southern California rallied to clandestinely suspend Woods and Billings, and Aileen vowed, "We'll close up the Olympic to wrestling before we allow Billings to referee any of our matches," at a hearing on November 8, 1955.

The California probe was one of the largest in professional wrestling history, but the subcommittee failed to cause the changes necessary to shake the NWA to its foundations. Outside fueling the animosity among the Eatons, Doyle, and Pasquale, and the admissions of two referees that wrestling matches were scripted, little had been accomplished. But on November 30, 1955, North Hollywood's Valley Athletic Club filed a $1.2 million damage suit against Cal Eaton and his cohorts. The charges were piling up.

According to a Justice Department communication from McGrath to Derr on November 9, Eaton hadn't responded or even acknowledged their letter of September 13. McGrath attached a rough version of the civil complaint arranged by the Los Angeles office: *United States of America v. National Wrestling Alliance*, for the United States District Court for the Southern District of California, Central Division.

The action named 35 defendants, including former NWA member Leonard Schwartz, Leroy McGuirk, who wasn't even a member, and new associates Billy Watson, Pedro Martinez, and "Doc" Sarpolis. Exempt were Canadians Stu Hart, Eddie Quinn, and Frank Tunney, and Salvador Lutteroth of Mexico City, all of whom could sleep comfortably at night without fretting about a pending tribunal.

The Antitrust Division told Muchnick they were ready to give him an opportunity to address officials on behalf of the Alliance, and Sam, with Soffer and Tunney (NWA vice president), appeared in Washington on January 3, 1956. The trio met Barnes and Derr, and began a series of deliberations that NWA representatives hoped would produce a reasonable judgment.

Soffer reiterated the group's collective eagerness to oblige the examiners in whatever way necessary, but a request for time to allow the Alliance to sort out their "house" privately was promptly denied. Derr and Barnes said that they wouldn't force the wrestling coalition to disband, but insisted upon a complete reevaluation of all Alliance resolutions. The conversation switched to the adoption of a consent decree to resolve the predicament, an idea everyone seemed to support.

The November 1955 draft complaint was reviewed by Soffer, and he admitted that Alliance members were guilty of many of the practices described. Muchnick denied any widespread strategy to blackball wrestlers, but conceded that such things had been, at one time, discussed. Soffer was curious about where a complaint would be filed, volunteering San Francisco, St. Louis, and Iowa as the fitting locations for such an indictment. Iowa, he explained, was appropriate because the Alliance had been incorporated there in 1951.

Three days after the convention, Derr and McGrath conferred. Derr said that "while there was a close question as to whether this should be both a criminal and civil case, it had finally been determined to proceed only civilly." The use of a consent decree to settle the matter was approved, if specific terms were agreed to in advance.

Talk of a consent decree was music to the ears of Alliance members. One was left to wonder how much of a part the NWA's political connections played in alleviating the pressure. After all, Muchnick's best friend was Mel Price, an influential member of the U.S. House of Representatives from East St. Louis. It is generally believed that Price was instrumental in creating a more moderate environment between the Justice Department and the NWA, paving the way for their negotiations. Incidentally, the case file held by the National Archive did not reveal who Cal Eaton spoke with in Washington in August 1955, and that shadowy political figure may also have had a bigger significance than previously suspected. Other contacts for NWA members in Washington included U.S. Senators Everett Dirksen (Fred Kohler) and Estes Kefauver (Nick Gulas and Roy Welch). Any one of these associations may have resulted in a recommendation of leniency.

Unfortunately for promoters of boxing, embroiled in a similar dispute, such a swift and peaceful solution was not forthcoming. On April 19, 1956, the U.S. Government brought charges against the International Boxing Club, citing antitrust violations, and alleging that there was a monopoly in professional boxing. That war began years earlier and had run the gamut, including a stop at the Supreme Court. The simultaneous boxing and wrestling investigations, and the resulting suits, put a stranglehold on the squared circle that lingered through 1956.

The Antitrust Division labored in the following months, building a formidable civil complaint against the NWA. Rather than naming 35 defendants, the suit was altered to, simply, the *United States v. National Wrestling Alliance*, and Disney proposed that the litigation be filed in Los Angeles. There was speculation that Soffer may have tried to sway him to stage the proceedings in Iowa, where the publicity would be limited. The bottom line was that wherever the case was launched, the NWA wanted it kept as quiet as possible.

Disney's recommendations were heeded, but the drafting of a viable consent decree would be painstaking. According to Disney (in his March 7, 1956, office memorandum to McGrath), the "departure" of George Derr, who was being transferred, was going to delay the matter. Derr was considered to be the "man most familiar in Washington with the facts," but unbeknownst to Disney, Derr had prepared an elaborate report, also on March 7, that resolved a number of lingering questions. His outline would serve as a companion piece for the complaint, and set Des Moines, the Southern District of Iowa, Central Division, as the site for the case.

As the clock ticked, witnesses, mainly Doyle and Pasquale, continued to struggle with the restraint of trade practiced by the Alliance. New plaintiffs were on the horizon with stories to tell, but on March 19 Disney notified his directors that "no further investigation [was] desired at this time." The complaint was being drafted, and the Antitrust Division had what it needed to secure an impressive settlement.

The cooperation of Muchnick was undoubtedly a key factor in the acceptance of a consent decree, which, by definition, meant: "A voluntary accord between parties, resulting in a judicial decree and end of charges, to a lawsuit; particularly an agreement made by a defendant to cease illegal practices as accused by the government instead of going through with a trial; defendant consents to not resume said illegalities in exchange for no criminal prosecution."

Muchnick and Soffer met with William D. Kilgore Jr., Chief of the Judgments and Judgment Enforcement Section of the Antitrust Division, in Washington on June 8, 1956. Since the Alliance was the sole defendant, Kilgore stressed to Muchnick that he was responsible for getting all members to sign the decree, binding them individually to the agreement. He also said that it would be easy to charge every member if problems arose. On June 25, a version of the complaint was approved by the Antitrust Division; it was signed by the Attorney General during the first half of July.

The NWA President and his lawyer returned to Washington on July 10 and aided in drafting the manuscript that spelled out the compromise. They were hoping to get the specific terms dealt with in a way that would be least harmful to professional wrestling, while still satisfying the treaty.

The NWA convention, Muchnick felt, was a suitable place to endorse the decree, and 25 members affixed their signatures at the annual gathering in St. Louis. Eight others (Maupin, Gunther, Clayton, Dusek, Lewis, Owen, Bowser, Sigel) got copies of the text in the mail, and by September 18, 33 of 36 members had signed. Al Karasick signed, while Joe Malcewicz, who was said to be critically ill, and Rod Fenton were threatened with banishment if they failed to consent to the settlement. Their signatures were added after the Iowa ruling. Alliance attorneys signed the documents, and sent them to Kilgore in Washington.

A civil antitrust suit, *United States of America v. National Wrestling Alliance* (Civil Action No. 3–729), was filed before U.S. Federal Judge William F. Riley on October 15, 1956, in Des Moines. The carefully composed suit spelled out the government's case, claiming the NWA had violated Sections 1 and 2 of the Sherman Act by working to "restrain and monopolize" the wrestling business.

As part of the overall conspiracy, the government identified eleven major infractions that breached the letter of the law:

(a) To recognize each member as possessing a territory;
(b) To refrain from competing with any other member in the booking of exhibitions in the other member's territory;
(c) To prevent any member from competing in the booking of exhibitions in another member's territory;
(d) To assist each member to exclude all nonmembers from booking exhibitions in the member's territory

(e) To control the booking markets constituted by the promoters in each member's territory

(f) To assist each member to induce or compel all promoters within his territory to obtain wrestlers exclusively from said member;

(g) To prevent others from booking professional wrestlers in the territory of any member;

(h) To exclude nonmembers from engaging in business as bookers;

(i) To blacklist and refrain from booking professional wrestlers who accept engagements not booked by a member;

(j) To discourage professional wrestlers from appearing in studio exhibitions; and

(k) To recognize only three world championship titles, advertise, feature, and book such recognized title holders as common property of the defendant and coconspirators, require any wrestler recognized as the holder of a world championship title to agree to wrestle only in performances booked by members as a condition of recognition, limit the percentage of the gate paid the wrestler recognized as the world's heavyweight champion, and fix a minimum admission charge for all public exhibitions of such champion.

The government also asserted that not only had the NWA outlined their objectives in an organized fashion, but had successfully achieved a monopoly. As a result of the restraint of trade, the following had occurred:

(a) Competition in the booking of professional wrestlers in interstate commerce and in the promotion of exhibitions throughout the United States has been suppressed and eliminated.

(b) Professional wrestlers and promoters have been compelled to subject themselves to the management and control of defendant and the coconspirators in order to obtain adequate interstate bookings.

(c) Promoters of unrelated promotions have been unable generally to obtain professional wrestlers of the same reputation and ability as those booked by members for related promotions.

(d) Wrestlers have been denied the right to seek engagements and championship recognition except under conditions agreeable to the defendant and the coconspirators.

(e) The benefits of competition among bookers have been denied to promoters, professional wrestlers, television stations, broadcast sponsors, advertisers, persons desiring exhibitions for television broadcasts, or theatre presentations, owners of arenas, stadia, and studios, and members of the public attending or viewing exhibitions."

United States attorneys summarized what changes they wanted made in the "Prayer" section of the complaint:

(1) That the Court adjudge and decree that the defendant NWA and the coconspirators have combined, and conspired to restrain and to monopolize, and have attempted to monopolize, and have monopolized the aforesaid interstate trade and commerce, in violation of Sections 1 and 2 of the Sherman Act, and that defendant be enjoined and restrained from continuing such violations or committing other violations of like character and effort.

(3) That the defendant and its members, their successors, officers, directors, managers, agents, representatives, and employees, and all persons and corporations acting or claiming to act under, through, or on behalf of them or any of them, be perpetually enjoined and restrained from entering into, adhering to, renewing, maintaining, or furthering, directly or indirectly, or inducing others to enter into, any contract, agreement, understanding, plan or program, or common course of action to:

(a) Attempt to exclude anyone from engaging in business as a booker or promoter; and
(b) Allocate any territory or territories among or between bookers.

(4) That the Court order defendant NWA and its members not to interfere with, hinder, deter, or obstruct the booking by nonmember bookers of professional wrestlers booked or managed by the defendant or any of its members.

(5) That the Court order defendant NWA and its members to take such steps as may be necessary to permit any booker who is duly licensed or otherwise qualified to engage in such business to enjoy full membership and participation in the NWA.

(6) That the Court enjoin the defendant and each of its members from agreeing with any booker, promoter, or professional wrestler to recognize as champions or featured wrestlers only those professional wrestlers who agree to work exclusively through or for the NWA or its members, and from agreeing with any booker or promoter to limit the amount to be paid to any wrestler for engaging in an exhibition, or to fix or establish admission charges for an exhibition.

(7) That the plaintiff have such other, further, and different relief as the Court may deem just and proper in the premises.

(8) That the plaintiff recover the costs of this suit.

In accordance with the planned settlement, the charges were answered by the defendant immediately, and attorneys for the National Wrestling Alliance submitted a rebuttal on October 15, 1956. Although the management of the NWA had deliberated closely with antitrust attorneys, and scripted the decree that would end the federal investigation, they weren't required to tender an admission to all of the government's accusations. On the contrary, their "answer" was riddled with denials.

The "First Defense" of the NWA boldly stated:

> This court lacks jurisdiction over the subject matter of the claims attempted to be set forth in the complaint for the reason that plaintiff attempts to base said jurisdiction upon the Act of Congress entitled "An Act to Protect Trade and Commerce Against Unlawful Restraints and Monopolies" (15 U.S.C. Sec. 4) as amended and commonly known as the Sherman Antitrust Act; the wrestling business and activities conducted by defendant and described in the complaint do no constitute "trade or commerce" between the states of the United States of America so as to vest the Congress of the United States with authority to regulate or enact legislation with respect to said business and activities of defendant.

The NWA, as a whole, denied "its acts as alleged constitute offenses against the Sherman Antitrust Act or any other act of congress," or that any members "claim an exclusive right to book wrestling exhibitions in any 'territory.'" Paragraph 12 of the complaint was rejected, with the NWA stating: "The promotion of professional wrestling exhibitions and the booking of professional wrestlers for such exhibition are not within the scope of the federal antitrust laws in that they do no constitute 'trade or commerce among the several states.'"

Most of the NWA's response was defiant, but was followed by a Final Judgment rendered by Judge Riley and signed by representatives of the Attorney General's office, the Antitrust Division, and the Alliance.

According to the agreement, NWA members agreed to void all existing bylaws, adopt new regulations in concert with the judgment, and agree to "admit to membership upon nondiscriminatory terms" if the individual applying for membership met a certain criteria. Those included having at least two years booking experience, being "financially responsible," and having "good moral character."

Additionally, the Alliance was prevented from authorizing or acknowledging a particular member's exclusive rights to a specific territory. They couldn't inhibit any bookers or promoters from "doing business" or force them to only work with affiliated members. Nor could they impede a booker or promoter from employing any available wrestler.

Part VII of the decree stipulated that the government had the right to assess the records and/or interview any consenting NWA member "for the purpose of securing compliance with this Final Judgment." Dignitaries from both sides concurred with the ruling, and Judge Riley endorsed the decision, ending the federal suit against the Alliance.

A statement was issued and carried across the Associated Press wire. The complete story, however, was not widely broadcast. Muchnick knew the NWA had been very fortunate in that regard, as the consequences might have been catastrophic. He was quoted in the February 1957 edition of *Wrestling Life*: "The case was officially closed October 15, 1956, with the consent decree entered in the United States District Court in Des Moines, Iowa. A consent decree means that the National Wrestling Alliance, as a body, does not admit to any violations, but agrees to change its bylaws to conform to the antitrust statutes."

The revision of the NWA constitution was in the works by November, and on December 19, 1956, East St. Louis attorney John Ferguson mailed Kilgore the adjusted bylaws for his approval. After receiving no answer by February 7, 1957, Ferguson sent a second letter, asking for a status update.

An interoffice FBI document (January 4, 1957) stated: "On January 2, 1957, Attorney Stanley Disney, Antitrust Division, Los Angeles, California, advised that a civil complaint in this matter against the National Wrestling Alliance was filed on October 15, 1956, in the Southern District of Iowa, U.S. District Court, Des Moines, Iowa, and on the same date, a consent decree was also filed in the U.S. District Court. Mr. Disney advised that the Antitrust Division file in this matter is now closed." The Antitrust office was commended for their triumph in the wrestling case, and had Disney, above all, to thank for his tireless efforts.

With the inquiry over and the NWA patiently awaiting certification of their modified bylaws, the Justice Department received two new missives from NWA detractors. The first, dated January 11, 1957, was from Katye Zaharias of Chattanooga, the wife of wrestler Babe Zaharias (Chris Davros). Babe, incidentally, died of a heart attack seven months after the letter was written. In her message, Zaharias protested the monopolies of Nick Gulas, Paul Jones, Jim Crockett, and Cowboy Luttrall. She said that Babe, the nephew of the legendary Zaharias Brothers, was unable to make a living in that part of the country because of a personal grudge, and that "Mr. Gulas [was] the Hitler of wrestling." Antone "Ripper"

Leone (1916–1994) was the author of the second complaint to the Justice Department, received in March. A wrestler who, by 1957, had 20 of his 40-plus years in grappling under his belt, Leone had a grudge against the Alliance and its members that was unequaled. His letters were verbose, but ultimately humdrum in their substance. Leone used words like "tyranny" and "slavery" in describing his plight, but his charges lost their impact in the midst of pages and pages of similar memos sent to government employees.

The FBI was well aware of Leone's grievances. Assistant Attorney General Victor Hansen, in a note dated April 12, 1957, asked Leone for any evidence that the Alliance deliberately barred him from wrestling. Their correspondence went back and forth for several months. On June 14, 1957, Leone met with an investigator in New York and discussed his dilemmas without physical proof. J. Paul McQueen, in his office memorandum of June 27, recommended "this matter be closed," and "in view of the complainant's obsessed attitude toward [the] NWA, I feel certain that as far as he is concerned, the matter will be a continuing one, and that we will continue to receive his lengthy missives from time to time."

Kilgore, on July 9, 1957, stated: "I agree with your conclusion that, if possible, this matter be closed. In view of Mr. Leone's obsession with [the] NWA, there is little that we can do to help him obtain employment through that organization."

Leone's gripes were remarkably bitter. In letters to Muchnick in 1956 and '57, he claimed that since his blacklisting in 1950, he had been unable to earn a "decent" living, and cursed the members of the coalition. He believed there was a master conspiracy against him, mentioned that Hugh Nichols, who committed suicide in 1956, had "blasted his evil head off," and how he looked forward to laughing when Malcewicz, Karasick, and Crockett died. The January 14, 1957, dispatch from South Africa had personal digs aimed at Muchnick, Kohler, Doyle, Eaton, Sandor Szabo, Jules Strongbow, Mike Hirsch, and Bill Longson.

Was Leone blackballed by the NWA or was his predicament the result of a problematic relationship with its members? In the years following his diatribes, he wrestled in numerous Alliance territories, including Texas, the Carolinas, Central States, Oklahoma, Calgary, and Florida, and battled the NWA world heavyweight and junior heavyweight champions.

While the Department of Justice had found common ground with the NWA, their prosecution of the International Boxing Club of violations of the Sherman Act went down to the bitter end. On March 8, 1957, the government won their case, and forced the I.B.C. to disband.

Hansen's reply to NWA attorney Ferguson on April 24 contained constructive suggestions about the tweaking of their regulations. On May 9, the Alliance countered, addressing the remaining criticisms and offering amendments to meet the required standards. Finally, Hansen wrote, on May 20, that "based upon the representation in your letter of May 9, 1957, this department has no further objections at this time to the proposed bylaws of the National Wrestling Alliance." The changes were finalized, spawning a new 16-page set of regulations that was ratified by the membership.

The consent decree had abolished the tactics that were once so useful to wrestling bookers. Muchnick watched his treasured organization sink into the doldrums, and realized that its dissolution was imminent. Membership dipped from 38 to 26 by March 1959, and was expected to continue to drop. Seeking refuge, Sam contacted Hansen, and told him about the bleak situation.

Hansen wanted someone to interview Muchnick in St. Louis, and on May 18, 1959, Raymond Hunter of the Chicago Antitrust Division met with the NWA president at the Claridge. To quote Hunter's memorandum, Muchnick surmised that the Alliance's "loss of membership is due to the fact that the National Wrestling Alliance no longer can offer the promoters anything of value for their fees."

The memo concluded: "He [Muchnick] stated that prior to the final judgment promoters respected the contracts between a promoter and a wrestler as well as territories in which a promoter staged exhibitions. Since the decree, according to Muchnick, which prohibits exclusive territories for the staging of wrestling exhibits, the National Wrestling Alliance can do nothing in disputes between promoters of wrestling exhibitions whether they relate to territory contracts or otherwise."

Muchnick wondered if there was "a possibility of the final judgment being modified in the interest of the industry." When asked what changes he would like to have made, Sam stated he wanted to confer with his lawyer and the members of the NWA. In his "Special Bulletin #7," Sam notified the remaining membership of his thoughts. He explained that there was a clause in the 1956 verdict that gave them the option to appeal for a "modification" or "termination" of statutes. Believing that such changes could prove helpful in a number of ways, Muchnick was, once again, without support. Only two members replied to his plea, and the reevaluation never took place.

Muchnick was frustrated by the Alliance's failure to rally around the idea of altering the decree to ease some of their problems. The lack of solidarity had him out on a limb, but didn't diminish his faith in either wrestling or the intentions of the NWA. Beyond trying to convince his fellow associates to follow his lead, mediating between the Alliance and the government, and the members themselves, booking the heavyweight champion, and running his own promotion, Sam offered to travel to Chicago or Washington to speak with officials. But he was losing his grip and was having doubts in the group's viability. He believed that after the 1959 convention in St. Louis, the membership could dip below 20 members. He was right.

In the post-decree wrestling world, the Justice Department heard complaints of a chronic restraint of trade, but never initiated a suit. Ted Thye moaned that Don Owen was violating the agreement in the Pacific Northwest in 1958, but Stanley Disney, who reviewed the documentation, decided the circumstances unworthy of additional study. Kilgore was alerted by William Victor "Tony" Olivas about the monopolistic actions of Bill Lewis in late 1959, and a broader conspiracy including Joe "Toots" Mondt (Capitol Wrestling Corporation) and Jim Crockett, three bookers who signed the 1956 pact. Despite drawing the Antitrust Division the closest to prosecuting a member of the NWA for violations of the decree, the investigation was abandoned and forgotten.

A multitude of accusations and insinuations concerning the Alliance's iron grip continued off and on through the 1970s. Because of the massive size and range of the group, there would always be disgruntled employees, some with personal gripes, others with genuine evidence of wrongdoing. Members at the top of the pyramid wised up to the consequences of their behavior, and shrewd decisions were made to conceal devious moves. Many of the complainants sought to use the 1956 judgment against the bookers that signed it, from Roy Welch to Don Owen.

The membership of the NWA may have wanted unchallenged rule over wrestling, but there was no way they could eliminate all competition. They bullied those they could, but had trouble with promoters and bookers who possessed the resources to resist. Among those capable of warding off the Alliance, at different times, were Ed McLemore, Ray Fabiani, Billy Sandow, Johnny Doyle, Jack Pfefer, Roy Shire, Cal Eaton and Jules Strongbow, and Pedro Martinez. Smaller independent operations existed under the control of Karl Pojello (Chicago), Tom Rolewicz (Chicago), Babe Bisagnano (Des Moines), Larry Kasaboski (Ontario), the Lorties (Montreal), Tony Santos (Boston), Anthony "Bert" Bertolini (parts of Pennsylvania), Frank Pasquale (Los Angeles), Sterling Davis (Houston), Ken Fenelon (Iowa), Eddie Williams (St. Paul), Jim Henry (Denver), Ed Faietta (Pittsburgh), and dozens of minor promotions that ran shows in clubs and assembly halls, and during carnivals and fairs.

In 1948, it was unthinkable to believe that the National Wrestling Alliance, a product of Iowa, would effectively rule the sport within a short span of a few years. The headaches caused by its bullying tactics eventually had people knocking on the doors of the Justice Department. Irate participants and spectators were moved to step forward with complaints. The allegations accumulated, prompting officials to tear down the barriers established by Alliance members.

But was the NWA entirely bad? Had the organization been comprised of crooks and thieves who held a negative influence over professional wrestling? Responses would vary, depending on who was asked. Sam Muchnick could spew a fountain of reasons why the Alliance was beneficial. On the other hand, Antone Leone could write you a ten-page soliloquy that disparaged every current, former, or future member.

The NWA did bring a new level of prosperity to wrestling, and it was the dedication of its wrestlers and managers that preserved whatever admiration it achieved in the marketplace.

In 1956, the United States Government reminded the NWA exactly where the lines of the law were, and warned them they would not be shown a second time.

CHAPTER TEN

SONNY MYERS V. THE NWA

The lawsuit brought by Sonny Myers against Paul "Pinkie" George in August 1955 didn't appear, at least on paper, to affect anyone other than the individual named as the defendant. It seemed unlikely that the members of the NWA would suffer any fallout. But the bitterness of an ugly feud between an aspiring promoter and wrestler and the NWA establishment set the table for two court cases and created a significant rift in the central states.

Harold Calvin "Sonny" Myers had been a wrestling star since the beginning of the Alliance, and had received much support from his vivacious mentor Gust Karras, a Greek promoter in St. Joseph, Missouri. Born on January 15, 1924, the son of an area farmer, Sonny labored long hours as a teenager assisting in the daily family chores. Excelling in football at Pickett High School, he had the tools to shine at the collegiate level. Instead, at the age of 20, he turned to professional wrestling under the tutelage of Karras, a carnival hooker in the 1920s and 30s, gaining experience in Missouri, Iowa, Nebraska, and Kansas. The regional favorite soon proved a draw outside of his home territory, capable of attracting fans on his merits as a wrestler alone.

Myers was an impressive adversary for the Midwest's most popular wrestler, Orville Brown, and a four-match series at Kansas City's Memorial Hall in November and December 1947 gave him credibility as a challenger for Brown's MWA world title. Little did the thousands of fans that attended the quartet of highly competitive bouts know, but Myers had defeated Brown in Des Moines on November 3, 1947, three days before their initial contest in Kansas City. With the win, Sonny took over Orville's National Wrestling Alliance title, a distinction exclusive to Pinkie George's territory. While Myers was challenging Brown in Kansas City for the MWA title, he was defending his NWA title against him in Des Moines through January 5, 1948, when Brown won a rematch.

After Leroy McGuirk's fateful automobile accident, which ended his career in February 1950, Myers became a prime candidate for the NWA junior title. Sonny advanced to the finals of a tournament for the vacant strap in Tulsa, but was defeated by Verne Gagne that November. On June 23, 1951, the bright future of Myers was nearly stolen by a paying customer following a bout with Rito Romero in Angleton, Texas. That night, he came face to face with death. While casually walking to the dressing room, Myers was grabbed by a man named Jackson, a spectator with a sadistic grudge, and viciously slashed along his right side and stomach with a knife.

Dr. William Holt needed 258 stitches to close the life-threatening 16½ inch gash. Sonny recovered from the wound astonishingly quickly, and returned to the ring. That year, counting the time he missed as a result of the assault, Sonny made $12,170 on the Alliance circuit, and drove 63,000 miles in his private automobile across ten states, spending more than 290 days away from his wife Elaine. In 1952, Myers earned $11,104 from wrestling, performing in the same number of states, and driving 46,000 miles by car.

In November 1952, Myers signed a three-year managerial contract with Jim Barnett, a representative of Chicago promoter Fred Kohler. Through Barnett and Kohler, Sonny was booked to promoters wanting wrestlers featured on the Marigold show across the DuMont Network. The deal included matches in the Northeast, and transformed Myers into a national celebrity. The decision to go with the Chicago combine had proven wise, and in 1953, he wrestled in 26 different states and grossed $18,629. When Leonard Schwartz finally got a date for NWA champion Lou Thesz to appear on his Rainbo telecast in Chicago on March 20, 1953, Myers was his challenger.

Myers invested in a carnival operation run by Karras in the summer of 1953, and eventually took over the business completely. The cavalcade of attractions featured by Sonny Myers Amusements at county fairs throughout Iowa and Missouri included professional wrestling matches. According to NWA rules, Myers was obligated to go through the organization's Iowa booking agent, Pinkie George, to obtain talent for his presentation at the Pottawattamie County Fair in Avoca on August 12.

Believing that Avoca wasn't under the NWA's jurisdiction because wrestling hadn't been promoted there since 1950, Myers was unhappy with being forced to compensate George. In fact, he planned to bring Karras's wrestlers down, and bypass George altogether. On July 14, Karras called Pinkie's Des Moines office and spoke with Jerry Meeker, explaining their strategy for Avoca. Irate at the incursion on his turf, George sent a letter to Gust, reaffirming his control over Avoca. Pinkie wanted Orville Brown to nip the entire situation in the bud by withholding grapplers from Karras.

The criticisms out of western Missouri were well known. Both Karras and Kansas City promoter George Simpson complained about the compulsory ten percent booking fee payments to Brown. An insignificant county fair might not seem like a big deal to most, but to George, it was an illegal foray onto sacred land. The move became fodder in the rivalry between Alliance bookers and area promoters.

Myers and Karras lined up several wrestlers, among them Ronnie Etchison and Joe Dusek, for the Avoca program, and the show went off without a hitch. Pinkie, however, expected a $100 payment for talent fees, even if he didn't directly participate. Iowa was his domain, and he took a slice of any affiliated shows. At that juncture, the story warps into a string of discrepancies. Myers asserted that he'd sent Pinkie a check for $75, which was refused, as was a payment of $100 mailed by Karras. Pinkie said neither check arrived. Myers divulged that during a meeting with George in the winter of 1953, he'd told him about his booking plans, and that they had come to an agreement, settling the dispute. Or so he thought.

Based on the popularity of wrestling at their annual community gathering the previous year, the administration of the Pottawattamie Fair, president Dr. Norman West and Maurice Van Nostrand, wanted to repeat their success. West, who had corresponded with Myers in preparation for the fair's matches in August 1954, was shocked to learn from Pinkie that he was the only point of contact for wrestling shows in the state of Iowa.

Keeping his end of the bargain, Pinkie not only booked eight wrestlers for each of the two programs, one on August 10 in Avoca, and the other the next night in Clarinda, but attended the initial show himself. At that event, he confronted Myers over their differences, and followed up with a letter to Van Nostrand dated August 16, 1954:

> In my 26 years of promoting and booking I have never been subjected to bodily threats, humiliation and accusations as I was at Avoca August 10.
>
> I was convinced after that experience, I don't want to ever have any more business dealings with Sonny Myers. I also feel that in view of the situation as developed the past two years, I do not have any desire to book any shows there in the future. Max Clayton, Castle Hotel, Omaha, has a reputable booking office such as mine, and I suggest you contact him next year if you want a show. Also, there are many such booking offices in the Middlewest, and if your committee wants the list I will be glad to forward them to you.
>
> So much for that. Regarding the check Myers claims to have sent me, you will find that no such check ever existed. He promised to go to St. Joe the night of the 11th and bring the cancelled check to you. I understand he changed his mind and was going to St. Joe Friday. The reason, that his carnival was to be only a few miles from St. Joe and it would be more convenient for him. I still say that was a stalling tactic and that there will not be any such bank-cleared check.
>
> I'd like to review the big points. When Myers was confronted about the extra $100 asked for last year, he said, he did not ask for the extra $100 but that Gust Karras had, and it was because they had to get two extra girls to wrestle which by his statement "cost more to bring in." When you challenged him on that statement and pinned him down, his story changed and the $100 was supposed to have been for me.
>
> From then on, the whole picture got so confused that I would take pages to review it. He accused me of lying, and that he had sent me a check for $75 and that he had the cancelled check to prove it. It was then that I challenged him $200 to $20 that no such check existed.
>
> The reason I came down there was to clear my name. I had not broken any contract. I had not asked for an added $100. But in spite of that, I returned the $100 because I felt you had been gypped and the board was entitled to their money. That may have been a mistake. Your statement to wit; "I don't know who to believe," makes it obvious that being fair and honest was not the proper course.

Myers mailed a letter to George, dated October 7, 1954, professing that Sam Muchnick was not using him in St. Louis, on account of their conflict and Sam's loyalty to the NWA booker. He conscientiously admitted mistakes in the past, but felt that Pinkie was also in the wrong. Seeking to reconcile their differences, Myers apologized, and added, "I would like very much to be your friend." The document had a distinct undercurrent of concern that he was blacklisted, and reminded George that he was "told many time (sic) that the Alliance does not bar anyone, and I would hate to think that such a method of barring a wrestler exists among Alliance members."

The squabble festered. Finally, a suit was brought by Myers against his adversary and the NWA on August 2, 1955, in the District Court of the United States for the Southern District of Iowa. The complaint, *Harold C. "Sonny" Myers v. P.L. George and the National Wrestling Alliance* (Civil Action No. 3–630), had serious implications and with the right kind of publicity, could harm the sport.

The plaintiff bravely maintained that the National Wrestling Alliance, of which George was associated, was violating the Sherman Antitrust Act by monopolizing pro grappling. There was a claim that the union of bookers had unmitigated control over the industry, and that an organized scheme eliminated opposition and restrained trade. Myers alleged that the cartel managed all wrestlers "of any prominence" and:

> If the said wrestlers do not follow the dictates of the defendants herein they can be blackballed from wrestling for other promoters who are members of said Alliance and lose their means or livelihood, or are refused and denied access to lucrative bouts and are thus coerced and by use of duress forced into line. That the members of said Alliance, including the defendant, P.L. George, have effectuated this conspiracy and monopoly by working together in such a way that a wrestler from one part of the country must wrestle under other members of the Alliance in order to make a living, particularly because he loses his box office appeal if he stays in one territory too long, and by necessity has to wrestle over a large territory encompassing several members of the Alliance. Thus the wrestlers become hopelessly dependent upon the members of said conspiracy.
>
> That when a wrestler decides to enter the field of professional wrestling, he is required by this conspiracy to contact one of the members of said Alliance and from that point forward becomes the "property" of that member, and is traded back and forth between other members of said Alliance for the use of

said other members as they see fit. Said individual wrestler has no voice what-soever in the place where he will wrestle, in the amount of his percentage of the gate upon which is determined his wage, nor is he even allowed to know the amount thereof, or to see any of the receipts from the people who attend the wrestling match.

Myers's complaint spoke of exclusive territories and the control of bookers over a certain region. He elaborated on how NWA members received fees from promoters for using wrestlers, emphasizing that grapplers had no recourse. Wrestlers were either to obey the regulations, or they would "have no place to wrestle and earn a livelihood. This has gradually increased until now it is absolutely impossible for a person out of favor with any single promoter to have any freedom of contract or to earn a livelihood, and no local promoter can book individually and directly."

The circumstances of the feud were outlined, breaking down Myers's side of the story. He acknowledged sending Pinkie $75 to cover the Avoca fees, and claimed George mailed the money back, demanding $100. Karras allegedly then sent the total amount to Des Moines, and again, George stubbornly refused to accept payment. Despite the tension, Sonny maintained that at some time in late 1953 he met with George, and it was agreed that he could, again, put on a show at the county fair in Avoca. The complaint said:

> That approximately at or before the date set for said wrestling match at Avoca, the defendant, P.L. George, notified the plaintiff that he was not going to authorize the matches and he had notified the wrestlers that they could not wrestle with the plaintiff acting as a promoter, and that if they did so he, the defendant, P.L. George, should see that they never wrestled again for any members of the Alliance. That when the plaintiff had been notified by P.L. George to this effect, he was told by the defendant, P.L. George, that the only way that the matches would go on would be that the defendant, P.L. George, would take all the profits therefrom and would pay the plaintiff for his work just like any of the other wrestlers, and he could never again promote any wrestling in the state of Iowa, but that it all had to come through P.L. George, or not at all, and for his insubordination he would see that plaintiff was hurt all over the country.

Myers claimed the illegal plot involved several Alliance members, freezing him out of the business, and causing "duress." The problems with George purportedly hurt both his income and "future earning capacity." His complaint concluded with: "Wherefore, plaintiff demands judgment against the defendants, and each of them, in the sum of $200,000 actual damages, which, under the provisions of Title 15, Section 15, of the United States Code, shall be increased threefold, or $600,000, together with costs, including reasonable attorney fees."

Pinkie was one of the founders of the NWA, but by 1955, he just was a small-town member of the organization and five years removed from the office of the presidency. The charges against him had evolved out of a personal grudge, but the bigger conspiracy and rumored blacklisting was another thing entirely. Since the Justice Department's ongoing investigation into the Alliance was dealing with many of the same issues, it seemed to them that there may have been legitimate weight to Myers's accusations.

On the other hand, the attitudes of Simpson and Karras toward the territories operated by George and Brown were hostile at best. The latter duo's entrenched positions threatened other people's livelihoods, and civil case 3-630 was the front line of a heated war between veteran Alliance members and angry promoters reluctant to pay booking fees.

The rest of the NWA went on as if nothing was happening. After all, why would Toots Mondt in New York, or Cal Eaton in Los Angeles, worry about a petty Midwestern promotional war?

In a sense, Pinkie was going to have to defend the NWA in the dispute with Myers. A response by his Des Moines attorney John Connolly filed on September 15, 1955, wanted the mention of violations of Section 1 and 2 of Title 15 of the United States Code (Sherman Act) stricken from the plaintiff's complaint, asserting it "is immaterial and prejudicial to this defendant, and Section 2, having to do with criminal penalties, has no connection with a civil case such as the case at bar."

George sought to have other elements erased from the complaint as well, including the contention that "wrestlers become hopelessly dependant upon the members of said conspiracy," because it was "an opinion and conclusion of the pleader, and is speculative." Pinkie wanted to know the names of all the NWA members Myers said were allegedly "not using" him in their matches, and provided a list of the towns in which he claimed he "could have promoted a large number of wrestling matches in southern Iowa in 1954."

Overall, Myers's suit revealed insider secrets about the business practices of the coalition. Any hint of monopoly attached to a particular corporation or industry attracted the attention of investigators in the Antitrust Division of the Department of Justice. With its charges of a monopolization of the entire wrestling business, possible interstate trade infractions, and control over millions of dollars, this was a little more than a simple court case in a small Midwestern city. It was a situation that could ruin lives and bury the sport of wrestling.

George denied all wrongdoing. Included in his legal team was the NWA's official lawyer Harry Soffer, a man growing increasingly familiar with such matters. In a detailed answer filed with the court on December 29, 1955, George and his attorneys stated:

> That this Defendant has at no time prevented this Plaintiff from wrestling, nor promoting, nor has he ever contacted any member of the Alliance complaining about this Plaintiff and in fact, this Plaintiff during the periods covered herein has appeared for, and wrestled for, this Defendant on shows which this Defendant has booked in the state of Iowa, and in addition thereto this Plaintiff has wrestled steadily throughout the Middlewest and southern states at wrestling shows.

Proving that George had asked Alliance members to effectively blackball Myers was going to be a tough sell. Could a grudge over booking payments, mandated in organization bylaws, inspire a nationwide boycott of a single wrestler? Did an NWA booker have the power to ban a man from making a living and providing for his family based on a simple quarrel?

Obliged to refute the claims of Myers, and with help from fellow NWA promoters, George submitted materials for the record that did just that. A collection of arena programs substantiated his claim that Myers had wrestled for numerous Alliance members during the time frame he claimed to be boycotted. Not only did he perform for Sam Muchnick, Karl Sarpolis, and Roy Welch, but Sonny also received strong pushes in various other territories. He battled NWA world junior champion Baron Leone on several occasions in closely contested bouts, and faced NWA world titleholder Thesz. On the Welch-Gulas circuit, he wore the southern junior belt, and in Amarillo, he teamed with Sterling "Dizzy" Davis to hold a version of the world tag title.

Further research showed that Myers had worked for no less than eight Alliance bookers from 1954 to '56. He even worked for George himself in Des Moines in the spring of 1954. Myers was a compelling fan favorite, usually billed as a TV star based on his Marigold and Rainbo appearances in Chicago.

As the court drama built, Pinkie's business in Iowa was in trouble, and he was quick to blame promoters in Kansas City and St. Louis. It already looked as if George was an NWA outsider rather than one of its founders. With an NWA attorney setting up a defense, Pinkie braced himself for the squall of controversy in Federal Court beginning November 20, 1958.

Witnesses for Myers consisted of former wrestler Alphonse "Babe" Bisignano and George Simpson, each efficient in getting their point across. The testimony was riddled with venomous comments from Judge Edwin R. Hicklin (1895–1963), who made it abundantly clear that he was embarrassed by having to preside over a case about professional wrestling.

According to the proceedings, printed in the December 3, 1958, edition of the *Des Moines Register*, Bisignano spoke about previously attempting to act as a promoter:

> [Sonny's lawyer] James G. McDowell: You tried to promote wrestling shows in Iowa?
> Bisignano: Yes
> McDowell: You know there are non-Alliance wrestlers as opposed to Alliance wrestlers?
> Bisignano: Well, it's like this.
> Judge Hicklin: Just answer yes or no.
> Bisignano: You take your orders or you're out of business.
> Judge Hicklin: The jury will disregard that conversation.
> McDowell: That's the essence of this lawsuit.
> Judge Hicklin: That remark will be stricken from the record.

Pinkie's attorney, George E. O'Malley, said that Bisignano's stabs at promoting wrestling in Iowa had occured before 1951, when the NWA was incorporated:

> McDowell: Now, Babe, just tell what you know, no hearsay.
> Bisignano: I'll tell you what's important to this case.
> Judge Hicklin: Just tell the facts.

Simpson asserted that he had been totally reliant on the NWA, saying he could not function without the approval of that association. He said that the wrestlers themselves assumed that "if they worked for us, they couldn't work for somebody else." His resentment toward the Alliance was much better explained in a letter to Wladek Zbyszko of Savannah, Missouri, written on June 30, 1955. He wrote that if promoters didn't adhere to the booker's demands, their businesses would fail, and that the NWA blackballed rebellious grapplers. He considered the National Wrestling Alliance "one of the strongest monopolies in the United States. They know that they are and boast about it."

An Alliance member earlier in the decade with Brown, Simpson said, "If I am called in as a witness, I certainly will tell the truth." When the Myers case came to trial, he stepped up as a voluntary witness for the plaintiff, and his testimony was potent. The courtroom shenanigans continued, and during the direct examination of Myers, the judge's sentiments became more vocal.

McDowell: Well, how did that [his operation of a carnival with Gust Karras] come about?

Myers: Well, at that time Mr. Karras and I was very close and it just happened that I do business with Mr. Karras. I did at that time. Although — there was a discrepancy here the other day when we were here last week over a booking fee for a hundred dollars that came up. Now this hundred dollars that was supposedly, as Mr. O'Malley has said, was to go to Mr. George for a booking fee for the wrestlers, which was not true, the hundred dollars that was put on extry (sic) was for the lady wrestlers. Now then, the fair board of Avoca, Iowa came to Barnard, Missouri, to see me and I didn't happen to be there at that time. Mr. Karras was at Barnard, Missouri, with my carnival, and the fair board from Avoca asked Mr. Karras what —

Judge Hicklin: Oh, no, not in your absence.

McDowell: Not what somebody else told you, Sonny.

Judge Hicklin: I would like to teach you wrestlers that you can't repeat everything here somebody else says.

Myers: Well, maybe I don't have a good education, your honor.

Judge Hicklin: I think that's common.

Myers: Well, probably so.

McDowell: Well, how much did you make down there at Kansas City?

Myers: Well, as I said yesterday, you take year in and year out, probably my average would be between fifty and seventy-five dollars a night that I worked. Naturally I had many, many main events there which had good payoffs.

McDowell: What do you mean "good payoffs?"

Myers: Well —

Judge Hicklin: Suckers.

Myers: As I said before, I made anywhere from twenty-five dollars in Kansas City up to three hundred forty five dollars. Two hundred thirty five dollars, I believe. Three hundred twenty five dollars, I believe it was.

McDowell: All right. Now, you say you were taken off of television. Why is that important to a wrestler?

Myers: Why is it important to a wrestler? It's probably one of the biggest monitors of publicity in the wrestling game today. If you are not on television at times, you don't do too well at all. In other words, television more or less puts you out in front of the people's eyes. They see who you are. If they like you or want to come see you, they will come and see you, because it's good publicity. If you just come in from out of a dark corner some place and be on a wrestling card as far as having —

Judge Hicklin: You mean by that, that the women in the home audiences can see the hair on your chest and come out if they want to see you, is that correct?

Myers: No, sir.

Judge Hicklin: Well, who does?

Myers: Either you have ability or you don't have ability. If you have ability that appeals to the public, why naturally they want to come and see you. If you don't, you might as well stay where you were.

Judge Hicklin: Well, I will stay home.

The judge's sarcasm was palpable; it was obvious that the man on the bench had a deep disgust for what professional wrestling was all about. During the cross-examination of Myers by O'Malley, the judge jumped in and the jury watched intently.

O'Malley: Now let's get to '56. I hand you what the reporter has marked Exhibit Z-16, and ask you whether or not those are two representations of wrestling programs you have been on in Amarillo, Texas.

Judge Hicklin: Mr. Myers, did you study the bricklaying trade or something like that in '55 and '56, along there? Had you had some other profession?

Myers: For my income?

Judge Hicklin: Yes.

Myers: No, sir, your honor, but I will explain that after a while.

Judge Hicklin: Well, I don't know whether you will or not. I sought to gain an explanation right then.

Myers: Right then?

Even NWA President Sam Muchnick was drawn into the fun:

McDowell: Now, Mr. Watson of Toronto, Canada, is a member of your alliance, isn't he?

Muchnick: No, sir.

McDowell: He was?

Muchnick: He was.

McDowell: When was he a member?

Muchnick: I don't recall the exact year, but I think in 1955–56.

McDowell: And he bought the northwest territory, is that correct?

Soffer: I object to the question, "bought."

Judge Hicklin: What has Mr. Watson got to do with this lawsuit?

McDowell: He is a member of the Alliance here, and I'm showing here that they do have that territory. I am hoping to. I'm attempting to.

Judge Hicklin: You may show that they have territory. But don't try to ask this witness to tell what was conveyed from one party to another or from the Alliance to any party, unless he has written evidence to back it up.

McDowell: Well, your honor, I believe the witness can testify that he knows of his own personal knowledge that Mr. Watson purchased the northwest territory.

Judge Hicklin: What is the northwest territory?

McDowell: Well, that's what I'll ask him. It's in Washington.

Soffer: That was by Lewis and Clark. They found that, if the Court please.

Judge Hicklin: Quite a little bit ago. Lewis and Clark. It would be a conclusion at most that you are asking from this witness, wouldn't it?

McDowell: I think it is a custom and usage, your honor, of which he is certainly an expert.

Judge Hicklin: Well, I have little faith in custom and usage. It's usually made by those who want it in their terms.

When Pinkie George was asked if he, at any time, had told anyone not to use Sonny Myers, he answered: "Never to my knowledge, ever. In the first place, I couldn't say that to anybody. The Alliance would have throwed me out on my ear if I had."

Instead of remaining impartial to the proceedings in the courtroom, Judge Hicklin interjected from beginning to end. The lawyer for Myers tried to win the jury over by portraying Sonny as a hard-working, well-liked wrestler who wanted nothing more but to work without hindrance. He talked about the NWA's ability to limit opportunities and the grand conspiracy to keep Myers from making a living. But would the three women and nine men on the jury panel believe it?

On December 8, 1958, a verdict — "We the jury, find for the defendants, P.L. George and National Wrestling Alliance, a corporation" — was announced and signed by the 12 jurors. Myers had lost.

After the verdict was read, Judge Hicklin spoke to the jury:

I want to say to the people who acted as jurors in this case that they undoubtedly acted with a great deal of wisdom. It was a case which was difficult for decision. But I think that they, having heard the evidence, they are entirely justified at having brought the verdict which they did bring in this case. The whole thing smacked of a grudge. Probably should have been transferred to the wrestling ring, and that would have been interesting thing to see how it came out. But it certainly had no place in a court of law. Unfortunately, we're bound to try these cases, these so-called public cases, no matter what the amount is that is involved in the case.

Of course, it was booted about by many that there was a $600,000 lawsuit. There was, of course, no such thing. We found of our own volition, and not our own choice, but of our own necessity that the plaintiff had not been injured in any way for a lack of wrestling, and it remained to be seen whether the so-called trust had operated to injure him in any way so far as promoting in southern Iowa was concerned; and I think that they justly and wisely brought in a verdict, and have decided that, so far as this contest is concerned.

Shortly after the decision was rendered, McDowell motioned for a new trial, outlining ten faults with the first trial and verdict. Number five was crucial: "That the uncalled-for and voluntary remarks of the trial court to the effect that the lawsuit was a 'farce' and was 'humerous,' (sic) and 'had no place in his court room' were extremely prejudicial to the plaintiff."

Three days before Christmas 1958, an unimpressed Judge Hicklin answered the motion by McDowell with a denial. He wrote, in a response to paragraph five: "Paragraph 5 of said Motion complains of certain statements made by the Court during the trial of the case. In the first place, the Court in its instructions very clearly told the jury to disregard any comments made by the Court. In the second place, viewing plaintiff's evidence in its most favorable light, plaintiff failed to introduce any evidence, based upon fact and not speculation, that would bring his alleged damages up to the jurisdictional amount of $3,000." Myers had sued for $600,000.

But the inappropriate remarks of Judge Hicklin earned Myers a victory in the U.S. Court of Appeals on November 23, 1959. McDowell pointed out particular statements he felt unfairly disadvantaged his client, including the judge allowing one of Pinkie's attorneys to submit: "If they [the NWA] were guilty of monopoly the government would have done something about it." As per the pretrial instructions, mentioning the government's investigation and the resulting consent decree of October 1956 was not allowed.

On November 23, 1959, judges Mickelson, Gardner and Vogel of the U.S. Court of Appeals, Eighth Circuit, determined: "It is earnestly contended that the trial court made a mockery of the trial by reason of certain remarks made during the course of the trial, variously referred to as unsolicited, jocular, belittling, witty, unjudicial, and prejudicial to the case of the plaintiff."

And finally: "We are convinced that plaintiff, by reason of the comments of the trial judge during the trial, was prevented from having a fair trial. The judgment appealed from is therefore reversed, and the case is remanded to the trial court with directions to grant plaintiff a new trial."

With a fresh start, a new jury, and more importantly, a less intolerant judge, Sonny Myers once against stood up against Pinkie George and the NWA. On January 8, 1962, part two of Civil Action No. 3–630, *Harold C. Myers v. P.L. George and National Wrestling Alliance, a Corporation*, went before District Court Judge Roy L. Stephenson. Pinkie, who had resigned as a member of the NWA in March 1959, and was now spending more time in boxing than wrestling, was represented again by O'Malley and Soffer. Myers changed his trial lawyer to Henry Haugan. The jury was brought in on January 22 and opening statements were issued. Soffer asked for a summary judgment in favor of the Alliance before going into his initial commentary, and was overruled by Judge Stephenson.

The plaintiff's case was much better defined the second time around. Myers was well prepared for his testimony, and elaborated on his financial losses while reportedly blackballed. A concentrated effort was made to compare Sonny's pre-grudge wages with what he earned and where he went afterwards. In fact, his income-tax returns were supplied from 1950 to 1960 (excluding 1957), showing a gradual increase in pay until 1954.

1950	$9,804.50	$2,044.53 (net profit)
1951	$12,170.00	$2,715.38 (net profit)
1952	$11,104.00	$3,379.16 (net profit)
1953	$18,629.00	$3,322.85 (net profit)
1954	$8,398.00	$1,331.09 (net profit)
1955	$8,237.00	$2,364.63 (net profit)
1956	$12,856.00	$5,855.03 (net profit)
1958	$6,270.00	$1,749.24 (net profit)
1959	$10,774.00	$4,070.79 (net profit)
1960	$7,704.50	$2,508.38 (net profit)

Myers spent $4,107.65 on plane, train, and car expenses in 1953 traveling to and from wrestling shows booked on the publicity garnered from his television exposure. In 1954, he spent only $1,515.90. According to his tax returns, Sonny experienced a major financial drop between 1953 and 1954. His attorneys used the term "outlaw" with regard to his standing in wrestling during the time in question, and alleged that members of the Alliance were warned not to book him. Whether they could get the jury to believe there had been widespread NWA discrimination was yet to be seen.

Muchnick was called to the stand, and testified that Pinkie had never told him not to "use Myers in any events." Al Bisignano, Jack Crawford, George Simpson, Joseph Davis, and Dr. Norman West were among the others to appear and speak before the five men and seven women on the jury.

Closing arguments were given on January 25, 1962, and deliberations began. The jury remained in closed quarters for an estimated four hours, after which they returned a decision: "We, the jury, find for the plaintiff, Harold C. Myers, on his claim against both defendants, the National Wrestling Alliance and P.L. George, and fix the amount of recovery herein against the defendant in the sum of $50,000."

The $50,000 figure was decided on the basis of $45,000 damages in loss of earnings as a grappler, and $5,000 for loss of profits as a promoter. Sonny was, in turn, awarded three times $50,000, giving him a $150,000 victory (plus interest of five percent per annum).

Insisting that there was no evidence showing the NWA had monopolized the wrestling business or had tried to stifle competition, Soffer filed a motion for a third trial on February 1, 1962. He laid out 24 errors with the case and verdict, calling the decision a "miscarriage of justice." O'Malley followed up with a second motion for a new trial on February 3. Judge Stephenson arranged a hearing for later in the month, and denied the motions of Soffer and O'Malley, tacking on an additional $10,000 in legal fees for good measure.

Soffer appealed to the United States Court of Appeals on behalf of the NWA on March 26, 1962. Eight days later, O'Malley did the same for Pinkie George. The struggle was not over.

The U.S. Court of Appeals for the Eighth Circuit, Judges Johnsen, Matthes, and Ridge, issued its statement on case No. 17,046, *National Wrestling Alliance v. Harold C. Myers* and case No. 17,047, *P.L. George v. Harold C. Myers* on January 10, 1964. What follows appeared in the records submitted by the court:

We can find no proof in the record of this case from which the jury could reasonably find that the Alliance, *qua* a corporation, *pro se* had "the power either to remove or to exclude or keep out, competitors from the field of competition" because of the business in which it was engaged, nor that it inherently "possessed' any such "power."

Additionally, the Eighth Circuit judges wrote, the "judgment in this case must be reversed," and, "we think this case must be returned *in toto* to the District Court for another trial." Also, "both before and after the Iowa incidents . . . , the evidence is that appellee wrestled for some members of the National Wrestling Alliance, including the appellant George."

Chief Judge Johnsen explained:

> Here, as the majority opinion points out, the National Wrestling Alliance was not entitively engaged in the business of booking, promoting, or exhibiting wrestling matches. Looking, however, at what I believe the evidence would have permitted it to be found that the nature and purpose of the Alliance really were — a group of bookers, promoters and exhibitors joining together for control and protection; the association not being intended to have any corporate functions as such; and the object of membership being to make their underlying agreement or understanding work — I am not certain but that the Alliance could be regarded as representatively having a competitive interest and a monopoly power as to the wrestling game.
>
> I do not deem it necessary, however, to deal further with this question. There was a lack of focus upon any definite theory on which the Alliance was contended to be a monopolist, so that no intelligible basis was afforded for the Court to submit the question generally and have the jury pass upon it in that manner. On the abstractness of the evidence and the instructions, I agree that the judgment is entitled to be reversed, for the Court's general submission of the issue.

Chief Judge Johnsen finished with: "I am unable to see how the jury could objectively come forth with a verdict of $45,000.00 as earnings lost."

In an order from Judge Stephenson filed with the court on March 6, 1964, he explained that no one from Sonny Myers's camp appeared for a March 4 hearing, and that the latter's lawyer James McDowell had no intention of pursuing the case any further. Judge Stephenon gave Myers until March 20 to respond or the case was going to be dismissed.

On March 11, 1964, after almost nine years of court battles, a victory, and several losses, Myers, through McDowell, dismissed "his cause of action against the defendants with prejudice." Judge Stephenson signed the documents on March 23, officially ending the case.

Sonny Myers remained a headliner in many Alliance provinces during and after his litigation against George and the NWA. From 1964 into the early part of the 1970s, Sonny was booked on top for promoters Karras, Geigel, O'Connor, and Muchnick in Missouri, Kansas, and the territory formerly operated by George. He was regional champion more than ten times, and after retirement, maintained a position as an NWA trouble-shooting referee. In December 1975, he acted as third man for the Funk-Brisco world title switch in Miami.

A lead journeyman, Myers was a credible wrestling champion in any part of the country. Known for his dropkicks, quickness, and strength, he could match holds with any of the sport's greats. He was conditioned and had a sincere baby face quality that endeared him to wrestling fans, especially in the central states. In 2000, he promoted All Star Wrestling in St. Joseph and, at 76, proved he still had the ability to entertain audiences.

Myers had successfully sued the National Wrestling Alliance and one of its founders, but saw the decision overturned and the suit dropped after years of legal combat. While the implications appeared harrowing early on, the case in Des Moines turned into a marathon feud with neither side giving an inch. As it had fended off the U.S. Government's inquest with little publicity, the members of the Alliance avoided any long-term difficulties stemming from the conflict between Sonny Myers and Pinkie George. The few sportswriters who mentioned the proceedings usually did it with the same sort of cynicism that Judge Hicklin offered at the first trial. In the end, the NWA, as a whole, was never put in any real jeopardy by the accusations made during this case.

CHAPTER ELEVEN

THE FOUNDING
FATHER RESIGNS

Almost 11 years after he sat at the head of a table and formed the most consequential professional wrestling body in history, Pinkie George was isolated, a victim of the constitution he helped pen. Admittedly, he was always a small-time promoter with modest aspirations, but his leadership moved the National Wrestling Alliance out of the pastures of the Midwest and into the world's spotlight. He supervised the initial arduous process that defined the group's role in the marketplace, but rather than being lauded for his inventive ideas, he spent years at war with an inner-NWA clique who eventually got the upper hand.

George discussed his criticisms in letters to associates, and his grievances with Alliance executives, specifically Sam Muchnick. Muchnick, like George, was well respected for his sincerity, and the culmination of what was suspected to be years of political maneuvering by the reigning NWA president gave way for the feud that prompted Pinkie to resign from the organization he created.

On January 22, 1905, Pinkie George was born Paul Lloyd Georgeacopoulos in Lowell, Massachusetts to Greek parents, Limberis "Louis" and Elizabeth Bolanis Georgeacopoulos. Pinkie and his younger brother Andrew, whose father had run a restaurant in Muncie, Indiana, were in their teens when they began to prosper on their own, following the family's migration to Black Hawk County, Iowa. Their last name shortened to George, Pinkie finished his schooling and took to boxing as an amateur, then as a professional, in the flyweight class. He engaged in more than 160 fights, with limited success, and a turning point came when he was knocked out in the second round by Speedy Dado on August 29, 1928, in San Francisco.

Pinkie married and embarked on a promotional career under the auspices of the American Legion Drum Corps in Mason City, Iowa. He moved his base to Des Moines, and later claimed that the first wrestling match he ever staged was Joe Stecher versus George Vassel in 1928. George's weekly program in Des Moines highlighted the era's best grapplers. He was one of a large contingent of promoters from across the U.S. to witness the Ed "Strangler" Lewis–Jim Londos contest at Chicago's Wrigley Field on September 20, 1934. He mingled with Jack Curley, Joe "Toots" Mondt, Ray Fabiani, Lou Daro, and Paul Bowser.

Pinkie recognized the profits that might be generated if professional football player Bronko Nagurski competed on the mat, and helped his good friend Tony Stecher of Minneapolis turn the Chicago Bear into a sensation. His interest in Nagurski gave Pinkie clout in the wrestling business at the same time, and he used that to further his pursuit of boxing fame as a promoter. He was constantly striving to bring important fights to Des Moines. A generous offer to Mike Jacobs fell on deaf ears when he attempted to secure the services of Joe Louis. Des Moines was an awkward place to stage the sort of matches Pinkie wanted, as representatives of the principal boxers usually steered clear of Iowa. As a manager, Pinkie held the contracts of numerous fighters, including Lee Savold, Johnny Paychek, Glen Flanagan, Henry Schaft, Abel Cestac, and Ricardo Lara.

The catalyst in the decision to create a collaborative of booking offices under the "National Wrestling Alliance" name in 1948, George operated closely with promoters in neighboring Nebraska, Kansas, Missouri, and Minnesota. He was an innovative thinker and believed in teamwork over individual interests. In a September 25, 1949, letter to Jack Pfefer on official letterhead from the "Office of the President," Pinkie described his idealistic intentions for the NWA:

The idea of the Alliance was originated here by this small-town country promoter. My thought in getting them all together was because I figured all the promoters in the Middlewest were neighbors and should work together — I had no interest nationally on this — my idea was for the Middlewest only.

Later it all got out of control, as many thought it was a combine to control wrestling. Frankly Jack, I didn't care who was the champion or who ran the organization. I became president because no one else wanted it. At the next general meeting my time will expire, and someone else will no doubt take over.

I hold no malice towards anyone. I figure our game gets enough abuse from newspapers and public without us abusing it too by fighting. This is honestly the one and only reason I tried so hard to organize the Alliance. I have no ambitions nor care who is champion or who makes the most money. All I desire is to stay in business and make a living for my wife and family.

By the end of 1950, the National Wrestling Alliance had 26 members from Montreal to Hollywood, and from Tampa to Honolulu. The roster included big shot promoters Toots Mondt, Fred Kohler, Eddie Quinn, and Paul Bowser. The association thrived well beyond Pinkie's imaginings and was quickly taking on a mind of its own. George was the president of the national NWA from 1948 to 1950, before amicably giving up his seat.

Pinkie expressed his intentions in a letter to Pfefer, dated June 8, 1950, stating: "In September, my term ends and Sam Muchnick will be elected, as I think he is the fellow deserving of it. He is a very capable guy, and a swell one who's word is his bond."

On November 29, 1950, George was honored at a banquet given by the NWA at the Des Moines Club and presented a $1,000 check and trophy by Muchnick and Max Clayton.

A clever magnate, Pinkie took a chance and brought a professional National Basketball League franchise to Iowa in 1948. The Waterloo Hawks failed to attract fans, and after losing $20,000 in less than a year, he sold it to his brother Andy and Charles Shipp. Pinkie invested in baseball and hockey in Des Moines, and remained alert for potential boxing draws.

The Iowa wrestling circuit was run in methodical fashion by Pinkie, and many talented grapplers earned their stripes in the territory. Wrestlers of the caliber of Joe Scarpello, Verne Gagne, Bob Orton, Johnny Valentine, Bob Geigel, and Pat O'Connor gained experience venturing across country once traveled by Frank Gotch and Earl Caddock. Highly skilled matches thrilled the spoiled fans, even as the dramatics of the more colorful characters seen on TV were changing the style of wrestling. Pinkie ran his own live television, but his market suffered, like most others, from the influence of the Saturday night DuMont feed from Chicago. The rush to acquire Kohler's workers was on. Pinkie George got in line.

On January 23, 1951, Pinkie incorporated the National Wrestling Alliance in the state of Iowa. The move, done initially for tax purposes, was opposed by a fraction of the membership, but Pinkie was insistent. The new code of ethics for the non-profit Iowa corporation were submitted to the Secretary of State.

Article III of the incorporation documents explained the overall purpose of the NWA:

> To promote good fellowship among its members; elevate the standards of wrestling generally; to promote the business and ethical interest of professional wrestling; to enlighten and direct public opinion with regard to the relation between professional wrestling and public welfare; to promote the science and art of wrestling and interest therein; to promote good will between members of this association with state athletic commissions in whatever states said commissions do exist; to promote fair play, sportsmanship, and a high standard of competition and interest in the wrestling profession.

Article VII stated that the corporation would exist "for a period of fifty (50) years from the date of incorporation, unless sooner dissolved by a three-fourths vote of the membership, and approved by a majority of the board of directors." Article VIII declared that "the officers of this corporation shall be a president, first vice president, second vice president, secretary and treasurer, who shall hold office for a period of one (1) year, or until their successors are duly elected and have qualified. A person may hold more than one office in the corporation."

The official board of directors would "consist of not less than three (3) persons, and not more than ten (10) persons, who shall hold office for a period of fifteen (15) years, or until their successors are duly elected and have qualified," according to Article IX. And the articles protected the original founders, proven in Article XI:

> Until the annual meeting of the corporation, to be held on the second Saturday of September, 1966, the following shall constitute the board of directors, subject to additions therein, if any, elected and selected by a majority of the present board of directors. The present directors are as follows, to-wit:
>
> Tony Stecher, Minneapolis, Minnesota
> Sam Muchnick, St. Louis, Missouri
> Orville Brown, Kansas City, Missouri

Max Clayton, Omaha, Nebraska
P.L. George, Des Moines, Iowa

The corporate documents were signed by Pinkie, his wife Elizabeth, and their attorney John Connolly. According to the text, George was to be a member of the NWA board of directors for 15 years with the four originators. Unfortunately, his chum Stecher died unexpectedly on October 10, 1954 and Clayton followed him in June 1957.

There was an obvious bond between Pinkie and Muchnick that strengthened in the first two years of the NWA's existence. Aside from being trusted associates, they were friends, and overcame many obstacles with a united front. A subtle animosity sprouted when the Alliance decided to pay Muchnick to book the heavyweight champion and perform the duties of the organization's president in 1951. Muchnick justified the stipend, citing the harsher demands on the office as compared to when Pinkie ran the coalition, but he also conceded that George had not only fathered the NWA, but had formulated the initial bylaws.

Tensions between Muchnick and George fluctuated as years passed, and Pinkie was never shy about expressing his grievances. In his anger, he withdrew from the NWA board of directors in 1951, and asked to be excused from participating in any committees on the basis that he now viewed the Alliance as nothing more than a social club. He often considered Sam's work to be commendable, and thought he was doing a "fine job" as president. But by 1955, his opinions of Muchnick and the NWA were at their lowest points, and his own problems with Sonny Myers were at the root of much of the bitterness.

Former heavyweight champion Wladek Zbyszko, a crony of Myers, Gust Karras, and George Simpson, mailed two messages in late January 1957. One was to Muchnick in St. Louis, and the other was to George. The Zbyszkos were known for their hatred of the NWA and contributed a scathing anti-Alliance piece to the *Savannah Reporter* (Missouri), their hometown newspaper, on January 4, 1957. Wladek's cryptic notes, including a comment that he'd soon be visiting the promoter in Des Moines, provoked George to write a letter "to whom it may concern" on January 30, 1957, that wasn't your average communiqué.

He wrote that on October 7, 1956, eight days before the federal judgment against the NWA, he'd received a phone call at his home that warned him to, "get out of the business you S.O.B. or we'll deliver your body to your wife some night." Pinkie also said "someone tried to do bodily harm or kill" Orville Brown while driving to Kansas City from St. Joseph on December 26, and that Brown had also received menacing calls at his home. The threats had moved George to purchase a gun, and give "photostats and other material to prove the . . . charges, should anything happen" to his wife Elizabeth.

"These incidents are tied," Pinkie wrote. "It is a wrestling war — a one sided war — by a combine who organized last fall. This combine includes Gust Karras and Harold Sonny Myers of St. Joe, and George Simpson of Kansas City.

"This suit by Myers was a well-timed camouflage, and part and parcel to the conspiracy to harass, scare, and discourage me out of the business. They timed the suit when they learned that the federal government had started investigation against the NWA for alleged monopolistic practices."

Myers's accusations paralleled others being investigated by members of the Department of Justice, and it was clear that the Alliance was heading for a date with disaster. Rather than feeling comfortable that his partners would stand with him, Pinkie's back was to the wall, and his options were shrinking quickly. To insiders, there was a visible link between Myers, Karras, Simpson, and Muchnick and that became more clear when the case went to trial in December 1958.

Simpson testified against Pinkie, saying he had had difficulty getting talent in the past because of the NWA system. He also said he'd recently straightened his problems out through a deal with Brown and Muchnick. Muchnick also testified as a witness for the plaintiff, but did little to seriously hurt Pinkie or the Alliance.

On December 8, the verdict was read in open court, with the 12-person jury finding for the defendants. Pinkie George and the NWA were off the hook. Sonny's attorney filed for a new hearing, and was denied by the judge. As their appeal was drafted, Pinkie considered his current situation, and his standing in the National Wrestling Alliance. There was no doubt he was fuming at the treachery of his cohorts, and targeted his anger at the once-sacrosanct armor of Muchnick. Sam, who was looking more and more mortal, apprised the membership of George's grievances in one of his normal bulletins. Pinkie responded in a letter:

> To Alliance membership: I herewith this day, March 3rd, 1959, officially resign from the National Wrestling Alliance. There are two reasons, both involving Sam Muchnick. A very small minority of the Alliance, including President Muchnick, are in violation of the government decree. Interlocking regional monopolies that control the champion endanger every member in the Alliance. (Better read the consent decree you signed.)

Shortly thereafter, a two-page memo was sent to NWA members by Pinkie. The following are excerpts from his detailed correspondence:

In accepting my resignation from the NWA, Muchnick's letter closed with these famous lines: "When I go to bed every night, I do so in good conscience," end of quote. Okay, let's review his conscience.

One, before the trial here [*Myers v. P.L. George and the National Wrestling Alliance*], the St. Louis and Kansas City territories merged. During the trial, Mr. Simpson, one of Sam's partners, appeared as a voluntary witness against the Alliance and me. As promoter in Topeka, Sonny Myers was a close associate of Sam's. What a farce and sham. Read on: During a three-day recess of the trial, Mr. Conscience called a meeting in St. Louis — all his St. Louis and K.C. partners. In this meeting he said, to wit, "I don't care about Pinkie George, it's the Alliance I want to save." Let him deny this. What Alliance was he saving? The Muchnick and Co. Alliance.

Except for an aside I'll close this subject. It's ironic that Sam's K.C. partners are taking over towns I used to book. I bet Sam's conscience don't bother him one bit when he cuts up the booking money. Conscience, you say?

Three. Not long ago Bruns (who likes to play Sec. of State for Sam) gave Orville Brown an ultimatum. This monopoly is trying to throw Brown out — put him out of the business he built. Again, how ironic. The first four people who agreed on the original Alliance was Stecher, Clayton, Brown, and myself. IT WAS BROWN'S INSISTENCE THAT BROUGHT MUCHNICK IN! Stecher and Clayton have passed away. I resigned. One more to go. How soon? It depends on Muchnick's conscience. Brother'. (sic)

Sam's territory in partnership with the Kansas City territory and Canadian partners (who are safe from the U.S. anti-trust laws) now comprise an interlocking monopoly that has made the champion and championship their own personal property. All championship matches are held either in Canada or St. Louis. Who knows when and where these matches are made? Did you know when the Hutton-O'Connor match was made?

With the presidency in Sam's hand and the power of the championship he can whip anyone in[to] line. As a matter of fact, it is a blackjack over every member's head. Many who are sick of the situation don't dare resign — wrestling is their business.

As long as the situation exists, I am going to shout from the rooftops and try to clean it up. Whether Sam wants to admit it or not, IT WAS I WHO WAS THE FATHER OF THE ALLIANCE. As a matter of fact, it was also incorporated here in Iowa with my lawyer, my wife, and I the incorporators. The Alliance was not intended only for the benefit of one man or a small group. It was intended to be a cooperative for the benefit of the whole membership. If I can't clean it up I am going to the Justice Dept. Some one has to.

Pinkie also wrote the following to Jack Pfefer in a letter dated April 15, 1959:

> The Alliance and Mr. Muchnick will get a big surprise next fall when they meet. I am going to time a legal suit against them just as they meet, no matter where they meet. Sam and his partners not only have put me out of business but now they are phone treats (threats) (sic) and further squeeze is put on me to shut me up. I am not going to suppress the truth.

Unafraid to speak his mind, George went on to outline perceived injustices beyond the central states quarrel. Ten years earlier, the compliments and praise flowed like wine. But the party was over. The bitterness was on a course to hamstring the NWA, and had become public enough to incite a government inquiry into antitrust violations.

Muchnick sent a letter to the Department of Justice, addressing the Pinkie-Myers case, and there was the potential for one side or the other to speak to the FBI about alleged infractions. Pinkie's place in wrestling crumbled. Whether from conspiracy, blackballing, or just fate, his Des Moines promotion was reduced to rubble. In a March 30, 1959, letter to Muchnick, he wrote: "Man, talk about the Teamsters Union. Your monopoly can give them cards and spades."

Always industrious, Pinkie fled the complex problems of the central states for Texas. There his buddy Jack Dempsey gave him a hot tip concerning a gifted 6´5´´ Argentine fighter named Alejandro Lavorante. George met the young boxer in San Antonio in 1959 and made two trips to South America to establish a repore with him and with his family. Returning to wrestling promotions, he worked with the Morris Sigel faction to promote the City Auditorium in opposition to Sigel's former associates, Frank Brown and Dorothy Livengood.

In November 1959, Lavorante was beaten by Roy Harris on points, but that didn't stop Pinkie's drive to make him a superstar. The duo went on tour, and Lavorante won 15 out of his next 16 fights. On March 30, 1962, at the Los Angeles Sports Arena, he was flattened in ten rounds by Archie Moore and carried from the ring in a bout that drew 12,500 people and a gate of $105,000. Several months later, on July 20, Pinkie led his prodigy into a scrap with the invincible Cassius Clay in Los Angeles — despite being in excellent shape, Alejandro was defeated in the fifth round. Clay dominated the fight and delivered numerous punches to his opponent's head.

Lavorante's third match of 1962 was on September 21 at the Olympic Auditorium in Los Angeles against a veteran, Johnny Riggins. He hoped to rebound from consecutive losses, and pundits saw him as the favorite. Through four rounds, he was ahead and appeared to be on his way to victory. Suddenly, Lavorante lost the conditioning he was known for, and began to fade. During the sixth round, Riggins took advantage of his weakened foe and applied a mighty wallop to the left side of Alejandro's head. Knocked unconscious, Lavorante fell to the mat. The fighter suffered a brain hemorrhage and went into a coma.

In the two months following the tragic affair, Lavorante underwent three brain operations and a tracheotomy at California Lutheran Hospital. George was at his young friend's bedside daily, sharing the pain with the boxer's mother and brother. "I feel like he is my own son," Pinkie was quoted as saying in the *Los Angeles Times*, on October 27, 1962. "Such a nice boy. Such a real gentleman. He was going to apply for a permanent visa and U.S. citizenship in December. I have no plans for myself for the future. I don't think I'll ever manage again. I must have handled 300 or 350 boys and never had a serious injury."

Pinkie, in November 1962, announced the formation of the First National Boxing Club of California, for which he'd serve as matchmaker along with promoter Joseph Bracker. Expecting to stage a Sugar Ramos–Davey Moore fight at the Sports Arena, Pinkie applied for a license, but was turned down by the California Athletic Commission in January 1963. The feeling was that because his new organization would be running in opposition to the influential Eaton-Olympic Auditorium group and the Joe Louis troupe, the commission had vetoed his efforts. Pinkie left Los Angeles for Kansas City, where a surprising opportunity presented itself.

Eager to solve the problems in the central states and to muzzle Pinkie, Muchnick teamed with Jim Barnett to bankroll George in Kansas City, Missouri. Both bookers sent grapplers for his debut on April 30, 1963, at the Municipal Auditorium, and the most "outstanding" heavyweight of the top two bouts would reportedly be in line for a match with Lou Thesz. George attended the NWA convention in August and all seemed well within the Alliance.

That is, at least on the surface. On September 18, 1963, Pinkie went before the Missouri Athletic Commission insisting that there was a monopoly controlling wrestling in Missouri, Iowa, and Kansas. He publicly named Gust Karras, George Simpson, Pat O'Connor, Bob Geigel, Fred Kohler, Wally Karbo, Verne Gagne, and Joe Dusek as conspirators in the syndicate, saying: "They are the cosa nostra of wrestling, working in a high-handed monopolistic fashion so the independent promoter cannot sign wrestlers, and they even make threats."

He followed up with a $200,000 damage suit in Kansas City District Court against the owners of Heart of Sports Attractions, Inc. of Kansas City on October 16, 1963, citing antitrust violations. The complaint, *Paul L. George v. Gust Karras,*

George D. Simpson, Robert Geigel, and Pat O'Connor, No. 14640-4, read:

The defendants are individuals doing business jointly and severally, as bookers and promoters for professional wrestling and by which the said bookers and promoters operate as a monopoly and do have a monopoly on all professional wrestling, the exclusive use of the talents of every wrestler of any prominence in professional wrestling, and that in the course of the dealings of the defendants, both individually and in concert, they have violated Sections One (1) and Two (2) of the United States Code.

That as a part of business of defendants they make a substantial utilization of the channels of interstate trade in commerce, to negotiate:

(a) Contracts with wrestlers advertising agencies, seconds, referees, announcers and other personnel living in states other than those in which the defendants reside;

(b) Lease suitable arenas, and arrange other details for wrestling contests, particularly when the contests are held in states other than those in which the promoters reside;

(c) Sell tickets to contests across the state line;

(d) Negotiate for the sale of and sell rights to make and distribute motion pictures of wrestling contests in other states;

(e) Negotiate for the sale of, and sell rights to broadcast and telecast wrestling contests to homes through both radio and television stations throughout the United States;

(f) Negotiate for the sale of and sell rights to telecast wrestling exhibitions to motion picture theaters in various states of the United States for display by large screen television.

That the defendants have so retained and monopolized the wrestling business, which is a trade or a commerce, through a conspiracy to exclude competition by restraint, in fact, today literally no competition, and all wrestlers, if they are to wrestle for pay, must wrestle for the said defendants, who have the exclusive rights under said conspiracy for the territory of the State of Iowa and the State of Missouri.

If the said wrestlers do not follow the dictates of the defendants herein, they can be blackballed for wrestling for other promoters, and thereby lose their means of livelihood, or refuse, and be denied access to, lucrative bouts and are thus coerced and by use of duress, forced to negotiate with these defendants.

That the said defendants have effectuated this conspiracy and monopoly by working together in such a way that a wrestler must contact one of their number in order to wrestle in the State of Missouri or Iowa, or he is unable to pay anyone to promote his said bouts and therefore, due to the monopoly, would be restrained from pursuing his livelihood within the states aforesaid. Thus the wrestler becomes hoplessly (sic) dependent upon the members of said conspiracy.

That when a wrestler decides to enter the field of professional wrestling, then the States of Missouri and Iowa are required by this conspiracy to contact one of the members, and from that point forward, [he] becomes the "property" of the defendants and is traded back and forth between the said members of the conspiracy for the use of the said members of the conspiracy as they see fit. Said individual wrestler has no voice whatsoever in the place where he shall wrestle, but is restrained for wrestling for any other promoter or booker and thus restrained by said monopoly the rights of other bookers and promoters to promote wrestling bouts within this area.

The plaintiff herein has been a booker and promoter for over twenty years, and was one of the top bookers and promoters in the field. That the plaintiff did, for years, promote and book wrestling within the confines of the State of Iowa at various arenas and for county fairs. In the course of said booking and promoting he arranged for wrestlers to appear and would promote said bouts for public viewing. That since 1959, up until the present time, the defendants conspired to put the plaintiff out of business in the following manner, to-wit:

(a) By contracting with all of the wrestlers whereby they would wrestle only for the defendants and not for this plaintiff;

(b) By tying up all personnel talent through their conspiracy and thereby eliminating the possibility of plaintiff being able to promote or book any wrestling talent;

(c) By corroboration of the conspiracy with other promoters and bookers from Omaha, Minneapolis, Chicago, and Kansas City, to restrain this plaintiff from obtaining any wrestling talent and thereby isolate the State of Iowa for the exclusive monopoly of these defendants.

(d) By violation of various state athletic commission regulations which prohibit any booker or wrestler from being directly or indirectly, interested financially in any wrestler, and which prevents the wrestlers from promoting wrestling matches in the state.

That they advised wrestlers that if they did shows for this plaintiff, they would be blackballed from wrestling within the State of Iowa, in the future.

That this plaintiff, prior to 1959, would promote and book, in excess of two hundred (200) matches a year, and has, since this conspiracy of monopoly by these defendants, been unable to book any shows in the State of Iowa since June of 1959.

That if the plaintiff had not been prevented, through the monopoly of the defendants, he would have been able to book many shows in arenas and fairs throughout the State of Iowa, but that due to the monopoly, plaintiff was unable to do so and this has caused damage to his income and affected his future earning capacity.

An answer to the suit filed by George was filed in court on January 13, 1964: "This defendant denies each and every allegation in plaintiff's complaint."

Counterclaims by Karras, Simpson, Geigel, and O'Connor were filed. Court documents contained the following counter accusation:

At the time of commission by plaintiff of the actions hereinafter mentioned, this defendant was and now is engaged in the promotion of wrestling exhibitions and had maintained a good reputation in the conducting of such business.

That on or about September 18, 1963, plaintiff in the presence of other persons whose names are unknown to this defendant, maliciously and with the intent to cause it to be believed that this defendant was a member of a criminal element, and was an unfit person to engage in the promotion of wrestling exhibitions business, and pursuant to a preconceived policy and intent to injure this defendant in his business and in his reputation, did say and publish of and concerning this defendant words as follows: "They are the cosa nostra of wrestling, working in a high-handed monopolistic fashion so the independent promoter cannot sign wrestlers, and they even make threats."

Asking for $25,000 damage for "reason of injury to [their] reputation, good name and character," and an additional $200,000 each for punitive damages, the potential penalty against Pinkie should he lose the case would be $900,000. George refuted the accusations in documents filed on January 22, 1964, and demanded a jury trial.

O'Connor issued a series of questions to Pinkie on May 13, 1964, through the courts, among them asking which wrestlers he "alleges were told they would be blackballed from wrestling within the State of Iowa if they did shows for the plaintiff."

Pinkie, on June 1, replied with the following list of professional grapplers: "Farmer Martin (sic), Pepper Martin, Big Bill Miller, Lou Thez (sic), Mark Lewis (sic), Jack Steele, Duke Keumuka (sic), Al Leilina (sic), Mike DiBiase, Fritz Von Erick (sic), Bearcat Wright, Buddy Rodgers (sic), Bill Melby, Frank Altman, Ken Finland (sic), Emile Dupre, Art Bull, Hans Schmidt, Bob Geigel . . . and Pat O'Connor."

Lawyers preparing the counterclaim scheduled all four defendants to testify. Muchnick and Charles Pian of the Missouri Athletic Commission were also going to be called to the stand. Submitted into evidence was a copy of the *Saturday Evening Post* dated November 9, 1963, with a feature on the mafia in Chicago. The attorney for Karras, Simpson, O'Connor, and Geigel said that by presenting the article on crime, they would demonstrate: "That the plaintiff's words were intended to 'prejudice' the defendants in their trade or business."

The Kansas City attorney emphasized the fact that Pinkie had been involved in two previous cases regarding alleged violations of the Sherman Act: *United States v. National Wrestling Alliance* and *Harold Myers v. P.L. George and the National Wrestling Alliance*.

Additionally, signed affidavits were tendered by wrestlers Bill Miller, Mike DiBiase, Jack Steele, Don Marlin, Pepper Martin, Fritz Von Erich, Duke Keomuka, Lou Thesz, Emile Dupre, Frank Altman, Mark Lewin, and Ken Fenelon, stating for the record that they had never refused to wrestle for George. Bookers Wally Karbo, Fred Kohler, Joe Dusek, Karl Sarpolis, Bobby Bruns, and Sam Muchnick denied that they had ever "refused to book wrestlers for Paul George in the State of Missouri or the State of Iowa." The group also said that they had never been "threatened" by O'Connor, Geigel, Simpson, or Karras, and hadn't signed any contracts to wrestle exclusively for them.

Pinkie spent most of nine months in the hospital, convinced that his talented protégé Alejandro Lavorante would eventually regain consciousness. But Lavorante's father obtained a court order, and transported his comatose son to Argentina on June 30, 1963. In Buenos Aires on April 1, 1964, Lavorante passed away. The *Los Angeles Times* quoted Pinkie following his death: "It's a tragedy they took him over there, because I don't think he got the care he was getting in the United States, probably just some rubbing. It's too late now. I have an awfully empty feeling. I think I'm going to leave town now and go some place where I can rest."

Aileen Eaton also spoke about Lavorante's death in the April 2, 1964, *Los Angeles Times:* "I'm terribly, terribly sorry. But I'm even more sorry he was ever taken out of this country. He was receiving such wonderful care and treatment here and we were certain he was on his way to recovery. He needed the treatment he was getting in a major hospital, but his father refused. I'll never be able to understand it."

While mourning the death of his friend, Pinkie failed to reply to several court documents, and a district judge gave him additional time on December 31, 1964. A week later, George submitted the proper formatted response to defendants Geigel and O'Connor.

On February 15, 1965, George filed paperwork to dismiss his indictment of Karras, Simpson, O'Connor, and Geigel, "without prejudice." That same day, the defendants also issued a motion to dismiss their counterclaim, and District Judge William H. Becker signed the order.

In the years after the legal wrangling in Kansas City, George bounced around the sports world from Houston to San Diego, returning to Des Moines, where he acted as the midwestern agent for heavyweight boxing contender Jerry Quarry (1945–1999). As late as 1971, with more than 40 years in promotions, Pinkie had the enthusiasm to establish a monthly boxing event in Des Moines. He became the supervisor of Waterloo's McElroy Auditorium in August 1975, but gave his notice when the bug to promote returned his focus.

Active through the early 1980s, Pinkie was on a shortlist to act as the Iowa State Commissioner of Athletics, speaking out against "toughman" contests. He retired and succumbed to cancer and Alzheimer's disease on November 1, 1993 at the age of 89.

Brother Andrew, who helped with Pinkie's Iowa endeavors, became the chairman of the Iowa State Tax Commission. With his wife Vivien (1938–1982), he lived in Waterloo until his death on January 14, 1997, at 90 years of age.

Pinkie George had a big heart and carried his 5'2'' frame proudly amongst the dignitaries of sports. His experience ran the gamut of professional athletics, from boxing competitively and managing a contending fighter, to participating in all aspects of the wrestling business. His imaginative mind saw beyond the limits of Des Moines, and his unassuming confidence transformed a simple trade agreement in the Midwest into the strongest union of wrestling promoters in history.

From his days in the College Hill area of Cedar Falls to the state capital, Pinkie was always on the go, and made many friends. Without his leadership, the National Wrestling Alliance would never have gotten off the ground, but in the end, the NWA grew beyond his control. By the mid-1950s, George's voice was barely heard, drowned out by his ambitious colleagues. Fed up with how things had changed, and of the NWA ignorning his numerous complaints, Pinkie walked away from the Alliance. While he revisited wrestling every now and then, participated in a few conventions, and associated with his old cronies, George pursued other avenues of promotions. The loss of George in 1959 was a crushing blow to a beleaugured organization.

CHAPTER TWELVE

THE EXPANSION OF CAPITOL WRESTLING

The National Wrestling Alliance had reached a pinnacle during the early 1950s that seemed unimaginable when it was founded. But by 1957, the organization was collapsing, and by 1962, it was facing complete destruction. The wise Sam Muchnick had held the Alliance together with his administrative skills, but two men would rise from the NWA's inner circles to economic heights that dwarfed their colleagues — Joe "Toots" Mondt and Vincent James John McMahon. With the prodigious McMahon leading the way as commander-in-chief, the duo's stranglehold on wrestling in the Northeast led to the famed Capitol Wrestling Corporation, and set a course that has slowly evolved into World Wrestling Entertainment today.

The celebrated journey of the McMahon family began with the arrival of Roderick and Elizabeth in New York City from Ireland in 1868, the first generation of the dynasty in the United States. The two idealistic twenty-somethings hoped for a new life in a postwar society, where they could raise children, and provide them both education and opportunity. In December 1875, they had a daughter, Mary Lauretta, and two years later, Elizabeth gave birth to Catherine. Roderick was running a hotel when his first son, Edward Joseph "Eddie" McMahon (1880–1935), was born. On May 26, 1882, they had their fourth and final child, Roderick James.

Edward and Roderick attended Manhattan College, where Rod graduated with a commercial diploma in 1899 at the age of 17. To support their widowed mother and sisters living at 1424 Amsterdam Avenue in West Harlem, the brothers were employed as bank clerks, though they expressed a wide interest in sports. By 1909, they were managing partners of the Olympic Athletic Club, and bookers, subsequently, at the Empire and St. Nichols Athletic Clubs, all in Harlem. Faced with a loss of public interest in professional boxing, the McMahons overcame a number of obstacles to appease the public with high-quality fights.

Already respected in the boxing world, the McMahons expanded their affairs in 1911, founding the New York Lincoln Giants, a championship caliber black baseball team. Touring with the talented squad, the siblings ventured to Havana, Cuba, where, in 1915, they acted in collaboration with the promoters of the Jess Willard-Jack Johnson heavyweight title scrap.

To supplement his income, Roderick sold furniture. He married a New York woman of Irish descent named Rose, and had three children between 1910 and 1917. Vincent, born on July 6, 1914, was the middle child, four years younger than brother Roderick, and two years older than his sister Dorothy. In 1918, as World War I raged abroad, the McMahon Brothers appeared before draft boards. Roderick faced a committee in September at Columbia University, but avoided active duty when the November armistice ended the conflict.

Roderick, known as "Jess," became a well-connected member of the boxing community. The illustrious George "Tex" Rickard, who engaged in many skirmishes against the likes of Jimmy Johnston, Humbert Fugazy, and Jack Curley, remained in control of the all-important Madison Square Garden in New York City. When he sought a replacement in October 1925 for matchmakers Leo Flynn and Frank Flournay, Rickard didn't have to look far, hiring his friend Jess.

McMahon and Rickard went to the table, negotiating to bring consequential matches to the Garden, but the ongoing hostilities prevented any of the major groups from gaining a clear advantage. They also had to contend with the guidelines prescribed by the stern New York State Athletic Commission. Piloting the new effort to entice audiences, McMahon had some intriguing ideas, including a bout between Gene Tunney and Jack Sharkey. In July 1927, he landed the Sharkey-Dempsey fight for the Garden, which Dempsey won in seven rounds. That same summer Rickard and McMahon made an unsuccessful pitch for the rights to the pivotal Tunney-Dempsey championship clash.

On September 5, 1928, Jess quit his Garden job and took over the comparatively paltry promotions at Starlight Park in the Bronx. Rickard's death in January 1929 stunned the sport, but if anyone had a similar ability to grab up attractive bouts, it was McMahon. With Bushey Graham versus Kid Chocolate in the main event, McMahon introduced boxing to Starlight's adjoining 32,000–seat New York Coliseum, on April 12, 1929. He leased the Coliseum for ten years and his backers expected a substantial return on their investment.

Showing how fragile the sport was at the time, McMahon's decade-long obligation at the Coliseum ended abruptly just prior to Christmas 1929, and the lofty goals of his financiers were never realized. In the years that followed, he bounced from position to position. He staged boxing at Ebbets Field in Brooklyn in 1930–31, the Philadelphia Arena in 1932–33, then anchored in Long Island, where he became the first McMahon to promote professional wrestling at the Municipal Stadium in Freeport.

The aforementioned boxing showdowns were nothing compared to the vicious wrestling wars. Battles over turf and power in New York raged in the 1930s. Unable to snag big-money earners, McMahon allied himself with another independent faction captained by Carlos Louis Henriquez. McMahon and Henriquez booked the Coney Island and Brooklyn Sports Stadiums, usually with Carlos as the main fan favorite.

The formation of the "Trust" calmed the New York territory enough for McMahon to have access to a larger pool of wrestlers for shows at the Hempstead Arena. There, he promoted Gino Garibaldi, Jim Browning, Hans Kampfer, Wee Willie Davis, Alphonse Bisignano, Mike Romano, the Duseks, Everette Marshall, Sandor Szabo, Tor Johnson, and Abe Kashey. By 1937, the popularity of wrestling waned, but while some bookers escaped the city for fresher ground, Jess dug in for the long haul. His contacts were extremely helpful, and he freely traded wrestlers with promoters in Pennsylvania, New Jersey, and Connecticut.

A perpetual force in the Northeastern sportsworld, Jess is generally more remembered for his spell as matchmaker at the Garden than for his 20 years as a wrestling promoter. He died of a cerebral hemorrhage at a hospital in Wilkes-Barre, Pennsylvania, on November 21, 1954.

The turbulent career of Jess McMahon was carefully monitored by his second son, Vincent. Vincent had a remarkable instinct for promotions, both in entertainment and athletics, and he was always mindful of his father's actions. Vince reportedly became involved with wrestling around 1933, studying under his father in Hempstead. He served in the coast guard during World War II, and was discharged honorably in 1946.

The six-foot-three-inch magnate and socialite moved from New York to Washington D.C. in the summer of 1947, and on December 3, 1948, was hired to manage Turner's Arena (14th and W streets). William "Joe" Turner, ex-middleweight wrestling champion, had owned and operated the facility from 1935 until his death on February 18, 1947. His widow, Florence, continued in boxing and wrestling, and married Joe's matchmaker, Gabe Menendez. McMahon concentrated his attention on promoting concerts, but was soon lured into wrestling, where cash was guaranteed on a weekly basis.

On December 18, 1952, Vince assumed the lease for wrestling at Turner's and officially bought the "territory" from Menendez for $60,000. He ushered in his brand of wrestling on January 7, 1953, with Primo Carnera, Lu Kim, the Zebra Kid, and the Golden Terror on the bill. He imported talent from New York's foremost booker Toots Mondt, Jack Pfefer, and Fred Kohler, whose DuMont television show was popular throughout the eastern part of the country. McMahon brought many headliners into Washington, including Antonino Rocca, Killer Kowalski, Gorgeous George, Gene Stanlee, Hans Schmidt, and Verne Gagne.

Tired of relying on a Bailey Goss–hosted program from Baltimore, McMahon plunged into producing television. During a hiatus in December 1955, he renamed Turner's Arena the Capitol Arena and prepped the building for cameras. On January 5, 1956, he debuted live wrestling on Washington's DuMont affiliate, WTTG (channel 5) from 10:00 to 11:00 p.m, sponsored by Gunther Brewery, with the spirited Bill Malone (William Malone Polglase) as commentator.

The launch of McMahon's television series was considered a risk, and he paid the initial two weeks of production costs out of his own pocket before fixed terms were settled with the initially skeptical DuMont organization. The arrival of his animated grappling on TV couldn't have come at a better time, as Ray Fabiani was running D.C.'s Uline Arena in opposition. McMahon was primed to defend his town.

Whereas McMahon pushed his cavalcade of stars weekly, Fabiani staged monthly programs with Buddy Rogers in the spotlight. Fabiani was getting national press for coercing former boxing champion Joe Louis into wrestling, but McMahon had a growing advantage and eventually won out. An accord came within a year, and Fabiani would become one of McMahon's staunchest allies.

There was speculation that television was going to hurt McMahon's arena business, but after several advance-purchase ticket sellouts, he told radio and TV columnist Lawrence Laurent of the *Washington Post and Times Herald* on March 10, 1956: "It's television. What else could it be? We are getting reservation orders from as far north as Chambersburg, Pennsylvania, and as far south as Staunton, Virginia. If this is the way television kills promoters, I'm going to die a rich man."

The sensation created by grappling in Washington was discussed quietly about in board rooms, and when Haskell Cohen's ten-month reign ended as producer of wrestling at Studio Five of DuMont's Telecenter in New York City, officials looked to McMahon's programming as a substitute. Vince announced on June 8, 1956, that his show was slipping into the prized 9:00-11:00 p.m. slot on WABD (channel 5) beginning on Thursday, June 21. The weekly program had the potential to influence gates across the New York metropolitan area, especially at Madison Square Garden, giving him an advantage over all other promoters in the region.

Thirty years before his son would earn positive and negative attention for his multifarious shenanigans, McMahon's TV program drew a copious amount of criticism for its violence by marks who believed what they were seeing. District of Columbia Boxing Commission Chairman Jocko Miller moved to regulate wrestling based on such complaints in October 1956. He claimed that viewers in New York, specifically, were outraged with McMahon's wrestlers and pushed the legislature to police the show. Angry citizens even mailed letters of protest to the White House.

McMahon, unfazed, was quoted in the October 27, 1956, edition of the *Washington Post and Times Herald:* "There is a simple solution for this. There is a knob on each TV set for changing channels. If the show doesn't appeal to you, all you have to do is flip the knob and watch something else. These people talk about juvenile delinquency. What about the lessons children get each day on TV in murder, robbery, arson, jail-breaking and barroom brawling? Is this good?" Commenting on the fact that detractors had blasted the pro-Nazi wrestler, Karl Von Hess, McMahon retorted: "Von Hess is no Nazi. He uses that silly salute to point up the fact he is the villain. Each wrestling exhibition has a hero and a villain."

McMahon's new clout in New York led to a personal managerial contract with Antonino Rocca, and "Argentina" was booked steadily in Washington and at the Garden. Banding together with Toots Mondt, McMahon devised a strategy to rule wrestling in the Northeast. They were forced into a compromise with Charley Johnston, his nephew Walter Smallshaw, and matchmaker Kola Kwariani, a group who controlled the promoter's position at the Garden, the St. Nicholas Arena, and various New York venues. Their sway could affect the future of Rudy Dusek, who was targeted, and forced to retire.

Mondt wanted control of the east's main booking office, an ambition that was shaped with the methods and determination of McMahon. Mondt had been to the top many times, governing profitable firms in New York and Los Angeles, but was often distracted and thrown off course. McMahon was a better point man, a sound thinker who laid the foundation for their success. And once Toots was focused and energized, there was a concentrated push forward. They also received critical assistance from a third associate, New Jersey promoter Willie Gilzenberg.

Johnston, Smallshaw, and Kwariani tried managing the Garden their way, but soon realized they needed the wrestlers of McMahon and Mondt to sell tickets. It wasn't long before the changes resonated with New York fans, as the second Mondt-McMahon Garden show drew 19,300, with Rocca teaming with Gagne against Karl Von Hess and Hans Schmidt on February 4, 1957. The gate was $61,250. A Garden spokesman noted at the time that the event drew the largest crowd in 25 years. As a symbol of his mounting importance in New York City, McMahon was given the formal matchmaker tab at the Garden, and Mondt was elevated to copromoter with Johnston.

The idea of creating a central booking agency and promotional headquarters came to fruition when the Capitol Wrestling Corporation was incorporated on August 5, 1957, in the District of Columbia. McMahon, Phil Zacko, and Johnny Doyle were the initial directors, with offices at 1332 I Street NW (Franklin Park Hotel). McMahon and Mondt each held 46 percent of the 1000 shares in the company, while Doyle had eight.

There was no question that Rocca was the Garden's principal celebrity, and the biggest wrestling attraction in New York since Jim Londos. He topped every Garden show from November 26, 1956, to January 23, 1961. The booking philosophy itself was predicated on the idea that he'd be in the main event. Rocca and Puerto Rican grappler Miguel Perez (Jose Miguel Perez Sr.) were an amazingly popular pairing, drawing well against all opponents. The ethnic tandem appealed to the wrestling audience immensely. It was pure gold for Capitol Wrestling.

An infamous night in Madison Square Garden history came on November 19, 1957. The seven-match program featured Rocca and title claimant Edouard Carpentier against Dr. Jerry Graham and Dick the Bruiser. Five minutes prior to the 11:00 curfew, the referee disqualified Bruiser and Graham as Rocca bled, and the audience charged the ring. In turn, Rocca drew blood from Graham. Bruiser, meanwhile, had to fight off a pair of fans who were not carrying pens hoping for an autograph.

Approximately 500 of the nearly 13,000 people in attendance began to riot, throwing chairs and instigating fights. Many attempted to take their aggression out on the hated heels. A handful were arrested by a gang of police officers who quashed the violence. All four wrestlers had performed expertly, whipping the crowd into a frenzy. Their actions warranted a joint session before the no-nonsense New York Athletic Commission, which was getting tired of wrestling's anarchy. The unrest did nothing to help gates, and the December 9 show drew a mere 9,264.

The tension between the Kwariani-Johnston and the Mondt-McMahon factions remained, but the collaboration was paying huge dividends. Attendance figures of over 15,000 at the Garden became common, and the men added slices of the $40,000-plus gates to their bank accounts. In 1958, they packed the arena to the rafters for five out of 11 shows, including a record-breaking effort on May 24, where a throng of 20,335 inside left 8,000 on the sidewalk. That mark was broken on January 26, 1959, when a standing-room-only crowd of 21,240 observed the tumble of the Grahams by Perez and Rocca. The $63,896 paid also shattered the old gate figure.

As if the trumpeting for wrestling at the Garden wasn't loud enough already, McMahon used the Bridgeport (Connecticut) Knights of Columbus Hall, run by a family friend, Joseph Smith, to set up a second television program feeding into New York City. The series, starting on February 11, 1959, would be broadcast on WNEW-TV (channel 5) from 8:30-10:30 p.m., and combined with his Washington show, gave McMahon extensive range. He was now reaching fans from Virginia to Canada.

Mondt, an imposing man who had weighed 185 as a grappler and 325 pounds as a booker, opened Pittsburgh in 1960 from offices at the Plaza Building. With Mal Alberts and later, Bill Cardille as master of ceremonies of his studio wrestling telecast on WIIC (channel 11), Toots drew exceptional stats at the Civic Arena and Forbes Field. Though his presence in New York and Washington continued, it was McMahon who spearheaded Capitol's remarkable growth.

The stay of Doyle in Washington was relatively short, but as he marched into a role as matchmaker for Paul Bowser and Eddie Quinn in 1958, he maintained an affiliation with Capitol, and booked Edouard Carpentier into their cities. By the summer of 1959, Fred Kohler, who had formerly supplied wrestlers for clubs in the east, was in need of talent in Chicago to ward off Quinn's invasion.

The Bridgeport show was sold to WNBQ (channel 5) in Chicago, and premiered as *Heavyweight Wrestling* at midnight on Saturday, September 19, 1959. Kohler advertised his live programs during the broadcast, and scored an instant boost. His October 23 production drew the biggest house of the year — 5,020 fans paying more than $12,000. The status of grappling in Chicago would fluctuate, then rebound completely with Kohler's drive and the mixture of McMahon's wrestlers and TV.

McMahon's television exposure now gave him unparalleled leverage, and astute sports writers were anointing him as the national wrestling czar. Controlling a roster of some 50 competitors who remitted booking fees to the syndicate, McMahon furnished wrestlers to many promoters within "Capitol territory," covering 11 states. In addition to the income from the contracts of wrestlers, the company earned a cut of all shows its talent worked. The kickback could be as steep as 50 percent of the gross.

Among the promoters who acquired grapplers from McMahon through the years were Kohler, Fabiani, Gilzenberg, Johnston, Mondt, Zacko, Frank Tunney (Toronto), Al Haft (Columbus), Harry Light (Detroit), Abe Ford, (Boston), Arnold "Whitey" Carlson (Island Garden Arena), Arnold Skaaland (White Plains), Tom Lockhart (Long Island Arena), Ed Contos (Baltimore), Harry Smythe (Baltimore), The Feld Brothers (Baltimore), Joe "Smitty" Smith (Bridgeport), Larry Gale (New Haven), Bill Witchi (Providence), Ace Freeman (parts of Pennsylvania and Ohio), Charley Hoffman (Paterson), Roland Hines (Asbury Park), Al "Boomie" Soifer (Atlantic City), Billy Darnell (Hagerstown), and Al Gore (sections of Maryland and Virginia).

To balance the traditional good guy vs. bad guy scenario for his promotion, McMahon obtained the services of Buddy Rogers. Known as a prominent box office draw, the Nature Boy was the perfect antagonist, an arrogant showman who spurred angry crowds, and turned peaceful citizens into raving lunatics. Rogers was a remarkable anti-hero, playing right into the pockets of promoters and making a fortune for himself as the least humble of all wrestlers. Enthusiasts were provoked to holler at the golden-skinned, blond-haired egomaniac, and he earned points for even the simple aspects of his keenly sculptured routine. Fans wanted to see him knocked from his perch as he contorted his neck to look down at the peons in the audience.

Born Herman Gustave Rohde on February 20, 1921, the son of Herman and Freda, Rogers served in the Navy, and turned to professional wrestling on the circuit of Frank and Ray Hanly in New Jersey in the early 1940s. Tutored by the likes of Fred Grobmier, Joe Cox, and Rudy Dusek, he quickly rose to performance heights shared by the likes of Gorgeous George, then surpassed all of his counterparts with his durability as a star. Perfecting a type of grappling that could not be matched, Buddy had a wealth of dramatic holds, exaggerated facial expressions, and gimmicks that put him high above his competition. Buddy just had that something special that propelled a man from a modest background in Camden to international notoriety.

By 1957, Rogers was reportedly making close to $100,000 a year as a wrestler, and profiting from his efforts as a real-estate broker (Herman Rohde, Inc.) from his offices at 2031 Wayne Avenue in Haddon Heights, New Jersey. Consideration was given to making him NWA champion, but Thesz wouldn't approve the idea. Instead, the title was entrusted to the unproven Dick Hutton. Hutton upheld the honor some saw in the NWA title, but with the Alliance in decline at the time, Rogers might have been a better choice.

With or without the prestigious title, Buddy did his job. Even after 15 years in the industry as a top earner, he didn't have an ego that prevented him from laying down and seeing the lights. Rogers was willing to put people over, and understood the importance it had for a wrestler's salary. That was part of his wrestling appeal. Fans paid to see him lose, not to be an unbeatable warrior. In return, promoters gave Buddy an abundance of logical victories, stalemates with NWA champs Thesz and Hutton, and assorted regional championship belts.

Rogers remained on the west coast for most of 1958, then made his way back to Ohio in December, where he began 1959 employed by Al Haft. On September 16, 1959, he grabbed the Montreal "world" title from Wladek Kowalski, and won an unpopular victory over "Jersey" Joe Walcott in a wrestler vs. boxer match on October 7, 1959, before an audience of 10,000.

Rogers had a financial impact on Capitol right off the bat, and McMahon's campaign to magnify Buddy's character on TV, going into his Garden return on May 21, was hugely successful. The dream bout against Antonino Rocca drew an estimated 18,000 fans to the Garden, earning a gate of $53,000. The CWC's previous Garden endeavor had taken in only 6,400 spectators and a gate of $19,000, with Rocca and Miguel Perez wrestling the Grahams. Following the $53,000 gate in New York City, Buddy drew a record 16,521 in Washington D.C. on July 18 versus Bearcat Wright, then 30,275 for the rematch at Comiskey Park in Chicago on July 29.

McMahon, who was admitted into the NWA several months after the 1959 convention, revelled in the special designation bestowed upon his superstar by the coalition as early as May 1960. Rogers was sanctioned as United States heavyweight champion, seven years after the association had rejected a similar endorsement for Verne Gagne, and was awarded the belt by president Sam Muchnick. Wearing the championship strap for appointments in Chicago, Milwaukee, Charlotte, St. Louis, and across the expanded northeastern circuit, Buddy was the foremost attraction for a gaggle of NWA members who reaped the rewards of his labor. Kohler's *Wrestling Life* magazine appropriately named Rogers "Wrestler of the Year" in 1960.

At the summer 1960 session of the Alliance in Acapulco, Mondt and McMahon explored the possibility of passing the "world" championship to Buddy with the organization's leadership. The idea intrigued the assembly, particularly Muchnick,

Kohler, and Morris Sigel. A mobile Nature Boy could benefit the whole fraternity, and no doubt members of the NWA expected Rogers to also go into many towns run by affiliated promoters. It was universally held that the Alliance champion would tour cities big and small, and any notion of a monopolization of the title-holder's bookings seemed crazy.

There were vocal naysayers who were against putting the belt on Rogers, and perhaps the most influential was none other than Buddy's perpetual foe, Lou Thesz. McMahon was a shrewd businessman, and some believed he had only his own best interests at heart, but most members saw him as a team player. He was part of their exclusive union, and enormously persuasive. At the end of the day, McMahon's overall influence made an impression on voters.

The myopic championship committee green-lighted Rogers, and Chicago was chosen as the host site for the switch. Comiskey Park was lined up for several big programs by Kohler during the summer of 1961, and with Capitol's television coming in from Bridgeport, everything was in place for promoting the bout. The publicity actually commenced on November 11, 1960, when the two wrestlers appeared at the International Amphitheater for title defenses. Rogers was the acknowledged U.S. champion, and Pat O'Connor was defending his NWA world title. The *Chicago Daily Tribune* even noted that O'Connor was the "hero" and Rogers was the "villain," and that it was fitting that they would go head to head at one point or another.

Downtown Chicago was besieged by wrestling addicts from all over the country for the June 30, 1961, extravaganza. An estimated 38,000 paid in excess of $125,000 to see Buddy dethrone O'Connor for the NWA title. In the middle of the ring, Buddy was presented the belt by Kohler. Rogers thanked the promoter, and responded by telling the crowd, in his classically presumptuous manner, "To a nicer guy, it couldn't happen." Never before had a newly crowned NWA titleholder begun his reign with such flamboyance.

The traditional parameters surrounding the NWA world heavyweight title included a belt deposit or performance bond that was increased by the Alliance specifically for Buddy from $10,000 to $25,000. In letters, Willie Gilzenberg and Jack Pfefer speculated about the forfeit amount. Gilzenberg mentioned that Rogers could have been forced to deposit as much as $40,000 to "behave himself," and wrote on September 18, 1961, that the champion "must be satisfied that none of the boys will bother him."

A projected cycle of Rogers-O'Connor rematches was surprisingly limited to a single bout at Comiskey Park on September 1, 1961. They drew 20,015, a gate of $63,326, and ended with the champion retaining the belt by countout in the third fall. A tremendous amount of excitement was created by having a colorful showman as NWA titleholder, and arenas in places like Pittsburgh, Washington D.C., and New York City were turning fans away at the gates. Those attending Madison Square Garden events were very comfortable with the Nature Boy headlining. A week before Buddy won the title 15,675 packed the facility, and 17,698 were there on July 28, 1961, when he debuted as champ.

With Rogers the world titleholder, weaknesses in the system were exposed. Muchnick was registered as the champion's booker, but it was McMahon and Buddy who dictated the day-to-day calendar. They controlled the champ's dates, and it allowed McMahon to dominate his touring schedule, adding to a growing volatility inside the NWA. The booking of Rogers clearly favored engagements in the Northeast on Captiol's turf, and then after that to the political hierarchy of the Alliance. That meant Kohler in Chicago, Muchnick in St. Louis, Sigel in Texas, and Tunney in Toronto were locked in for dates.

Many other dues-paying members eagerly awaited Buddy's visit, but anticipation soon turned into acrimony and resentment. Sporadic visits to key locales in Texas and the Midwest eased some tension, but many regions were bypassed completely. It seemed clear that Mike London (Albuquerque), Salvador Lutteroth (Mexico City), Dr. Karl Sarpolis (Amarillo), Roy Welch and Nick Gulas (Nashville), Leroy McGuirk (Tulsa), Jim Crockett (Charlotte), Stu Hart (Calgary), Don Owen (Portland), and Cowboy Luttrall (Tampa) ran the nonessential territories of the NWA, and this group comprised half of the entire Alliance membership. Champions Thesz, Hutton, and O'Connor had met the needs of the whole membership, but Buddy's handlers were engineering a new trajectory that was doing more to divide the organization than unite it.

The Alliance was spinning into a complex web of animosity. At the expense of their associates, McMahon and his partners were getting wealthy off the hard labor of Rogers and the unique credibility that came with the title. The backlash from Capitol's monopolization had promoters threatening to break off and recognize their own champions. The mess endangered the stability of the NWA.

Did any of it necessarily matter? The dismantling of the Alliance was already on some promoter's minds, and the controversial reign of the Nature Boy may have been the excuse they were waiting for to finally get the job done.

As champion, Buddy was astonishing. He was a relentless worker, giving 100 percent, and audiences appreciated it. Playing to crowds, bleeding to sell the drama, and strutting around with the championship belt, Rogers was beloved and cursed simultaneously, sometimes by the same people. Between May 1960 and May 1963, he drew over a $1 million in gates in both Chicago and New York City. *Ring*

Billy Sandow, long before he was the manager of Ed "Strangler" Lewis, wrestled as "Chicago Sandow" on barnstorming tours, and was a talented middleweight.

Ed "Strangler" Lewis (left) and Billy Sandow (right) controlled professional wrestling for a period during the 1920s, effectively monopolizing all big-time grappling until the double-cross of Wayne Munn in 1925.

Before turning to wrestling full time, Toots Mondt (bottom) and his brother Ralph worked as clown comedians, mixing colorful antics and athletic exhibitions.

Toots Mondt displays his brute strength during a public training session.

The stipulations for a 1930 match at Madison Square Garden are reviewed before New York State Athletic Commission chairman William Muldoon (middle, sitting), as competitors Jim McMillen (second from left) and Jim Londos (second from right) look on. Promoter Jack Curley (far left) and his associates are also present (back row).

Tom Packs (middle), the Midwestern promotional czar, oversees a contract signing between Joe Stecher (left), who is accompanied by his brother Tony (left back), and Jim Londos (right), accompanied by promoter Joe Coffey (right back), for a match in St. Louis.

The "Golden Greek" Jim Londos was one of wrestling's most popular superstars, and a performer who outshone his contemporaries during the 1930s.

In wrestling history, they didn't come much tougher than the "Tigerman" John Pesek of Ravenna, Nebraska.

The Dusek Clan (Ernie, Emil, Rudy, and Joe) of Nebraska were also known as the Riot Squad for their wild tactics in and around the squared circle.

A student of wrestling in his youth, Al Haft was an avid proponent of legitimate grappling skills and taught many future legends at his Columbus, Ohio, gymnasium.

A promoter arranged a comical black tie photo-op for ten of his star grapplers on the sidewalk in front of his Chicago office, circa 1933. Fred Kohler is second from right.

The kingpin of women's wrestling, Billy Wolfe earned a notorious reputation for his questionable exploits with the women he traveled with, but took the form of grappling to new financial heights.

Mildred Burke, the Queen of Wrestling, had to deal with many inequities in the NWA system, especially the one barring women from annual conventions.

On behalf of the Tom Packs promotion and the
National Wrestling Association, Sam Muchnick
(left) presents new titleholder Ray Steele the
valuable championship belt in 1940.

"Wild" Bill Longson was a three-time National
Wrestling Association champion during the
1940s and the decade's top draw.

When Buddy Rogers (left) jumped
from the promotion of Tom Packs
(right) to Sam Muchnick in 1948,
the tides in the St. Louis wrestling
war began to shift.

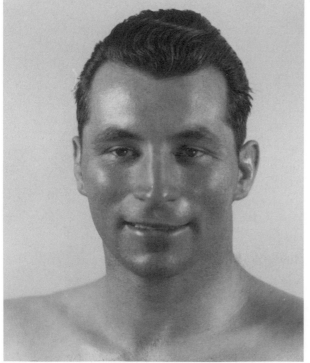

A former Olympian, Roy Dunn
was the first wrestler to be named
National Wrestling Alliance champion
in 1941 by promoters in Kansas.

Hungarian Ede Virag was an independent superstar and held the National Wrestling Alliance title in Kansas for most of 1942–46.

Ed McLemore, the Dallas promoter who boldly stood up to the NWA in 1953–54, presents a championship belt to Lillian Ellison, better known as The Fabulous Moolah.

Jack O'Brien (left) and Roy Graham (right) were unafraid of the possibility of being blacklisted and remained loyal to Dallas promoter Ed McLemore in 1953 in a bitter war with the NWA.

NWA champion Lou Thesz (left) and Ed "Strangler" Lewis (right) traveled together extensively in the 1950s and, in many ways, Lewis mentored the champion.

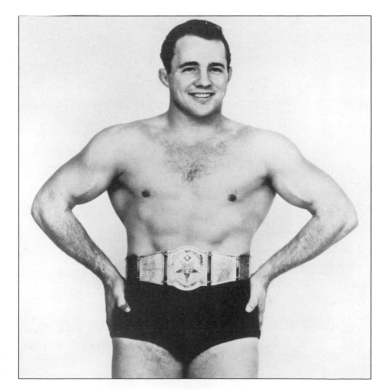

Verne Gagne, once regarded as a possible heir to Lou Thesz, never got a chance to be NWA champion. He was, however, AWA champion on nine occasions.

Michele Leone immersed himself in the "Baron" persona, taking wrestling's popularity in Southern California to a new plateau, then topping the previous national record with the first ever $100,000 gate in 1952.

U.S. Senator, presidential candidate and wrestling fan Estes Kefauver (left) shakes hands with his good friend "Argentine" Antonino Rocca. Kefauver and Senator John McClellan were regulars at the Capitol Arena in Washington.

After a tough match at Madison Square Garden, WWWF World Champion Bruno Sammartino shakes hands with the promotion's founder Vincent J. McMahon (left) and president Willie Gilzenberg (right).

Willie Gilzenberg (left), Toronto promoter Frank Tunney (middle), and Capitol Wrestling minority shareholder Bob Marella (Gorilla Monsoon, right) dine with their wives in Miami Beach.

In the Tampa office, Buddy Rogers (right) formally agrees to a match as promoter Cowboy Luttrall (left sitting) and matchmaker Eddie Graham look on.

High-flyer Edouard Carpentier was co-NWA champion for 71 days in 1957, but had his claim erased from the books when the Alliance decided to rewrite history.

Popular Wilbur Snyder was a clean cut California grappler with a diverse wrestling repertoire. He is seen here wearing Fred Kohler's controversial United States title belt.

NWA champion from 1966 to 1969, Gene "Big Thunder" Kiniski was a skilled wrestler, outstanding performer, and talented speaker. There was never a dull moment with him in the ring.

Fritz Von Erich was a shining star in wrestling circles and a successful promoter in Dallas. In 1975, he succeeded Sam Muchnick as NWA President.

Magazine named him Wrestler of the Year in 1961 and '62.

Throughout Buddy's run as titleholder, McMahon had to deal with the unexpected. On November 27, 1961, Rogers suffered a fractured arm in Washington and was out of commission for weeks. He then broke his right ankle early in a match with Killer Kowalski on November 21, 1962 in Montreal, an injury that kept him from the mat for almost two months. He was constantly pushing his body, wrestling a grueling itinerary, so mishaps were inevitable. But on the evening of August 31, 1962, he was yanked into a spontaneous backstage scuffle with two of the heaviest hitters in the business. It was no accident.

Rogers was in Columbus at the Fairgrounds Coliseum for a ordinary bout with Johnny Barend. Everything was going according to plan, when uninvited guests Karl Gotch and Bill Miller entered the dressing room and interrupted Buddy's discussion with promoter Al Haft. The calm environment quickly escalated to the point of violence, and the 75-year-old Haft was in no position to get between the temperamental grapplers. Rogers and Miller had a history, and had battled on numerous occasions in Ohio for Haft, while Gotch was an ex-Olympian trained by Billy Riley at Wigan.

The confrontation rapidly deteriorated into a lopsided fistfight. Rogers, the blustering loner, suffered an injured left arm and wrenched neck, and was treated at University Hospital. Each of those involved had a different version of events, but Buddy's conversation with police and Franklin County Prosecutor Bernard Chupka was the one that held the most consequence. Charges were filed against Gotch and Miller, and an arrest warrant was issued. On September 2, the wrestlers turned themselves in to police and were released on $25 bond.

Rogers spoke to reporters at the Montreal Forum and he was quoted in a column in the November 8, 1962, edition of the *Montreal Star*: "It's a mystery to me. I was in my room, when these two guys walked in, and said they had come to make a challenge. Before I could ask them what challenge, one grabbed me from behind, the other started hammering me in front. They dragged me over to the door of the room, jammed my left arm in, and then began slamming the door against it. Obviously they were trying to break my arm, but before they could do that, I got free, but fell, and they gave me the boots. My arm was very badly bruised. Why, I don't know. But I do know I've had all I want of Ohio for wrestling purposes. I sold my home there, and moved back to Camden, New Jersey. Promoter Al Haft, of Columbus, has telephoned me several times to come back, but never again."

Miller denied that the trauma to the champion's arm had been deliberate. He admitted that Buddy was slapped by the two men, but denied they intended to harm him. But the intimidation by Bill and Karl did its job, and Rogers was true to his word that he wouldn't revisit Columbus as NWA champ. He distanced himself from Haft and the city he once ruled.

The tough man ruling Capitol had a political mind and kept open communication with promoters across the country. He attended conventions and understood the bottom line of the Alliance. Thirteen months into the reign of Rogers, and notwithstanding the weak position of the NWA, McMahon was honored by the coalition. In August 1962, he was elected second vice president at the annual meeting in St. Louis. McMahon served with president Doc Sarpolis, the Amarillo promoter who had never received a single booking for the Nature Boy.

Muchnick appealed to the always-durable Lou Thesz on behalf of those in the NWA longing for a clean slate and a new move toward unity. McMahon wasn't alarmed. He knew promoters were looking to oust Rogers, but still didn't see the advantages of having the championship on Thesz. The territory was thriving, and Capitol wanted to explore other options for a heavyweight king.

McMahon understood that Rogers losing the title was inevitable. Instead of following the Alliance into the next phase, Vince took his corporation and assembled his own bloc of promoters. It wasn't set up so much in opposition to the NWA, or even in spite of the NWA, but he envisioned a territory that fell under his sanctioning authority, supporting a champion he approved, and watched the television he produced. Capitol Wrestling was now big enough to run its own, private champion, permanently.

Rogers missed a scheduled match with Thesz on November 29, then the final Madison Square Garden show of the year on December 10, due to the ankle injury he suffered in Montreal. With his belt deposit at stake, Buddy was compelled to wrestle Thesz in Toronto on January 24, 1963. The deed was done, and despite the loss, Buddy returned to the Northeast as the Capitol titleholder. The match in Toronto was ignored. It was a bold move, yet fundamental to McMahon's plans. The early whispers out of Capitol's camp suggested that Rogers retained his title over Thesz because the bout had only gone one fall, but had to take a different route when Buddy lost in three falls on February 7.

A story was conjured up and disseminated: Rogers won the "World Wide Wrestling Federation" (WWWF) title in a tournament at Rio de Janeiro. It was all kayfabe. To give Rogers credibility as champion, McMahon needed to create a new series of events to highlight their split from the National Wrestling Alliance, and the Northeastern populace proved very open to his imaginative concept. McMahon had an excellent earner in Rogers, Rocca was still in the fold, and he was making a play to pull Bruno Sammartino out of Toronto.

McMahon was first introduced to Bruno Laopardo Franceso Sammartino, an extraordinarily strong athlete from Pittsburgh, in 1959. He saw potential greatness. A short while later, Sammartino made his inaugural appearance at the Garden on January 2, 1960, he was in a bout second from the top, confirming Capitol's high expectations for the young phenom.

Although inexperienced, Sammartino held his own, matching with Kowalski, Mighty Zuma, and Karl Von Hess. He teamed with Rocca to beat Great Antonio and Pampero Firpo at the Garden on June 4, 1960. They partnered again at the Garden on August 6 and August 27, 1960, triumphing over Dr. Jerry Graham and Firpo, and the Tolos Brothers, and wrestled each other twice on October 24 and November 14. The first bout ended with Rocca winning via disqualification. The rematch was a draw.

Burdened by the travel demands, Bruno scaled back his commitment to wrestling to spend time with his family. He was impressed with the money, however, and through February 1961, was an essential player at the Garden. Very much out of character and possibly against the wishes of McMahon, Sammartino joined Rocca for an assignment in San Francisco on March 4, 1961.

The west coast excursion forced Sammartino to miss a date in Baltimore, resulting in the Maryland State Athletic Commission's referral of his suspension to the recharged National Wrestling Association. On March 6, 1961, the Association banned Bruno in member states until the situation was resolved. McMahon eventually stepped in and assisted Bruno in clearing his name. Sammartino was a diamond in the rough, a grappler worthy of having a promotion built around him, and McMahon was as enthusiastic about him as Toots was about Rocca 15 years earlier.

In late 1962, McMahon made additional accommodations with Cleveland promoter Larry Atkins. Their union called for the establishment of the World Wide Wrestling Association (wwwA), headed by Mondt and Gilzenberg. Cleveland had promise, and McMahon believed the new organization could provide another vital stop for talent traveling back and forth between the Northeast and Chicago. With the new venture still in the preliminary stages, McMahon sent workers to breathe life into the idea.

Rogers was billed as the champion in Cleveland in matches with Bobo Brazil, Edouard Carpentier, and Killer Kowalski until losing his wwwA title to Dory Dixon on March 28 at the Arena. Atkins announced that he was trying to arrange a mixed bout between boxer Cassius Clay (Muhammad Ali) and Rogers that might demolish attendance records.

On April 11, 1963, Buddy wrestled Sammartino at a Capitol Arena TV taping for broadcast on April 18. The anticipated match ended in a no contest, and Rogers was given a championship belt sanctioned by the World Wide Wrestling Federation. The prize wasn't entirely unfamiliar to Buddy, as it was his old United States strap, the trophy he'd been lugging from town to town after dropping the NWA title.

Around the same time, Cleveland newspapers reported that promoters were designing a belt for the victor of the Dixon–Karl Von Hess World Wide Wrestling Association championship affair on May 2, won by Von Hess. Capitol Wrestling had two new wrestling organizations, and, within a short period, had awarded championship belts to the respective champions.

Buddy's life took a sudden twist after the loss to Thesz. In Ottawa for a contest with "Bulldog" Brower on April 16, 1963, Rogers felt an overwhelming pain in his chest and went to a hospital. The intense stinging he felt had grown in the weeks and months prior, culminating in a sudden need for medical aid. He braved a flight the next day to Pittsburgh, where he was booked in a six man tag-team match at the Civic Arena, but a doctor refused to grant authorization following a pre-bout checkup and Rogers's admission of sustained chest pain.

On the morning of Thursday, April 18, Rogers was thoroughly examined at Mercy Hospital in Pittsburgh, then went to Cleveland, where he was scheduled to wrestle WWWA champion Dory Dixon. Unable to compete in Cleveland, Rogers was hospitalized for the third time in three days. He stayed in Cleveland through the weekend, missing a match in Boston on Saturday.

Booked in Ottawa on April 23, Rogers pulled out and was replaced by Jolly Charlie against Bobo Brazil. The morning of the program, the *Ottawa Citizen* reported he had suffered a heart attack Sunday at a Cleveland hospital. In fact, no one was quite sure what had happened, but a heart attack seemed to be the simplest explanation. Buddy's prognosis was grave, and for the resilient grappler, the health scare frightened him to his core. He was in absolutely no condition to wrestle, and doctors wanted him stabilized and resting. Pressured to return to grappling, Buddy was back in the ring less than two weeks later, but in a restricted capacity.

The news was devastating to Capitol Wrestling. McMahon immediately changed course, and hastened the push of Sammartino. The newfangled plan certainly required Buddy's assistance. It was essential that the wrestler's illness was kept quiet, and nobody outside a small circle could know exactly what had happened. Only a few media outlets had mentioned his medical condition since mid-April, and that was the way McMahon needed it to avoid a detailed evaluation by the New York Athletic Commission.

McMahon was also an "associate member" in the National Wrestling Association, a group of athletic-commission appointees known for their scrupulous regulation of medical conditions. The NWA regularly suspended wrestlers at the slightest sign of a health issue or infraction.

If word of Buddy's condition got out, the Association would not hesitate to add his name to the list of the indefinitely suspended, and preclude him from performing in any member states. The New York Commission would certainly respect that judgment, and kill any chance for a match that passed the title to Sammartino at the Garden. Buddy was just months removed from being on the NWA's disqualified list for ankle and knee injuries. Officials would not think twice about barring the Nature Boy for his current physical problems. In the meantime, Rogers couldn't miss a scheduled booking because that, too, would have triggered a ban.

Rogers was secretly examined at several facilities, and after a few brief appearances in essential cities, he fulfilled the date at the Garden on May 17, 1963. He squeezed past a house physician, entering the ring as the defending champion in front of a sold-out house. McMahon and his cohorts had hidden the illness brilliantly, and pushed Buddy into the ring for a match that Rogers later claimed could have killed him. The struggle lasted a whopping 48 seconds. Buddy submitted to a bear hug, and Sammartino won the WWWF title. The way in which Sammartino captured the belt helped put him over with the New York audience and endeared him to fans worldwide.

McMahon was the second vice president of the NWA when the WWWF was founded, and kept his fellow promoters apprised of what was going on in his territory. On June 3, 1963, Mondt promoted Bruno's first match as champion in Sammartino's native Pittsburgh. In the crowd were NWA members Muchnick, Frank Tunney, Morris Sigel, and Jim Crockett, and promoters Gilzenberg, Fabiani, Quinn, Ned Irish, and Jules Strongbow. In August, McMahon was replaced in his Alliance position by Crockett. Although the WWWF was now its own entity, Vince kept ties to the NWA, attending meetings, sharing talent, and extending his friendship to affiliates.

Capitol Wrestling no longer needed Rogers around, and a series of bouts between the ex-champ and Sammartino for the summer were cancelled. Buddy would leave under shoddy circumstances with a serious grudge, but his time as an attraction was over, due to his health concerns and an injury suffered at a spa in South Florida. He tried several comebacks, but was hampered by pain, and in 1979, he passed the torch to "Nature Boy" Ric Flair.

At the age of 68, in July 1989, Rogers encountered a man verbally harassing two employees of a sandwich shop. He bravely stepped in, and the exchange turned violent. The 30-year-old aggressor threw a chair, resulting in 14 stitches to Buddy's lip, but Rogers regrouped, and pummeled the man until he begged for mercy.

Afterward, he told the *Fort Lauderdale Sun Sentinel*, in his confident style: "That guy couldn't hurt me. I could be dead six months, and they could stand me up, and I'd still be able to beat him." The often imitated, but never duplicated Buddy Rogers passed away on June 26, 1992 at the age of 71.

As matchmaker, and later promoter, at Madison Square Garden, McMahon soon generated more revenue with Sammartino than during his days with Rocca and Rogers. What were the chances he'd discover a better draw than Argentina Rocca or the Nature Boy? But because he had, his wrestling company flourished more than any other in the United States.

Rocca also parted ways with bitterness, and ran opposition in New York with the proprietor of the Sunnyside Gardens. The small promotion was no match for McMahon's ventures. Vince's plans for Chicago, and for the WWWA in Cleveland ceased in 1963 after a refocusing of objectives closer to home.

In January 1964, McMahon's lease of the Capitol Arena expired, and he was given the opportunity to relocate by the Washington Orphan Asylum, the owners, who planned to raze the structure. Vince moved his weekly programs to the National Roller Skating Rink, also known as the National Arena (17th street and Kalorama Road), in July 1965.

Noted sportswriter Morris "Mo" Siegel took over the television analysis from Bill Malone for the D.C. show in early October 1956. However, fans of the program, among them J. Edgar Hoover and numerous members of congress, saw the bulk of the announcing supplied by Ray Morgan (Raymond Storrs Morgan). Morgan was the host on WTTG from the late 1950s until May 1966, when the station abolished the Thursday offering because of declining popularity, continuing on WDCA (channel 20) through August 23, 1970.

The ever-changing television environment regularly required McMahon to reconfigure his vast empire. His Thursday night Washington program was shown live in New York from June 21, 1956, to October 8, 1964, on WABD/WNEW (channel 5) and with the Bridgeport telecast, *Heavyweight Wrestling from Connecticut*, (initially in prime time on Wednesdays, then switched to Saturday nights) gave Capitol exposure to a massive segment of the television wrestling audience.

The Bridgeport show was presented on WNEW from February 11, 1959, until April 30, 1966, in a variety of time slots. The loss of TV in New York persuaded McMahon to suspend all Garden events from late March until November 7, 1966, and then depend on his new Saturday afternoon program on WOR-9, which debuted on August 20 with Washington tapes.

Much to the chagrin of Capitol, executives at WOR shifted wrestling from Saturday afternoons to 12:30 in the morning on Sundays, beginning April 23, 1967.

The Washington show stayed in that slot until it was cancelled on August 13. McMahon's October 23, 1967, Garden card, without TV, drew 6,612 fans, and the numbers weren't likely to improve.

It was a former wrestling play-by-play man from Newark, Fred Sayles, who brought television coverage back in New York City. Sayles, program director of the ultra high-frequency station WNJU-TV (channel 47), had worked for Gilzenberg at WATV in the halcyon days of television, and made arrangements with McMahon to broadcast his tapes from Washington. Commencing on November 11, 1967, National Arena footage was on Saturdays at 7:00 p.m and was the primary show promoting wrestling at the Garden.

The Washington tapes continued on channel 47 until May 31, 1969, when McMahon's telecasts were erased from the schedule once again. His June 30, 1969, Garden event drew less than 5,600 without the added publicity, which prompted cancellation of a show planned for July 21. On August 30, 1969, Vince introduced footage from Philadelphia in New York City on Saturdays in prime time on WNJU and the market began to redevelop. Within a year, he was selling out the Garden and attaining gates in excess of $70,000.

"It's bigger than ever," McMahon said regarding wrestling in his region in the *Washington Post, Times Herald* on November 7, 1969. "I have a territory of some 15 states and the District of Columbia and it's like a franchise would be in football or baseball. I tape weekly wrestling shows right here in Washington and these are syndicated. We bicycle them around the country. Sammartino has never earned less than $100,000 a year for the last ten years, and the average wrestler can make between $40,000 and $50,000 a year."

In September 1971, financial problems terminated McMahon's standard Washington programs, which were bringing in $1,000 per week, commercially, $1,500 less than when they started at the National Arena six years earlier. McMahon assumed the drop in attendance was related to a general anxiety about the venue's neighborhood.

The rental costs of buildings in the metropolitan areas of Washington, New York, Baltimore, and Philadelphia were now far too expensive to fit Capitol's needs. McMahon and Zacko found cheaper buildings in Hamburg (Fieldhouse) and Allentown (Agriculture Hall) that were used to tape for broadcast in larger cities. That way, their overall income easily exceeded expenditures, with equal results on the programming side.

While there were failures and controversies, the WWWF maintained its worth as a wrestling promotion. With creative booking, an impressive list of enemies to pit against Sammartino, and a colorful cast of grapplers, McMahon's operations prospered throughout his tenure. On January 29, 1968, Capitol held the final wrestling program at the "old" Madison Square Garden (8th Avenue), and the first at the modern venue on 33rd street, above Penn Station, on February 19, 1968.

In 1971, McMahon and Sammartino, worried about overexposure, decided it was time for Bruno to step down. Sammartino dropped the title on January 18 to Ivan Koloff (Oreal Donald Perras) before 21,106 fans. The next major fan favorite to rise to the WWWF title was Pedro Morales, who captured the championship at the Garden on February 8.

Mindful of the pros and cons of being a member, McMahon rejoined the NWA at the 1971 convention in Mexico City. One requirement by the Alliance was that Morales's WWWF championship be recognized as a regional heavyweight title, and not a "world" title. The alignment with the NWA would be especially beneficial after McMahon was introduced to a 6´11´´, 400-pound wrestler from Grenoble, France, by way of Quebec. Frank Valois brought Andre Rene Roussimoff, identified as Monster Roussimoff and Jean Ferre, to McMahon's doorstep in 1973, and Vince rapidly signed Andre to a contract.

McMahon spoke about Andre, in the December 21, 1981, issue of *Sports Illustrated*:

> My initial thought was, "My god. I never saw such a man." I'd seen photographs and videotapes, of course, and I knew Andre was 7´4´´ (sic) and over 400 pounds, but I simply wasn't prepared for how he looked up close. He was unlike anything I'd ever seen before, and I knew he could become the number one draw in wrestling. I saw right away that Andre needed to be booked into a place no more than a few times a year. Most of our men work one of our circuits for a while and then move to another. It keeps things fresh. A guy may work New England for a few months, for instance, go from there to the south, and then on out to spend some time with Verne Gagne in Minneapolis.
>
> But Andre's different. The whole world is his circuit. By making his visits few and far between, he never becomes commonplace. Now, wherever he goes, the gates are larger than they would be without him. I book him for three visits a year to Japan, two to Australia, two to Europe, and the rest of the time I book him into the major arenas in the U.S. The wrestlers and promoters all want him on their cards, because when the Giant comes, everyone makes more money.

At the 1973 meeting of the NWA, McMahon proposed that Roussimoff, renamed "Andre the Giant," make a tour of the entire Alliance, similar to that of the NWA champion himself. With his exaggerated height and billed as the "Eighth Wonder of the World," Andre realized the potential McMahon saw in him. Embracing his national fame, Andre appeared on the *Tonight Show* with host Joey Bishop in August 1974, and was considered for a spot as a linebacker for the Washington Redskins in the summer of 1975.

The Garden ran between nine and twelve shows annually, and, in terms of gate figures, stood as the single most successful wrestling venue in the country. On September 30, 1972, the first of three Shea Stadium events were held by McMahon, but inclement weather diminished what could have been an astronomical crowd for a match between Sammartino and Morales. Still, 22,508 fans paid a record $140,923 and watched their idols wrestle 75 minutes to a draw.

The acclaim for Morales was similar to that of Sammartino, but in December 1973, Bruno regained the heavyweight championship, winning the belt from interim champion Stanley Stasiak (George Stipich). In the years that followed, Sammartino had notable feuds with Killer Kowalski, Nikolai Volkoff, Spiros Arion, Chief Jay Strongbow, Waldo Von Erich, and George Steele. On June 25, 1976, Sammartino battled his arch enemy Stan Hansen, the man blamed for fracturing a vertebrae in Bruno's neck in April, at Shea Stadium. That night, 32,897 fans watched the champion retain his championship, a three-round boxer vs. wrestler match between Andre the Giant and Chuck Wepner, and then the lethargic Muhammad Ali-Antonio Inoki 15-round draw on closed-circuit television.

"Superstar" Billy Graham (Eldridge Wayne Coleman), a sophisticated eccentric, enjoyed a nine-month reign as wwwf champion from April 1977 to February 1978. He ended Sammartino's final stretch as titleholder, and proved that a heel champ could again pay off at the box office. On a recommendation from Muchnick, McMahon hired Bob Backlund in 1977, and Backlund was able to sell his Midwestern personality to Northeastern audiences. He went over Graham on February 20, 1978, beginning a lengthy run as wwwf champion.

For marketing purposes, the World Wide Wrestling Federation became the "World Wrestling Federation" in the spring of 1979. McMahon's innovations and creative booking produced a North American gate record for the wwf's Showdown at Shea on August 9, 1980. The heated rivalry between Sammartino and his protégé Larry Zbyszko drew 40,717 fans with a gate of $537,421.

On June 6, 1982, McMahon, Arnold Skaaland, Robert Marella, and Phil Zacko sold their stock in Capitol Wrestling to Vincent Kennedy McMahon of Greenwich for a reported $1 million. Vincent Kennedy, called "Vinnie" or "Junior," was the second son of Vincent and Victoria Elizabeth "Vicky" Hanner McMahon, and was the president of Titan Sports, Inc. Born on August 24, 1945, in Moore County, North Carolina, Vince was the product of a broken home, and endured much abuse in his youth. His middle name, Kennedy, was taken in honor of his maternal grandmother Victoria Kennedy Hanner.

Joining his father in the grappling business following his graduation from East Carolina University in 1968, McMahon was an entrepreneur in every sense of the word, and his purchase of Capitol showed his enthusiasm for professional wrestling. He did not respect the venerable territorial barriers that had been protected by promoters for decades, and the NWA was in real jeopardy with him on the prowl. After the purchase, Jr. became the president and treasurer of Capitol, while his wife Linda functioned as vice president and secretary. His father remained attached as an advisor.

Known for always being on the telephone discussing business, McMahon Senior dabbled in boxing, even holding a stake in light heavyweight champion Bobby Foster in the late 1960s. Vincent was an insightful gentleman, and his ability to carefully select the right people to handle important tasks gave him a crucial advantage. In a universe of thieves, he found trustworthy allies who treasured his friendship. The people around him were essential to the daily operations of Capitol, and without them, McMahon would not have achieved the same level of success. In return, he never abandoned his most loyal allies.

Toots retired as a member of Capitol Wrestling's Board of Directors in 1969. He served as the company's vice president from 1958–59, then from 1961 to 1969, and after leaving the business, kept close to McMahon as an consultant.

Outside of Mondt, McMahon's most influential partner in the expansion of the WWWF was William "Willie" Gilzenberg, the federation's president from 1963 to 1978. Gilzenberg, born on October 24, 1901, became a pioneering promoter with Thomas "Babe" Culnan part of Newark's Laurel Sports Activities, Inc. Exceptionally experienced in TV production and smartly connected, Gilzenberg was a respected leader in professional sports. His promotional license was renewed by the New Jersey Athletic Commission for more than 50 consecutive years, and he managed the WWWF main office in Newark. He passed away in Miami Beach on November 15, 1978, leaving his wife Lillian and daughter Holly.

Philip Paul Zacko was Capitol secretary from 1957 to 1982 and vice president from 1971 to 1982. He held promoter's licenses in Pennsylvania and Maryland, staging shows in Philadelphia, Baltimore, Landover, and Harrisburg. In the Washington office, veteran booker and assistant Herbert Freeman performed secretarial duties from 1963 until his death in April 1966. James Dudley, a native of Baltimore, was another devoted friend of the McMahons, and managed the Capitol Arena in the 1950s. He was a second for Bobo Brazil, chauffered dignitaries, and was a gate collector. Capitol Wrestling's bookkeeper was Bernard Yockelson, and McMahon relied heavily on publicity work from Joseph Holman and Dominic Consentino.

Edward "Ned" Irish was the executive director at Madison Square Garden and instrumental in the popularization of amateur and professional basketball. He was also involved with wrestling at the Garden, dealing with McMahon and Charles Johnston. The Johnston Family had been associated with wrestling at the Garden since 1949, and Charley took on the pivotal role of promoter following the death of his brother Bill in 1950.

The Johnston's corporate office (Johnston Enterprises) at 1476 Broadway, room 809, was managed by nephew Walter Smallshaw, often incorrectly listed as "Walter Johnston," a sibling of the famous tribe: Charley, William, Ned, and Jimmy Johnston. Smallshaw operated the Glendale Sporting Club that presided over the St. Nicholas Arena, and was occasionally referred to as the Garden wrestling promoter in newspapers. Charley Johnston and Smallshaw were dependent on matchmaker Kola Kwariani — a sharp former wrestler who regularly bumped heads with McMahon — and received additional aid from publicist Vic Scutari, Bertie Briscoe, and George Moxley. Charley maintained his position until his death on September 16, 1969.

In 1971, Vince McMahon Sr. and his second wife Juanita relocated their primary residence from Gaithersburg, Maryland, to Plantation, Florida, in the suburbs of Fort Lauderdale. On Sunday night, May 27, 1984, he died of cancer. At the time of his death, his son was systematically dismantling the National Wrestling Alliance, and replacing it with a potent monopoly of his own.

From room 751 of the Franklin Park Hotel in Washington, Vincent McMahon had run a $2 million-a-year wrestling business, formed the WWWF, and mentored his clever son. At present, Vince Jr. is the chairman of the board for World Wrestling Entertainment, Inc., a publicly traded company with annual revenue of over $350 million.

CHAPTER THIRTEEN

NWA WORLD HEAVYWEIGHT CHAMPIONS

(1948–1975)

Recognition by the members of the National Wrestling Alliance as world heavyweight champion was acknowledged as the pinnacle of professional wrestling for more than 40 years. While great credibility was brought to the AWA and WWWF titles by champions Verne Gagne and Bruno Sammartino, respectively, the NWA world heavyweight title remained the most cherished crown in the industry. Wrestling purists appreciated the fact that NWA champions proudly wore their laurels as they traversed numerous states, territories, and countries. The circuits of the AWA and WWWF were distinctively localized, and even when the NWA began to downsize, their champion maintained a more challenging itinerary than any rival titleholder.

Lou Thesz weathered the excessive touring, one of the harshest aspects of professional wrestling, and made it look easy. Sam Muchnick was comfortable in booking Thesz for dates in such diverse locations as the Olympic Auditorium and the International Amphitheater, and then in towns like Sparta, Illinois, or Hannibal, Missouri. He was a rock-solid workhorse who would wrestle his heart out in a town with a population under 5,000, perhaps in front of a few hundred, exactly as he would before 10,000 at an arena in St. Louis.

The selection process for a heavyweight champion required a certain amount of foresight. NWA members scrutinized the candidates, examining each individual's likely effect on their businesses and the wrestler's ability to adapt to the daunting role. The nominee usually necessitated a clean-cut image and couldn't rely on an overly elaborate gimmick. Wrestling was full of offbeat characters, but the champion's eccentric behavior had to be minimal. Charisma was a plus, as was an ability to relate to audiences.

The ability to shoot, or wrestle a "real" competition to safeguard the championship, was a requirement. Thesz was a monster hooker with few rivals, and Pat O'Connor's amateur credentials also measured up to the standards. Not only was Dick Hutton an NCAA champion and an ex-Olympian, he was a mammoth grappler who could demolish a foe if pushed the wrong way. Whipper Watson and Buddy Rogers were more performers than shooters, but tough enough to wiggle out of a sticky situation if caught in a double-cross. The need for legitimate skills diminished as years passed, and by the 1980s, it was almost a non-issue.

Stamina was essential. To cover the extensive circuit of NWA members, the touring champion had to be able to handle the most grueling schedule in pro wrestling. The constant traveling was physically and mentally taxing, and the athlete who held the position had to balance a whole range of responsibilities. Sustaining a healthy lifestyle, conditioning, and training while touring various towns was exceptionally difficult.

The matches themselves were another series of challenges. The champion needed to be able to fluctuate between being the all-encompassing "good" guy and a heel, depending on the night's specific opponent. He was responsible for boosting the esteem of the local headliner, and, rather than come off as an invincible superhero, was to make his rival look as if he was capable of winning the prized championship.

"Broadways," or one-hour draws, were used by promoters to sell a story, and, again, set up the critical second bout. It was imperative that the champion have the endurance and skills to wrestle a technical 60 minutes, or a five-minute brawl, depending on the evening's assignment. The champion had to be a master of psychology, and proficient in all areas of marketing, from mainstream interviews to pre-match promos. It didn't matter if he was in Waco or Los Angeles, the mat king had to preserve the position's integrity, projecting an image that could be admired by fans.

With these expectations in mind, the members of the board voted based on their opinions, and some champions were able to match those pre-conceived goals, while others exceeded them and more. Despite a tremendous workload, the heavyweight titleholder pushed his limits to meet the constant demands of affiliated promoters. No matter how they stood in comparison to their peers, the NWA champions wrote their names into the history books forever, and hold a distinction less than one percent of all wrestlers share.

The NWA, beginning in 1948, created a new title lineage with no ties to Frank Gotch or Jim Londos, but one that set a benchmark for all of professional wrestling. These are the heavyweight champions of the National Wrestling Alliance. . . .

When the National Wrestling Alliance expanded from the backyard of Pinkie George in July 1948, **Orville Brown** was the champion of record. He was endorsed as the champion by both George's Des Moines version of the Alliance, and by the Midwest Wrestling Association in Kansas City. People were unaware Brown had been the central states' most influential booker since the early 1940s. His position as the leading wrestler *and* booker gave him unparalleled power, but Orville was smart about it. He never abused his status, but creatively scripted scenarios that were less like squash matches and more like the evenly contested bouts audiences thrived on.

Brown conspired with George and Tony Stecher to create a sanctioning body that recognized and promoted a single heavyweight champion. The close connections of those involved in the Alliance would help the movement of wrestlers from territory to territory, and instead of multiplying the number of turf wars, it had the potential to nip them in the bud. Brown not only became the Alliance's world champion from the outset, but was the central states initial member-booker.

Orville was born on March 10, 1908, in the Cedar Township of Barber County, Kansas, near the city of Sharon, southwest of Wichita. He was the fifth child of farmers Clarence (1870–1936) and Ellen Elizabeth Brown (1878–1920), who had moved from Eureka during the 1910s. Before Orville turned two years of age, his father vanished. His mother struggled to provide the necessities for her five young children, and farmed extensively in the Nippawalla area to make ends meet. After losing his mother as well in 1920, Orville lived with his brothers, and attended high school.

An adroit rancher, Orville took home district rodeo honors. On October 13,

1927, he married Grace Charlotte, the daughter of William and Violet Springer of Riley County, Kansas. When the 1930 census was recorded, Orville and Grace were living in the Springer household with their infant son Richard, born on July 17, 1929. Orville labored as a road worker, and studied to become a blacksmith. Within months, he moved his family across the state to Wallace, where he took up his new occupation.

Orville's physical size made him a natural for professional wrestling, and a 42-year-old farmer and wrestler named Ernest Brown (no relation) of Harrison took to training him in the basics. The education Orville received under the watch of Ernest quickly paid off. On September 2, 1932, he beat veteran Alan Eustace (1891–1972) for the state championship. Within a year, he was active in the Northeast, where he was exposed to a level of showmanship he'd never seen before.

Brown went to a number major wrestling cities, including Chicago, Detroit, St. Louis, Houston, Philadelphia, and New York City, building his range as a grappler and as a performer. Both skills were necessary to make serious money in the profession. Putting in his time, he progressed from a preliminary grappler to a semi-finalist, and settled in as a perennial main-eventer. Brown began making regular appearances in Kansas City, where George Simpson ran weekly at the Memorial Hall. On June 13, 1940, he beat Bobby Bruns for his first "world" title, and his popularity continued to skyrocket.

During the tumultuous 1940s, Orville was a steady source of entertainment for the public. He traded his MWA title a number of times with high caliber opponents, demonstrating that he wasn't one to sit on his laurels. Brown knew that title movement, and even losses, fueled a wrestler's draw if booked correctly. Kansas City exchanged wrestlers with Pinkie George in Des Moines, and Pinkie became Orville's staunchest supporter. Brown's fame spread throughout the central states, and facilities were packed with his name on the bill. The innovative system of booking helped keep business brisk.

A number of things were done to protect Brown's affairs after the expansion of the Alliance in July 1948. As NWA champion, no one could know that he was also the matchmaker in Kansas City. To hide that fact, Brown employed Pearl Millard Christy (1915–2000) as his office manager. Christy, originally from Clear Creek, Ohio, was married to Hazel, the sister of Orville's wife Grace. In addition to the duties in the Kansas City booking office at 3908 Baltimore, Christy promoted Sedalia, and later ran Wichita after the departure of Bill Atkinson. Orville was referred to as "Wallace" on all correspondence mentioning booking or the promotions of matches.

While champion, Brown toured the enlarged NWA circuit, including

Hollywood, Salt Lake City, Minneapolis, Winnipeg, Calgary, and Houston. In St. Louis, Brown appeared for Sam Muchnick, a promoter then in a booking war with National Wrestling Association champion Lou Thesz. Thesz and Muchnick signed a peace accord in mid-1949, and the two outfits merged. The move led to the planning of a unification match between Brown and Thesz to determine a single "NWA" champion. A bout was arranged for St. Louis on November 25, 1949, and the preparations were underway when the unthinkable happened.

The *Bethany Republican Clipper* (Bethany, Missouri) reported on November 1, 1949, that an accident occurred at 1:00 that morning on U.S. highway 69, three miles north of Eagleville. Two professional wrestlers were driving from Des Moines to Kansas City when their 1949 Cadillac sedan ran under the bottom of a stalled tractor-trailer on the side of the road. At the wheel of the car was NWA champion Orville Brown. His passenger was his best friend and ring enemy, Bobby Bruns. They both survived the crash, but awestruck people at the scene, seeing what was left of their automobile, wondered how. The wrestlers would not walk away unscathed.

Taken to Bethany Hospital, Brown and Bruns were in dire need of medical attention, and Orville's condition was much more critical. Little did anyone know at the time that his ring career was already over. Orville had numerous cuts on his forehead, scalp, right forearm, right hand, and an injury to his right eye. He was conscious during the initial treatment, but soon fell into a coma that lasted five days. A suspected brain injury was revealed and Orville was paralyzed on his right side. Bruns suffered a fractured right shoulder and strained neck. Represented by William Varner Mayse, Orville was awarded a $35,000 settlement for the accident in Harrison County (MO) Circuit Court on May 16, 1950.

Bruns bounced back from his injuries and resumed wrestling. Not so fortunate, Orville's rehabilitation took months. Though it was soon clear that he wouldn't be the athlete he once was, he never gave up trying to recover. An attempt at a comeback in October 1950 was gallant, but proved conclusively that his wrestling days were over. The Alliance, at its convention in November 1949, awarded the title to Thesz, and Brown returned to life as a booker.

Always ambitious, Orville formed a corporation with Pinkie George, Brown-George Wrestling, Inc., in September 1955 that combined Brown's booking agency with George's Iowa operations. Their increasing influence troubled many promoters in the region. Orville's "co-directors" in the central states booking office, Simpson and Gust Karras, were already outspoken critics of the purported monopoly held by Brown, George and the NWA, and backed Sonny Myers in his court case against Pinkie. They wanted nothing more than to destabilize the enterprises of Brown, and accomplished that when they aligned themselves with Muchnick. The merger, essentially a double-cross, secured wrestlers for Kansas City and St. Joseph without Brown's direct participation.

The betrayal wouldn't be enough to oust Brown. He was the nucleus of the territory, and although Pinkie's Iowa towns were being raided by the inter-Alliance faction, his business was safe. Orville, whose son Richard became a wrestler in 1953, had a good track record with grapplers, and the "boys" understood what they were getting when he ran the show. The unscrupulous politics eventually got to him, and with his son retired, Orville left wrestling behind in 1963. The resignation of Pinkie in 1959, and Brown's desertion in 1963, left the Alliance with only one remaining founder, and it was undoubtedly true, the NWA had grown bigger than originally intended, a talent-sharing organization for the promoters in the Midwest.

Brown and his wife Grace retired comfortably, and he enjoyed fishing and the outdoors. Other than maintaining ties with Ronnie Etchison, Lee Wykoff, and Lou Spandle, Orville distanced himself from wrestling altogether. They lived at the John Village Retirement Center in Lee's Summit, Missouri, in their later years, where Brown passed away on January 24, 1981, at the age of 72. His son Richard was well educated, and became a school principal.

Orville Brown was a champion wrestler, a hard-working booker, trainer, friend, and father. To those who knew him, he was a kind person who gave 100 percent to whatever he strived for. Brown had a devotion to professional wrestling and earned the title of "legend" in a territory that honored both him and his achievements to the very end.

Frank Tunney estimated that **"Whipper" Billy Watson** drew more than five million people in main events of shows in Toronto. He was undoubtedly the most popular wrestler in that city's history, from his debut on October 3, 1940, until his last match on November 28, 1971. That was a commitment of 31 years, breaking bones and entertaining crowds with his charisma. Outside the ropes, he was dedicated to charities, helping numerous causes and willing to give back to the city that had given him so much. He'd sign autographs until everyone who wanted one had one, and appreciated the fans who idolized him.

Watson was born William John Potts on June 25, 1915, in East York, Ontario to an English born father John (1891–1918) and Canadian mother Alice Mary Wilken (1891–1951). Living at 1 Rosevear Avenue, the Potts family was faced with the onset of World War I in Europe, and John, a Mansfield ammunition employee, was sent overseas as part of the Canadian expeditionary forces. In fact, John had already enlisted in the Sportsmen's Battalion four months before Billy was born, went overseas in October 1915, and was killed in the line of duty in September 1918. Alice would be married again to Ernest Chezzie (1894–1956), a political organizer with whom Billy had a hard time bonding as a child.

For four years as a teenager, Billy sold the *Toronto Daily Star* at the corner of Danforth and Dawes Road. He was convinced by his brother George to play hooky from piano lessons one Saturday afternoon to attend a wrestling session some of the neighborhood kids were having at the All Hallows' Anglican Church gymnasium. The impromptu truancy set in motion a series of events that changed Billy's life forever, and without it, he may have ended up down a very different path. He furthered his grappling education with lessons from Phillip Lawson at the Bowles Athletic Club and later the Central YMCA.

Watson developed into a six-foot, 175-pound athlete with cunning skill. He moved into the professional ranks, and joined a contingent of wrestlers traveling to the United Kingdom. With him were Harry Joyce, Tommy Nelson, Al Korman, and Ken "Tiger" Tasker. Wrestling in England was a little different from the kind of action regularly seen at the Gardens. It was a more brutal world of competition that often involved hard-nosed shooting. Shortly after his arrival, and adopting the ring name "Billy Watson," he was sidelined for six months with a variety of injuries, including a fractured shoulder and numerous broken ribs. Booked by former Olympic gold medallist George de Relwyskow, who also took an interest in training him, Billy traveled throughout England and Ireland.

The triumphs in Europe had Watson motivated about his return to Toronto. Gathering up newspaper clippings and promotional pieces, he mailed them to Tunney in advance with the hopes that he'd be impressed. Instead of finding an enthused promoter, Watson learned that Tunney had completely disregarded the package. Weighing 190 pounds and using the "Irish Whip" move made famous by Danno O'Mahoney, Watson was sometimes billed as being from Belfast. Tunney gave Watson his first shot at the Gardens on October 3, 1940, a victory over Lee Henning.

Press writers boasted about the applause Whipper had earned, but Tunney refused to give him a push. By April 1941, Toronto's promoter began to encounter outside pressure for not using Watson in matches higher up on the bill, and fans were tired of a heel Roland Kirchmeyer (Masked Wolf) "crippling" opponents. In response, he booked a tournament on May 1, 1941, that saw Whipper beat Wolf by default, Wallace Musovich by disqualification, Jack Claybourne, then Cy Williams to become the number one contender for the world's title. The event pushed Watson past a pivotal hurdle, and marked the turning point of his career.

The aura of the Whipper electrified Toronto's wrestling fans. The audience admired his virtuous style — even when his ring "ethics" would cost him a match, they ate it up. Watson's brilliant quickness and showmanship drew drama from both sides of a wrestling contest, the hero and the villain. He could carry matches against opponents of all sizes, sold the hysteria, and gave the people reason to cheer. The fact that he was a normal guy who seemed beatable only added to his mystique.

Tunney may not have known what he had with Whipper Watson, but he went with it. Watson feuded with Nanjo Singh leading up to a British Empire title win on April 30, 1942. With his title win over Singh, Whipper climbed to a level of popularity that no wrestler in Toronto's history had ever reached before.

The tides turned, and all who entered Tunney's lair had to deal with the cloud of Watson's presence. He faced NWA champion Bill Longson, Thesz, Sexton, Robert, Managoff, Casey, and Savoldi. He'd work against opposing favorites, brawl with heels, and most importantly, was willing to lose clean in the ring. He projected an everyman image people could relate to, and Toronto fans responded to him. The city's regional title, the British Empire championship, would be passed around, but always came back to the Whipper.

Tunney cut Watson in on the business side of the Toronto franchise, and Billy's political power rose. Their combined booking efforts built private fortunes beyond anything they could have imagined. A link to St. Louis promoter Tom Packs, who managed the National Wrestling Association world title, also abetted the growing notoriety of Watson. On February 21, 1947, Billy ended Longson's four-year reign as champion with a disqualification victory at the Kiel in St. Louis.

St. Louis was a home away from home for Watson. Packs brought hometown boy Thesz in to challenge him for the championship on April 25, 1947, and more than 10,000 fans packed the Kiel to see the title switch hands. In June 1948, Packs retired, and Tunney was a part of a group of individuals who bought a piece of the valuable NWA title and the St. Louis office. It was a smart business move for Tunney, because it not only sealed up dates for Watson in St. Louis, but created an open road between Missouri and Ontario for the champion, whoever it might be.

Watson added to his business ventures and became one of a small group of active wrestlers to have actual membership in the NWA. In 1955, he bought the Seattle franchise from Bob Murray, and grapplers from the Toronto market, Doug Hepburn and Sky-Hi Lee, headlined at the Trianon. Ken Kenneth administered the operation locally from an office at 2230 7th Avenue, bringing in talent from San Francisco. But the Watson venture in the Pacific Northwest lasted just a few months before folding.

The Whipper had ended Longson's four-year spell as titleholder in 1947 and when Thesz had to drop the title after more than six years as NWA champion,

Watson was the man they trusted to do the deed. The Toronto star captured the belt in front of 15,000 fans when referee Jack Dempsey reached ten as Thesz laid outside the ring ropes on March 15, 1956. As Alliance champion, Watson traveled the circuit, including stops in Amarillo, Los Angeles, and Memphis, beating Gorgeous George, Pat O'Connor, Dick Hutton, Bobo Brazil, Hans Schmidt, Fritz Von Erich, Killer Kowalski, and Buddy Rogers. On November 9, 1956, he gave the NWA title back to Thesz in the same manner that he had won it, a countout finish in 37:05 in St. Louis.

Well aware his popularity extended beyond the wrestling mat, he considered a stint with the Edmonton Eskimos football squad in 1950, and tested the waters of the political arena in 1965. Whipper was known for his customary thin mustache, and was always a candidate for advertising campaigns by companies yearning for a boost in revenue. He even branded his own soft drink. When Billy wasn't pitching items or pummeling foes, he was giving to charity, donating and raising millions of dollars for campaigns like the Easter Seals and a safety club that convinced 150,000 kids to join. Watson took pleasure in the company of fans, and his acts of kindness were not isolated.

On November 28, 1971, he teamed with Bulldog Brower at the Gardens in Toronto to beat Dingo the Sundowner and Man Mountain Cannon in less than five minutes. During the afternoon of November 30, Watson was placing a fireplace screen into his automobile's trunk on Rogers Road in Toronto. An out-of-control car skidded on the ice and into him, running into his left leg. He suffered no broken bones, but his knee was injured so severely he would never wrestle again. After a three-hour surgery at Northwestern Hospital, Watson recovered, but dealt with the pain for the rest of his life.

Hovering at about 220 pounds when the accident occurred in 1971, Watson weighed 350 by 1983. He remained focused on fundraising, supporting causes for the people of Toronto until his death on February 4, 1990, at an Orlando, Florida, hospital. Wrestling had lost another legend.

Of all National Wrestling Alliance world heavyweight champions, none were more accomplished in the amateur ranks than **Richard Hutton**. He was born on October 4, 1923, to Bailey (1902–1975) and Gladys (1904–1989) in Amarillo. Shortly after he was born, his parents moved the family south of Tulsa, where he and his brother Jerald were raised. Dick attended Daniel Webster High School and was a standout wrestler for the Warriors under Frank "Snake" Briscoe. With many scholarships on the table, Hutton accepted a place on the Oklahoma A&M roster based on Briscoe's recommendation. Briscoe knew the 6′1′′, 235-pound

Hutton would thrive under the tutelage of the school's renowned coach, Art Griffith. He was right.

Hutton served in World War II, and helped the allied forces conquer Italy. By March 1947, he was back in wrestling form and ready to make an impact at the NCAA competition in Champaign. On March 29, Hutton beat Ray Gunkel of Purdue, 5-3, in overtime to take the heavyweight division. Despite Hutton's win and being a recognized favorite going into the tournament, Oklahoma A&M came in third place as a team. The next year in Bethlehem, Hutton successfully defended his championship over Thurman McGraw, and Griffith's Aggies captured the NCAA Title. At the same tournament, in the 191.5 weight class, Verne Gagne of Minnesota placed first and Bob Geigel of Iowa placed third.

The road to the 1948 Olympics went through Ames, Iowa, for dozens of wrestling hopefuls. Hutton, eyeing a spot on the team led by his own coach, Griffith, wrestled four tough rounds, and on April 30, eliminated Gunkel to make the squad. A victory at the Olympics in London over Iran's Sakdhari won Hutton early acclaim in what appeared to be a legitimate medal bid, but consecutive losses to Josef Ruzicka of Czechoslovakia and James Armstrong of Australia concluded Richard's run for a medal. He was forced to default the final bout against Armstrong because to a broken blood vessel in his right arm.

The collegiate achievements continued for Dick when he returned to competition and was projected to collar his third straight NCAA heavyweight title in Fort Collins. He was upset in the decisive match by his Olympic team buddy, Gagne, by decision on March 26, 1949. Dreams of winning four straight heavyweight titles were gone. But on March 25, 1950, in Cedar Falls, he beat Fred Stoeker of Iowa State Teachers College to win his third NCAA heavyweight championship.

After graduation, Hutton fulfilled an obligation to the military as an officer, and sat by as his college mates, Gagne, Gunkel, Geigel, Mike DiBiase, and Joe Scarpello turned professional. Dick contemplated turning pro himself, impressed by the money being made at that level.

Hutton hooked up with LeRoy McGuirk, who trained him at Tulsa's police gym, and made his debut on May 11, 1953 (versus Frank Altman in Tulsa), supplementing his earnings with work at his father's construction company. "He has a fine chance to get into the big-money brackets. He has a lot to learn, but has the natural qualifications and I won't be surprised at anything he may accomplish," McGuirk said of Hutton in the May 10, 1953, edition of the *Tulsa Daily World*. The venerable Ed "Strangler" Lewis, quoted in the *Odessa American* in the Sunday, January 5, 1958, edition was also impressed: "When I first saw Hutton in a gymnasium work out in Tulsa, I saw a future champion."

Weighing as much as 250 pounds, Dick was a monster on the amateur mat, and it was McGuirk and Lewis who shaped him into a feared professional. Before adopting the abdominal stretch as a finisher, Hutton used the "Strangler Lewis" headlock to put away foes. He went to Columbus for booker Al Haft, who had a special place in his heart for wrestlers with amateur experience, and Hutton developed his abilities.

Training at Haft's gym with the likes of Bill Miller and Ruffy Silverstein certainly honed Hutton's technical skills. The Ohio tour introduced him to many facets of wrestling, from consistent traveling to generating heat. He found a gimmick that put over his amateur qualifications and gave him a confident swagger, agreeing to take on all comers for one dollar a minute. The Oklahoma grappler debuted in Toronto on April 26, 1956, and was praised in the press for his proficiency. Toronto, like Ohio, gave Hutton an outlet for the growth of his wrestling personality, and within his first week in the city, they started a famous "Beat the Yank" series that put up $1,000 to anyone that could pin Hutton in 20 minutes.

Hutton was a headliner by June, and had three matches at Maple Leaf Gardens against NWA champion Billy Watson during the summer. Though he lost all three bouts by countout, and their feud was not drawing as they expected, Hutton's push continued. He teamed with Hard Boiled Haggerty on September 20, 1956, in Toronto and won the Canadian open tag title and George Richards trophy from the Brunettis. Several months later, he was partnered with the territory's top heel, Gene Kiniski, and the duo impressed Frank Tunney. On January 31, 1957, Hutton was pinned at the East York Arena, losing $1,000 to Watson, only to have the check torn into pieces by Kiniski.

The tandem of Hutton and Kiniski proved profitable, especially matched against Watson and O'Connor, and Dick learned much about performing on both sides of a match. Kiniski rubbed off on Hutton, but it was clear that Dick was not going to work purely as a heel. When he returned to Ontario after a several-month layoff, Hutton had a more scientific approach, but was still aggressive. The methodical and impassive Tulsa grappler was on a very short list of candidates to succeed Thesz as NWA champion, and it was Lou, instead of the board of directors, who made the final call.

Tunney had a compelling marketing plan in place for Hutton vs. Thesz, held on November 14, 1957, at the Gardens. Instead of putting up his usual $1,000, Hutton upped the prize to $2,000, with half the cash going to charity if he lost. The bout would have no curfew and Sam Muchnick was going to be ringside. Fans who read the daily newspapers could easily see something was up. This wasn't a typical championship match.

The Hutton-Thesz affair drew an estimated 10,000 fans, and the fortunate witnesses watched the champion submit to an abdominal stretch in 35 minutes, giving Hutton the NWA world title. Supported by the organization's influential members, Muchnick, McGuirk, Tunney, Thesz, and Lewis, Hutton was thrust into a role many believed he was unprepared for. Surprisingly, Hutton's appeal hadn't been established in St. Louis prior to his winning the championship, and a rematch against Thesz drew a meager 6,200 on November 22.

Various promoters had complained about Lou's lack of color, but even more grumbled about the stoic Hutton. He offered a high degree of credibility, but there were promoters who didn't want that. They wanted drama, and, if necessary, flying chairs and blood. Muchnick knew that selling Hutton was going to be a chore, and expressed his concern to fellow associates. Running the circuit in the shadow of the Alliance leadership's ploy to split the title in June 1957, when Edouard Carpentier went over Thesz, gave Hutton an unparalleled chore, and, by himself, he was unable to bring unity to the title. A fraction of the country now recognized Edouard as titleholder, and rejected Dick's claim altogether.

More than half of the 28 members still welcomed Hutton into their territories, and he did what he could to maintain the prestige of the title at a low point in Alliance history. His tenure was lackluster in terms of excitement and fan support, and Carpentier was generally regarded as a more electrifying performer. Still, Hutton had the mat prowess to easily outshine his rival, and would have demolished him in a straight match. The decision to divide the championship five months before he rose to the top of the NWA severely hindered Hutton's ability to draw spectators to the arena. That misjudgement wasn't something he could be blamed for.

Because Thesz owned the belt he wore while NWA champion, Hutton was forced to use a strap he received in college during his reign. Muchnick claimed in the April 5, 1958, edition of his St. Louis arena program that "our organization has never owned such a belt. But we certainly intend to get one and present it to the champion at some future date." Hutton's nearly 14-month run ended prior to any such ceremony, but, notably, the Alliance did issue his successor a brand new, contemporary championship belt.

On January 9, 1959, Hutton was dethroned by Pat O'Connor in a one-fall match, surrendering the NWA title before 4,896 people in St. Louis. When it was all said and done, Hutton had built a case for himself as the most technically gifted NWA champion of the 39 official titleholders between 1948 and 2006.

Nicknamed "Cowboy," Dick campaigned in Texas, California, and Japan in the five years after losing the NWA championship. He was married twice and had three children. Hutton was inducted into the Oklahoma State Athletic Hall of Fame, the National Wrestling Hall of Fame (1995), and the Professional Wrestling Hall of Fame at the International Wrestling Institute and Museum (1999). He died at the age of 80 on November 24, 2003.

A sheepherder once held the NWA world title. It might be hard to believe or sound like something made up by a wired promoter for a gimmick, but it wasn't. **Patrick John O'Connor** was born in Raetihi, New Zealand, on August 22, 1924, one of three sons of John Frederick and Isabella O'Connor. During his schooling years at Feilding Agricultural High School, he tended to sheep and cattle on his parents' large farm. He reportedly attended Massey University, and for six months in 1945, served as a member of the New Zealand Royal Air Force.

Former amateur champion Dave Scarrow was Pat's original wrestling coach in Raetihi. Moving to Wanganui to pursue his interests in wrestling and rugby, O'Connor joined a local gym, and was trained by owner Don Anderson. He used his skills as a blacksmith to pay the bills, and focused on the 1947 amateur wrestling tournament at Rotorua. The defending heavyweight champion, Richard Hrstich, was matched up with the mysterious newcomer, and Pat was impressive in a loss. Einar Lynneberg, chairman of the Dominion Wrestling Union, recommended that O'Connor train with the Wellington wrestling team, and, if he was willing, enroll in the famous gym of Anton Koolman.

Koolman was known for transforming dedicated grapplers into champions, and immediately knew he had a rising star with O'Connor. In October 1948, Patrick dominated at the national tournament in Dunedin, winning the heavyweight championship. Touring pro Joe Pazandak was bowled over by the dexterity of O'Connor, and made it known that the New Zealander could make a fortune wrestling in America. Reporters, and the camp of Koolman, believed O'Connor should protect his amateur status through the 1950 British Empire Games, where a victory in the heavyweight class seemed assured.

There were so few amateur heavyweight wrestlers in New Zealand that Pat had only one match at the national tournament on October 18, 1949, in Gisborne. O'Connor beat Edmonds on points and took the title. Earning his way onto the New Zealand wrestling team competing at the British Empire Games, Pat faced off with Australian heavyweight Jim Armstrong on February 5, 1950. Things took a shocking turn when O'Connor was pinned in less than a minute at Auckland's town hall. O'Connor won his second match, then beat Ken Richmond of England. Armstrong also beat Richmond and took the gold. O'Connor had impressed, but also displayed an undisciplined eagerness in the loss, and had to settle for runner-up. Armstrong, coincidentally, was the same man who had eliminated Dick Hutton (though by forfeit) from the 1948 Olympics.

Pazandak hadn't forgotten about O'Connor, nor had Patrick lost interest in going to America. Pazandak returned to New Zealand with Butch Levy — a second envoy from the office of Tony Stecher in Minneapolis — to wrestle and scout O'Connor. Following the Empire Games, and after strings were pulled by promoter Walter Miller, O'Connor sailed for the U.S. in August 1950. The American style of wrestling was taught by Pazandak, Stecher, Levy, and Verne Gagne. Additionally, it was arranged for Pat to train under famous University of Minnesota wrestling coach David Bartelma. O'Connor built up his fundamentals, conditioning, and speed, preparing for his professional debut.

O'Connor was introduced to the U.S. audience in September against Stan Myslajek. Accompanied by Pazandak on the road, he chose an approach that provided a comfortable living. Using a flashy dropkick and flying tackle, O'Connor's work was praised by Stecher before the members of the NWA at the 1951 convention. In 1952, he got over in Chicago with television exposure that boosted his profile nationwide, and was quickly booked for a Wrigley Field bout with world champion Lou Thesz on June 27, 1952. The darling of fans, O'Connor lost in three falls in front of more than 12,000, paying a gross gate of $34,218. Chicago promoter Fred Kohler had O'Connor under contract, with Jim Barnett acting as his manager.

O'Connor was compared to Thesz and Gagne, acknowledged as two of the best, but was bigger and stronger than the latter. He was aggressive on the mat, something that was more instinctive than anything else; it was not something he could have picked up from a collegiate coach. When he debuted in St. Louis, Sam Muchnick gave him the top spot, headlining with the Mighty Atlas on September 19, 1952. Of all the associations Pat had with American promoters, from Kohler to Toots Mondt, none were more consequential than what he had with Muchnick. Muchnick thrived on legitimate wrestling, and O'Connor demonstrated an ideal balance of science and speed. He felt at home in the ring and was able to inject personality into his matches.

On February 15, 1954, Pat beat Sky-Hi Lee in his initial appearance at Madison Square Garden, and the next night in Denver, won the Rocky Mountain title from Reggie Lisowski. In Montreal, Pat beat Wladek Kowalski for the area world title on July 21, 1954, and wrestled important bouts against Thesz, Bobby Managoff, Yvon Robert, and Buddy Rogers. In 1955, he held the Montreal title a second time, captured the world tag title with Roy McClarity and briefly held the Ohio State title. He received good press in Toronto in 1956, and won the vacant British Empire title over Lord Athol Layton on March 29. In September, he journeyed to New Zealand for the first time in six years, then engaged Edouard Carpentier, Dick Hutton, and Gene Kiniski upon returning to Ontario. Kiniski eventually took the British Empire title.

The NWA was almost ungovernable between 1957 and 1959. The dilemmas facing Alliance executives were multiplying, and where the organization had once controlled the number of roaming champions, the claimants were now increasing. At the convention in St. Louis in August 1958, O'Connor's name was mentioned as a replacement for the uninspiring Hutton as champion. Muchnick agreed with the decision, as did his allies in Kansas City. The balloting went in favor of Patrick, and on January 9, 1959, in St. Louis, he beat Hutton in one fall for the NWA championship with less than 5,000 fans in attendance. A $10,000 performance bond was handed over to the NWA treasury.

Unlike Hutton-Thesz in November 1957, with Dan Parker of the *New York Mirror* forecasting the switch 12 hours in advance, having learned of the change through the grapevine, the O'Connor-Hutton exchange took several ranking NWA members by surprise. That revelation was certainly not good, given the challenges facing promoters, but after O'Connor took the title, there was a widening sense of unity and expansion after several years of infighting.

Chicago, for example, recognized the Carpentier lineage stemming from his June 1957 match with Thesz. After a prolonged grudge, Kohler brought O'Connor in, on January 8, 1960, against Billy Watson, and again on February 19 for a show that drew more than 8,000 and a gate of $21,009.

O'Connor also went into the Northeast for Vince McMahon, wrestling at the Garden and the Capitol Arena in D.C. On December 26, 1960, he wrestled Antonino Rocca in an anticipated match in Philadelphia, and both the Pennsylvania Athletic Commission and the National Wrestling Association gave him sponsorship as champion. That was the same association that had suspended O'Connor for 16 days in March 1961 for missing a match in New York.

While there was a blossoming harmony among members, there was a genuine neglect during O'Connor's reign for many of the booking regulations that were once sacred for the NWA. These violations came in the form of accepting dates for nonmembers (Roy Shire, Barnett, and Doyle), booking matches under the main event (New York City, San Francisco, Miami, Detroit), and ignoring their previous conviction that the champion should not wrestle on programs which also involved midgets or women grapplers.

Hutton's reign had included a shifty work that threatened the credibility of the NWA title (October 1958, Amarillo, versus Dory Funk), and so did O'Connor's. On July 11, 1959, in Calgary, during the Tournament of Champions at the Stampede

Corral, Thesz pinned Pat in a controversial match for the title. But promoter Stu Hart stated that the champion's legs had been outside the ropes, thus Lou didn't have a clear claim to the belt. The referee, "Jersey" Joe Walcott, stood by his decision, awarding the championship to Thesz. On July 17, O'Connor won a one-fall rematch in 26:20, beating Thesz by disqualification, and the *Albertan* newspaper in Calgary billed Thesz as the "seven-day champ."

The 1960 convention in Acapulco ended with a strategy for giving the world title to Buddy Rogers, but O'Connor still had nine months left as champion. A faithful worker, he met the demands of the Alliance membership from New York to Mexico City, with only periodic breaks. The successful promotion of the O'Connor-Rogers match at Comiskey Park broke records, and on June 30, 1961, Pat lost the title in three falls.

Members lauded O'Connor for the job he'd done as champion, and the NWA was structurally better when he left than when he arrived as champion. At the August 1961 meeting in Toronto, he was sanctioned as United States champion, a lineage that had no links to the Barnett-Doyle or Farhat versions, and was booked by Muchnick and Bobby Bruns. He toured Japan from March 23 to April 24, 1963, and wrestled Antonio Inoki, Shohei Baba, Kokichi Endo, Toyonobori, Kim Ill, The Great Togo, and Rikidozan for the International Title.

O'Connor was part owner of Kansas City from 1963 to 1987, and St. Louis from 1972 to 1987. On January 1, 1982, Muchnick retired, and O'Connor fittingly wrestled what was billed as his last match, beating Bob Sweetan in St. Louis, where Pat had contributed to the booking since 1969. Later in the month, he worked for All Japan and wrestled in New Zealand in October and November 1982, where he teamed with Steve Rickard and held the Commonwealth title for a day. In 1987, he came out of retirement to compete in the "old-timers" battle royal at the Meadowlands. O'Connor maintained many friendships from his wrestling days, especially with Geigel, and was planning to promote under the NWA banner with Rickard when he passed away suddenly at the age of 65 on August 16, 1990.

The first NWA world heavyweight champion with football as a big part of his resumé was "Big Thunder" **Gene Kiniski**. Colorful, innovative and captivating to watch as he prowled the squared circle, Gene performed masterly as a contender, then carried the belt proudly across the territories of the NWA.

Eugene Nicholas Kiniski (derived from Knihnicky) was born on November 23, 1928, outside of Edmonton, Alberta, one of six children born to Nicholas (1890–1968) and Julia (1899–1969). His father was employed as a barber, making less than $10 a week, while his diligent mother walked two miles to classes at the

University of Alberta. Educating herself, Julia opened her mind to civic concerns, and after 11 attempts to become an Edmonton alderman, she accomplished the feat in 1963. She drew attention for her unusual optimism until her death in October 1969.

Over six feet tall by age 17, Gene wrestled and played football at St. Joseph's High School. In March 1947, he entered the annual Edmonton Schools' Boxing and Wrestling Tournament at Westglen gymnasium. Because of his size, he was the lone heavyweight wrestler competing, and didn't have a match. He was coached at the Edmonton YMCA by Leo Magrill and won various amateur wrestling tournaments in the years that followed.

Annis Stukus, scouting for the reestablished Edmonton Eskimos professional football squad of the Western Interprovincial Football Union in 1949, looked over the wrestlers at the Sales Pavilion, and when training camps commenced in May, promoter Al Oeming and Stu Hart were among the grapplers asked to try out. Twenty-year-old Gene, standing 6'4'', was also in contention, and his spirited play secured him a spot on the starting defensive line. Kiniski's enthusiasm earned him a scholarship to the University of Arizona, where he was enrolled from September 18, 1950, until January 26, 1952, and distinguished himself on the gridiron for Bob Winslow. Recruited into professional wrestling in Arizona, Kiniski trained under promoter Rod Fenton, and had his first match in early 1952.

In Edmonton for the football season, Kiniski's promising career for the Eskimos was interrupted when a torn kneecap sidelined him during his team's first game against Saskatchewan in August 1952. Surgery ended his season. In March 1953, Kiniski announced his retirement from football, recanted his decision in July, and enjoyed one final season as an Eskimo before devoting his life to pro wrestling.

To say he was a competent two-sport athlete would be an understatement. Kiniski had amateur credentials and an instinct for the role of heel that frightened audiences and wrecked havoc around the squared circle. His exuberance as a lineman, which had been noted by panicked sideline reporters, translated perfectly to the wrestling ring, where such antics were appreciated. In southern California in 1954, Kiniski got television time with future legends Wilbur Snyder and Bobo Brazil, and won the local tag title with John Tolos. A budding talent, Kiniski headlined at the Olympic with NWA champion Thesz on November 3, 1954, and was defeated in two straight falls.

Using the backbreaker as a finisher, Kiniski was pushed in Toronto and Montreal in 1957, and his participation in angles with Billy Watson, Edouard Carpentier, Pat O'Connor, and Yukon Eric drew well at the Maple Leaf Gardens and Forum, respectively. Warranting suspensions along the way for his outrageousness, Gene won the British Empire title from O'Connor on May 2, 1957, and the Montreal version of the world title from Carpentier on June 12, 1957. On the evening he lost the Montreal title to Wladek Kowalski on July 17, 1957, 21,000 plus fans were in attendance at the baseball stadium.

On July 11, 1961, Kiniski won the AWA world title from Verne Gagne in Minneapolis, but lost it less than a month later. Kiniski reportedly weighed more than 260 pounds when he magically became world champion in West Texas in March 1962, and following a fourth reign as British Empire titleholder, he made headway as a challenger to Bruno Sammartino's WWWF title. Thinking he had scored a winning pinfall over the champ on November 16, 1964, at Madison Square Garden, Gene took the belt and left the ring area, only to be counted out. Kiniski kept the strap until a rematch on December 14 cleared up any questions about who really was the proper champion.

Speculation about an heir to Lou Thesz as NWA champion ended with the board of directors' vote going to Kiniski. On January 7, 1966, two weeks after giving up his WWA (Indianapolis) title to Dick the Bruiser, Gene went over Thesz in St. Louis in front of 11,612 fans at the Kiel Auditorium, and won the NWA title.

Kiniski's role as champion deviated from that of Thesz, and Gene comfortably delivered as a "bad guy" night in and night out. He could curb his methods to stay within the rules and still equal the viciousness with any growling heel, then shine against any number of favorites. A provocative wrestler, Kiniski was well conditioned, and known for his trustworthiness. Promoters couldn't question either his dedication to the championship, or his competence, as he matched up against the best heavyweights in the business. During his tenure as mat king, he wrestled Dick the Bruiser, Bobo Brazil, Johnny Valentine, Bill Watts, Carpentier, O'Connor, and the Funks.

Exhausted from traveling the circuit, including stops in Tokyo, Honolulu, and becoming the first NWA champion in more than eleven years to appear in Los Angeles in November 1968, Kiniski told Alliance members at the 1968 convention that it was time for him to step down. A friend of Dory Funk Sr. and his boys, Gene agreed to lose the championship to Dory Jr., and went down to a spinning toehold on February 11, 1969, in Tampa. His 37 months as heavyweight champion had been profitable for NWA members, and promoters were appreciative of his service.

Kiniski continued to be a draw through the 1970s, especially in St. Louis, where he was a close confidant of Sam Muchnick. He wrestled often in Vancouver, owning part of the territory with Sandor Kovacs, and held the international title in Japan in 1970. He made a handful of public appearances as his career wound down, from guest referee at Starrcade 1983 to participant in a legends' battle royal in 1987.

On February 25, 1992, he participated in his final match in Winnipeg, then was inducted into the wcw Hall of Fame in 1993. He prepared sons Kelly and Nick for pro wrestling, and upon retirement, ran a tavern in Point Roberts, Washington.

There is a long history of fathers pushing their sons to success in the world of wrestling. Twenty years before Jack Adkisson booked his Dallas territory on the marketability of his children, Dorrance Wilhelm Funk opened the door for his son and namesake, **Dory Funk Jr.** to headline within weeks of his pro debut. Dory was a top-flight athlete, as he showed in four years of college, and had all the attributes to spark attendance figures. Within three months of his debut, Dory Jr. had claimed the world title. His win over the previous champion was so convincing it left fans no doubt that he was a force to be reckoned with.

Dorrance Earnest Jr. was born on February 3, 1941, his brother Terry, a few years later. The Funks, after Dory Senior's service in World War II, traveled as a family while he pursued pro wrestling as a vocation. Late in the decade, he came into contact with premier junior heavyweight promoter, Dory Detton, and civic leader Cal Farley in Amarillo. Farley, a prominent former light heavyweight wrestler and principal of the famed Boys Ranch, hired Funk to be the superintendent, and the Funks had a new home.

Between 1949 and 1955, outside of a few jaunts to other regions, Dory was the number-one grappler for Detton in West Texas. Funk exemplified toughness in brutal matches with diverse opponents, and through his creativity helped turn Amarillo from a basic, run-of-the-mill wrestling community into a world center for all grapplers.

In 1955, Karl Sarpolis and Dory Sr. bought Detton's booking office. Sarpolis assumed NWA rights, and the territory expanded with help from television. A stint as NWA world junior champion preceded Funk's jump to the heavyweight class, and he took on all of the era's superstars, including Lou Thesz, Mike DiBiase and Fritz Von Erich. Dory Jr. was a varsity athlete at Canyon High School in wrestling and basketball, but it was on the football field for coach Bill Davis that he shined the brightest. He was a tackle at West Texas State, and the Buffalo eleven won their 1963 Sun Bowl game against Ohio.

Trained by his father, Dory Jr. made his wrestling debut on January 10, 1963, at Amarillo's Sports Arena. In the crowd were members of the West Texas football team, with Jerry Logan handcuffed to Jim Dalton, the "brother" of Dory's wrestling opponent, Jack Dalton (Don Kalt). Funk won the match in 4:30. Victories over Bud Cody, Rick DiBiase, Moose Cholak, and even a forfeit win over his father in a tournament on March 21, 1963, earned him a world title shot against

Gene Kiniski, who had claimed the championship in Amarillo in the absence of the official NWA titleholder.

Seventy-seven days after his professional debut, "Dunk" was in a position to capture a somewhat prestigious belt. On March 28, 1963, he was disqualified in the first fall by referee Danno O'Shocker for not releasing a spinning toehold after 34:10. He then won the second and third falls when Kiniski couldn't continue. The 22-year-old Dory was added to a list of "world" champions that included Thesz, Gagne, and Buddy Rogers. Undefeated for months, Dory didn't even lose a fall to any of the veteran wrestlers he was going over.

Funk wrestled Gagne in a title vs. title match in Amarillo on May 30, 1963, and the two went 60 minutes to a draw. Surprisingly, Junior got the opening fall by submission. Gagne gave him his first loss of a fall, putting Dory away with a sleeper. Several weeks later, Dory beat Pat O'Connor, again winning with a toehold in the third fall of an even match. Dory's streak was impressive, and publicity agents pushed the possibility of a unification match against NWA titleholder Thesz. His career was guided and protected by his father, who had an interest in every angle, every match, and every fall his son participated in.

Dory's championship was quietly phased out, and losses to The Sheik and Lou Thesz wiped the slate clean. With his father, he began to venture to other territories, and the NWA title was on the elder Funk's mind. He knew that getting his son out to wrestle in front of the assorted NWA members could only help him when future decisions about champions were made. Two of the more important opinions in the NWA were those of Thesz and St. Louis promoter Sam Muchnick. There was no way Dory Sr. could have shored up the votes for Dory to win the strap from Thesz. Nor would Thesz have dropped the belt to him. But in January 1966, Lou did pass the NWA title to a man who might.

On January 7, Kiniski won the world title in St. Louis. Around that same time, the Funks were appearing regularly for Muchnick, and Dory Sr. had become a close friend of the influential promoter. The Funks were prime members of the St. Louis wrestling community, and both sons were popular with the local audience. On March 1, 1968, Dory Jr. wrestled a no-decision with Thesz in the main event of a Kiel show. Several months later, Kiniski told Funk Sr. he was ready to get off the throne, and Dory went to work on the NWA board of directors.

Dory's obvious talent would have taken him to the summit of wrestling by itself, but it was the maneuvering of his father that made it happen as quickly as it did. Funk Sr. was smart enough to get his sons into St. Louis and, with Muchnick impressed, had sealed up support from the most significant man in the Alliance. The board voted, Junior was given the nod, and a $25,000 deposit was made. On

February 11, 1969, six years after Kiniski did the job in Amarillo, he did it again in Tampa. Dory won the NWA world title with a spinning toehold before an estimated 7,000 fans. His proud father was in his corner.

Funk was a dependable traveler as champion and a valuable asset to the NWA. He wasn't the shooter Thesz was, or as brutally tough as Kiniski or Harley Race, but he was as scientific as they came. Funk could brawl, match grips, and make opponents look good, no matter if his rival weighed 185 or 385 pounds. Combining a youthful appearance, astounding conditioning, and a capacity to vary his mat performance, Dory was an inspiring champion. Promoters were thrilled with his adroitness, and Dory gave them no reason to make a change. His father and brother often preceded him into territories, wrestling his opponents in advance, and setting the table for his arrival.

But by the August 1972 convention in Las Vegas, Dory was burned out. He wanted to give up the title, and the two names that came up to replace him were Race and former NCAA Champion Jack Brisco. Race, a heel, was considered by Funk Sr. to be the better of the two choices, because there was the opportunity to have a controversial finish. Dory being pinned fairly wasn't something the Funks wanted.

Race had other sponsors, but Brisco eventually won the board over. The match was booked for Houston on March 2, 1973. On February 28, Funk was rounding up cattle at the Double Cross Ranch in Umbarger when his truck fell over a six-foot bank, flipping into a creek. The Associated Press reported that Dory Sr. had pulled his son from the vehicle and that he was treated at Canyon Hospital for a severely injured shoulder. Initial indications were that Dory would be out of the ring for anywhere between six weeks to two months. It wasn't far from the truth. The Brisco match was cancelled, as were any plans for a rematch.

With a proclamation already issued by the NWA to get Brisco the title, a new script was written. In May, Dory returned to the ring, losing a match to Race in Kansas City on May 24, 1973. Referee Richard Moody was knocked out in their match, with Funk applying what would have been the deciding pinfall if the official had been awake to see it. Harley recovered as Dory argued with Moody, capitalized on the situation, and landed a suplex. Race's pin was counted, and the title changed hands. In total, Dory's reign had lasted 1,563 days, the second longest in Alliance history. Nine days later, Dory Sr. suffered a heart attack and died. He was 54.

Funk was semi-active into the early 2000s, furthering his legend worldwide. From teaming with Terry in Japan, to being All-Japan's booker, to winning championships in Florida, and wrestling as "Hoss" Funk in the WWF, Dory has seen just about everything wrestling can deliver — the good, the bad, and the ugly. From 1975 to '77, Terry was the NWA champion, making the Funks the only brothers to have both held the coveted title. In 1981, the two men actually wrestled to a 54-minute draw in Japan. West Texas A&M University (formerly West Texas State) inducted Dory into their Athletics Hall of Champions in 1990, and he was also honored by the Panhandle Sports Hall of Fame in 1998. Today, he coaches up-and-comers at his wrestling school in Florida. More information is available about him at his website: www.dory-funk.com.

A key personality on the NWA circuit in the 1970s and '80s was **Harley Race**, an intelligent grappler from northwestern Missouri. Born to Jay (1902–1981) and Mary Frances Stevens Race (1921–1986) on April 11, 1943, in Quitman, Harley Leland was one of six children: four girls and two boys. He attended Quitman High, but an altercation with a faculty member got him expelled. Standing six-one and weighing 200 pounds, Harley toiled at area carnivals taking on all comers, prior to meeting Stanislaus and Wladek Zbyszko, the famous former world champions who had a farm in nearby Savannah. The brothers proceeded to toughen and discipline Harley, preparing him for the harsh wrestling world.

Race became the driver for wrestler William Cobb, a 750-pound wrestler who went by the name "Happy Humphrey." Carting the hefty wrestler around the Midwest was not an easy task, but for the chance to meet some of the grapplers he admired, it was well worth it. Harley took his first paying gig in 1959, and was given dates in the central states by Gust Karras. In 1961, he went to Tennessee as part of a made up brother combination with Johnny Long. Harley was known as Jack Long, and it was during this tour that he suffered a serious leg injury.

Following rehab, Harley went to Boston for the Santos-Pfefer combine, where he was renamed the "Great Mortimer," a silly jab at the WWWF's the Great Mortier. As he increased his knowledge of how the game was played, Race did plenty of losing as a preliminary worker, and his size and strength was a terrific equalizer for his lack of experience. He was, perhaps, the toughest of the new blood in the business.

Race teamed with Larry Hennig in Minneapolis, and on January 30, 1965, the tandem dethroned Bruiser and Crusher for the first of three AWA world tag titles. In West Texas, he morphed his "Handsome" moniker to "Mad Dog" and proved to be a top solo heel whose brawling made headlines. It was apparent that Race, along with the Funk Brothers, was going to lead the wrestling industry for years to come.

By 1971, Race was the focal point of the Heart of America promotion, and for Muchnick in St. Louis. Wrestling needed a dominant heel, and Harley fit the part perfectly. He could be pitted against any number of wrestlers, from Jack Brisco to

Bob Geigel, and had the ability to draw fans to his side as a middle-of-the-road grappler. In fact, Race was quite popular in Missouri, while appearing as a heel elsewhere. Fans were able to see his skill and toughness, and promoters were confident in his abilities to draw as a regional champion.

Harley began to stack up titles, winning three central states and the Muchnick-promoted Missouri title (in a tournament final over Pak-San on September 16, 1972, at the Chase Hotel) before being scheduled into a bout with NWA champion Dory Funk Jr. on May 24, 1973, at Kansas City's Memorial Hall. That was a match he would also win.

The first reign of Race lasted a month and a half, serving as a bridge between the championship runs of Dory Jr. and Brisco. At the Coliseum in Houston, Brisco beat Race in two-of-three falls on July 20, 1973, capturing the NWA belt. In St. Louis on October 13, Race beat Gene Kiniski for the Missouri title. The Missouri State crown was always seen as the championship that propelled a man to the NWA title, and it did so for three people (Race, Terry Funk, and Kerry Von Erich). Four others had already held the NWA title prior to wearing the Missouri belt (Kiniski, Dory Jr., Brisco, and Ric Flair). In the case of Race, the Missouri title set up his initial NWA title reign, but he would go on to hold the strap on six other occasions from 1973 to 1985. Harley gave the title a sense of importance, and every defense was made with an intense grit that preserved the illusion of legitimacy.

Race was locked in to replace Terry Funk as NWA champion, after losing a close vote to him at the August 1975 convention. A year later, a date and location for the switch was decided, February 6, 1977, in Toronto. That night, Harley made the champion submit to an Indian deathlock in 14:10, taking the belt at Maple Leaf Gardens. Whereas his first reign had lasted a mere 57 days, his second would last more than 900. Race traveled the entire circuit, including three treks to Japan, and made good on the promise to preserve the championship's integrity. As a gift to promoter Eddie Graham, Race lost the title to Dusty Rhodes in Tampa on August 21, 1979, then regained it five days later in Orlando.

Between October 31, 1979, and May 1, 1981, Race traded the NWA title twice with "Giant" Shohei Baba in Japan, and with Tommy Rich in Georgia. On May 1 in Gainesville, he won his sixth NWA title, at the time regarded as a record-tying victory. The so-called record of Lou Thesz was wrestling lore. In fact, Race was just lengthening his own record, as Thesz had actually won the Alliance world title just three times. Rhodes beat Race for the title at the Omni in Atlanta on June 21, 1981, and dropped the strap to Ric Flair several months later.

On June 10, 1983 in St. Louis, Race beat Flair to capture the NWA title for the seventh time, breaking the "record" of Thesz. As the Alliance began to crumble and booking offices were consolidated, Race, Flair, and Rhodes stood as the top three heavyweights. Upon the retirement of Muchnick, Harley bought into St. Louis, but sold out in 1986.

Flair regained the NWA title in Greensboro at the inaugural Starrcade, promoted by Crockett Promotions on November 24, 1983. The "Nature Boy" won a dramatic cage match in 33:29. Four months later, Harley and Flair exchanged the belt again in New Zealand and Singapore, but the switches were not acknowledged by the Alliance until years later. In a class with Johnny Valentine, Race won more than just a few wrestling championships during his long career. Outside of his eight NWA titles, he held the Central States championship eight times, the Missouri title seven times, the United States, Southern, Mid-America, Caribbean, Georgia, North American, and Australian titles. He was also world champion in Japan and Indiana, and a multiple tag titleholder. From 1986 to 1988, he was known as the king of the WWF.

In the colorful world of wrestling, Harley Race looked like a hard-nosed grappler. He wasn't there for comic relief, although his tenure in the WWF offered more of that style than at any time in his past. Race gave the appearance that he wanted to torment his opponent by any means necessary, and could hold his own with anyone, including the mammoth Andre the Giant. After his retirement in 1991, he functioned as a manager in WCW, acting as a second for Lex Luger, Mr. Hughes, Big Van Vader, and Steve Austin. A car accident and hip injury in 1995 forced him out of competition for good. In 1999, he founded World League Wrestling, a promotion running in conjunction with his central Missouri wrestling school. His website, www.harleyrace.com, gives an in-depth review of his wrestling achievements, and the training he provides in Eldon, Missouri.

CHAPTER FOURTEEN

DISTINGUISHED WRESTLING CHAMPIONS

As a unified group, the National Wrestling Alliance sanctioned a heavyweight (205 pounds and over), junior heavyweight (180-205), and light heavyweight (165–180) champion for more than four decades. The championships were regulated by the Alliance board of directors with unequivocal cooperation from the supporting committees. Those wearing the distinctions crossed territorial boundaries and were available to wrestle for all members, if the latter agreed to pay the associated fees and adhere to the rigid regulations. Since the heavyweight and junior heavyweight champions were always busy with their schedules, and the light heavyweight title was typically limited to Mexico, policies were written into the bylaws authorizing members to book regional titles.

The establishment of member-controlled championships was a crucial factor in the success of individual territories. Regional audiences were predisposed to a championship system unique to their territory; and it built public interest in specific wrestlers, feuds, or matches. The Alliance member in charge of the territory instituted the assorted championships and selected wrestlers to send along to promoters on the trail.

Each region would normally have a primary singles championship, which could vary from a United States title to a state championship, accompanied by a tag-team belt. In larger regions, such as Florida and Texas, members found it practical to create a range of minor championships to include junior heavyweight and television titles. The titleholders fell under the Alliance umbrella, but were in no way NWA champions.

Members relied and expected visits from the NWA heavyweight and junior heavyweight champions, and the traveling titleholders commonly engaged regional champions in local main events. The NWA-appointed champions were responsible for boosting the image of local grapplers, thus helping the membership. A good showing by a district star against one of the top champions usually paid considerable dividends, and the credibility earned through a draw with the heavyweight champion could be remarkable.

In wrestling, not unlike other professional sports, egos often got in the way. Some NWA heavyweight and junior heavyweight champions took their own view of how they should handle their jobs, and were unwilling to concede anything to regional grapplers or champions. That attitude hurt territories and worked against the principles of the union.

The nuisances of wrestling and the political spats inside the National Wrestling Alliance were many and varied. Grievances between wrestlers and promoters, unruly or vain champions, and quarrels over finishes were dealt with individually, and the lack of scrutiny regarding local championships gave members a sense of independence in the management of their territories. There was one edict the hierarchy of the NWA insisted that members comply with: under no circumstances could a regional titleholder be labeled a "world" champion of any kind.

The structure of the tag-team division, and how the NWA should observe recognition, was vehemently debated by members for the greater part of 25 years. Tag-team championships did not fall within the same parameters as singles belts, and any affiliated member could name their two-man team "world" titleholders. It was commonly done, but frowned upon by members who wanted a universal claimant backed by the board of directors. Sam Muchnick was increasingly fond of the approach, and even pitched the idea at the 1971 convention in Mexico City.

The board shot down the suggestion, leaving the booking of tag champions to members. During the 1990s, with membership in single digits, members finally approved a measure sanctioning a single world tag-team championship.

Guidelines governing women's wrestling by the National Wrestling Alliance were restricted to the whims of Billy Wolfe. However, the NWA supported his wife, Mildred Burke, as the undisputed champion from 1950 to '53. Wolfe and Burke had a substantial falling out and their grudge saw Billy try to undermine the credibility of Mildred's championship. He kept membership in the NWA, while pushing his alleged new girlfriend Nell Stewart as United States champion and his daughter-in-law June Byers as "world" titleholder. Members at the 1953 convention decided they would no longer regulate women's grappling, nor formally support any single champion.

The standard for professional wrestling in the men's junior heavyweight class was set by **Leroy Michael McGuirk**. A cordial and reasonable man, McGuirk was involved in wrestling for 50 years. He was born on December 13, 1910, in Garvin, Oklahoma, the third child of John William and Anna McGuirk. Suffering the loss of his father before he was 12, and the sight in one of his eyes in a swimming mishap, Leroy overcame great adversity to become a superlative grappler. His education in wrestling began at Tulsa Central High School and continued at Oklahoma A&M, from 1928–32, under Edward Gallagher.

Edged out by a referee's decision in the quarterfinals by Phillip Berry at the 1930 NCAA Tournament, McGuirk rebounded to take the 155-pound title on March 28, 1931, in Providence. A year later in Bloomington, he lost in overtime to Robert Hess at 174 pounds. Several months after his graduation from college, McGuirk made his pro debut for Tulsa promoter Sam Avey. On March 5, 1934, he beat Hugh Nichols in Tulsa for the world light heavyweight title, and was endorsed by the National Wrestling Association.

Bobby Chick (Roberts) won the championship in December 1936, and McGuirk regained the strap by defeating Danny McShain on May 16, 1938. The NWA sponsored a 190-pound championship (later raised to 200) known as the junior heavyweight title, which Leroy corralled on June 19, 1939, from John Swenski. On a circuit between Tulsa and Hollywood, McGuirk dominated the junior heavyweights, but at least three other junior champions were recognized in the 1940s. An excellent leverage grappler and master of the rolling double-wrist lock, McGuirk trounced Billy Goelz on December 28, 1949, at KRNT Theater in Des Moines to unify his National Wrestling Association junior title with Goelz's National Wrestling Alliance version.

On February 7, 1950, on a wet night in Little Rock, McGuirk was being driven to a restaurant by his wrestling pupil Robert "Bob" Clay. Trying to prevent a collision, Clay locked the car's brakes and McGuirk was thrown against the front windshield, shattering the tinted glasses he wore because he was self-conscious about his blind eye. Ironically, only the side of the glasses covering his good eye fractured, blinding him permanently. McGuirk's days as a wrestler were over, but Avey was more than happy to keep Leroy around as his partner.

Leroy served as the second vice president of the NWA from September 1950 to August 1956, and from August 1959 through August 1960. He was appointed honorary vice president in 1957 and '58. From his office at the Expo Pavilion, McGuirk dictated the course of the junior heavyweights, booking the champions for a quarter of a century. McGuirk's territory included most of Oklahoma and Arkansas, parts of Missouri (Joplin and Springfield), Louisiana (Shreveport), and Texas (Wichita Falls and Tyler).

On January 4, 1958, McGuirk took over the Tulsa business when Avey retired. He was one of the longest surviving NWA members, affiliated from 1949 until '82, and relied heavily on his matchmaker, a role held at various points by Clay, Leo Voss, Sam Menacker, Rip Tyler, Bill Watts, Wayne Martin, and George Scott. McGuirk had many friends in the television and newspaper business that helped publicize his wrestling shows, and the wealth he accumulated as a booker and promoter allowed him to purchase 800 acres in Rogers County.

McGuirk and Ed "Strangler" Lewis were responsible for instituting the NWA Leader Dogs for the Blind annual charity functions, and Leroy was inducted into the Oklahoma Athletic Hall of Fame in 1977. His Tulsa operations ceased in 1982, leaving the city open for Watts and his Mid-South Wrestling Association. McGuirk passed away on September 9, 1988, in Claremore at the age of 78, leaving his wife Dorothy and two daughters.

A decade after McGuirk's accident, **Daniel Allen Hodge** of Perry, Oklahoma, rose to the top of the junior heavyweights. Like Earl McCready, McGuirk, and Hutton, Hodge's amateur background out of Oklahoma schools paved the way for a extraordinary professional career. Danny built his skills at the University of Oklahoma, but his wrestling education in the Sooner State started much earlier than his arrival in college.

Hodge was born on May 13, 1932, to William Edward ("Bill") and Hazel Blanchard Hodge, and weighed 13 pounds at birth. In his first year at Perry High School, he joined the wrestling squad led by John Devine. Educated in all facets of amateur grappling, Danny's passion for the sport grew. His strong instincts also began to shine as he conditioned and strengthened his body. The repute he earned as a wrestler in high school preceded him when he enlisted in the U.S. Navy in 1951.

At Ames, Iowa in April 1952, Hodge survived the U.S. Olympic wrestling trials, and secured a spot on the team, coached by Naval Academy instructor Ray Swartz, in the 174-pound division. On July 20 in Helsinki, he was pinned by Russia's David Cimakuridze in 5:58 in what was hyped as the initial match between Russia and America in an Olympic contact competition. Hodge returned to commitments at the Great Lakes Naval Training Center near Chicago, and scored the National AAU Championship in April 1953 at Toledo. He repeated the feat at 174 pounds in 1954.

Going into the May 1956 wrestling trials for the U.S. Olympic team, Hodge was the favorite in the middleweight class. Undefeated since his loss to Cimakuridze, he prevailed through six rounds at the Hollywood Legion Stadium. It seemed that he was going to coast onto the team going to Melbourne, but on May 2, Danny was pinned in 2:37 by William Smith and eliminated from participation in the Games. Fate would intervene, though. Smith, nominated to captain the Olympic squad, was embroiled in a controversy with the Central AAU, ending in his removal from the team altogether. Hodge was his substitute, and went to Australia, where he took a silver medal in the freestyle event.

Representing the University of Oklahoma, Hodge snared three Big Seven and NCAA Championships from 1955–57 at 177 pounds under the tutelage of the distinguished Port Robertson. He also repeated as AAU Champ in 1956. Interested in evolving his athletic resume, Danny participated in the March 1958 National Golden Gloves tournament in New York City. In the finals, he beat Charley Hood in 2:23 of the second round for the heavyweight boxing title at the Garden. Following the tournament, he balanced the possibilities of turning professional in boxing with competing as both a wrestler and boxer at the 1960 Olympic Games. Convinced by boxing manager Art Freeman, and the hype that he was a "better prospect" than Rocky Marciano, Hodge debut as a pro boxer on June 10, 1958, in Scranton with a first-round knockout victory over Norman Jackson.

By July 9, 1959, Hodge had won eight of ten pro fights, and subsequently announced his retirement. Trained, in part, by McGuirk and Ed Lewis, he debuted in October as a wrestler, and a crafted push by promoters in the tri-state area built a steady fan base that resulted in profits across the territory. Danny's feud with NWA junior champion Angelo Savoldi in the spring of 1960 saw a bizarre incident occur involving his father.

Bill Hodge Sr. attended a program in Oklahoma City headlined by a ten-round boxing match between Hodge and Savoldi on May 27. In the fifth round, Bill jumped into the ring and stabbed Savoldi with a penknife. Savoldi bled excessively from injuries on his arm and back, requiring 70 stitches at a local hospital, while Danny's father was arrested. In what appeared to be a complete lack of awareness of the dramatics of wrestling, Bill attacked the heel pummeling his son with blind anger. The unscripted moment was captured in the minds of all who witnessed it, and, of course, played perfectly into the promoter's cashbox.

An estimated 6,000 fans watched Hodge shellac Savoldi for the NWA world junior title on July 22, 1960, at the Stockyards Coliseum in Oklahoma City. Danny became the principal headliner in McGuirk's territory and successfully made his way across the Alliance. By 1962, he was making upwards of $80,000 annually as a pro wrestler, compared to a modest teacher's salary, an occupation he contemplated embracing.

Hodge's acute wrestling knowledge, combined with his strength and agility, made him a feared shooter. From 1960 to March 15, 1976, when his career was cut short in a car accident, he was the superstar of the NWA's junior heavyweight class. Forced to retire as champion, Hodge has since been honored by numerous committees for induction into their Halls of Fame.

Among the dozens of other wrestlers to hold the world junior title were Verne Gagne, Baron Leone, Edmund Francis, Mike Clancy, Hiro Matsuda, Roger Kirby, Dory Funk, Mike DiBiase, Ivan the Terrible, Joe McCarthy, Lorenzo Parente, Sputnik Monroe, Pat Barrett, Roger Kirby, Nelson Royal, Ken Mantel, and Al Madril.

The bylaws of the National Wrestling Alliance were amended in September 1952 to include the sanctioning of a world light heavyweight championship. At that juncture, there were several versions of the title, and the NWA wanted to reduce the number of champions to better regulate the division. **John "the Great" Balbo** was Pinkie George's claimant in Iowa, and Andy Tremaine was holding a version on the basis of a victory in Southwestern Texas. Gypsy Joe (Joe Dorsetti) beat Balbo on November 6, 1952, at KRNT Theater in Des Moines, and on January 11, 1953, at an NWA meeting in St. Louis, was given official recognition by the Alliance. Instead of being asked to lose a unification match, Tremaine retired.

The 185-pound championship was deemed less valuable than the junior title, and few promoters wanted anything to do with it. Pinkie administered the booking of Dorsetti until March 29, handing over the obligation to Tex Hager at a special Alliance gathering at the Blackstone Hotel in Chicago. Hager, the man who supervised wrestling for the NWA in Idaho, Montana, and parts of British Columbia, Oregon, and Washington, had a replacement for his friend Dorsetti in **Frank Stojack**. Stojack was born in British Columbia in 1912, the second son of

Mike and Sophia Stojack, Polish immigrants from Austria. Moving his family to Tacoma in Pierce County, Washington, in 1919, Mike was a laborer and saw to it that his children were well educated. Frank was applauded for his football and wrestling prowess at Lincoln High School and with the Washington State College Cougars in Pullman from 1933 to '35.

As a grappler, Stojack gained conference honors at 175 pounds and was a prime candidate for the Olympic wrestling squad. He was a preeminent guard for football coach Babe Hollingbery, and gained a physical education degree. In August 1935, he was signed by the Brooklyn Dodgers professional football team. He played 12 games in the NFL that year, and 11 the next. In the off-season, he made his pro wrestling debut to earn extra cash. He was a member of the Tacoma City Council (1950–1956) when he received Hager's push, and subdued Dorsetti in Spokane on August 10, 1953, for the NWA light heavyweight title.

The NWA supported Stojack's claim until inactivity forced the organization to strip him of the title in 1958. Considerations for a national tournament were granted to an affiliated promoter in Nevada who, without membership in the NWA, saw his efforts completely wasted. Ted Walker's awarding of the vacant championship to Moe Smith on October 29, 1958, in Carson City was rejected and the title dropped from the Alliance's list of fundamental endorsements. Instead, exclusive booking of the title was taken over by Salvador Lutteroth of Mexico City.

Formal recognition was offered to the winner of a bout between a second-generation grappler, Al Kashey, and the adopted son of Mexico, **Dorrell Dixon**, at an arena in the Mexican capital that reportedly held as many as 20,000 fans on the night of February 13, 1959. Proclaimed "Mr. Jamaica" in 1953, Dixon was a gifted wrestler and an accomplished bodybuilder, and his defeat of Kashey for the championship proved worthwhile. At 25 years of age, he became the new world light heavyweight champion, backed by both the National Wrestling Association and the National Wrestling Alliance, and given a belt by Association President David Ott. Since 1959, this edition of the light heavyweight title has been defended and traded in Mexico, with more than 30 different grapplers holding the strap.

Danny McShain was a versatile, three-division champion, having held the National Wrestling Association world light heavyweight title, the National Wrestling Alliance world junior title, and an abundance of regional heavyweight titles. His road to wrestling stardom started in Little Rock on October 30, 1912, born into a poor family headed by Charles and Evelina Savage Shain. He spent his early childhood in DeBastrop Township in Ashley County, Arkansas, prior to his family's relocation to Tujunga, California, just north of Glendale. He participated in sports at Glendale High, and turned pro wrestler in 1933 as a middleweight. Using the name Danny "McShain," he played up a gimmick that suggested Ireland as his homeland.

By 1937, he was a respected light heavyweight, and moonlighted in Hollywood at R.K.O. Radio Pictures. Managed by actor and future television commentator Richard "Dick" Lane, McShain was a lively and innovative performer. He sold everything in the ring, from exaggerated expressions to the hysteria before and after skirmishes. He vanquished "Wild" Red Berry in Hollywood on October 11, 1937 for his first world light heavyweight title and wore the championship no less than ten times. In Memphis on November 19, 1951, he won the second and third falls from Verne Gagne to take the belt symbolizing the NWA world junior title. Danny mastered Rito Romero and unified the latter's junior laurels with his own on June 25, 1952, in Los Angeles.

McShain was the first official NWA titleholder to be double-crossed in the ring by a rogue wrestler. On July 24, 1952, he battled Henry Harrell, a shining member of the Nick Gulas–Roy Welch circuit, at Chattanooga's Memorial Auditorium. Wearing the Southern junior heavyweight championship, Harrell was in the midst of his biggest push, and was given a bout with McShain as an example of where hard work could get you. The defending world junior champion was scripted to win the match, and would, by making it a spirited affair, boost the credibility of Harrell.

Nevertheless, the challenger was uncooperative from the very beginning, suggestive of an in-ring betrayal. The initial fall ended when the NWA titleholder was counted out by referee Lucky O'Rourke. In the second, Danny was disqualified and the *Chattanooga News Free Press* described the bout as a "disappointing fizzle." The newspaper also pointed that the title couldn't change hands on a DQ, a ruse Sam Muchnick later claimed wasn't officially adopted by the NWA until April 1953. Appalled at what had transpired, Welch sent his brother Herb into the ring with Harrell the next night in Knoxville, and stripped the desperado of his Southern championship. It is not likely that match was altogether clean either.

The stunt had been inexcusable and sent shock waves across the organization. Muchnick subtly mentioned it in a bulletin, and members were reportedly warned, in private, to stay away from Harrell. There was a belief Gulas had put Harrell up to the trick, and that this was the reason why the Nashville promoter was later denied entry into the NWA. Needless to say, the Department of Justice got wind of the story, and, in inner-office messages, showed interest in discussing the situation with Harrell. They wanted to know why he wasn't backed as the new titleholder, and if he had been blackballed in any way by the Alliance for winning a match "against instructions."

Despite their interest, investigators never reached him for an interview. While Harrell found some work with affiliated bookers after the episode, it was clear that he had been relegated to undercards as retribution for his adventure in Chattanooga. Double-crosses were indeed possible, and the NWA leadership were well aware of the ramifications.

McShain wore the championship until August 17, 1953, when he lost the belt to "Baron" Leone in Memphis. Long stints in California and Texas, with expansive television coverage, gave "Dangerous" Danny a national reputation as being a wild man of the mat. A brawler, he was able to mix comedy into his matches, adding to his persona. At the same time, he could fight in the brutal Texas style that drew blood and perpetuated sheer violence. McShain retired after three decades on the mat, only to invest in promotions in Albuquerque and Austin. The latter endeavor cost him $15,000, and his stay in New Mexico included a promotional war with NWA member Mike London. In April 1969, he marred Sally Lewin, the sister of wrestlers Mark, Donn, and Ted Lewin. He died on July 14, 1992, at the age of 79.

Edouard Carpentier was the NWA's choice in June 1957 to take a controversial match from Lou Thesz, splitting the championship and introducing a new twist to wrestling's legacy. Born Edouard Wieczorkwicz on July 17, 1926, outside Lyon, France, Carpentier was one of three children raised by his Russian innkeeper father and Polish mother. From a young age, he excelled in athletics, and demonstrated his bravery by fighting with the French Resistance at age 16 during World War II. Decorated for his valor, Carpentier pursued gymnastics after the war, specifically the rings and trampoline, and was an alternate on the 1948 French Olympic squad in London.

Carpentier said in an interview with the *Montreal Star* on December 18, 1957, that he had met Verne Gagne, a member of the U.S. wrestling team, in London during the Olympics, and that Gagne was an early mentor. In 1950 and '51, Edouard participated in amateur Greco-Roman tournaments and learned much from 1924 Olympic gold medallist Henri DeGlane. Under the alias "Eddie Wiecz," he turned pro in 1952, and beat Felix Miquet for a version of the European heavyweight title in 1954. Aside from modeling clothing in Paris, he entered the world of cinema, acting as a stuntman and in small roles in at least six French-language films, beginning in 1955. Three of his movies were *Les Truands, Folies Bergere*, and *Ca Va Barde*, starring Eddie Constantine.

On a jaunt through Europe with Yvon Robert, Larry Moquin, and a contingent of midget grapplers, Eddie Quinn and Frank Tunney stopped in Paris and saw a November 14, 1955, wrestling program at the Palais des Sports. The two NWA members witnessed Wiecz in action and were astounded by his resemblance athletically to Antonino "Argentina" Rocca. Robert acted as a mediator as Quinn extended an invitation to the Frenchman for exhibitions in Canada, and large amounts of money were promised.

Edouard accepted the proposal, adopted the name "Carpentier," and came up with a falsified ancestry to former boxer Georges Carpentier that spiced up his profile. According to Carpentier, his arrangement with Quinn soured the moment he stepped off a plane in Quebec, and nearly quashed their business dealings even before they got off the ground. Further schooled by Robert and Moquin, Carpentier made his Montreal debut on April 18, 1956, against veteran Angelo Savoldi. Carpentier vanquished his opponent and gained the admiration of the estimated 8,000 fans at the Forum.

Quinn was astute, and knew the potential income with Carpentier on the payroll was going to pad his bank account nicely. He was quoted by the *Montreal Star* as saying Edouard was better than Rocca. The press reports on Carpentier in Montreal helped sell his talents, and hyped him over established stars. Among Carpentier's victims in Montreal were Lenny Montana, Ernie Dusek, Pat O'Connor, and Don Leo Jonathan. On June 13, 1956, Edouard received his first chance at Wladek "Killer" Kowalski's world title. The duel ended in a draw with one fall apiece, at the 11:30 curfew.

Beloved in Montreal, Carpentier was ready to make his mark in Ontario, and then debut in the United States. Telegrams and correspondence by Quinn to allies offered up his import's services, and Edouard soon was making an impact in Chicago and St. Louis. Always accompanied by his road agent, Bob "Legs" Langevin, Carpentier built a loyal fan base and entertained audiences with his acrobatics. On May 8, 1957, in Montreal, Edouard threw Kowalski for the local world title, winning the first and third falls, the final by countout.

Two years after failing to double their revenue with duel heavyweight title claimants, the members of the Alliance approved the failed measure again under slightly different conditions. The decision was spurred by a hunger to make money during Lou Thesz's expedition to the South Pacific and Asia in the fall of 1957. With Thesz unavailable for two months, members were concerned about losing the sizable gates he'd normally be bringing in. But Thesz was committed to the tour, optimistic that it was going to be financially beneficial in the long term, and with NWA President Sam Muchnick garnering a percentage, the NWA braintrust was satisfied.

Recycling the Leo Nomellini angle used in 1955 allowed the Alliance to claim two champions simultaneously. While Thesz was overseas with his belt, a short-term champ could be accessible to any of the 30-plus members in the union. Thesz was on board if the man he was defeated by met his own personal criteria, and the loss did not conflict with his travel plans or damage his reputation. The NWA crown added tremendous value to his image overseas, and there was no way he was going to be stripped of that title clean.

Satisfied Carpentier could successfully handle the Alliance circuit, the powers-that-be chose him to accommodate disgruntled members in Thesz's absence. Thesz agreed to the selection of Edouard, an ambassador of Quinn's empire, and the plan was a go. Quinn covered the $10,000 mandatory performance bond, and the idea of having a secondary titleholder came to fruition. Carpentier dropped his Montreal belt to Gene Kiniski on June 12, then went to Chicago for the defining match of his career.

On June 14, 1957, in Chicago, a mere 5,682 fans attended Fred Kohler's International Amphitheater program headlined by Thesz and Carpentier, a match which could easily have drawn twice that in Montreal. The historic encounter opened with the first fall going to Thesz in 17:22 with a flying body press. Carpentier rebounded to win the second in 3:39. An onslaught by the nimble grappler forced Thesz into a defensive position, and the champ's incessant bouncing, off the ropes and from corner-to-corner, during the third fall compelled referee Ed Whalen to act. Whalen called the match when it was apparent that Thesz, who professed a back injury, could no longer ward off the attacks of his rival, and named Carpentier the victor by disqualification.

The *Chicago Tribune, Montreal Star*, and Kohler's magazine *Wrestling Life*, a publication with nationwide distribution, each reported that Carpentier beat Thesz for the "National Wrestling Alliance" title. The basis for his claim in 43 states and parts of Canada stemmed from the fact that Whalen had halted the match, not for a violation of a rule, but because the defending champion couldn't continue.

The use of the word "disqualification," under these circumstances, was a deliberate tactic to confuse things. By NWA standards, the title could not change hands by DQ and accounts in several Alliance territories made reference to that fact. The *Toronto Star*, on June 22, 1957, billed Carpentier as the "number one contender" based on the Chicago victory. Muchnick followed that same reasoning in St. Louis, and as the coalition's president, he adhered to official policy.

But on the side, Muchnick was a full-fledged player in the plan to run two champions, even publicly affirming Carpentier's championship status in the July 27, 1957, *Montreal Star* following a rematch between the two grapplers on July 24 at a Montreal baseball stadium. The match ended in a bona fide disqualification when Carpentier threw referee Yvon Robert to the mat.

On August 23, 1957, Carpentier worked a semifinal in St. Louis on the undercard of Thesz's title defense versus Pat O'Connor, and was acknowledged as a claimant. Winning his match against Fritz Von Erich impressively, Carpentier displayed his magnetic style for the NWA members in town for the convention. The showing was essential to expanding his booking schedule throughout the organization, and profitable appearances lay ahead. However, the next day, his pilot, Quinn, stormed out of a luncheon at the Claridge Hotel after learning outlaw promoter Jack Pfefer had also been in attendance. Quinn was furious Muchnick had invited his foe, withdrew his membership, and effectively destroyed his working arrangement with the NWA.

In other words, Carpentier was no longer available to Muchnick for bookings, and the previous agreement allowing duel titleholders was terminated. Hoping to avoid a potential quagmire with a straightforward declaration, Muchnick announced that the NWA "does not, and at no time has recognized Edouard Carpentier as world heavyweight wrestling champion." Any and all references to the French athlete ever having a claim to the Alliance title was erased from the books, although he had been co-champion for 71 days. The Alliance rewrote history on a dime, but members weren't getting off that easy. There were going to be consequences, and just like the Nomellini scheme, no return payoff.

Quinn wrote a letter to Muchnick dated September 4, 1957 that addressed his objections:

> I would like to explain to you again, if it is possible to get the message thru, that for the past 20 years I have been fighting the Cancer of the Wrestling Business, Jack Pfefer. This is the same man who tried to kill the Alliance, and he has loused up quite a few territories of NWA members, including New England, where I have a $25,000 investment.
>
> You, as president of the Alliance, know that everybody in it despises Pfefer, and what he stands for. You, as president of the Alliance, trying to play politics with everybody in it, must realize that sooner or later you have to face the barrier. At times you are much weaker than others. If you think it is good business for the Alliance to have Jack Pfefer consorting and in partnership, or in collusion, or working with, certain members of said Alliance, I think it is your duty as a man to bring this to the attention of the rest of the members. Remember, the first thing you asked me before the Alliance meeting is what did I think of the Alliance. I told you all, that business-wise, it was no good, as the government takes care of that. I did express my thoughts that it was a worthwhile social group, but that we should get together more often to become better acquainted on matters pertaining to business. But when you have the bold audacity to inflict Jack Pfefer on the

members of the Alliance, socially, it is a little too much for me.

Yes, I did tell Larry Moquin that I was sick, in fact, I was nauseated by your conduct in allowing our common enemy to mingle with the Members, thus causing them much embarrassment. I am sure when Lou Thesz hears about this incident, it will only convince him that he did the right thing when he left you, and St. Louis, and the meeting behind him.

The reason I wished to get out of the St. Louis promotion is firstly, the promoter or promoters have shown no ability to promote for the past two years. I know you spend your time knocking Thesz as a poor businessman and Longson as a dope, but sooner or later you will have to take the blame on your own shoulders. Another thing I did not like at the meeting was when that loud-mouthed blatant individual, Cliff Maupin, a garbage collector of the old school, kept knocking Thesz about his forthcoming trip. It struck several of us very funny that you did not stand up and defend Lou, who by the sweat of his brow has been paying your salary as long as he has been champion, and was making you money when he was your partner in promotion.

Getting back to Carpentier, you seem to overlook the fact that Carpentier is my personal property. He does not belong to you or the National Wrestling Alliance. He is not recognized by you and neither does he claim to be NWA champion. He met and defeated Lou Thesz June 14 in Chicago via disqualification. In a return match in Montreal, he met and was defeated by Lou Thesz July 24. You should be able to add two and two. On the next meeting, held in Chicago, I understand the match was a draw.

I have consulted my attorney on the matter and they suggested that I write to you and have you return Edouard Carpentier's $10,000. What you are holding it for, no one seems to know. If this money has not been returned within ten days from this date, I will have my attorneys turn this matter over to the U.S. Department of Justice and the St. Louis police, c/o the Bunco Squad. My attorneys seem to think this is a combination of blackmail, extortion, or grand larceny. Hope this will clarify everything.

On a slow news weekend, Dan Parker, the colorful sportswriter for the *New York Mirror*, reprinted Quinn's scandalous missive in its entirety on November 16, 1957. He said that Quinn "had posted [$10,000] with Muchnick as a guarantee that Carpentier would lose the 'title' back to Lou Thesz, Sam's champion, if Thesz would first let him win it for prestige."

Carpentier was already irritated with the way Quinn was disbursing the money he was bringing in, and the break from the NWA increased his displeasure. Alliance members wanted dates on him whether he was a titleholder or not, and Quinn planned to monopolize his bookings. That was until Fred Kohler got Carpentier's ear and persuaded him to leave Quinn's stable and work directly for him. The double-cross infuriated Quinn, and would later prompt his 1959 invasion of Chicago. Kohler made Carpentier available to the NWA, and sent him to many important towns, including New York City, Denver, St. Louis, and Philadelphia.

By 1958, news outlets, depending on their original source of information, offered contradicting reports on who was the rightful titleholder, Carpentier or Thesz's successor, Dick Hutton. It was a media game, and as Kohler and Johnny Doyle marketed Carpentier, Muchnick spent time ballyhooing the attributes of both Hutton and the NWA. Taking some of the responsibility for recognizing Edouard as world titleholder was the National Wrestling Association, beginning in October 1958, a shocker seeing as it hadn't recognized a separate champion from the Alliance in almost a decade. This was a turning point in the Association's attempts to restructure with any sort of national credibility.

Carpentier's accomplishments were mounting in some of wrestling's biggest cities. Frank Mastro's article in the *Chicago Tribune* on January 5, 1958, stated that Carpentier was "responsible" for drawing over 71,000 fans at the International Amphitheater and Marigold Arena in 1957, and, with Antonino Rocca, drew a $62,000 gate at Madison Square Garden on September 16, 1957. In Montreal, he was regularly packing 10,000 into the Forum and in excess of that number for summer spectaculars at the baseball stadium.

The distinction of "National Wrestling Association" champion was attached to Carpentier by Quinn's Montreal public relations department through the first week of March 1958, and was long forgotten by the time he suffered a loss to Mike Sharpe on April 23. Local titleholder Wladek Kowalski stood singly as king of Quinn's promotion without any mention of Carpentier's once-highlighted championship, proving once again that titles often meant very little in wrestling.

In the years that followed, Edouard was obliging to promoters, and his victory over Thesz was manipulated to establish world title lineages in Boston (Wladek Kowalski, May 3, 1958), Omaha (Verne Gagne, August 9, 1958), and Los Angeles (Fred Blassie, June 12, 1961). Demonstrating his enduring appeal, the Los Angeles bout with Blassie drew a gate in excess of $40,000 at the Sports Arena. A new attendance record for a wrestling show in Canada was established on July 21, 1960, when Carpentier wrestled and beat Buddy Rogers at Montreal's Delorimier Stadium. On July 20, 1961, with Hans Schmidt, Edouard lured 20,618 fans to the same venue. Carpentier and Rogers also brought in a gate of $55,719 at Comiskey Park on July 27, 1962.

Three years later, on May 10, 1963, Carpentier was involved in a serious head-on car accident near Louiseville, Quebec, but his excellent physical conditioning not only allowed him to walk away from the hospital within a few days time, but return to the mat and continue his career. Carpentier remained one of the most popular wrestlers in the world and a top box-office attraction. It didn't matter if he was at the Forum in Montreal or roaming across the Midwest for Gagne's AWA. Following his retirement, he trained future grapplers, and today lives in Quebec — unenthusiastic about modern professional wrestling.

Laverne Clarence Gagne, some believe, would have been a better choice than Dick Hutton to replace Thesz as NWA champion in November 1957. Born on February 26, 1926, in Hennepin County, Minnesota, he was the second son of Clarence (1898–1966) and Elsie Gagne (1902–1938). He participated in football and wrestled at Robbinsdale High School, receiving attention from many college coaches, especially David Bartelma and Bernie Bierman at the University of Minnesota. Beginning on June 19, 1943, Gagne was enrolled at Minnesota, and competed between the 175-pound and heavyweight divisions. The 1943 squad walked away with the all-conference football title, and Verne won a Big Ten wrestling championship in 1944. In the finals of the National AAU Tournament on March 18, 1944, he was pinned by Dr. M.A. Northrup.

Enlisting in the marines in 1944, Gagne played football for Lt. Col. Dick Hanley at El Toro, and returned to college in 1946–47. On March 8, 1947, he beat Dan Dworsky for the Big Ten heavyweight championship, but placed third in the NCAA tournament at Champaign behind champion Dick Hutton and Ray Gunkel. He captured his first NCAA title at 191 pounds in Bethlehem on March 20, 1948, defeating LeRoy Alitz of Iowa State Teachers College. In London, Gagne was an inactive alternate on the 1948 U.S. Olympic wrestling team, and a year later, avenged his 1947 loss to Hutton with a referee's decision for the NCAA heavyweight title at Fort Collins.

In total, he collected four Big Ten titles, two NCAA championships, and an AAU title. He graduated from Minnesota on June 12, 1948, and wrestled through the 1949 season in his last year of eligibility. Considering turning to the National Football League as a vocation, Gagne was courted by Minneapolis promoter Tony Stecher into pro wrestling. He was tutored by Stecher and Joe Pazandak, and debuted on May 3, 1949, at the Minneapolis Auditorium. 2,724 fans witnessed Gagne's victory over Abe Kashey by disqualification in 22:10, with his future business partner Wally Karbo acting as referee.

Gagne toured eastern Texas (where he learned from Paul Boesch), the central states, and got television time in Chicago. He was pushed toward the world junior title, and took the vacant championship in a tournament on November 13, 1950. The elevation to junior champion boosted his fame and gave him a valued badge to wear for more than a year.

In the months after his title loss to Danny McShain, Gagne became a heavyweight and was a challenger for NWA champion Lou Thesz, a man ten years his senior. The professional competitiveness of the Thesz-Gagne rivalry was revered by fans, and Verne's backers saw him as a potential successor to the titleholder. *Ring Magazine* agreed, predicting he would be the next heavyweight champion of the world in its December 1951 issue. Thesz and Gagne went 60 minutes for a stalemate on January 25, 1952, at the Amphitheater in Chicago before a mob of nearly 11,000 and a gate of $25,136. According to the *Chicago Daily Tribune*, Gagne was in control for most of the match, indicating the respect Thesz had for him.

The following night at the Marigold, Verne was honored by the *Police Gazette* for his "contribution to clean and scientific wrestling in 1951." The accolade was symbolized by a sterling silver belt, an award presented by Arch Ward, the *Chicago Tribune* sports editor, in a ceremony televised on WGN and DuMont. Verne was designated "Outstanding Professional Wrestler of 1952," and furnished a second *Police Gazette* trophy.

Twenty NWA members participated in an election to name the principal contenders to the heavyweight title in March 1953, and Gagne prevailed with ten first-place votes and 65 total points. Killer Kowalski came in second and Antonino Rocca, third. In a letter from Muchnick to Fred Kohler dated March 12, 1953, he wrote: "The reason I sent these out was to get a cross-view on the thinking of Alliance members, and in the event of an accident or serious injury to the champion, it would give us an idea on how to proceed from there."

Gagne and Thesz fought to a draw again in 60 minutes, this time at Boston on April 7, 1953, in front of an estimated 8,000 people. In September, Gagne was awarded the "United States" championship, a distinction that would become the crown jewel of wrestling on DuMont. The contentious title was never sanctioned by the Alliance, and was considered by Kohler to be a "sectional" championship, much like the British Empire title or any number of other state belts.

Kohler, a cunning impresario with limitless promotional savvy, may have unconsciously impeded Gagne's climb to the NWA world heavyweight championship by being so stubborn in his endorsement of the U.S. title. Muchnick and Thesz believed that Lou's houses were weakened by the existence of a United States belt, and fans were second-guessing the validity of his claim to wrestling's top prize. The many TV outlets run by Kohler were giving Gagne more coverage than anyone else, and made Verne an industry-wide superstar.

The most powerful people in the Alliance continued to be piqued by Kohler's manipulations. After publishing an "NWA Official Calendar" which celebrated Gagne, but failed to mention that Thesz was even a titleholder, Kohler was threatened with legal action if it wasn't corrected. Such moves perpetuated an unsteady tension among Kohler, Muchnick, Thesz, and, ultimately Gagne, and diminished the prospects of everyone involved. Conceivably, under the right conditions, Gagne and Thesz could have been matched at an outdoor park and achieved Thesz–Leone-like figures, perhaps even greater.

Between October 1953 and March 1954, Gagne headlined Madison Square Garden five straight times, drawing a gate of in excess of $50,000 on October 27. Compared to Thesz, he was a superior draw in New York and Chicago, and brought prestige to the U.S. belt for 31 months, establishing its place as second only to the NWA heavyweight title. Was he in a strong enough position, politically, to get the NWA championship, or were the bridges already burned?

By 1958, the shift to Gagne still hadn't been made. In fact, it was his Olympic teammate, Dick Hutton, who was chosen to replace Thesz. Hutton was given the daunting task of restoring universal faith to the heavyweight class, but was unsuccessful. Verne, meanwhile, sold hundreds of thousands of tickets in Minneapolis, Chicago, Omaha, Denver, and Milwaukee, with stops in Washington, Boston, and New York. He teamed with Argentina Rocca to lure the largest wrestling crowd to the Garden since Londos was on the marquee. On February 4, 1957, 19,300 fans paid $61,000 to see the two favorites beat Karl Von Hess and Hans Schmidt, and an estimated 5,000 fans were turned away.

Nearly seven years after *Ring Magazine* prophesized he would be the next world heavyweight champion, Gagne finally got his chance. The Minnesota product took the title from Edouard Carpentier on August 9, 1958, at Omaha's Municipal Stadium. Gagne was a compelling attraction and likely would have served the Alliance better if he'd been given the strap when Thesz stepped down. Whether or not it was a private rift that eliminated him from contention, no one will know for sure. Gagne was a competitor at heart but, historically, lived in the shadow of Thesz.

Gagne was at the forefront of an idea to construct an independent body that cooperated with the NWA on many levels, but had its own champions and guidelines. With Wally Karbo, he bought the Stechers family's shares in the Minneapolis territory (Minneapolis Boxing and Wrestling Club) and formed the American Wrestling Alliance. For storyline sake, AWA "officials" gave NWA champion Pat O'Connor 90 days to defend his belt against Gagne. When that bout failed to materialize, Verne was proclaimed inaugural AWA world champion in August 1960. The members of the NWA were not threatened in any way by what was a friendly "rival" organization, and the AWA's brass frequently attended Alliance gatherings.

For 30 years, the AWA enthralled audiences across the upper Midwest. Booking was done by Gagne and Karbo from their offices at the Dyckman Hotel. Gagne held the AWA title on nine occasions, the offshoot (Carpentier lineage) of the championship five times, the AWA tag title four times, and various regional belts. With Dick the Bruiser and Wilbur Snyder, Gagne owned a piece of the Chicago promotion (Chicago Wrestling Club), and in 1976, bought into St. Louis. In the early 1980s, as cable television was reshaping professional wrestling, marketing schemes took over the old-school mindset of those involved with the sport. Those willing to conform to the ever-changing times remained afloat, and others sank.

Verne had four children, Gregory Allan, Kathleen Ann, Elizabeth Mary, and Donna Lynn with wife Mary Ardith Marxen Gagne (1926–2002). His son Greg was a talented football player at Minnesota and followed his father into wrestling. A heralded champion, Verne offered pro grappling great credibility. Popular and astonishingly quick, he was not naïve about the political side of the business. Gagne watched the birth and death of the organization he created, and his celebrated athletic career is still remembered by his fans today.

On April 7, 1956, **Wilbur Snyder** ended the lengthy stretch of Gagne as U.S. champion at the Marigold Arena in Chicago. Wilbur, a product of Santa Monica, was born to Firman and Lola Irene Snyder on September 15, 1929. He displayed a mastery of football at Van Nuys High, which led him to the University of Utah, and then the Edmonton Eskimos of the Western Interprovincial Football Union in 1951. Snyder, a dependable lineman, changed positions to become one of Canada's top place-kickers. In 1953, he established two WIFU records with best convert-kicking percentage, 100 percent on 31 kicks, and set the record for the longest kickoff at 83 yards.

Snyder's wrestling debut occurred during the off-season in 1953, and he was coached by Sandor Szabo and Warren Bockwinkel in southern California. In 1954, Snyder decided to retire from football and wrestle full time. He informed Eskimo coach Al Anderson of his decision, and the team released him in May. Using football tactics combined with a growing array of mat skills, he garnered a lot of national attention. Wilbur was fresh off a reign as champion in Montreal when he nabbed the U.S. title in Chicago, and was evolving into a superstar of a circuit that included Indianapolis and Omaha.

A regional champion in a myriad of Alliance territories, Snyder copped an offshoot of the world title from Gagne on November 15, 1958, in Omaha. He invested in Indianapolis following the departure of Jim Barnett, founding Championship Wrestling, Inc. on April 27, 1965, with Dick Afflis (Dick the Bruiser). Wilbur's wife Shirlee, identified as "S. Snyder" on the articles of incorporation, was the registered agent. The directors were listed as S. Snyder, L. Afflis (Bruiser's wife Louise), and M.A. Johnston (Bruiser's mother Margaret), and it was done that way to keep Wilbur and Bruiser's ownership secret.

Snyder beat Mitsu Arakawa for the WWA title in September 1967 and was champ for nearly two years. He was a ten-time U.S. champion between 1956 and '62, having extended battles with the Bruiser and Hans Schmidt. He held the WWA world tag team title 13 times, and during a tour of Japan in 1969, won the JWA international tag team title with Danny Hodge. Wilbur was married to Shirlee Ann Hanson Snyder from 1948 until his death on December 25, 1991, in Pompano Beach, Florida at the age of 62.

Kohler also gave **William Richard (Dick) Afflis** a stage on which to perform on his circuit around the Great Lakes. William, the son of a World War I veteran, William Walter, and an influential political figure, Margaret, was born on June 27, 1929, in Carroll County, Indiana. His father, who died when Dick was in his teens, ran a drugstore in Delphi, the hometown of Margaret, and the Afflises lived an affluent lifestyle. After playing football at Shortridge High, Bill attended Purdue University in West Lafayette. In 1950, he transferred to the University of Nevada at Reno, and demonstrated his athletic skills on the football field. He was taken in the 16th round of the 1951 National Football League draft by the Green Bay Packers.

As an offensive lineman, Dick Afflis was a member of the Packers from 1951 to '54, earning a reputation as a tough guy. In the summer of 1954, he made his wrestling debut in Reno and joined the promotional wheel of Kohler, training under Leo Nomellini, Joe Pazandak, and Gagne. Afflis chose wrestling as a full-time occupation in August 1955, leaving the Packers with a self-imposed retirement. Several months later, he signed a three-year contract with Jim Barnett and worked as a heel who slowly started to win over fans. In Chicago, Indianapolis, Omaha, and Milwaukee, Bruiser became a draw against Schmidt, Snyder, Gagne, Don Leo Jonathan, Bobo Brazil, Bob Ellis, and Yukon Eric.

On December 13, 1957, Dick the Bruiser captured the main version of the United States title from Snyder at the Amphitheater in Chicago. He dropped the championship to Gagne on April 11, 1958, at the same venue with a gate of $17,668.39. In Barnett strongholds Indianapolis, Denver, and Detroit, Bruiser was a fixed main-eventer, and lofty attendance numbers were commonplace with him on the bill (10,896 fans saw Bruiser win his second U.S. title from Snyder at the Olympia in Detroit on May 23, 1959). In total, he won U.S. championships 13 times from 1957 to 1963. He also gained attention for a feud with recently banned NFL defensive tackle Alex Karras.

Bruiser engaged in an infamous public brawl with Karras at the latter's tavern (Lindell A.C. Bar) in Detroit on April 23, 1963. A police officer trying to break up the struggle suffered a broken wrist. Dick needed five stitches to close a wound under his left eye, was charged with assault and battery, and received a $400 fine. The fight, of course, built toward a match at the Olympia four nights later, and a huge throng was expected for the supershow. But the stacked program was a dud, drawing much less interest than promoters had hoped.

Before Bruiser went to Los Angeles and sold out the Olympic with Fred Blassie on April 22, 1964, he bought the Indianapolis territory. Incorporated as Championship Wrestling from Indiana, Inc. (2208 N. Meridian), the business was sold to the audience as being the promotion of L. (Louise) Afflis, Bruiser's wife, with Johnny King as matchmaker. Newspapers reported that the two wrestlers had taken over the wrestling enterprises, but kayfabe kept later assessments of the promotion quiet.

While in Los Angeles, Bruiser won the Worldwide Wrestling Alliance title, a championship that would become the centerpiece for the WWA in Indiana. Although he lost the title in Los Angeles in July, Dick remained titleholder in the Hoosier State until losing the belt to Gene Kiniski on August 21, 1965. The WWA was successful in its promotions, expanding into parts of Illinois, Michigan, Kentucky, and Ohio. Bruiser, in an arrangement with the Kohler Family, put money into Chicago, then purchased the entire operation when Fred retired in 1965.

Bruiser formed a tag team with the Crusher (Reggie Lisowski) and captured the AWA world tag title on five occasions. Additionally, they were WWA champions six times and held the JWA international tag title in Japan. He was WWA world titleholder a total of ten times over a 21-year period and wore the Missouri title three times. The Bruiser passed away on November 10, 1991, at the age of 62. A little more than six weeks later, his friend and business partner Snyder died, also at 62.

"Cowboy" Bob Ellis was a popular champion across NWA territories and a U.S. champion three times beginning in 1960. The third child of hardworking parents John and Rose Ellis, Robert Ellis was born on March 15, 1929, in Tom Green County, Texas. He went to San Angelo High School from 1944 to 1947, and played football for coach Joe Hamrick. The tallest guy on the team at 6'2'', Ellis was a standout at fullback, and had similar achievements on the McMurry

College squad at Abilene. He enlisted in the army during the Korean War, and wrestled at the San Angelo YMCA. Around 1956, he was courted into the pro mat game by Ed "Strangler" Lewis. Under the name "Bob Elliott," Ellis debut in 1957.

The "bulldog" headlock was a maneuver Ellis picked up from Lewis, a variation of his famous stranglehold. On January 19, 1961, he lost to U.S. champion Bruiser at Denver's City Auditorium, a match that drew a local record gate of $20,000, with 8,000 fans in attendance and 2,500 turned away. He headlined Madison Square Garden five straight times between February and July 1962, with three singles bouts versus NWA champion Buddy Rogers that averaged 18,000 per show and a gate exceeding $58,000.

Ellis was known for his ability to sell for an opponent, and often bled profusely in contests. He was a heavy draw in Detroit, Chicago, New York, St. Louis, and Los Angeles, and was a regional champion throughout the NWA. In 1964, he stopped the Destroyer for the WWA title in California. He held the IWA world title for a week in Australia in February 1969, and had two spells as WWA (Midwest) champion in 1973–74. Ellis was caught up in two scandals involving horse racing, and retired from wrestling in 1978.

In the footsteps of Jack Claybourne and King Kong Clayton, **Bobo Brazil** forged a legendary career as an African-American wrestler. He was born Houston Harris on July 15, 1924, in Wilson, Mississippi County, Arkansas, and endured the loss of his father at the age of seven. Raised by his mother Ruby and aunts and uncles, who labored in the cotton-farming industry, young Houston had an inclination for sports, especially baseball. By 16, he'd lived in Gilmore, then spent a little time in East St. Louis before settling in Benton Harbor, Michigan, where his grandfather resided. In 1949, when he made his pro wrestling debut as "Huston Harris," he stood 6′4′′ and weighed 220 pounds.

Adopting the tag "Bobo Brazil," and occasionally listed as being from Cuba, Harris debuted in Chicago in 1950 for promoter Ray Fabiani and received television exposure at the Rainbo Arena. He got his first major break as a headliner in Toronto for Frank Tunney in 1952, teaming with Whipper Watson and clashing with Bob Wagner, Hans Hermann, and Fred Atkins. Bobo, using his "coco-bump" headbutt against opponents, referees, and anyone else who got in his way, proved that talent would prevail over prejudice if given the opportunity. Tunney gave him that chance, and Brazil went right to the top. Jim Mitchell, the "Black Panther," took Bobo on the road with him, and helped him get into Los Angeles for booker Cal Eaton.

Brazil paired with Wilbur Snyder, also a novice, and learned from Sandor

Szabo. On September 6, 1954, Bobo and Snyder defeated Lord Blears and Gene Kiniski in a tournament final for the international TV tag team title in Hollywood. His southern California exploits parlayed into job openings elsewhere, and his notoriety was growing. Backward promoters still refused to use him or any other black wrestlers, and wrestling in some territories was still segregated. Brazil had traveled to San Francisco, Ohio, and Toronto by 1958. At Maple Leaf Gardens, he teamed with Watson on May 22, 1958 to win the Canadian Open tag title from the Lisowskis by disqualification.

As part of the Doyle-Barnett syndicate, Brazil acquired the U.S. title from Dick the Bruiser on January 28, 1961, in Detroit. Brazil and Bruiser traded the belt on February 28 in Detroit, and again the ensuing night in Denver, which drew 8,000 fans, with another 3,000 turned away. On March 29, Bruiser regained the championship in front of 8,528 fans paying $22,711, the two figures setting new records for wrestling in Denver. Bobo was signed by Vince McMahon, and appeared in main events as a fan favorite with Edouard Carpentier and Art Thomas in Chicago and at Madison Square Garden during the summer of 1962.

In Newark, Brazil was booked into a scenario devised by Willie Gilzenberg that allegedly tainted the NWA world title, and drew the ire of promoters who lived and died by the Alliance bylaws. In the short term, the angle would enhance a marketable feud between Bobo and champion Buddy Rogers, and increase ticket sales. On August 18, 1962, 6,112 fans at the Newark Armory watched Bobo win a one-fall match over the Nature Boy in 18:20. Brazil won the bout by countout, with the champion lying incapacitated in the middle of the ring.

There were suggestions that Brazil had captured the title, but the *Newark Sunday News* reported that Bobo declined the belt because he hadn't pinned Rogers, confirming the status of the champion. Speculation that Alliance members were fuming at the unfair booking of their valuable titleholder was refuted eight days after the Newark exhibition, when McMahon was elected the NWA's second vice president.

The seedy booking practices of August 1962 had actually been started in Toronto by Tunney on August 2. Bruno Sammartino routed Rogers and seemingly took the NWA title, only the Italian from Pittsburgh refused the belt on a technicality.

Capitol bookers had no intention of using Brazil as their top heavyweight, but Buddy's injury in Columbus on August 31 sparked serious debate about calling Bobo titleholder in the interim. Affiliated promoter Arnold "Whitey" Carlson, in his local publicity buildup for a show at the Long Island Arena, billed Brazil as the "newly crowned" champion in September, even though Bobo had already dropped a rematch to Rogers.

Newspapers boasted of Bobo's $50,000-plus annual income, and he was featured prominently at Madison Square Garden, wrestling with Gorilla Monsoon, Killer Kowalski, the Grahams, Waldo Von Erich, and Bill Watts. Bobo, on loan to Jules Strongbow, went to Los Angeles and beat Buddy Austin for the WWA title on September 2, 1966.

Brazil was vital to the WWWF in the Northeast from 1963 to '68, and often wore a United States title belt into the ring. On January 12, 1968, in Los Angeles, he again conquered Austin for the WWA title. Mike LeBell joined the NWA later that year, and Brazil's championship was retired. However, he grabbed the "Americas" title following a victory over El Mongol. Bobo challenged Gene Kiniski for the NWA title on December 18, 1968, at the Olympic, and the two wrestled to a deadlock before 10,127 fans.

The 46-year-old Brazil netted his third (non-WWWF) United States title, the first in the Detroit promotion of Ed Farhat (The Sheik), from Farhat himself on May 29, 1971, at Cobo Hall. The Brazil-Sheik feud, which had bloomed in Los Angeles in 1969, would become a primary battle across Michigan. The violence and bloodshed in their matches was on a primitive, almost fictional level, and pioneered the so-called hardcore style.

Bobo retired from wrestling in 1993. An important member of the Benton Harbor community, Brazil was known for his generosity and kindness. His son, Houston Harris Jr., was also a pro wrestler. On June 9, 1994, the WWF inducted Brazil into their Hall of Fame in Baltimore, the site of many of his impressive bouts. Bobo died on January 20, 1998, at the age of 74.

Born on August 16, 1929 in Jewett, Texas, **Jack Barton Adkisson** was the son of Benjamin Rush (1907–1995) and Coren Bessie Newberry Adkisson (1905–1999). He attended Crozier Tech High School in Dallas, and played football at Southern Methodist in 1948–49. On June 23, 1950, Jack married Doris Juanita Smith, and furthered his collegiate education and reputation as a football player at Corpus Christi University. Adkisson signed with the Dallas Texans of the American Football League in June 1952 as a guard, but was later cut.

Standing 6′5′′ and weighing 230 pounds, Jack was convinced to give wrestling a shot by Dallas promoter Ed McLemore. He made his professional debut under his proper name in January 1953, and competed in preliminaries for promoters McLemore and Maurice Beck at the original Sportatorium. By the end of the year, Adkisson was on the road, working as Nazi disciple "Fritz Von Erich." Possessing the size and skill to excel on the mat, Adkisson showed the potential to make a substantial fortune as a wrestler.

The German gimmick stirred spectators into a constant frenzy, and Von Erich drew incredible heat in tag teams with Karl Von Schober, Hans Hermann, and Gene Kiniski. His act created controversy and the seized the ire of audiences everywhere, and television only spread the hatred for his character. He collared championships in innumerable territories, including the United States title twice for Barnett and Doyle, in 1961 and '63. He warred with Dory Funk Sr. over the North American title in 1962, then beat Verne Gagne for the Nebraska world title on July 31 in Omaha. On August 25, Gagne regained the title in a cage match.

Von Erich captured the AWA and Nebraska world titles from Gagne on July 27, 1963, and dropped the former title to Gagne on August 8 in Amarillo, and the latter to Gagne on September 7 in Omaha. He wrestled stints in Dallas in March and April 1958, then from April 1961 to March 1962, but Adkisson kicked off a run in February 1964 that lasted the remainder of his career. Partnered with McLemore, he opened Southwest Promotions, Inc. on September 23, 1966, and severed ties to Houston booking agent Morris Sigel, prompting a promotional war. The dispute concluded with McLemore and Adkisson not only protecting their Sportatorium interests, but gaining booking privileges to Houston and a number of other Texas cities.

McLemore, who Jack regarded as a "master at crowd psychology," and treated like a member of his own family, mentored Adkisson in all aspects of promotion and booking. But he suffered a heart attack in February 1968, leaving Adkisson in charge of the company. Adkisson hired his father to be the manager of the Sportatorium, and Ed Watt to serve as the "front" matchmaker for the Dallas Wrestling Club, as he continued to actively wrestle through the 1970s.

From 1966 to 1982, he held the American title, the main belt of his promotion, 15 times, and was a key challenger for the NWA heavyweight championship. Adkisson had six sons with wife Doris Juanita Smith, and, by 1993, only one still survived. Kevin, David, Kerry, Michael, and Chris followed their father into wrestling, using the "Von Erich" moniker, but this time as fan favorites and teenage icons in Dallas. A member of the NWA from 1967 until 1985, Jack had the distinction of replacing Sam Muchnick as the organization's president on September 1, 1975.

World Class Championship Wrestling provided some of the best action in the country, with angles built around Adkisson's sons. He sold his interests in the promotion in December 1987, and retired. In July 1992, after 42 years of marriage, Jack and Doris divorced, and he passed away on September 10, 1997, of cancer. The famed Sportatorium McLemore and Adkisson had brought all of wrestling's superstars to, and the arena that the Von Erichs were celebrated in, was torn down in 2003.

NWA members earned ample paydays with **Wladek "Killer" Kowalski**, a

Canadian grappler. Walter was born on October 13, 1926, in Essex County, Ontario. He graduated from Lowe High School in Windsor, attended the University of Detroit, and was employed at the Ford Motor Plant. Having put muscle on his 6′5′′ frame bodybuilding in school, he was discovered by promoter Bert Ruby at the Hamtramck YMCA. Ruby was always on the lookout for a moneymaker, and trained Kowalski prior to his debut in 1948. A match with NWA champion Orville Brown in Detroit opened the door for a shot in the central states, and "Tarzan" Kowalski made headlines from Des Moines to Wichita. He ventured to Chicago, where he got important television exposure.

Walter impressed promoters Muchnick and Tunney, and during the summer of 1950, he was billed as "Killer" Kowalski in Houston, while keeping the alias "Tarzan" in Kansas City. On January 25, 1951, he became the second Heart of America champion by whipping Bill Longson. Known as "Wladek" Kowalski in Montreal, he defeated Bobby Managoff for the local world title on April 2, 1952. Over the next decade, he won that championship 11 times and drew consistently in Quebec as the dominant heel.

One of wrestling's most fabled stories was played out on the mat of the Montreal Forum on the evening of October 15, 1952. Kowalski wrestled Yukon Eric, his out-of-the-ring pal, in what was surely to be a hotly contested bout with plenty of audience reaction. Of course, what was about to happen was completely unexpected. Kowalski scaled the top rope for a devastating knee drop onto the prone grappler, but instead of missing, as he'd planned, his knee accidentally sliced across the right side of Holmback's head. The cauliflowered ear of Yukon was torn away, and blood gushed from the open wound.

Referee Sammy Mack, seemingly unaware of what had occurred, stepped on the ear by mistake, then causally picked it up and put it in his pocket. Holmback was rushed to the dressing room, and Mack gave the ear to a Quebec Athletic Commission doctor. Taken to Western Hospital, Eric was operated on, and doctors suggested his days as a grappler were likely finished. But Yukon bounced back to campaign against Kowalski in what would be a lifelong feud, always using the Montreal blunder as a promotional instrument.

Some of Wladek's better drawing matches were with Thesz, Rocca, Kiniski, Carpentier, Pat O'Connor, Manuel Cortez, Tarzan Zorra, Great Togo, and Buddy Rogers. After losing the Montreal title to O'Connor on March 9, 1955, Walter became ill. He noticed a difference in his performance and an unexplained loss of weight was taking a toll on him mentally and physically. Diminishing from 275 to 210 pounds, he was a shell of his former self, and suddenly disappeared from the mat scene. For nine months, he devoted himself to healthy eating and weightlifting at Billy Hill's gym, preparing for a triumphant return.

Kowalski took a claim to the world title with a win over Edouard Carpentier at the Boston Garden on May 3, 1958, before 10,267 fans. The belt went to Bearcat Wright on April 4, 1961, at the same venue on a show for Tony Santos. Between May 1958 and April 1961, Killer lost and rewon his Montreal championship, but maintained this Boston version. In March 1962, he was booked as world champion in Alberta for Stu Hart and Rocky Wagner, during the time in which the territory was denied the sanctioned NWA titleholder, only to lose the championship to Ronnie Etchison in Saskatoon in June.

A heated angle in Montreal set up a title bout for Kowalski against Rogers on November 21, 1962, at the Forum. In the first fall, and less than a minute into the match, Kowalski dashed at the champion and Buddy leapt from the ring apron. Rogers landed wrong, and twisted his right ankle. The duel continued, and Kowalski pinned the NWA king following consecutive bodyslams. A Forum physician halted the affair and ordered Rogers to Montreal General Hospital for further examination, where an X ray revealed a fracture. Promoters, who now needed to fill many of Rogers's bookings while he was on the shelf, wanted to replace him with Kowalski.

Morris Sigel and Toots Mondt made separate moves to shift the spotlight from Rogers as heavyweight champion to a substitute. Kowalski was in the center of both attempts. Mondt, in his effort to garner attention for a program, tried to get official Alliance sponsorship for a Kowalski–Bruno Sammartino match in Pittsburgh on December 3, 1962, but was denied. Sigel acknowledged Walter's controversial win in Montreal over Rogers, and billed him as the new world champ. The *Houston Post* listed Kowalski as the defending champion for a tussle with Lou Thesz on December 14 at the Coliseum, and reported that a representative of the NWA was going to be there to "certify the verdict." Kowalski and Thesz drew in 90 minutes.

The NWA wanted to take the championship from Rogers as soon as possible, but according to the accepted practice, the organization's board of directors needed to wait for Buddy to recuperate from his injury before coercing him into a mandatory booking versus Thesz. They would not support Sigel or any other promoter in their endorsement of a different champion. Kowalski was pinned by Rogers at Madison Square Garden on January 21, 1963, in what was seen by some as a unification bout, but the New York Athletic Commission didn't recognize wrestling titles. Kowalski's reign in Houston lasted until February 1, when he was thwarted by Thesz, who by then was wearing the legitimate Alliance crown.

In Australia, Kowalski was local "world" champion on six occasions from 1964 to '67. He held a U.S. title in Hawaii, the Americas title in Los Angeles, the Southern title in Florida, and several championships in Quebec. In 1976, he acted as a member of the Masked Executioners and won the WWWF tag title. He now lives in the Boston area and coaches aspiring grapplers at his distinguished wrestling school.

Johnny Valentine, the seasoned ruffian from Hobart, Washington, was well known for his toughness and brutal fighting methods. The second of four children born to Theodore, a war veteran and carpenter from Pennsylvania, and Ida, a homemaker from Montana, Johnny was born John Theodore Wisniski on September 19, 1928. Growing to a little more than 6′2′′, he was a standout football player at Tahoma High School, and tested his nerve as a boxer in local gymnasiums. His instincts for ring combat were simmering just beneath the surface.

Around 1943, John met Stanislaus Zbyszko during a training session in Seattle and was sold on the idea of traveling with the former champion to his farm in Savannah, Missouri. Against the wishes of his parents, he consented, and journeyed east. He enrolled in a Missouri high school, and studied wrestling under Stanislaus and his brother Wladek. The teachings of the Zbyszkos would be life-altering.

Although his future remained uncertain, Johnny felt a passion for the sport he was now learning. The Zbyszkos urged their young prodigy to voyage to South America to compete for their "nephew" Karol Nowina beginning in October 1947. Wisniski agreed based on the ideas that he would not only make money and gain experience, but that he would also return to the U.S. an improved prospect.

Following appearances in the Caribbean, and taking the pseudonym "Valentine," John wrestled his way across the upper Midwest in 1949 with Nick Elitch, a friend of the Zbyszkos, as his agent. He toured Florida in the summers of 1949 and '50, trading the Southern title with Danny Dusek in Tampa. Booker Al Haft hired him for programs in Columbus and Chicago, where he was featured on ABC-TV from the Rainbo. At that time, he was booked as "Jim" Valentine or "Honest" John Valentine, a fan favorite. Over the next ten years, he worked through Texas, southern California, St. Louis, Ohio, Illinois, and finally, the Northeast.

A preeminent star for Capitol Wrestling, Valentine drew good houses in Chicago, Newark, Pittsburgh, Washington, and New York City. He became so imperative to the territory, that after word came down that promoter Pedro Martinez had offered John a large guarantee to abandon Capitol and join him in 1962, McMahon took Valentine and his wife on an all-expenses-paid trip to Puerto Rico. The gift was extremely unusual, particularly in a day and age that saw promoters counting every nickel and dime, and some even short-changing their employees.

Johnny was one of the most decorated wrestlers in history, winning championships everywhere he went. He held state honors in Texas, Georgia, and Florida, the American belt in Dallas, and a variety of United States titles. In Toronto, for Frank Tunney, he was U.S. champion off and on for most of the five years between 1962 and '67. He was also a world title claimant in Montreal and for Martinez's NWF.

Fifteen days after his 47th birthday, Johnny's career came to an abrupt end in a plane crash near an airport in Wilmington, North Carolina. Suffering a broken back in the wreck, John retired quietly, and endured many years of rehabilitation. He left a legacy with the people who had wrestled him and the audiences that either cheered for, or hated him with a passion. His performances in rings across the world showed his true dedication to the sport he loved. Johnny passed away on April 24, 2001, at the age of 72.

"Argentina" Antonino Rocca was a household name in his day. He was a spectacular performer, appealing to fans of all persuasions. Relying on acrobatics, he was admired for his athleticism and changed the way people thought about wrestling. Outside of Buddy Rogers, no grappler generated more money from 1949 to 1963 than he did. At the same time, no wrestler had their earnings more carved up by promoters than Rocca, and that includes Primo Carnera, which is saying a lot.

Using the ethnicity of wrestlers to spike turnout was a tactic known by promoters in the early 20th century, and grapplers were regularly provided illegitimate credentials to fit a needed character profile. In the case of Rocca, his mixed bloodlines combined his Italian birthplace with his childhood spent in Buenos Aires. Antonino Biasetton was born in Treviso, Italy on April 13, 1921, the son of Antonio and Angelo Basso Biasetton. A proficient swimmer, Rocca developed his athletic skills and coordination by playing soccer and rugby. He weighed 200 pounds by the age of 16, and when he stopped growing, he stood six foot, with a size-13 shoe.

"I am, as you know, from Argentina," Rocca told *New York Times* writer Arthur Daley for a column printed in the January 26, 1958 paper. "I go there at the age of seven from Italy, where I was born. When I am 17, I weigh 220 and am the greatest rugby player in Argentina, the captain of the national team. I am getting my degree in electrical engineering from the University of San Rosario when Kola Kwariani, a Russian, teaches me how to wrestle in private training. At the end of six months, I can beat him, and I enter the championship tournament at Buenos Aires. No Argentinean ever qualified for it before. I win it."

Wrestler Nick Elitch saw Rocca's potential in South America, and called his old pal "Doc" Sarpolis in Dallas, a matchmaker for the Texas Wrestling Agency. The glowing review sparked his curiosity, and Sarpolis wanted Rocca in Texas as soon as possible. In July 1948, Elitch accompanied Antonino and his wife to Dallas, and Rocca made his U.S. debut on July 29, 1948, in Galveston with a two-fall victory over Gorilla Macias. Rocca already knew the ring well, but was humble enough to put in the time studying the American style of wrestling from Sarpolis and Paul Boesch.

Elitch was an agent representing Kwariani, who wanted credit as the manager for the imported athlete. Conquering "Dizzy" Davis, Rocca became the Texas champion eight days after his debut. His push was not restricted to Texas, as by the middle of September, he was facing Lou Thesz on a telecast from Chicago. It was apparent to savvy promoters looking for their next sensation, that whoever held the contract of Rocca stood to make a significant amount of money.

Rocca returned to Argentina once his six-month visa expired, and a short time later, received a personal visit from Toots Mondt, administrator of the renowned Manhattan Booking Agency. While Kwariani had what he thought to be a firm deal with his protégé, Mondt's hardline negotiations got the upper hand in a reworked agreement as the wrestler's manager. To appease Kwariani and Sigel, who also considered himself a stakeholder, Mondt gave Kola a salaried spot as the grappler's agent, and settled with Sigel by allotting early dates on Rocca in Texas.

Dazzling crowds, Rocca turned notoriously slow and uncomfortable matches into a speed show. His maneuvering made him a celebrity from coast to coast, and when Mondt and his partners reopened Madison Square Garden on December 12, 1949, 17,854 paid $50,639.28 to see Antonino beat Gene Stanlee in the main event. The program outdrew a previous attempt to revitalize the Garden in February by more than 13,000 fans.

Bags of cash were generated with Rocca in Chicago and Los Angeles, but New York City was where Antonino made his mark. In a rematch with Stanlee on March 6, 1950, at the Garden, they drew 16,979 paying $51,962.81, proving that he was no flash in the pan. Rocca turned around a territory that was losing money, and helped make it the spotlight of the wrestling world, amassing a fortune for his handlers, and seeing only one-third of his reported $100,000 plus annual income. Throughout the 1950s, he was a pawn in the power moves of Mondt, Kohler, Martinez, and lastly, Vince McMahon. The 25 percent of Garden gates he earned were broken up by the shady crew handling his affairs. Unable to wiggle free from his handlers, Rocca made hundreds of thousands of dollars for bosses who watched over him like hawks.

Among Rocca's achievements in wrestling were the Cleveland version of the AWA title in 1953, the Montreal world title in May 1954, and finally the United States "world" tag title, recognized by Capitol Wrestling. He was a mainstream media figure and appeared on notable talk shows, sharing his views on physical fitness. In August 1962, he was featured in the comic book *Superman*, issue 155, titled "The Downfall of Superman," and was pictured on the cover. He wrote the book *Antonino Rocca: Self Defense and Physical Fitness* (1965) and retired from active wrestling in 1968. Twelve years removed from a promotional war with Capitol Wrestling, Rocca mended fences with McMahon, and was a color commentator with the Vince Sr.'s son in 1975.

Rocca made several comeback attempts, notably for shots in Los Angeles and Puerto Rico. In the Caribbean, he reformed his famous team with Perez, and won the North American tag title in September 1976. On February 17, 1977, Rocca was honored in Staten Island on a card promoted by Tommy Dee. "Rocca Night" included an in-ring ceremony and presentation, and Antonino refereed the main event between Tor Kamata and Ivan Putski. He was admitted to Roosevelt Hospital two days later, where he died on March 15. The WWF inducted Antonino into their Hall of Fame on June 24, 1995. He was survived by his wife and three children.

CHAPTER FIFTEEN

PROMOTIONAL
WARS

For those who knew cunning independent promoter Jack Pfefer, the men and women who cherished his friendship and guidance, there was an understanding about his kindness. But in amazing contrast, there were also an awful lot of people in professional wrestling who despised him. They wanted nothing more than for him to fail in every endeavor and die a bankrupt and miserable old man. Eddie Quinn, the veteran Montreal promoter, referred to Pfefer as the "cancer of the wrestling business" in a historic letter to Sam Muchnick in 1957. Pfefer was involved in many donnybrooks in his 40-plus years in wrestling; in fact, he was an expert at bickering with rivals. A permanent mark was made in his mind when someone crossed him, and those who did would never live it down.

Jacob "Jack" Pfefer was born on December 10, 1894, the son of Shoel and Faiga Lichtenstein Pfefer, outside of Warsaw, Poland. A story of him crossing Siberia with a small group escaping the escalating tyranny was told later in life, and he was quick to add that he was the only one of the five men to survive the trip. Pfefer first arrived in the United States in 1921, but he was not planning to settle permanently. He got a job with the Russian Grand Opera, who performed through South and Central America, and Europe. Legend has it that he also toured with the San Francisco Opera Company, and had once claimed to have been apart of the Philadelphia Philharmonic Orchestra.

The wily provocateur first brought his familiarity with international culture to professional wrestling beginning in 1924 as a guide for foreign wrestlers. Gearing his operations towards multilingual fans, Pfefer approached wrestling like no other manager or promoter in America. Although he had an idea of what he was looking for in a "star" grappler, and possessed an uncanny intelligence as a scout, none of Jack's wrestlers made a real dent in America. Jack Curley, a New York promoter, hired him in 1929 as an intercontinental hunter of talent, and Pfefer began assembling a diverse group of characters.

In 1930, wrestling flourished in New York and many other large cities, and the need for exotic grapplers to popularize the sport with the recently arrived became paramount. Curley wanted ethnic wrestlers to lead the revival, and wasn't disappointed by Pfefer's transatlantic finds. The syndicate earned a fortune. Behind the back of Pfefer, Curley and other influential promoters devised the "Trust," a cohesive unit that shared the prosperity, in November 1933. His exclusion bothered Pfefer immensely, and he wanted revenge.

Speaking to *New York Daily Mirror* sportswriter Dan Parker, Pfefer explained the trade secrets of grappling, breaking the unspoken rules, and finally giving weight to the perception that it was all fakery. The public, while not entirely surprised by the news, found Pfefer's diatribe deplorable, and pro wrestling suffered at the box office as a result.

Pfefer, from that moment forward, maintained his freedom from the bigwigs of wrestling and sought new ways to wound his ever-increasing list of enemies. He got in the middle of the double-cross on Danno O'Mahoney in 1936 and then organized the "hit" on Ali Baba by Dave Levin. Unions of any kind alarmed him, and the formation of the NWA in 1948 definitely caught his attention. Mindful of being purposely excluded once again, Pfefer was overly conscious of when meetings were held, and awaited word from cronies to tell him whether or not his name had been mentioned. While booking Buddy Rogers, he was constantly worried about someone trying to steal away his top star.

The members of the NWA did discuss Pfefer, and the debate was usually over whether he was hurting or helping the business. The question of whether he should be cut off from doing business with members was a regular point of contention, and Jack was well aware of that. But going back to the presidency of Pinkie George, and continuing with Muchnick, it was spelled out to Pfefer in clear English that any NWA member had the right to charter his grapplers no matter what anyone else thought. Neither Alliance head wanted to stop him from making money. Muchnick relied on Pfefer so profoundly when he was starting out that there was an everlasting debt.

Pfefer jostled with a procession of wrestling luminaries, among them Curley, Rudy Dusek, Eddie Quinn, Paul Bowser, Jim Londos, Ray Fabiani, Tom Packs, and Buddy Rogers. He had cordial relations with Doc Sarpolis, Morris Sigel, Ed "Strangler" Lewis, Gust Karras, Hugh Nichols, Fred Kohler, Cliff Maupin, Sam Avey, Dave Levin, Leroy McGuirk, Mildred Burke, Mike London, and Willie Gilzenberg. He was considerate to close acquaintances, and often sent gifts for their wives. Stu Hart was so overwhelmed by the regularity of Pfefer's interest in his family that he asked Jack to be the godfather of his tenth child and seventh son, Ross Lindsay Hart, by letter in January 1960.

It is hard to believe that the 5′5′′ Pfefer influenced wrestling so greatly given that he had no formal education. The lessons he received traveling with wrestlers during his early years were experience enough for him. He got a taste for big-time booking and moneymaking, and polished his skills running his own New York clubs in the 1930s. For the next 30 years, he migrated from town to town as a less-than-subdued entrepreneur. He served as a booker for promoters with a throng of heavily gimmicked athletes under his thumb. The Swedish Angel, Elephant Boy, the Zebra Kid, Lord Pinkerton, and the Blimp were some of the characters Pfefer rented out.

Pfefer was infamous for casting wrestlers in roles that mimicked the sport's idols: Jumping Rococo (Antonino Rocca), Bruno Sanmartino (Bruno Sammartino), and Lou Kesz (Lou Thesz). The mockery made Pfefer few friends. He was known for degrading wrestlers verbally, calling them "palookas," and his unvarnished remarks occasionally came back to haunt him.

Pfefer was the king of wrestling conflicts, often seeking them out when there wouldn't have been one otherwise. Being obsessively skeptical played a part, and the fact that he was somewhat graceless, vengeful, and callous didn't help his image. The high quality service he provided as a booker was usually dwarfed by his inability to fit in and the cloud of negativity that followed him. It was always raining above Jack Pfefer, but even water couldn't wash the foul smell from his tattered clothing. With thousands in his bank account, Jack refused to invest in clothes, nor did he wash the articles he wore. He had poor hygiene, chain-smoked cigars, and praised himself as a wrestling historian-philosopher. There was a place in the business for Pfefer, but it wasn't as a member of the National Wrestling Alliance.

The Texas wrestling scene fell under the monopoly of Morris Sigel, a quiet former office clerk. Sigel's lucrative enterprises out of Houston became a staple of Texas sports. In addition to his weekly wrestling programs on Friday nights at the City Auditorium, Morris ran the Texas Wrestling Agency, a booking company that earned shareholders a percentage of wrestling shows across the state. Income from the popular Houston events were handled with incoming cash-filled envelopes, passed down from promoters in Dallas, San Antonio and Galveston. This method of payment to a central booking office kept the peace in Texas, but there were many people searching for a way to circumvent the entrenched system with the hopes that they'd save money in the long run.

Besides having the two venues in Houston locked up, and a solid booking office that would soon have National Wrestling Alliance membership, Sigel did the one thing that finalized his domination over eleven counties in Texas and one in Louisiana. Grapplers who came into the territory had to sign three-year contracts that forced them to wrestle exclusively for him. Part IV of the contract read: "Wrestler agrees and herby obligates himself to offer his services as a wrestler exclusively to Promoter and Agent in the localities herein specified, and that he will not wrestle for or under the auspices of any other promoter or agent or for any other person in said localities, or in any of them during the period of this contract."

By 1950, Sigel reportedly had 140 wrestlers signed. Often spoken about, but never proven, rumors ran rampant through dressing rooms that Sigel had connections in the Texas Labor Commission, the body that issued licenses to promoters, and that could reject applications tendered by prospective rivals. Altogether, the Gulf Athletic Club and Texas Wrestling Agency combined to have one of the strongest monopolies in professional wrestling history.

One wrestler under contract had ambitions to open his own Houston franchise outside of Sigel's control. His name was Sterling Blake Davis, known to the wrestling community as colorful performer "Dizzy Davis." Born on November 8, 1914, in Houston, Sterling was the product of a broken home from before he was five years old. He was a troubled youth, attended Allen Academy in Bryan and later Texas A&M. Having engaged in countless neighborhood fights, he became a wrestler on a semiprofessional circuit around Houston in his early 20s. During

World War II, Dizzy became a headliner for Sigel and was a technical grappler, also known for his many violent and bloody matches.

The "dandy" gimmick Davis used became a prototype for the routine of Gorgeous George Wagner, a Houston pal. Sterling wore extravagant robes and easily stood out against the dingy backdrop of smoke-filled arenas. On April 18, 1949, with funding of $30,000 and a rental contract for the Olympiad, a new structure in Houston, Davis applied for a promoter's license to Texas State Labor Commissioner M.B. Morgan. Sigel was livid, immediately getting the attention of the Wrestler's Association of Texas, and called upon his lawyer Russell Bonham, the former vice president of the Gulf Athletic Club, to be present at the hearing that would decide the fate of Dizzy's application in the offices of the Highway Commission in Austin on June 30, 1949.

In front of an arbiter, Sterling declared that his formula for promotion would have 50 percent of the net going to the talent after taxes. He adamantly insisted that he was not interested in running a booking office, and would not take money for sending grapplers to promoters in other towns. Even under heavy examination by Wrestling Association representative Aubrey Roberts, who twisted words and tried to catch Davis off guard, Sterling was calm in his testimony, freely admitting that he discussed plans to work with other promoters, including Karl Sarpolis and Ed McLemore of Dallas. Sarpolis, despite owning one-third of Sigel's agency and a stake in the Dallas office, listened to Davis's proposal, and volunteered a Friday slot at the Sportatorium if things went well in Houston. Dizzy was also in contact with potential partners in the budding configuration in Fort Worth and San Antonio.

The 50 percent to wrestlers was an attractive lure, and Davis wanted to take care of the "boys" first and foremost. He knew what it was like to scrape by with a paycheck determined by sticky-fingered promoters, and felt that a set procedure for payment could be beneficial. National Wrestling Association champion Lou Thesz was facing the expansion of the Alliance in 1948–49. When Sigel jumped aboard, Thesz even considered the prospects of siding with Davis, but everything was still at the preliminary stage. By the time the court case was filed by Davis, Lou had joined the Alliance.

A scathing portrait of wrestling in Texas had been published by Nat Terence in his weekly *Houstonian* newspaper, informing the public about the controversies surrounding Sigel. Davis replied "no" when asked by Roberts if he had contributed to the article. While everyone denied mass mailings of the paper, someone had sent copies to every member of the Texas Legislature, to the Governor, and to oil tycoon Glenn McCarthy, who, with his brother Bill, happened to be a good friend of Davis.

Early in the Austin hearing, Sterling was asked if the McCarthys were bankrolling his efforts, and again, Davis said no. However, he had asked Glenn to send a personal letter to Texas Governor Beauford Jester regarding his application to promote. Asked if he ever told "anyone that the [Texas Labor] commissioner was on the payroll of Mr. Sigel," Davis said no, but claimed it was "rumored about."

One of the more startling revelations was the criminal record of the individual applying for the permit. Roberts concentrated on that segment of the deposition, curious about Davis's 1936 stay in Los Angeles. Lieberman rebutted the attempted character assassination of his client:

> Your honor, at this time we wish to call to the court's attention that some 14 years ago, 13 years ago, when Sterling Davis was 18 or 19 years old, he got into several difficulties one place or another. He had the occasion at one time to hit a house police officer when he was a kid. He is 34 years old now. And consequently he had been picked up numerous times in Houston. In other words, when some crime or something might have been perpetrated, why, Sterling would be picked up. Never put in jail and never convicted.

Sterling was insistent in his own defense: "I have never been convicted in my life, California or elsewhere." Roberts inquired about whether he had been picked up on seven instances, and Davis argued that it had only been once. With an ace in the hole, Roberts asked Davis to confirm that he had understood his earlier oath, and the wrestler did.

Evidence was then revealed that Davis had been investigated for criminal activities 18 times between March 1933 and April 1936, including a February 1935 felony burglary charge of robbing a store that ended in a guilty plea. The Criminal District Court of Harris County had ordered Dizzy to spend five years in the state penitentiary, and then suspended the sentence. When asked about the specific case, Sterling said, "I don't remember."

Sterling Davis's application to promote at the Olympiad was denied by commissioner Morgan on July 2, 1949. If that wasn't bad enough, within a week, both his neon-sign business and his home suffered tremendous damage in two separate fires. An unlikely coincidence. What was Dizzy going to do? He failed to get a license, had no proof that Sigel was pulling the strings of the commission, and had busted open a can of worms that may have led to the suspected arson of his property.

Davis, 18 days after his rejection by the Labor Commission, filed a civil suit against Sigel in U.S. District Court for the Southern District of Texas in Houston, Civil Action No. 5119. The petition cited infractions of the Texas and Sherman

Antitrust Acts and mentioned the use of exclusive contracts.

Accusations were made that Sigel had contacted bookers Johnny Doyle of Hollywood, via Ed "Strangler" Lewis, and Sam Avey of Tulsa, warning them not to support Davis in any way. That meant Davis's promise to bring in Gorgeous George was off the table. A little-known fact was that Sterling had offered George one-fourth of his company.

Part (e) of the violations alleged in the July 20 submission to the courts stated:

> That Defendant Morris P. Sigel, upon information and belief and Plaintiff so charges, exercises a baneful influence over and upon the Commissioner of Labor Statistics, M.B. Morgan, as best expressed in a letter dated April 29, 1949, addressed to Plaintiff herein which, in part, reads as follows:

> "We might at times lay down a rule or regulation or exercise arbitrary power under the authority we believe that we have if, in our opinion, it is to the best interests of the boxing and wrestling profession, which could conceivably be interpreted to be outside of our legal authority or that we might be accused of showing partiality by upholding and following a policy adopted by the department which might be considered by some to be arbitrary and against some particular person or member of the profession."

> That said excerpt from the mentioned letter was written and executed by the said M.B. Morgan in which said public official of the State of Texas advised Plaintiff herein that he (Commissioner of Labor Statistics) would not believe it advisable for another promoter in addition to Defendant Sigel, to promote wrestling matches here in Houston, but that said Commissioner of Labor Statistics would take Plaintiff's application for a wrestling license under consideration.

> That a purported hearing was held in the office of the Commissioner of Labor Statistics subsequent to Plaintiff's application for a promoter's license at which time and place Defendant Sigel through his duly authorized representatives, bitterly and vehemently contested the application of this Plaintiff; in substance, stating to said Commissioner that this Defendant had long ago secured the exclusive right to use all of the arenas in Houston, Texas, and elsewhere, for the purpose of holding and staging wrestling contests and exhibitions and that no one was permitted, under any circumstances, to exhibit and stage any such exhibition at the only public places available in Houston, Texas, at any time when such public places were not in use by this Defendant.

> That said hearing was a farce from the beginning to end in that the hearing

was dominated and controlled by Defendant's representatives and authorized agents, and as a result this Plaintiff was denied his application for a wrestling promoter's license, without any valid and legal reason for so doing.

Davis was suing for $99,000, plus $10,000 for his lawyers. The attorneys for Sigel answered with a motion for a summary judgment, hoping that the district judge would toss the case out. Sigel's team pointed out that the Labor Commission had the right to deny a permit to promote, particularly when the person applying was of "questionable character," and that Davis had committed perjury in his testimony. "This was of itself a crime, the crime of perjury, that he could have been and should have been prosecuted for." This part of the statement was printed in all caps, highlighted in the defense document.

Sigel denied any violations of Texas law, and any wrongdoing. The defense avowed that the entire suit was based around Davis's disappointment over not getting a license. Of course, Dizzy's attorneys had a reply, insisting that Sigel had told his friends to blackball Davis either from wrestling, or from obtaining talent if he received a permit. On September 9, 1949, a federal judge dismissed the suit because of lack of jurisdiction. Davis and his lawyers filed with the United States Circuit Court of Appeals (Fifth Circuit) ten days later.

The ambitions of Dizzy Davis, the promoter, died in a conference room, but there was a more successful opponent in the crusade to topple Sigel. Hugh Benbow rented the Olympiad to Davis's ally, Bill McCarthy. McCarthy joined Houston National Bank President Joseph Meyer, and H.H. Townsend, to form the Olympiad Sporting Club in November 1949, and with the backing of Bill's influential brother Glenn, obtained that elusive license to promote in Houston. A debut of March 22, 1950, was planned, with Davis and Gorgeous George in the main event, and Juan Humberto and George Penchoff on the undercard.

Sigel's partner Frank Burke sought an injunction from the courts to prevent Davis from wrestling at the Olympiad, and supplied a signed contract with the wrestler that said he could only work for them. A second speed bump materialized when Gorgeous George reneged on the booking, and stayed loyal to the NWA.

Two days prior to the Olympiad debut, a judge rejected Burke's motion, and Davis went ahead and wrestled "Lumberjack" McDonald. Burke proceeded with a lawsuit against Humberto (District Court of the United States for the Southern District of Texas, Houston Division, *Frank J. Burke v. Juan Humberto,* Civil Action No. 5536), another wrestler he alleged broke his contract not to compete for any other Houston promoter when he grappled for Meyer.

A trip by Davis to New York City to negotiate with Toots Mondt proved worthwhile for the ostracized promotion, and enhanced their prospects tenfold. Meyer announced his valuable new connection to the Manhattan Booking Agency. Ray Fabiani, who was also manipulating things in Chicago, would become the general manager for wrestling at the Olympiad, and handle bringing in superstars Jim Londos, Gene Stanlee, Primo Carnera, and Antonino Rocca. The deal, in addition to the superior political and financial power of Meyer, McCarty, and Townsend, gave the "outlaws" an advantage, and it seemed that if anyone could break Sigel's monopoly, it was this trio.

The audience for wrestling at the Olympiad increased dramatically when Londos performed on April 19, 1950, and the momentum of the Houston promotion was building. Sigel booked Thesz and Killer Kowalski at the Coliseum under the banner "Parade of Champions" on May 5, and 10,000 fans turned out, said to be the largest crowd ever to see wrestling in Texas. Needless to say, the opposition couldn't match that kind of event. The May 10 Olympiad bill featured capable wrestlers, but lacked the stars the Manhattan Booking Agency guaranteed. Even Davis was missing from the marquee. Something was amiss, and where the independent promotion once appeared to have the connections and will to fight Sigel, the enthusiasm was gone.

Davis's appeal was still in the courts when he made a dramatic reemergence on the May 19, 1950, City Auditorium show promoted by Sigel. Confronting Danny McShain, he set the table for two programs in which they headlined together in exceptionally bloody matches. But his appeal was dismissed on May 29. The Olympiad was closed to wrestling on May 10, and was rededicated to boxing and roller-skating. To confirm that the hatchet was buried, Sterling found employment for Ed Don George, then toured Chicago, Indianapolis, St. Louis, and southern California for Alliance affiliates before his homecoming for Sigel in 1951.

Another wrestling war in Texas actually broke through the mighty Sigel combine. Wealthy Dallas promoter Edward McLemore (1905–1969) found himself on the outside of a wrestler's strike targeting his profitable television enterprises. According to the indignant grapplers, McLemore repeatedly violated an agreement that promised them $5 per airing of matches they appeared in and limited broadcasts, in Texas. The matmen stressed that the telecasts were diminishing gate receipts and that they were tired of promoters keeping all of the income from advertisers. The wrestlers' angst turned to action on December 10, 1952, when they refused to wrestle in San Antonio before TV cameras.

McLemore, convinced that the contracts in place would shield his interests, initially shrugged off the strike, and warned that "no wrestlers will be used here who will not agree to have their matches televised." Texas Labor Commissioner Morgan jumped into the fracas. He believed wrestlers should be compensated for their matches on TV, and arranged a meeting between McLemore and the three owners of the Texas Wrestling Agency, Morris Sigel, Doc Sarpolis, and Frank Burke.

The Texas Wrestling Agency was negotiating on behalf of the wrestlers in the argument, while McLemore had television deals both nationally (on the CBS network) and throughout Texas. Sigel and McLemore had argued vociferously at the September 1952 convention in Santa Monica over an arrangement for $50,000 that would give Sigel two-thirds interest in any wrestling films taped from the Sportatorium. McLemore snubbed the idea, and believed any current hostilities stemmed from that suspected insult. Already paying the agency for rights to use the wrestlers, McLemore wanted to maintain the previous arrangement, and any supplemental fee to the grapplers themselves was not something he'd bargained for.

The Austin confab ended with a preliminary agreement to give wrestlers a percentage, but McLemore felt railroaded. After all, he had a binding agreement with a clear-cut format for profit distribution. On December 29, 1952, a suit was filed by eight wrestlers, led by Red Berry, against McLemore, Sarpolis, KRLD-TV in Dallas, and the Texas Rasslin' and Dong King Advertising Agency over the signed contracts. A judge ruled that the previous obligations did not stand up, and McLemore was left with little recourse.

In protest, McLemore cut relations to Sigel, the Texas Wrestling Agency, and the National Wrestling Alliance, officially detaching him from all of the sport's top wrestlers. Such a defining move would have finished the career of the average promoter, but McLemore wasn't your regular gent. He showed the tenacity needed to function without Sigel's outfit or the NWA. At the same time, Sigel and his partners were not about to let go of Dallas, and a spokesman for their agency told the *Dallas Morning News* that they would continue booking their wrestlers in opposition to McLemore.

The Houston office named Norman Clark their representative in Dallas, with Sarpolis acting as his matchmaker. They would use Pappy's Showland as their staging ground and, like McLemore, would run on Tuesdays in direct competition. McLemore, unwilling to step aside in any capacity, announced that in addition to his usual Tuesday night spectacle at the Sportatorium, he'd have a Thursday evening card administered by Maurice Beck. The program would help the wrestling audience familiarize themselves with the array of wrestlers that were entering the city, most of whom were unknown.

The talent McLemore brought into Dallas beginning on January 6 was a combination of Jack Pfefer's crew and a series of independent grapplers. His main star was Olympian Roy Dunn, who was managed by the legendary Billy Sandow.

Dunn claimed to have gone unbeaten in six years, and held a version of the world title. McLemore had no illusions and knew that he was at a disadvantage. The Texas Wrestling Agency was going to dispatch a wave of superstars, while McLemore was reliant on those brave souls willing to risk being blackballed by the NWA. Three wrestlers remained after the shift: Jack O'Brien, Roy Graham, and Jack Kennedy.

On Tuesday, January 6, 1953, the head-to-head duel began, and McLemore spotlighted Dunn and Jack Bernard. On the other side of the fence, it was NWA champion Lou Thesz versus Mr. Moto. Both men kept their belts, winning in straight falls. Filling out McLemore's show was Graham, O'Brien, Kennedy, "Gorgeous" George Grant, Tommy Phelps, and Elephant Boy, while Clark had the benefit of having Texas champion Cyclone Anaya, Texas women's champion Nell Stewart, world negro champion Woody Strode, and Texas tag-team champions Ray Gunkel and Ricki Starr.

Threats were reportedly made, and Clark responded by a restraining order against McLemore. In April 1953, the two promoters issued public challenges to each other, and hammered home their claim to a wrestling champion while damaging the credibility of the other.

First, McLemore bought advertising space in the April 21, 1953 *Dallas Morning News*, reaffirming the title of Dunn. The piece claimed that Dunn had won the world title from Everette Marshall on November 1, 1940, in Wichita, and that he had defeated NWA world champ Thesz. The following was written in that promotional section:

> Thesz is associated with a St. Louis wrestling group which has refused to employ Roy Dunn's services because Dunn won't take orders. Thesz meets only Alliance stooges, many of whom he has beaten many times. The National Wrestling Alliance is a self-serving organization who named Thesz champion behind closed doors in a meeting in September (sic) of 1949. Dunn won his title in the ring.
>
> This Tuesday, McLemore's opposition has announced a Texas heavyweight championship bout between Ray Gunkel, the alleged Texas heavyweight title-holder, and Duke Keomuka. Promoter Ed McLemore announces that he will give $1,000 in cash to anyone able to get the synthetic champion Lou Thesz, and the winner of the Texas heavyweight championship bout Tuesday night, to meet Roy Dunn. Dunn agrees to beat both alleged champions on the same night, and to donate his share of the purse that night to any reputable charity.

"Mat Fans! Don't be foiled again!" was written at the bottom of the advertisement.

Clark countered the propaganda on behalf of the NWA in the April 28, 1953, edition of his arena wrestling program, *Dallas Wrestling*. The article corrected the claim that Dunn beat Marshall for his title on November 1, 1940, in Wichita, reminding enthusiasts that Thesz had captured Everette's laurels on February 23, 1939. Giving in to the challenges of his foe, Clark added a special attraction to that evening's Pappy Showland show — Dunn versus Gunkel. Dunn didn't show up to accept the proposition, but he had no reason to. It was very similar to the dare Sandow issued to Ray Steele on Roy's behalf in 1941.

A courageous shooter, Dunn had been shut out of the syndicates for a decade, and his wrestling prowess was respected by fellow grapplers. Purportedly wearing Sandow's $10,000 championship belt, also held by Marshall and Thesz in the 1936–39 timeframe in St. Louis, Roy's reign more likely had commenced with his April 29, 1946, victory over Ede Virag in Wichita, and not the fictitious 1940 Marshall bout. His win ironically earned him the Kansas lineage of the National Wrestling Alliance championship.

Perry Bash, an original member of the Kansas Alliance and chairman of the wrestling committee for the Thomas Hopkins post of the American Legion in Wichita, wrote a letter to Sam Muchnick on November 2, 1953, that praised Dunn's credentials and asserted "that Roy Dunn more than Lou Thesz is the rightful heavyweight wrestling champion." He pointed out that the National Wrestling Alliance "was formed here in Wichita," and that "the proper way to clear up the issue is a showdown between Dunn and Thesz. Dunn is ready; if Thesz refuses, we will let the public be the judge."

Dunn and Thesz had wrestled worked contests in the past, and each was very familiar with the style of their adversary. Their final match, on May 4, 1949, was staged in Wichita, where Thesz supposedly demanded that the referee (Benny Ginsberg) who had accompanied him from St. Louis be allowed to officiate. It was surmised that Thesz feared a double-cross, and wanted the protection of a trustworthy arbitrator. Their exhibition ended in a draw, without incident. Indictments went the other way, too. NWA officials were quick to remark that Dunn had ducked legitimate matches with Thesz, Gunkel, and Dick Hutton in Dallas.

During the month of April, McLemore's empire expanded when Bob Kline acquired a license to hold shows on Monday nights in San Antonio, and later added affiliated programs in Corpus Christi, Laredo, Del Rio, Marshall, and Tyler. A dagger to the heart of Sigel's promotion was struck on April 25, 1953, when Sarpolis abandoned ship and joined McLemore. Sarpolis had been a longtime ally of Sigel, a matchmaker in Houston, and had even wed in the promoter's office in 1936. But feathers were ruffled, and the once balanced union was further carved into pieces.

That Tuesday, Clark's Texas Wrestling Agency card drew a gate of $964.30 for five matches, with Sterling Davis as half of the main event. In comparison, McLemore earned less than half of that figure with six matches of mostly underachievers, and one future superstar, Jack Adkisson. Dallas wrestling would change forever by the end of the week, and like Davis's 1949 troubles in Houston, fire played a part.

At 12:35 a.m. on Friday, May 1, 1953, an inferno was purposely started on the southeast corner of the Sportatorium on Cadiz Street and South Industrial Blvd in Dallas. It was a five-alarm blaze, and the building was completely destroyed within 40 minutes. Following the fire W.T. Cox, a spokesman for the owners, said that arsonists had tried three or four times previously to obliterate the structure. He mentioned that 15 gallons of kerosene had been "planted in the back" several weeks prior, but that the criminals had failed to accomplish the job. Dallas's most famous wrestling site, insured for $52,500, while needing $150,000 to reconstruct, was wiped off the map by someone who investigators assumed had a personal grudge.

The next day, McLemore showed optimism in spite of the horrendous events. He announced that the Sportatorium would be rebuilt, and his Tuesday night shows would move in the interim to the Livestock Pavilion at Fair Park. With Sarpolis, a wrestler-friendly matchmaker at his side, he signed away workers from the NWA circuit, including Ellis Bashara, Farmer Jones, Sterling Davis, and George Bollas. Talent from Pfefer always helped his cause, and the Amazing Zuma and Slave Girl Moolah (Lillian Ellison) became big hits in the summer of 1953.

The cause of the blaze was confirmed to be arson by Dallas County Fire Marshal Hal Hood, and speculation about motive ran rampant. Evidence suggested a credible conspiracy among a group of men, all with different backgrounds, different versions of the story, and no obvious ties to professional wrestling. The link in the chain burst when a snitch being detained in Athens, Texas, on other matters revealed information regarding the fire. That data led to the Los Angeles arrest of Alfred Huey McCrory, charged with an attempted arson of the Sportatorium months before the actual blaze. The arrest was kept out of the local press, and when Hood returned to Dallas from a jaunt to Chicago on Friday, August 21, he had custody of Roy Houston Tatum. Tatum was the man who ultimately confessed to burning McLemore's venue.

A summary of the third arrest was reported in Chicago, then the story broke on the lead page of Saturday's *Dallas Morning News*, detailing the intricacies of the alleged plot. Tatum and McCrory's stories matched on one important point: they each were hired by William Theodore Moncrief. Moncrief, of Denton County, Texas, had been arrested and charged Friday night with being the mastermind of the scheme.

In his written confession, Tatum explained that he and Moncrief had bought tickets for McLemore's April 28 show at the Sportatorium, and that they'd considered burning the structure that evening. Rain thwarted their plans, but the two went forward after midnight on May 1. According to Tatum, he used gasoline and shears provided by Moncrief, sparked the fire, and joined the latter in escaping while the building was destroyed. Moncrief made it known that McLemore's office was the central target. To achieve that goal, Tatum cut a hole in the metallic wall exposing the room, and spread gasoline to guarantee its obliteration. The compensation he received for torching the Sportatorium and causing in excess of $150,000 damage was $100, paid with two fifties.

The two promotions in Dallas continued their clash as if nothing else was going on. McLemore opened the new Sportatorium, a 6,400-seat fireproof structure at Cadiz and Industrial, on September 22, 1953. In attendance was former world champion Stanislaus Zbyszko, a vocal critic of the National Wrestling Alliance, who was presented with an award from the promoter for his legendary career. For his charitable work, McLemore would also be honored, while Moolah, Zuma, Phelps, and the Lady Angel carried the weight of the program.

With suspects in custody and the court phase of the case to come, people were still curious if the wrestling war in Dallas had had anything to do with the fire. It was easy to assume that one way or another, it was at the root of the arson. The prosecution of Moncrief began on December 8, 1953 in front of Criminal District Judge Henry King. In his testimony, Tatum said that Moncrief told him specifically to burn McLemore's office and wipe out "TV films." Fortunately, McLemore didn't store his wrestling films at the arena. They were stored elsewhere, in a special fireproof vault.

If ruining McLemore's wrestling films were at the center of the conspirator's intentions, one had to wonder about the motive behind the plot. It could have been purely wrestling-related, or a private vendetta. During the trial, as noted by the *Dallas Morning News* on December 10, 1953, a "mysterious Tony" from Houston was mentioned several times. This individual didn't have a full name or identity for the jury, investigators, or McLemore, but reportedly had the ear of Moncrief, and may have been behind the arson from the very beginning.

On December 9, 1953, following 40 minutes of deliberation, the jury found Moncrief guilty of conspiracy, and he was subsequently sentenced to five years in jail, the maximum punishment. Tatum pleaded guilty to burning the

Sportatorium, and was sentenced to four years, while McCrory was given probation on January 20, 1954. In November 1954, Moncrief went before the Texas Court of Criminal Appeals in Austin, and his conviction was upheld.

The Texas war had been extremely costly. McLemore estimated that he lost $80,000 from January 1953 to May 1954, but his promotion survived the desertion of key athletes and the destruction of his facility. His resilience and the devotion of his Dallas area fans was enough to pull him through. A modern Sportatorium was erected at the same location, and the engineers behind the attacks on his promotion were in jail. Anyone who'd thought that McLemore would crumble at the sight of adversity had been proved wrong.

After two months of intense NWA pressure to settle their differences for the sake of the business, a peace accord was reached by Sigel, the Texas Wrestling Agency, and McLemore on May 22, 1954. The deal gave McLemore 50 percent of the Dallas promotion, and another 50 percent share of all wrestling films with Sigel and Burke. McLemore remained a constant target for lawsuits, and was sued by a promoter in Corpus Christi, Duke Keomuka, and Ray Gunkel in 1954–55. When the Justice Department came looking for information about the Alliance's shady exploits in June 1955, he hid the skeletons.

The Dallas quarrel was one the NWA wanted to forget, and Muchnick's announcement to members (NWA Bulletin #11, June 1, 1954) was made with great satisfaction: "Let's hope that the alignment again of Sigel and McLemore proves beneficial to Dallas and to Texas wrestling, and to the Alliance."

Chicago saw two significant wrestling disputes revolving around promoter extraordinaire Fred Kohler. The first started in 1949 during a time in which wrestling was booming and Kohler's influence was growing. Benefiting from the spoils of a seminational TV show featured across the ABC network, Kohler's Wednesday offering from the Rainbo Arena (4836 N. Clark Street) was not only his top priority, but the most popular with fans. Wrestling's renewed impact in Chicago meant a financial upswing, but Kohler was finding the new ownership of the Rainbo less than accommodating.

From the $500 television revenue from ABC, Fred pocketed $200 per show, and $260 went to owner Leonard Schwartz, who, since purchasing the Rainbo, had tripled his rent, angering Kohler immensely. Weary of the exorbitant overhead, he decided to move his operations to the cheaper Marigold Arena on July 20, ending his 15-year relationship with Schwartz's venue. Schwartz countered to keep things status quo, lowering his rent to $175 and his percentage of TV profits to $250. The compromise was a temporary solution, but Kohler was intent on allowing his Rainbo lease to expire.

Schwartz was unwilling to let Kohler walk away with all of the Rainbo's wrestling tradition, or sour the ABC deal, and filed for a promoter's license with the Illinois Athletic Commission, which was approved on December 13, 1949. Leonard was new to the sport, and to give his promotion the necessary experience, he aligned himself with longtime promoter Carl Schaller. He depended on Jack Pfefer for four weeks, beginning on January 4, 1950, then switched to Al Haft's Columbus booking office. Notably, Kohler also got wrestlers from Haft.

Although he was a member of the National Wrestling Alliance, Kohler recognized local titleholders, including Walter Palmer, Cyclone Anaya, and finally, Don Eagle. Eagle, under contract to Haft and Paul Bowser, became a sensation in Chicago, and Kohler used his expertise to push the grappler's success. The night the "Chief" won the championship on November 18, 1949, the International Amphitheater was sold out, with 10,745 in attendance and a gate exceeding $24,000.

After personally investing in excess of $10,000 in the marketing of Eagle, Kohler saw Haft book the Indian grappler for a show by rival promoter Ray Fabiani on February 3, 1950. Fabiani's Chicago Stadium effort, headlined by Londos-Carnera, drew a sizable crowd, and represented the third wrestling troupe in the city. Kohler wrongly assumed he had exclusive rights to Eagle in Chicago, and was furious when Don was booked below the main event, where he had extablished him.

Kohler was even more irate at the help Alliance members were giving his enemies, and his animosity intensified when Schwartz obtained a booking for NWA champion Lou Thesz on March 22, 1950. Both Kohler and Schwartz had to reckon with Fabiani's stake in the territory, with bonds to Toots Mondt, the Manhattan Booking Agency, and Jim Londos. But things turned in Schwartz's favor when an arrangement with the Fiddler brought an army of choice names to the Rainbo.

Schwartz, from his office at 134 N. LaSalle, teamed with Fabiani and several investors to incorporate Clark Sports, Inc. on April 13, 1950. Besides the Rainbo, Leonard and his brother David owned the outdoor Sparta Stadium. The newly structured consortium began at the Rainbo on May 3, with Fabiani listed as the promoter of note in publicity. Their ABC deal expanded to 26 markets including New York City, St. Louis, Milwaukee, Denver, Omaha, Minneapolis, New Orleans, Kansas City, and Oklahoma City.

In defense of his territory against the all-out strike, Kohler put on a Coliseum show on May 23, 1950, with all fans getting in free. He was running the Amphitheater, Midway Arena, Madison Arena, and the Marigold, and his NWA membership gave him links to a number of leading wrestlers. That in itself would have pushed out a normal invader. But the Fabiani-Schwartz cartel was impressive enough to buck the NWA's monopoly.

The two Amphitheater programs by Kohler in May 1950 were letdowns financially, but showcased a match between the recently crowned "AWA" champion Eagle and Gorgeous George on May 26. A humdrum affair changed before the spectator's eyes, turning suddenly into a rare double-cross. Kohler inspired the move with the purpose of damaging the credibility of Eagle, which in turn would have economic repercussions for Haft and Schwartz. He was prepared to dismiss months of booking his promotion around the Indian grappler as a main-event star.

Eagle, titleholder for three days, was betrayed in the ring after two falls, when referee Earl Mollohan declared George the victor after an unexpected three count. Don was stunned, expecting another finish altogether, never anticipating a swindle. In reaction, he punched the referee as George ran for cover. Police presence prevented the estimated 5,200 fans from trashing the building, and among those arrested was the former AWA champion. Eagle was charged with disorderly conduct, and let out on $25 bail.

Kohler's effective double-cross hurt his opponents, but following a 30-day suspension for hitting Mollohan, Eagle returned to Chicago for Schwartz-Fabiani. His title claims in the city were erased, but Eagle's AWA title hadn't been Kohler's target. Nor was he acting as part of an NWA conspiracy to eliminate an opposing title lineage. Eagle ignored the Chicago loss and remained champion in Haft country, then beat George on August 31, 1950, in Columbus to resolve any lingering questions.

The quarrel in Chicago went on, with Alliance members and the Manhattan Booking Agency sending their wrestlers in for what was guaranteed money. Still fuming at the level of Alliance help going to Schwartz, Kohler impulsively severed ties to the NWA. The feud was brought before the Alliance at a special meeting in early 1951 at a Chicago hotel that saw Schwartz inducted and Kohler readmitted into the group. Schwartz, because of his network television deal, and the fact that he was the most successful active indie promoter, was welcomed with open arms, and the hostilities that had dominated Chicago's wrestling scene ended with conditions favoring Kohler. Specifically, he'd be the only local promoter to get bookings for the recognized NWA champions.

Schwartz was okay with that, instead booking AWA champions from Haft. He was also strengthened by holding an exclusive license to Argentine Rocca. The series of matches Ruffy Silverstein had in Chicago defending his version of the world championship were highlights of Rainbo telecasts in 1951. Kohler used a core of wrestlers, led by Thesz and a young Verne Gagne, who promptly turned mediocre Marigold crowds into sellouts. Shortly after the death of his 13-year-old son Roland in a motorcycle accident on September 28, 1951, Fabiani phased out his presence in Clark Sports, and considered relocating back to Philadelphia.

Kohler and Schwartz coexisted in Chicago and the NWA from 1951 to 1955. Their individual television programs made them rich, but the key difference between them was that Kohler ran an international booking agency. Schwartz, however, outlasted the set parameters that prohibited Alliance titleholders from wrestling on his shows, with appearances from NWA light heavyweight champion Gypsy Joe and NWA champion Thesz in February and March 1953. The fallout from billing Gagne United States champion gave Schwartz an iron grip on all of Thesz's Chicago title bookings, but Kohler was too preoccupied with the national picture and the accomplishments of his agency to take any real offense.

In May 1954, when Morris Sigel resigned from his position as chairman of the NWA television committee due to illness, Schwartz was appointed to the vacancy. Three months later, Leonard himself faced grave health concerns after a sudden heart attack. The Rainbo was seeing more and more of Kohler's workers, and abruptly went dark to TV after the September 15, 1954 card headlined by Reggie Lisowski and Art Nielsen versus Steve Novak and Juan Hernandez. The loss of his heralded Wayne Griffin-hosted broadcast on WBKB (channel 7) in Chicago, and affiliates of the ABC network, crushed Schwartz's efforts to maintain financial stability.

While Schwartz was recuperating in Miami, Schaller ran the Rainbo on four more occasions. His last attempt to spark interest, with decent publicity, was on October 15, and featured stars Bill Miller, Bill Longson, Don Eagle, Ruffy Silverstein, and Dick Hutton. Schwartz was getting pressure from his wife and brother to resign from wrestling entirely, and anxiety about his health was weighing on his mind.

Schwartz staged three shows in Chicago in 1955. The first, on July 8, exploited the recent ruling of the Illinois Athletic Commission authorizing women wrestlers. Ironically, Silverstein versus Thesz, the match he'd been trying to land for years, was the main event of his final venture on August 19. A disappointing 1,438 fans were present. Leonard's days as a wrestling promoter were finished. The Rainbo was without wrestling for the first time in decades.

In 1959, wealthy Montreal promoter Eddie Quinn felt almost obligated to take his grudge with a certain old buddy 851 miles through Canadian terrain and across Lake Michigan. With a hometown boy, Bobby Managoff, acting as a booking agent, Quinn set his sights on the city of Chicago and Kohler. His resentment had been brewing since Kohler had cut into Edouard Carpentier's managerial contract in 1957, and a showdown was inevitable.

On the ropes, Kohler was vulnerable to an invasion. That spring, any semblance of cordiality between Chicago and Montreal ended, and Quinn went to work devising a plan to solidify his place in the Windy City's wrestling scene. He coordinated with the owners of the Chicago Stadium Corporation and its subsidiary, National Boxing Enterprises, to launch a new wrestling promotion. The compact, made with Chicago Stadium vice president William Burke, Chicago Blackhawks general manager Tommy Ivan, and NBE vice president Truman Gibson, would include a television tie-in on the Columbia Broadcasting System.

Quinn, Managoff, matchmaker Ben Bentley, and CBS commentator Bruce Roberts were among a contingent to speak before the Illinois Athletic Commission with the application to promote live wrestling from the CBS studios on May 27, 1959. The commission approved their proposal, and weekly matches from the WBBM-TV studios on channel 2 would begin Saturday, June 20. This would give them ample buildup for their premiere Stadium show on August 1. Saturdays in Chicago were once reserved for Kohler's Marigold broadcast, but with that program gone, Quinn won over a public still longing to watch wrestling's hysterics from their couches.

The war in Chicago would come down to talent and television exposure. Even before he staged his first match, Quinn held a decisive TV advantage, and his brigade of preeminent wrestlers included Carpentier, Managoff, Lou Thesz, Buddy Rogers, Gene Kiniski, Karl Krauser (Istaz), and Pepper Gomez. Kohler, on the other hand, was destitute, having lost his top earners, and in need of firepower to remain competitive. He was compelled to make a deal with Vince McMahon to bring the best of Capitol Wrestling to Chicago. Using tapes from Bridgeport, superstars like Antonino Rocca and Miguel Perez paraded into the Amphitheater beginning on August 21.

On December 15, 1959, Quinn, who'd paid his NWA dues for 1959–60, transmitted a somewhat shocking Western Union telegram to Muchnick at the Claridge Hotel. The message contained the text, "discontinue booking Pat O'Connor," stating that he was "under exclusive contract to me." Muchnick then received a piece of registered mail from Louis DeZwirek, a lawyer and partner in the Montreal office, indicating that O'Connor had signed a ten-year managerial contract with Quinn on November 10, 1954. The document claimed that Quinn's approval was needed on any matter having to do with O'Connor as a pro wrestler.

The tactic was sly and malicious, but Muchnick's legal representatives believed Quinn possessed a worthless contract. Illinois Athletic Commission Chairman Frank Gilmer concurred after reviewing the details, citing that Quinn hadn't performed as O'Connor's manager at any point in 1959, the first year of Pat's reign as NWA titleholder. Eddie's attempt to snatch up O'Connor actually expedited the resolution to the endless bickering between Kohler and St. Louis regarding the champion, and on January 8, 1960, O'Connor headlined at Chicago's Amphitheater versus Billy Watson.

Kohler's business picked up. Television was beamed in from Bridgeport, and introduced fans to the likes of the Kangaroos, the Bastiens, and the Grahams. A large audience was enthused about the two promotions during the first half of 1960, with Kohler drawing 8,025 on February 19 at the Amphitheater and Quinn at the Stadium on February 26 in front of 5,422. On April 1, 1960, Bearcat Wright and Johnny Valentine sold out the Amphitheater with thousands turned away, providing Kohler with a $31,000-plus gate, his biggest in years. Attendance spiked across the board, and Quinn took in 8,981 on April 9.

The seesawing of popularity continued, with Kohler bringing 7,130 to the Amphitheater on April 29, and Quinn getting 8,003 into the Stadium on May 7 with Kowalski and Don Leo Jonathan against Thesz and "Big Daddy" Lipscomb. Quinn used a weak substitute in an important main event two weeks later, and faced the consequences. At that juncture, Kohler pulled ahead and never looked back. He rented Comiskey Park three times, achieving gates of $89,675 (July 29), $52,350 (August 19), and $81,549 (September 16). Finally, in August 1960, after 19 shows in Chicago, Quinn folded. The cooperation Kohler received from the Alliance and his link to Capitol Wrestling effectively repelled the Montreal invasion.

A potpourri of territorial battles in Detroit divided the market and compelled entrepreneurs to constantly raise the bar. In 1961, rogue promoters Jim Barnett and Johnny Doyle were blitzed by wrestlers from Toots Mondt, Vince McMahon, and Fred Kohler, via Harry Light. Bruno Sammartino, Antonino Rocca, Don Curtis, Mark Lewin, Angelo Savoldi, and Haystack Calhoun wrestled at the Olympia on October 7 in what was labeled the "Greatest Card Ever Presented in Detroit." A week later, Barnett and Doyle ran the Cobo Arena with Verne Gagne, Dick the Bruiser, Wilbur Snyder, Bearcat Wright, Fritz Von Erich, Bobo Brazil, and Bob Ellis. The different factions wrangled on, with an edge held by the established group through the middle of 1962.

Dick the Bruiser already had financial interest in Indianapolis and Chicago when he encroached on Ed Farhat's Detroit promotion in 1965. Farhat was better known to fans as The Sheik, a wrestler who spent more time launching fireballs and gouging the foreheads of his opponents with forks than performing wristlocks or leg takedowns. His wildman antics scared audiences worldwide, but when the chance came to succeed Barnett and Doyle as the "owner" of Detroit's territory, Farhat took it, and joined the NWA. Bruiser, meanwhile, remained an independent under the World Wrestling Alliance banner.

The tensions between Bruiser and Farhat resumed in October 1971, and the second feud lasted three years. Alliance bookers aided in Farhat's defense, and just as Bruiser was getting off the ground, Farhat ran a show with grapplers from Toronto, Atlanta, Tampa, St. Louis, and Los Angeles. The tranquil Sam Muchnick, in an act of solidarity, banned Bruiser from wrestling in St. Louis. Bruiser put up with the inconveniences of being an outlaw of sorts until 1974, when he left Detroit and fell back into the good graces of the NWA.

The Eaton-LeBell combine's authority in southern California survived conflicts with Johnny Doyle and Frank Pasquale, and by early 1968, had been separate from the National Wrestling Alliance for almost nine years. Mike LeBell and his matchmaker Jules Strongbow submitted the necessary paperwork to return Los Angeles to the Alliance, and was approved at the 1968 convention. An association with the NWA allowed the best of the Alliance to appear at the Olympic Auditorium. Even more crucial was the relief LeBell obtained from the NWA when Jack Kent Cooke and promoter Don Fraser opened the Forum to wrestling in the summer of 1969.

The Cooke-Fraser franchise worked out a Saturday telecast at 1:30 p.m., which made its debut on August 2, 1969, with announcing from legendary Los Angeles Laker commentator Chick Hearn (Francis Dayle Hearn). The program was beamed in from Minneapolis, where it was taped by Verne Gagne under the auspices of his American Wrestling Association. On Saturday, September 6, the inaugural Forum show was headlined by Gagne and Dick the Bruiser, and featured Lou Thesz, the Vachon Brothers, Bill Watts, Wilbur Snyder, Larry Hennig, and Hard-Boiled Haggerty. Gagne won his match with a third fall disqualification of Bruiser. "Cowboy" Bob Ellis had been booked to wrestle Haggerty, but failed to show.

NWA membership had its privileges, and at the annual convention only weeks earlier, LeBell had informed his fellow associates of the invasion and received unprecedented support. Offsetting the premiere of Fraser's promotion, LeBell ran the Olympic the night prior with NWA champion Dory Funk Jr. successfully defending his crown against Buddy Austin in a bloody three-fall bout. His show, in total, offered 20 wrestlers and seven matches, including an Americas and Women's world title match.

A week later, the NWA hammered the AWA troupe again, promoting a Parade of Champions event under the guise of a salute to Strongbow. This time, the full resources of an organized Alliance campaign against a rival was clearly evident, as troops from eight territories flew to Los Angeles for the event. LeBell featured Atlantic Coast tag-team champions Rip Hawk and Swede Hanson, The Sheik,

Terry Funk, Florida champion Dale Lewis, Southern champion Buddy Fuller, International champion Shohei Baba, and world junior heavyweight champion Danny Hodge. Capitol Wrestling had also planned to send Gorilla Monsoon, who was booked to wrestle Baba, but he didn't show. In the main event, Baba and The Sheik fought to a draw.

The second Forum show was planned for October 13, but was rescheduled for November 25, and Gagne beat Luke Graham while the Vachons took care of Red Bastien and Billy "Red" Lyons. Unimpressed with the numbers, and basically outgunned in every possible sense, Cooke and Fraser closed the Forum to the AWA.

The mêlée lasted four months in total, and the Olympic saw NWA champion Funk five times, demonstrating the organization's resolve when pitted against an adversary. LeBell had the Alliance to thank for their considerable support, as did promoters in numerous territorial conflicts over the years. In the aftermath of the Los Angeles war, battles in Detroit, and along the east coast during Eddie Einhorn's International Wrestling Association run, were perfect examples of a united Alliance front against nonmembers. While there were many disagreements within the NWA, combating the threat of outsiders was an issue all members agreed on, and they were always willing to go the extra mile to help an ally.

In 1960, with the formation of the American Wrestling Association in Minneapolis, it seemed that the NWA's once-threatening monopoly and alleged violations of the Sherman Antitrust Act, were concerns of the past. The AWA and NWA would coexist without an exhausting territorial war. Promoters on both sides traded talent freely and usually minded their own interests in the face of any dispute. Three years later, a second regional promotion emerged independently of the NWA, this one known as the World Wide Wrestling Federation, an organization that evolved into today's World Wrestling Entertainment (WWE).

The three sanctioning bodies often overlapped, but in the case of the 1969 AWA vs. NWA encounter in Los Angeles, it was essentially a skirmish between area promoters and not a national clash. While those on the outside of a major clique were persistent in their entreaties to the Department of Justice, promoters at the top of the organizations in control counted their money, and consciously hid paper trails of their activities from prying eyes. The NWA, AWA, and WWWF, respectively, dominated professional wrestling in their affiliated territories, and their collaborations only boosted their bottom line at the box office, and that, of course, was all that was important to them anyway.

CHAPTER SIXTEEN

BOOKING
WRESTLING'S FUTURE
The Members of the NWA

The official National Wrestling Alliance letterhead included the motto: "A Cooperative of Wrestling Promoters in the United States, Canada, Hawaii, and Mexico — Affiliates in Other Countries." A synergy among the diverse personalities running the individual booking offices was often difficult to find, and the mix of eccentric characters and intelligent entrepreneurs kept controversy hot. Some were ex-wrestlers, others were college educated, with no athletic credentials. Each seizing traits from P.T. Barnum, they fought and scratched for leverage inside the NWA, and annual conventions generally appeared more like battle royals than diplomatic business meetings.

There was a chain of command in the Alliance, and outside of the officers, constituents who ran the most profitable territories usually had the clout. In other instances, those who were friendly with influential leaders saw decisions go their way. Some members balanced hypocrisy and greed, and threw in a lack of sympathy for the wrestlers themselves for good measure. Forgetting that the grapplers in the ring were paying their bills, these cold-hearted businessmen gave the NWA a bad name, and presented what was wrong with professional wrestling behind the scenes.

The public, however, was usually only exposed to the positive aspects of the Alliance's work. Representing an estimated 500 promoters across the world at the organization's height, the members of the NWA did more to boost the sport's esteem than any group in history. Fans rewarded their accomplishments, repeatedly demonstrating their satisfaction with the level of wrestling by establishing new annual records for attendance and revenue.

The Midwest Wrestling Association merged with the newly founded National Wrestling Alliance during the summer of 1948. Led by **Albert C. Haft**, the MWA had been organized in an effort to curb the growing power of the National Wrestling Association in the early 1930s. The refusal of major syndicates to acknowledge John Pesek's title aspirations caused Haft to construct his own union that recognized the Tigerman as heavyweight champion, and the MWA expanded into cities from West Virginia to Kansas.

Haft was the oldest original member of the National Wrestling Alliance, born in Buffalo on November 13, 1886, the son of Albert and Carrie Haft. Following an amateur wrestling career that saw him win regional honors in Erie County, he moved to Columbus, where he lived with his wife. By 1910, he took ownership of the middleweight championship of Ohio and competed under the alias "Young Gotch," a moniker used by numerous wrestlers over the years. Despite a reputable resumé, Haft would never lay a claim to any undisputed championship. He had an exceptional mind for wrestling, a unique outlook, and a scientific approach others did not share.

On May 15, 1918, Haft enlisted in the army. He went to Central Officer's Training School at Camp Gordon, Georgia, meriting an infantry commission on October 15, 1918. Discharged in December, Al concentrated on the promotional side of wrestling back in Columbus. He took to managing and training grapplers, and considered his importation of heavyweight contender George Kotsonaros into Columbus as a turning point in his career as a promoter.

Haft was named the first-ever wrestling coach for the Ohio State Buckeyes in 1921, and led the squad to an 8–0 record in 1923. On his professional shows, he featured light heavyweight and welterweight matches, with exhibitions by Clarence Eklund, Jack Reynolds, Hugh Nichols, Ray Carpenter, Matty Matsuda, Ted Thye, and Ira Dern. When the "Trust" materialized in 1933, Al found himself on the outside. He collaborated with Billy Sandow, Adam Weissmuller, and other independents in the war against the nation's leading promoters, and hyped Dick Shikat after his double-cross of Danno O'Mahoney in March 1936.

Busy with his many business interests, Haft missed the inaugural meeting of the NWA in July 1948. He was, however, one of the most important members of the new club, albeit a little dubious about what such a group could possibly achieve. Nonetheless, Al threw his name into the hat, and was eager to address his concerns at a gathering in Chicago in October. He would end up leaving the meeting comfortable with what had transpired. Known for his intellect, he originated studio television wrestling with help from executives of the Crosley Broadcasting Corporation, and added to his remarkable wealth using the new medium's exposure.

Haft was the initial vice president of the new coalition, and recognized Don Eagle as "AWA" champion in direct violation of NWA bylaws. He was adamant about balancing his territory with two titleholders, but Sam Muchnick refused to book Lou Thesz in Columbus. Al didn't protest too much. His region was thriving with his own stars and championships. He frequently booked Eagle, Frank Sexton, Ruffy Silverstein, Frankie Talaber, and Marvin Mercer, and agreements were in place with Paul Bowser and Eddie Quinn. In October 1951, Haft signed "free agent" Buddy Rogers, establishing Columbus as his new headquarters.

Between November 1949 and February 1952, Haft received only a handful of appearances by Thesz, but the tension was alleviated when Haft dropped his local "world" champion. In early 1954, the Alliance kingpin worked 12 dates for Haft, on a circuit from West Virginia to Indiana. But animosity about his scheduling of women and midgets on the undercard of Billy Watson and Thesz's matches two years later suspended NWA title contests in Columbus completely.

Rogers, in October 1961, broke an almost five-year period for Columbus during which they went without a showing by the NWA champion. Over that time, there was never a lack of championship-level wrestlers, or title matches. Al's stubbornness proved that his town could boom without appearances by the Alliance's heavyweight titleholder. Needless to say, the Columbus audience did pay a price, and both sides of the "battle" might have benefited from the potential returns.

Haft possessed a good eye for amateur talent, stemming from his true fascination with the fundamentals of wrestling, and a multitude of college athletes were lured into pro wrestling and schooled at his famous gymnasium on third floor of 261 S. High Street. Some of the best wrestling matches occurred there, hidden away from the public, and Haft's gym was a place where reputations were made and destroyed. Silverstein, Bill Miller, and Karl Gotch stretched young up-and-comers, and a host of future legends gained instruction they would carry for their entire careers.

Haft was a tenacious promoter, and his passion helped create a premier wrestling city. But using athleticism as a selling point, Haft kept a band of tough shooters on the payroll. He also pushed the performance aspects through characters like Buddy Rogers. In addition to acreage in Reynoldsburg, Haft was the proprietor of a restaurant and a motel, and was a horse aficionado. His promotion bottomed out in the late 1960s, and he died at the age of 90 on November 10, 1976.

A prominent wrestling matchmaker was **John James Doyle**, the son of a famous newspaper publisher. Doyle was instrumental in the progression of wrestling on television, the development of international superstars, and earned a record gate for a grappling spectacular. Even before he became the top matchmaker in California and after his departure from the state, he was always exceedingly successful. In fact, he was involved in sports promotions for more than 30 years, from smaller arenas in the upper Midwest and New England, to the South Pacific.

Doyle was born on April 6, 1909, the first child of LaSalle, Illinois, *Daily Post* editor James Gabriel and Eva Bowater Doyle. In 1921, the family relocated to an affluent neighborhood in Pasadena, California, and James worked for the Hearst Corporation as the publisher of the Seattle *Post-Intelligencer*. Educated at Los Angeles Junior College and the University of Southern California, John joined his father in the newspaper industry as a salesman.

By the mid-1930s, Johnny had taken a job as an assistant promoter of wrestling in Wilmington and later, in Jersey City. On behalf of Ray Fabiani, he contributed to the promotion of the famed international tournament in Los Angeles, along with Lou Daro and Toots Mondt. He did business on both coasts for Fabiani and Mondt until landing a gig managing the Eastside Arena in Los Angeles.

Doyle picked up tidbits of wisdom from his two mentors, Mondt and Floyd "Musty" Musgrave (1899–1948), who booked grapplers to Johnny at the Eastside Arena, Ocean Park Arena, and the Embassy Auditorium in the Los Angeles area. Mondt's move to New York prompted Doyle and Musgrave to fuse interests and buy out Nick Lutze, solidifying their control of the territory's main booking agency.

Faced with sour numbers at the Olympic and a general aversion to wrestling in Los Angeles, Johnny and his associate laid the foundations for a system that recharged pro grappling in the city. Musty passed away during the implementation phase, and Doyle took the wheel as Los Angeles shot to the forefront of wrestling in the United States. Handling primarily heavyweights, Doyle booked to the Olympic, and expedited the fortunes made off the abilities of Gorgeous George Wagner, Primo Carnera, and Baron Michele Leone.

Cal Eaton of the Olympic and Mike Hirsch of the Ocean Park Arena in Santa Monica bought into Doyle's booking agency, which, prior to January 1950, was a rival of Hugh Nichols's operations in Hollywood and San Diego. The unification of outfits, and an agreement that split booking fee revenue four ways, monopolized all big-time grappling in the region. Their agency would represent over 90 percent of the wrestlers in the territory, a tremendous boon for the ambitious National Wrestling Alliance.

Ring Talent, Inc., owned by Doyle, Hirsch and Eaton, was the company that processed valuable television contracts and distributed profits. Created in April 1950, the corporation silently strangled opponents, and from inside the bubble, met the demand of local stations. For each program, the combine earned upwards of several thousand in advertising, while paying grapplers as little as $25 per match. Nevertheless, Johnny was close with his wrestlers, especially Wagner, and invited many to his house for card games and dinner.

Accusations of restraint of trade became common in southern California, starting with Morris Cohan and Nick Lutze at the Pasadena Arena, and continuing with Benny Rubin at Pico Palace, Harold Gartner at the Valley Garden Arena, Ernie Steffen at the Wilmington Bowl, and Frank Pasquale at the South Gate Arena. Rumors of wrestlers who grappled for a non-NWA promoter being black-listed were rampant, and discouraged free enterprise. The syndicate was so tightly knit that even the threat of inquiries and lawsuits failed to change their practices.

The matchmaking skill of Doyle and the promotional capabilities of the Eatons worked together perfectly, and Johnny was responsible for the brilliant booking of Michele Leone, whose "Baron" gimmick attracted ample attention in California. Leone rose through the junior heavyweight ranks, and beat Enrique Torres for the state version of the "world" title, all in preparation for a bout with NWA champion Lou Thesz.

Doyle's marketing plan was impressive, and 25,256 paid a record $103,277.75 to see Thesz beat Leone on May 21, 1952. The eyes and ears of wrestling opened to Doyle's views following his unprecedented accomplishment, and his good luck continued. In October 1952, Johnny brokered a deal that sent tapes of Wednesday night Olympic shows to 11 western states across the ABC network. The multi-million-dollar contract began on January 7, 1953.

Eaton and Doyle went into a rocky period, and when Johnny shifted his office from the Olympic to the Legion Stadium on March 11, 1953, it looked as if their partnership was finished. But Doyle denied there was any trouble. He told the *Los Angeles Times* on March 12, 1953, that, "I moved my office to Hollywood as a matter of convenience. Most of the wrestlers, besides myself, live on the west side of town. Sure, Eaton and I have had, and have now, differences of opinion on operational procedures, but they had nothing to do with moving my office. As a matter of fact, I hope eventually to move my office to a neutral site." He also insisted that "the transfer will have no effect on the caliber of wrestling now being presented at the Olympic."

The problem dividing Doyle and Nichols and the Eatons grew into the summer, and in June, the two bookers decided to swap the Olympic feed with a live broadcast from San Diego. Nichols switched his weekly San Diego wrestling event from Tuesday to Wednesday to meet the new scheduling demands, and went head-to-head with Eaton. Cal attempted to go it alone, then petitioned the NWA for his own membership card. The dispute was smoothed over at the September conference in Chicago, and the best of the NWA returned to the Olympic.

Persistent problems in Los Angeles compelled Doyle to seek employment elsewhere. With a position opening for his former boss Toots Mondt, and a plan to film 13 half-hour wrestling shows in New York, Doyle sold out to Nichols, Eaton, and Hirsch for an estimated $27,000 on January 22, 1954. The conditions in the Northeast were horrid, and by September, Johnny was staying with his brother in Malibu and thinking about going into real estate.

Wrestling was his business, and despite the "no-compete" clause (until October 1, 1955) fixed in the January pact, Doyle resurfaced on the Los Angeles independent scene. He was anxious to run opposite the Eaton troupe, and believed he had the stamina to weather the political fallout. Booking with outlaw promotions, Doyle's efforts to scale the mountain proved difficult. With his wide assortment of connections, Johnny found TV coverage for his endeavors, including stations in South Gate, Las Vegas, and Salt Lake City, but the Eatons fought tooth and nail to keep him down.

With no other choice, Doyle took his grievances to investigators for the Department of Justice, and, in October 1955, provided testimony to the California State Assembly subcommittee. The quick-witted gentleman spoke out again about the California wrestling scene, this time in February 1957 before the State Athletic Commission, and neither statement helped Eaton's reputation. By the end of the year, Doyle was on to bigger and better things. He moved his family to Virginia and became the vice president, secretary-treasurer, matchmaker, and shareholder of the Capitol Wrestling Corporation.

Though there was plenty of room for varied personalities in the Capitol

Wrestling office, the combination of Doyle, Toots Mondt, and Vincent McMahon broke down almost immediately. Doyle abruptly left Washington for Boston, where he took the book for title claimant Edouard Carpentier, endorsed by the National Wrestling Association and promoters Quinn, Bowser, and Fred Kohler.

Doyle reached an agreement that sent Bowser's Boston talent to the Sunnyside Garden in Queens for promoters Haskell Cohen and Kola Kwariani with television on WNEW on Tuesdays at 9:00, starting on September 30, 1958. He also attained a slot for original programming from Boston into New York City beginning on November 7, 1958, on Fridays at 9:15 on WOR-9. Looking for malcontents, he contacted NWA promoters in an effort to set up dates for Carpentier to appear as champion, and got many to take the bait. Doyle made the case that Edouard was a superior draw than the Alliance's titleholder, Dick Hutton, which was true.

When the calendar turned to 1959, Doyle moved on again. He teamed with an old friend named James Barnett, who was now booking in Indiana, and the two set their eyes on Detroit. They formed Barnett-Doyle Corporation on March 31, 1959, and each owned 150 shares of the common stock. 700 shares were held by a front for various other investors, among them NWA first vice president Frank Tunney. Indianapolis, the city Barnett based his operations from, was partially owned by NWA president Sam Muchnick and Tunney, but during the stretch Barnett and Doyle were outlaw promoters, neither man could get Alliance membership. There was too much anger about the growth of their promotions among members to allow them in.

From record gates in Detroit and Denver, to the launching of television in NWA markets (a shrewd and aggressive move), Doyle and Barnett began to scare some affiliated promoters. In 1961, Doyle went back to Los Angeles to organize resistance to the Eatons from the Sports Arena, and run TV from the KTLA Studios. He encouraged Roy Shire's project in San Francisco, and warred briefly with Jack Pfefer in Denver. Johnny and Barnett were making a lot of enemies, but were dangerously close to creating the strongest national promotion, to that point, in American wrestling history.

Exceptionally good in social situations, Doyle was a proponent of using squash-type matches on TV to build anticipation for arena programs. The Los Angeles revival, with Tuesday night offerings on KTLA, faded in January 1962, and poor attendance in Denver caused Johnny to sell out in the spring of 1963. Detroit was sold in 1964 to Ed Farhat and his father-in-law, Francis Fleser, for $50,000, prior to Doyle and Barnett's expedition abroad. Their desire to take over an entire country was realized when they settled in Australia and commenced promoting in October 1964. Their migration to the South Pacific was carefully planned, and

Doyle and Barnett brought television outlets aboard before their arrival with tapes from Windsor to warm the territory.

Capitalizing on local laws, they split their time in Australia to save on taxes, each spending five months and 25 days in charge of the office. Barnett and Doyle looked into starting up wrestling in the Philippines, but the treacherous political conditions nearly cost John and his wife their lives at the beginning of the Marcos Dictatorship. Doyle, an adventurer, traveled extensively, and left behind complex booking arrangements for Barnett in his absence, using his decades of experience to develop their empire.

Around 1968, Johnny retired to Palm Springs with the intention of focusing on his two hobbies, golf and the flying of planes. The 60-year-old businessman passed away from cancer on October 9, 1969, at Loma Linda Hospital. Attending his funeral were Barnett, Billy Varga, Mike Mazurki, and Hardy Kruskamp, and donations were sent from Thesz, Farhat, Verne Gagne, Sam Menacker, and Wally Karbo.

The addition of **Paul Frank Bowser** in November 1949 boosted the NWA's senior leadership. Paul, born on May 28, 1886, in Kittanning, Pennsylvania, was the son of Marlin and Nancy Aretta, and grew up on the family's Armstrong County farm. A graduate of Beaver College, Bowser was a clever grappler, wrestling professionally as early as 1910. Within two years, he was holding the disputed middleweight championship, and had put down roots in Newark, Ohio. He embraced the job of promoting matches, and supported the career of his wife, women's champion Cora Livingston.

In 1922, Bowser took over the reins of Boston's Grand Opera House. For the next 38 years, he was New England's wrestling maestro, acting as both promoter and booker. His American Wrestling Association frequently clashed with the National Wrestling Association, and although he joined the National Wrestling Alliance in 1949, he had been given special permission to recognize a "world" champion other than Lou Thesz. In the fallout of the 1957 angle that saw Edouard Carpentier win the world title, Bowser severed his ties to the NWA. Boarding up his booking office, Bowser relied heavily on wrestlers from Montreal and the skills of matchmaker Johnny Doyle.

Paul and his brothers Walter and Roy were horse enthusiasts, and raced champion thoroughbreds. He owned a large farm in Lexington, Massachusetts, and invested money in horse racing in Foxboro. On Friday, July 15, 1960, Bowser's last promotional venture was staged at the Boston Garden with the tandem of Thesz and Carpentier grappling Killer Kowalski and Hans Schmidt. Three days prior, Paul suffered a heart attack at his home and was taken to Concord's Emerson

Hospital. A surgery was performed and it looked like he would recover. Paul died on Sunday, July 17, after a second surgery at Massachusetts General Hospital. He was 74. Bowser was buried at Westview Cemetery in Lexington.

The promoter of little big men, **Sam Avey** went from laboring as a merchant in a family grocery in the small Kansas town of Cherryvale to running a fan-friendly wrestling outfit. Son of nomadic parents Joseph and Susan Avey, Samuel was born on February 5, 1895, in Kingfisher, Oklahoma, the youngest of nine children. Joseph had taken his family from Ohio and through Indiana and Nebraska before pitching a tent in Oklahoma. He wasn't finished moving. By 1900, the Aveys were living in Kansas and found life in Cherryvale to be exactly what they were searching for. The family all contributed to their business, and the youngest boys, Edward and Sam, delivered groceries to the townsfolk.

No one will know for sure if Sam, on one of his routes, stopped by the cottage of Cherryvale's most prominent sports celebrity, Billy Sandow, the manager of Ed "Strangler" Lewis, but it is certain that the two became cronies while they both were living in Montgomery County. Following duty in World War I, Avey was lured into wrestling by Sandow. He traveled as a referee, shielding the champion from a double-cross. Plugged into Tulsa to promote Lewis's championship matches, Avey, whose surname was often misspelled "Avery," learned a lot as a member of the tribe.

Oklahoma was a breeding ground for wrestlers, and Avey benefited from living in the backyard of several exceptional collegiate programs. His main star was a Tulsa kid named Leroy McGuirk, an outstanding grappler for Oklahoma A&M. After turning pro, McGuirk took over the light heavyweight division, and wrestlers from across the country came into the territory for matches. There were outlets in Oklahoma for non-heavyweights, but it wasn't until Hugh Nichols was entrenched in Hollywood that Avey had a formidable partner.

When McGuirk was forcibly retired in an auto accident, Sam gave his colleague points in the company and named him matchmaker. In September 1950, the NWA awarded both men executive positions, appointing McGuirk to be the second vice president, and Avey treasurer because of his banking credentials. McGuirk's duties increased, and by 1953 he was the primary booker for the junior heavyweight champion, and coordinating talent from southwestern Missouri to Little Rock, across Oklahoma, and into parts of Texas.

Avey was the owner of the Tulsa Oilers of the United States Hockey League in the 1940s, and in 1942, purchased the Tulsa Coliseum for $185,000. Regularly hosting prestigious political events and boxing-and-wrestling championship matches, the Coliseum was Avey's headquarters. Even the radio station he owned, KAKC, broadcast from the facility's basement. On September 20, 1952, the Coliseum was gutted by fire, destroying a landmark and leaving Avey without a wrestling venue. Lightning was to blame, and the building's wooden roof unfortunately accelerated the complete and total destruction.

In January 1958, Sam sold out to McGuirk to concentrate on his role as senior vice president of Farmers and Merchants State Bank. He remained linked to the NWA as treasurer through August 1960. Active in the community, he was director of the Tulsa Chamber of Commerce, president of the Rotary Club, and involved in numerous charities including his annual Milk Fund wrestling spectacular every March, and his celebrated Christmas party for children. With over 30 years in the business, Avey gave the Tulsa audience a structured promotion, and the territory continued under McGuirk with great success. Avey died on August 9, 1962, at the age of 67.

There were two National Wrestling Alliance members in the Los Angeles metroplex from 1949 to '56, who represented dozens of area promoters. **Hugh Nichols** booked light heavyweight grapplers from his Hollywood office, while Doyle scheduled the heavyweights to the Olympic and other facilities from Santa Monica. The tandem also supervised wrestlers for California's million-dollar television industry.

Hugh Clifford Nichols was born on December 6, 1898, in Cedar Rapids, Iowa, the second child of George Clifford and Lucile "Lucy" Aungst Nichols. George labored on the railroads, specifically the Cedar Rapids and Iowa City Railway, and Hugh was a machinist, a profession that helped his physical development. Based on an introduction by a local welterweight wrestler, Jack Reynolds, Nichols was trained by "Farmer" Martin Burns. He learned additional techniques from Clarence Eklund, and was a huge admirer of legendary catch wrestler Dan McLeod.

Settling south of Dallas in Mexia, Nichols gained experience in the Lone Star State. He ended the decade with a share of the splintered world middleweight title, and jumped to the light heavyweight division to enter the National Boxing Association elimination tournament, held to determine a single titleholder in 1930. On April 4, 1930, he beat Joe Banaski in Cincinnati to win the championship. In March 1933, he lost a controversial match to Frank Wolff in Dallas that saw the latter claim the title, but Hugh recaptured it in May. On March 5, 1934, in Tulsa, he was dethroned by Leroy McGuirk.

A nightmare turned into reality for Hugh on August 9, 1933, en route to matches in Oklahoma City with wrestlers Joe Shimkus, Jack Kogut, and George

Sauer. Nichols, the auto's driver, accidentally hit and killed a five-year-old girl who was running across the street on a highway south of Purcell. The tragedy crushed Hugh, whose daughter Betty was also five. Nichols was cleared of any criminal liability in the accident. Another blow came in September 1935 when Nichols fractured his legs in a parachute jump at the San Diego Exposition. He would be out of action for almost a year, and forced to retire prematurely.

On November 9, 1939, Nichols was named matchmaker for the junior and light heavyweight divisions at the Legion Stadium in Hollywood. Trading talent with Sam Avey, Nichols promoted all of the top stars in the non-heavyweight category. He booked the most credible version of the world light heavyweight title and rarely did the championship change hands outside of Hollywood during the 1940s.

Nichols profited from the exposure of television, beginning on June 30, 1947, on W6XAO (changing to KTSL in May 1948). A contract with KTSL concluded in May 1950, and grappling on television from the Legion Stadium went missing until Monday, April 2, 1951, when Ring Talent, Inc. (Doyle, Hirsh, Eaton) introduced a series on KTTV. The program was hosted by Bill Welsh and Roy Maypole, and kinescopes (motion picture film) produced by Jerry Fairbanks, were sent to the ABC network's eastern affiliates from Texas to New York. ABC guaranteed the combine $7,500 a week, equal to $57,000 a week in today's dollars.

Nichols negotiated a six-year deal with CBS for a national program from Hollywood (hosted by Jules Strongbow), debuting on February 6, 1954, broadcast on 103 stations, and worth an estimated $5 million. After all this success, Hugh often found himself in the middle of quarrels concerning TV and booking arrangements, and leaned on his Alliance connection when necessary.

On December 15, 1956, Hugh committed suicide at his home at 2126 N. Bronson Avenue, shooting himself in the head. A toe on his right foot pulled the trigger of a shotgun. Speculation about why he ended his life ranged from depression after failing health to the demise of his San Diego promotion. The 58-year-old had been involved with wrestling for 35 years. He was survived by his wife Betty, and daughter Betty June. Hugh's funeral at Hollywood Memorial Park Cemetery was attended by more than 500 people.

Harold Light's Detroit agency had a special responsibility, and that was to supervise and regulate the booking of little people grapplers to NWA territories. A protégé of Adam Weissmuller (cousin of Johnny, swimmer and famous Tarzan actor), Harry was born on September 17, 1898 in Paris, France, and became associated with sports promotions around 1929. At the 5795 Woodward Avenue address of the Arena Gardens, Harry was educated in all facets of the business, from usher and cashier, to a position in the office of Weissmuller Sports Enterprises. Following the death of Weissmuller in March 1937, Light became an assistant to Louis Markowitz and Eddie Lewis.

Light seized the Gardens after World War II and formed his own company, the Harry Light Wrestling Office, which, along with partners Jack Britton (Gabriel Acocolla) and Bert Ruby, controlled grappling in the Detroit area for nearly 20 years. With Capitol Wrestling and Fred Kohler, Light promoted in opposition to Johnny Doyle and Jim Barnett at Olympia Stadium in 1961–62. The war against Barnett and Doyle ended peacefully, and the lines for talent opened across the board. Ruby was regarded as an excellent trainer and booker, and Britton traveled on the road as an agent for many of the midget wrestlers their office represented. Light retired quietly, and passed away on October 29, 1971.

The casual, refined **Morris Pincuss Sigel** operated one of the best wrestling ventures in the world. A product of Russian immigrants, and born in New York City, Morris was four years younger than his brother Julius. In 1909, the Sigels migrated to Harris County, Texas, and lived on Lubbock Street in Houston. Morris, according to reports, made three dollars a week as a teenage office boy for the *Houston Post*, prior to becoming a clerk for the Kirby Lumber Company. In September 1918, Morris registered for the national army, but with the armistice in November, he saw no combat.

In 1924, Julius made headway as a sports promoter in Houston, and tried to stage wrestling with a sense of legitimacy. He promptly expanded to other towns, and incorporated the Gulf Athletic Club, Inc. on November 15, 1926. In 1930, he relocated to Shreveport, and left the task of promoting Houston to Morris.

When Texas Governor Miriam Ferguson signed a new law legalizing boxing, and placing boxing and wrestling under the jurisdiction of the State Labor Commission effective September 1, 1933, Sigel sought to reorganize the old Gulf Athletic Club. In August, he relaunched the corporation with Russel Bonham and brother-in-law Frank Burke (1901–1983). The regulatory body issued its first licenses for boxing and wrestling to Sigel, and they would be renewed annually for the next 33 years.

Sigel fought his way through the 1930s as an affiliate of the "Trust" and the National Wrestling Association. Alliances with decision-making promoters Tom Packs and Paul Bowser provided Houston talent while he built his own stars, like Leo "Daniel Boone" Savage (Edward Civil), with creative booking. During the war years, Sigel presented some of the country's best grappling, with Thesz, Bobby Managoff, Yvon Robert, and Bill Longson headlining. Promoting at least five matches per show, supporting the new tag-team fad, adding state championships, and relying heavily on very smart wrestling minds, Sigel drew thousands regularly.

Sigel, Burke, Sarpolis, and Ed McLemore were all shareholders in the Dallas Wrestling Club, and associates in other cities made the Houston syndicate a powerful territory. The Texas Wrestling Agency, the central booking company for the Sigel Empire, pushed grapplers to sign exclusive contracts, and earned him financial percentages of shows outside Houston. The supplementary income was making Morris and his friends wealthy. His involvement with the National Wrestling Alliance, beginning in 1949, gave the organization valuable credibility.

Texas wrestling debuted on KLEE-TV in 1949 and Morris's nephew Sid Balkin, son of famed promoter Leon Balkin, was hired by the station as part of a trade agreement that allowed them to broadcast the shows for free. From rooms 502–504 of the Milam Building, the Houston promotion ran weekly, usually 52 weeks a year, on Friday nights at the City Auditorium or Sam Houston Coliseum. Their television show later moved to KTRK (channel 13), and finally onto KHTV (channel 39).

Sigel suffered a heart attack in 1952, and quickly came to the realization that things in his life had to slow down. Burke, his right-hand man, took on more of the daily burden, and traveled on behalf of the promotion. Of all the territorial and courtroom battles he withstood, against Dizzy Davis, Juan Humberto, Joseph Meyer, and Frank Brown, it was his feud with McLemore in 1953–54 that was the most agonizing. The clash left scars that never healed, even after peace was made.

Sigel reorganized the Texas Wrestling Agency in April 1955 with Frank and Ronnie Burke, and his signature was affixed to the Department of Justice consent decree in 1956. In 1959, the Texas State Legislature ratified Senate Resolution No. 328, applauding the lengthy career of Morris, and honoring his "conscientious and faithful service to Texas." The members of the NWA honored Sigel at the August 1960 convention in Acapulco. Paul Boesch, who admired the qualities of his boss, estimated that Morris contributed financially to 170 different groups.

Quoted by the *Houston Chronicle* on December 28, 1966, Boesch said this about Sigel: "He had a great promotional mind. He invented tag-team matches. He was the first man to put a fence around the ring. He had a million ideas. He made a lot of money, he gave a lot away and he was a thoroughly honest man."

Besides the Burkes and Boesch, Sigel was assisted in his promotion by Leon and Sidney Balkin, Paul Jones, and Doc Sarpolis. Late in the summer of 1966, at about the same time a heated war broke out between the Gulf Athletic Club and McLemore in Dallas, Sigel fell ill. He expired two days after Christmas at the age of 68. His wife Irene and daughter Shirley sold his stock in the promotion to Boesch.

Ed Don George (Edward Nichols George Jr.) was the only member of the NWA to have participated in an Olympic Games event. Born in the farming community of North Java, in Wyoming County, New York, Ed attended St. Bonaventure College in Olean, where he played football, and both competed in and taught wrestling. George transferred to the University of Michigan, and in 1926, placed third in the Big Ten Conference Wrestling Tournament. After taking a year off, Ed won AAU heavyweight titles in 1928 and '29, the Big Ten title in 1929, and achieved three letters for wrestling.

In 1928, George made the U.S. Olympic squad as a freestyle wrestler. At the Games in Amsterdam, he beat Swiss grappler in the semifinals of the unlimited class, then matched with Johan Richthoff of Sweden in the gold-medal contest. In 4:41, Richthoff beat George and captured the gold. Ed finished fourth. He was a favorite going into the 1929 NCAA Tournament, but was unable to compete due to an injured elbow.

Recruited and trained by Bowser in New England, Ed debuted professionally under the name "Ed Don George." George was quickly groomed for the heavy-weight throne, and took the championship from Gus Sonnenberg on December 10, 1930, in Boston. Naive or overconfident, George was double-crossed by Ed "Strangler" Lewis on April 13, 1931, in Los Angeles, and lost the world title. Bowser maneuvered the title back to him and George had a more than two-year stint as AWA champion from February 1933 to July 1935.

In the scramble to unify the championships, Ed passed his crown to stablemate O'Mahoney, the new idol of wrestling. During a tour of Europe, George beat Al Perreira on April 5, 1937, in Paris to capture the European version of the world title. He had a third run as AWA champion with a victory over Steve Casey in April 1939. After the onset of the American presence in World War II, he joined the navy and trained pre-flight cadets at Chapel Hill in wrestling and judo. In 1946, he was discharged as a commander, and returned to fulfill part-time duties as a wrestler.

The Upstate Athletic Club was incorporated in New York on July 31, 1947, and George opened a booking office in Buffalo. He soon expanded his promotional enterprises to include Rochester, Syracuse, Albany, Binghamton, and ten other cities. George was perhaps the most educated promoter in the country, and the problems with money that dogged many of his brethren did not affect him. Instead of spending excessively, Ed was saving, and by 1955 he was a millionaire.

George was an indispensable member of the National Wrestling Alliance, functioning as first vice president in 1951–52 and chairman of the rules committee. A majority of his towns saw record numbers with him as director, proving that the instruction he received from Bowser and Jerry Monahan had paid off.

George depended on Ignacio "Pedro" Martinez as a matchmaker until an argument in 1954 shattered their partnership. In late August 1955, Ed sold the Upstate A.C. to Martinez for $100,000, and retired from wrestling. With his wife Joanne, he traveled the globe, living off his investments and sizable fortune. They had several children, and he followed grappling for the remainder of his life.

In 1981, he was honored by the University of Michigan with induction into the school's Athletic Hall of Honor. Additionally, he was enshrined into the St. Bonaventure Hall of Fame, the Big Ten Hall of Fame, and the Professional Wrestling Hall of Fame at the International Wrestling Institute and Museum. George died on September 18, 1985, at the age of 80.

The NWA was represented north of the border by **Francis Martin "Frank" Tunney** and **Edmund Regan "Eddie" Quinn**, whose spots on the roster were practically guaranteed after Lou Thesz settled his conflict with Sam Muchnick. There were many parallels between Tunney and Quinn, and they navigated the pitfalls of sports promotions to become very rich. Often traveling together with their wives, the duo stood above the laws of the U.S. Sherman Antitrust Act, and brought a distinct confidence to the NWA.

Eddie was the third child born to John and Margaret Quinn on May 22, 1906, in Waltham, Massachusetts, and was ten years younger than his closest sibling, John. His father, the son of Irish immigrants, was a respected carpenter in Middlesex County. By 1930, Eddie was living in Waltham with his wife Gertrude and daughter Doris, and was an apprentice to his father.

Frank was also a third child, born on November 12, 1912, to Thomas and Anne Tunney. He was educated in the Markham area of Ontario, and after graduation, went to a business college. Excelling in typing, he earned his diploma around 1931. The motivated, mild mannered young man answered a classified ad for the Queensbury Athletic Club, and was hired on as a secretary by boxing and wrestling promoter Jack Corcoran. Tunney was an inexperienced member of the troupe when Corcoran opened up wrestling at Maple Leaf Gardens in November 1931.

After an amateur boxing career, Quinn made contacts in the Boston sports field, and an association with Paul Bowser persuaded Eddie to start his own promotional venture in Waltham. When Bowser needed a shrewd second for Quebec sensation Yvon Robert, he enlisted Quinn, and Eddie held the position from 1935 to '39. In 1936, Quinn moved into Boston to promote a weekly wrestling program at the Mechanics Building. His events subsidized Bowser's income, and were successful in slicing into Charley Gordon's Arena attendance, as the two went nose-to-nose on Wednesday nights.

With cooperation from Bowser, Quinn departed for Montreal and took over the local promotion. A legion of bad decisions had hurt the overall popularity of wrestling in Quebec, and Bowser conspired with the manager of the Forum, Tommy Gorman, to push Jack Ganson (John Karabinas) out. On July 27, 1939, the Montreal Athletic Commission granted Quinn a license to promote, and he debuted on August 8, 1939. It wasn't long before the plummeting wrestling operation was righted, and Quinn's innovative concepts not only solidified the interest of existing fans, but enticed tens of thousands more into the bedlam his grappling incited weekly.

Tunney facilitated Corcoran's employment of his older brother John as a matchmaker on the wrestling side of the athletic club. Corcoran counted on John to manage his wrestling assets in Toronto through much of the next five years, but, in 1939, was obligated to sell off his grappling enterprises with the Tunneys because of illness. John Tunney would direct the matchmaking duties with notable assists from Bowser, Jack Ganson, and Jerry Monahan, while Frank handled the bookkeeping. On January 19, 1940, the 32-year-old John, a father of four, suddenly died of influenza.

The unexpected loss dumped everything into Frank's lap. Despite a tough sell some weeks at the Gardens, he averted the pending disaster, and newspapermen were quick to praise Bill Longson for aiding in the renewed appeal. The debut of "Whipper" Billy Watson in 1941 was a momentous step in the prosperity of Francis Tunney.

In June 1948, Tunney and Quinn invested in St. Louis and gained control of the National Wrestling Association world title. St. Louis was being pulled apart in a wrestling war between Tunney's ally Thesz and an acquaintance Frank first met in 1936, Sam Muchnick. Muchnick and a crew of Midwestern promoters configured the National Wrestling Alliance in July, but the struggle in St. Louis prevented the membership from adding hubs in Toronto and Montreal. Tunney and Quinn entered the NWA at the November 1949 confab, several months after peace reined down.

Tunney had a non-threatening personality, but fraternized with more controversial promoters. He felt more comfortable putting money into another territory than trying to further any kind of personal aspirations. Because of his calm demeanor, Tunney was the clear choice to chair the Alliance's grievance committee, and was always a leading member of the heavyweight championship committee. He was selected to be the NWA's first vice president six consecutive years beginning in 1954, and in 1960 at the annual meeting in Acapulco, was voted president. Invested in Detroit and Indianapolis, Frank was closely aligned with Doyle and

Barnett, and preserved his stake in St. Louis until 1974.

Future Alliance world champions used Toronto as a barometer to measure their drawing power. Even after Bruno Sammartino won the WWWF title, Tunney used the hero much to the delight of his audience. The tactic proved that over and above membership in the NWA, Tunney would do what was necessary to keep his fans happy. The accident that injured Whipper Watson in 1971 marked the end of an era, and 30 years of Tunney-Watson wrestling stranglehold.

Quinn's phenomenal system of booking paid impressive dividends. The popularity of Robert was balanced out by a master heel, Wladek Kowalski, a man the Montreal promotion revolved around. Kowalski wore the championship for Quinn on at least 11 occasions and repeatedly drew more than 10,000 fans to the Forum and baseball stadium. All the greats of the 1950s went to Montreal, and Quinn staged some of the best matches anywhere in the world on a consistent basis. His contests featured original angles, bloody violence, and all the turmoil and carnage spectators grew to expect.

Original programming emanated from the Forum and Palais des Sports on CBFT, channel 2, with Michel Normandin providing commentary. Aside from Bowser and Robert, shareholders in Montreal were Bobby Managoff and Louis DeZwirek, a lawyer who served as the vice president of Canadian Athletic Promotions. Among the others on Quinn's payroll at different times were Abraham Ford and George Linnehan, associates in Boston, assistant matchmakers Frank Orlando and Lucien Gregoire, boxing matchmakers Nat Rogers and Raoul Golbout, and agents Larry Moquin and Bob Langevin. In addition to his investment in the Montreal and St. Louis wrestling businesses, Quinn had $25,000 in Boston.

A wise friendship with Montreal sportswriter Elmer Ferguson (1885–1972) gave Quinn credibility in the newspapers and released any tension that was festering underneath the mats of pro wrestling. With Ferguson, his partners, and acquaintances in the city, Quinn established a lucrative organization almost unequaled in North America. Aside from important alliances with men carrying Tommy guns, and aliases like "Jimmy the Gent," Quinn seized the opportunity to make acquaintances inside the Quebec political structure. Donations were given, charitable events were held, and decisions were made that were favorable to his promotion.

Quinn's promotion could only have safe harbor for so long. Quebec Liberal senator Cyrille Vaillancourt spoke out against wrestling and boxing in July 1958, and hoped to pass a bill banning them from television. He argued that children were being influenced by the violence, and his words began to hit home with the public. Later in the year, Eddie found himself in trouble with the athletic commission after a series of demands were made by the commission's chairman prior to a boxing match between Archie Moore and Yvon Durelle. The commission wanted a $10,000 deposit and five percent of the television rights revenue ($95,000) in advance, much to Quinn's disgust. He was so offended at the requests, he decided to take the commission to court to fight the proclamation.

The commission threatened to deny a permit for the affair, and Quinn would have forfeited thousands. Eventually, the parties settled and the fight went on. Problems with the athletic body persisted, but Quinn brought much of the controversy in 1961 onto himself. Thirteen hours before the Robert Cleroux-Archie Moore match in December, Eddie cancelled the bout, saying that the "box office is sick." With less than 3,000 tickets sold and an expected loss of as much as $60,000, Quinn called off the fight and faced the consequences. The penalties for his actions were huge. Montreal Mayor Jean Drapeau immediately called him to his office and scolded him verbally, then the athletic commission issued an indefinite suspension. Although his boxing license would not be renewed, the commission did allow him to return to wrestling in February 1962.

The cigar-smoking industrialist was involved in several nightclubs in Montreal, including the original el Morocco at Metcalfe and St. Catherine streets, and the newer version on Closse. Colorful and boisterous, Eddie retained his Boston attitude and persona until the day he died. Those who knew him understood his flair for the dramatic and eagerness to cash in with his next show. He had lasting friendships with Thesz, Managoff, Tunney, Jack Dempsey, and Jack Sharkey, and was usually the focus of any party.

After being a member of the NWA from 1949–57 and 1959–63, Quinn retired from wrestling and sold his house in Mount Royal. Eddie and his wife moved to Northampton, New Hampshire, in late 1963 where he died unexpectedly on December 14, 1964. His funeral was attended by Sharkey, Ford, Moquin, Orlando, Linnehan, Frank Scarpa, Gerry Heffernan, Clarence McFarland, Les Ryan, Rip Valente, Tom Johnson, and Elmer Ferguson.

Toronto was a highly rewarding wrestling city, but the always-honest Tunney was never in it just for the money. He wanted to sustain his promotion by keeping the sport hot at the Gardens, and endured many ups and downs. At the low end, in 1965, his weekly attendance sank below 2,000, but soon rebounded with adroit booking. The appearances of champions Thesz, Watson, Sammartino, Gene Kiniski, Johnny Valentine, and The Sheik kept his loyal fans on the edge of their seats with heart-pounding wrestling entertainment. Ed Farhat (The Sheik) and George Scott booked the Gardens in the 1970s and into the '80s, and an arrangement with Crockett Promotions imported the stars of the Mid-Atlantic to Ontario cities.

On a trip to Hong Kong, Frank passed away in his sleep on May 10, 1983, at the age of 70. Survived by his wife Lorraine and three children, Tunney was buried in Mount Hope Cemetery. His funeral was attended by Watson, Muchnick, Kiniski, Barnett, Scott, Jim Crockett, Vincent J. McMahon, Fred Ward, and Athol Layton. Frank Tunney Sports, Ltd. was continued by his nephew Jack, who had been in the racket since 1956, with financial interest going to Tunney's son Edward. In July 1984, the Tunneys made a deal with the World Wrestling Federation. Jack Tunney acted as the promotion's president, albeit as a figurehead, from 1984 to 1995. Toronto was affiliated to the NWA for 35 years.

The chore of training and managing women professional wrestlers was taken on by **William Harrison "Billy" Wolfe**. Wolfe was the second child born to John and Lucinda Wolfe on July 4, 1896, in Daviess County, Missouri. His father worked hard labor as a farmer in the town of Jackson, leaving his mother to raise Billy, his older brother George, and younger sister Jennie. The family was living in Phillipsburg Township, Kansas, by 1910, where John had taken a job as a rural mail carrier, and Billy was joined by a second sister, Hazel. The two Wolfe boys were drafted into the military during World War I, and Bill began pursuing the craft of wrestling at a Kentucky duty station.

A middleweight grappler, he claimed the Missouri State title in 1923 and was a solid challenger to champion Charles "Midget" Fischer of Wisconsin. A dangerous competitor, Billy was revered by his peers for doing whatever was necessary to defeat an opponent. He married Margaret Johnson, and on February 22, 1922, celebrated their first child, George William Wolfe, branded "Billy Wolfe Jr." After a second child, Violet, arrived, the family moved to Kansas City, and Billy decided to start instructing women at his local gymnasium.

Following a divorce from Margaret, Billy married women's wrestler Barbara Ware, known for competing with men on the mat. Their marriage failed, and while training at his Kansas City gym, his attention was drawn to a pretty young brunette named Mildred Bliss. Bliss, an office stenographer by day, wanted to become a wrestler, and displayed outstanding muscle development. Wolfe tutored her, soon realizing he had found the prospect he'd been searching for. The close proximity of their training evolved into a relationship, and ultimately marriage. Changing her name to Mildred "Burke," the talented athlete found her niche on the mat, and she took the top women's championship from Clara Mortenson in January 1937.

Wolfe booked Burke to a growing number of promoters throughout the nation, and the touring women's champion was always a reliable draw. In late 1949, Billy became a member of the National Wrestling Alliance, and made his stable of 30 women available to fellow associates. For each show, he received a percentage, and with that came considerable riches that slowly evaporated in extravagant living and gaudy jewelry for himself and his wife. On one plane, he stood as a father figure for the girls he mentored, but on another, he earned a reputation as a womanizer. The Wolfe-Burke marriage wasn't monogamous, and when they were apart, Billy enjoyed the companionship of the women he traveled with.

There was a breaking point. The relationship soured to bitterness and then to all-out combat. In 1952, the couple went their own ways, with Mildred losing a bundle of money in the process. Wolfe froze her out of wrestling along NWA channels, and in need of funds, she wired Jack Pfefer for help. The Alliance attempted to reconcile the couple, appointing a special committee to assess the different positions, and there was only one solution. One would buy the other completely out of the business.

Burke volunteered to sell out for $50,000, but was rebuffed. Instead, Wolfe, on January 26, 1953, sold all of his interests in booking women to Mildred and her financiers, who in turn founded the company Attractions, Inc. The deal was for $30,000, waived all alimony owed, and barred Wolfe from participating in wrestling for five years. That pledge lasted only a few months. Wolfe and his son recommended their booking of women from Columbus in opposition, tempting many wrestlers to his agency by offering talent 50 percent of all proceeds. To thwart his move, Burke upped her payments to 60 percent, and Wolfe finally settled on giving 75 percent to the women in his employee. The move was successful in luring scores of important grapplers to his stable.

While on the road struggling to preserve her share of the market, Attractions, Inc. went into bankruptcy, and into the hands of the receiver, James Hoff of Columbus. Eight months later, Hoff named Wolfe as administrator and the decision was approved by Franklin County Judge William Bryant.

In a memorandum to wrestling promoters across the nation dated August 20, 1953, Wolfe announced that he was the booker for Burke and 27 women wrestlers from the newly attained Attractions, Inc. He was also booking June Byers (DeAlva Eyvonnie Sibley), Nell Stewart, Violett Viann, and Mary Jane Mull.

Burke disputed his claims in a letter to promoters on August 26, 1953, stating that she hoped to get the entire mess straightened out in the courts. Her contract with Wolfe prohibited him from acting in any capacity in wrestling, and he was in breach of that binding agreement. In addition, he was confiscating what she had paid $30,000 for. Aligning herself with booker Leroy McGuirk, Burke expected to be vindicated by the Alliance at their September 1953 meeting in Chicago.

There were many inequities in the NWA system, and some promoters had a measure of hostility for anyone who wasn't an Anglo-Saxon male. Intolerance didn't infect the entire membership, but a significant number had successfully gotten women banned from yearly conferences, and diminished the importance of female wrestlers on the circuit. Aside from being in a fight for her livelihood, Burke was forced to sit in the lobby of the Blackstone Hotel in Chicago as male dignitaries argued inside closed doors about her future. It wasn't unusual that Wolfe had taken advantage of the situation and used the Alliance to influence things in his favor. His voice was the only one heard by the membership.

Although the Alliance declined to recognize women's wrestling after the convention, Billy regained his dominant stake. He touted his son's wife June Byers as world champion following a tournament in Baltimore, and his girlfriend Nell Stewart as the Women's U.S. titleholder. Some women grapplers chose to stay loyal to Burke, even going into a self-imposed retirement rather than wrestle for the Wolfes.

In a letter to members on November 4, 1953, Burke refuted Wolfe's claim that she would only wrestle one woman grappler. She listed 12 competitors, including Stewart and Byers as "girls I will be very happy to work with." Wolfe proceeded to eliminate possible jobs for her in NWA territories, and a run in the Southeast with Cowboy Luttrall and Paul Jones in 1954 fizzled.

Mentally and physically exhausted, Mildred was forced to wrestle Byers on August 20, 1954, in Atlanta on short notice, and there was genuine heat. The match was a shoot, with tremendous odds against her. Wolfe had the local commission in his corner, and slid a friendly referee in to call the match his way. Burke later admitted that she gave up the legitimate first fall with intentions to start the second strong. The second fall didn't have a finish. Officials stopped the match, and Burke left the ring understanding that her title was safe because she hadn't lost two falls. The resulting publicly spin claimed Byers defeated her for the belt, and the validity of Burke's championship was weakened significantly.

The Wolfe promotional machine used every opportunity to undermine Burke's credibility, and their feud was one of the most vicious in grappling history. Billy Sr. maintained membership in the NWA through 1957 and promoted women's wrestling until his death on March 7, 1963. At a restaurant near Opal, Virginia, Wolfe suddenly became sick, and died at Fauquier Hospital in Warrenton. His funeral in Newark, Ohio, was attended by a number of his peers and a contingent of women grapplers. The 42-year-old Billy Jr. passed away on August 8, 1964, in Newark.

The elder Wolfe's morals, or lack of them, have been criticized, but no one was more responsible for making women's grappling into a functional and profitable business. Women in wrestling were discriminated against, and for years viewed strictly as a sideshow, but Wolfe tried to make it respectable. Instead of mud match-type shenanigans, there were fiery contests for the women's championship. He introduced a tag-team title, and integrated African American women wrestlers into his growing monopoly. Wolfe furthered women's professional wrestling more than anyone before or since.

Justifiably paranoid, Burke traveled with an escort for the rest of her career to ward off potential trouble. She founded International Women's Wrestlers, Inc. with Bill Newman with offices in New York City, San Francisco, and Sydney, that served as both a booking agency and training center. The expansion internationally accelerated the spread of women's wrestling to Japan and numerous other countries, and brought about the World Wide Women's Wrestling Association (WWWA), and a singles championship that is still active today. Mildred was connected to athletics into the 1970s. She died on February 18, 1989, in Northridge, California at the age of 73. In 2002, she was posthumously inducted into the Professional Wrestling Hall of Fame.

Joe Malcewicz, an effective and sincere promoter from San Francisco, was a member of the NWA from 1949–62 (not counting a slight break in 1956–57 when he delayed in signing the consent decree). He was liked by wrestlers and known for his fair payoffs. Bright and extremely old school, Joe was the first child born to Anthony and Helen Malcewicz in Utica, New York, on March 17, 1897. The Malcewicz Family lived at 1 Hoyt Street, in a Polish Community, and Joe showed a natural wrestling ability, testing his skills by the age of 16 on Utica shows.

In 1917, Malcewicz went to New York City and entered the international tournament at the Lexington Theatre. He turned heads as an energetic battler, and made a trip to Omaha to learn from the legendary Farmer Burns. Malcewicz was a top grappler in Paul Bowser's troupe and affiliated with Ed Lewis when the Strangler wore the championship in the mid-1920s. Dissatisfied with the current product in San Francisco, Toots Mondt and Bowser swapped Jack Ganson with Malcewicz in 1935, and Joe bought out Dan Koloff for exclusive booking rights to a dozen towns in Northern California and Nevada.

Malcewicz devised a powerhouse promotion in San Francisco that featured great wrestlers, talented performers, and a striking level of excitement that captivated fans throughout the region. The Pacific Coast heavyweight and world tag team championships made for well-shaped feuds that regularly sold out the Auditorium, and the Sharpe Brothers and Leo Nomellini earned their fortunes bone-crushing for Malcewicz. A valued member of various NWA panels, from the board of directors to the heavyweight championship committee, Joe was looked to for his leadership and his opinion was trusted.

However, he was unwilling to change with the times. In 1961, Malcewicz was targeted by Johnny Doyle and Roy Shire, who were going to use television to oust their competition in the Bay Area. Joe was losing money hand-over-fist, and shifted his programs from the Civic Auditorium to the Kezar Pavilion in an attempt to stay in business. Joe died on April 20, 1962, at the age of 65.

An incomparable promoter, Malcewicz was genuinely kind and refrained from excessive hype or bullishness. Joe's aid to Bill Longson after the wrestler suffered a broken vertebrae in his back on January 5, 1937, offers a perfect example of his compassion for grapplers. The injury put Longson on the shelf, and Malcewicz provided financial help to him and his family. In the cold, cruel wrestling world, that sort of kindness was remarkable, and said a lot about the man he was.

Atlanta's **Paul Jones** was a childhood friend of legendary shooter Ray Steele in Lincoln, Nebraska. Born Andrew Lutziger on June 23, 1901, in Russia, Paul was the second son of Jacob and Elizabeth. Two years later, Lutzigers migrated to the United States and Lancaster County, Nebraska, shortened their name to "Lutzi," and had four additional children. Jacob worked on the railroad, and sons Jacob Jr. and Andrew followed in his footsteps. Around 1920, Andy began grappling at the Lincoln YMCA, training with Peter Sauer (Ray Steele), and learning much from legends Farmer Burns and Clarence Eklund.

Lutzi ventured to Texas under the assumed name "Paul Jones," and was the Sigel Brothers' most exceptional young athlete. He headlined in Los Angeles with Dick Shikat, Jim Browning, Joe Stecher, and Nick Lutze, and had a series of matches with Jim Londos in 1926 and 1927. By 1930, he was living in Houston with his older sibling Jacob, and making a decent living on the pro mat. Traveling with George Kotsonaros from Nashville to New Orleans for a match, Jones was almost killed when their automobile flipped outside Eutaw, Alabama, on July 13, 1933. Kotsonaros, the driver, died at the scene.

In Houston, Jones was a fire inspector, occasionally wrestled, and refereed dozens of bouts for Morris Sigel. After the war, he moved to Atlanta, where he picked up the wrestling franchise in January 1944. Jones joined the NWA in November 1949, and in the early 1950s, sold a piece of the territory to wrestler Donald J. "Don" McIntyre (1911–1990).

McIntyre wasn't the first wrestler to buy into the Atlanta office. Fred M. Ward (1914–1992), a wrestler billed as "Tommy Ward," was Jones's partner and promoter of record in many Georgia cities, including Columbus, Marietta, and Macon, for more than 30 years. Live television emanated from WLWA-TV (channel 11) on

Saturdays from 6:00-7:30 p.m., and grapplers were given dates from the central A.B.C. Booking Office at 76 Houston Street in Atlanta.

Wrestling matches at the Auditorium in Atlanta were kept lively with McIntyre, Freddie Blassie, Art Nelson, Al Massey, Babe Zaharias, and Ray Gunkel. The Atlanta office maintained a working relationship with Chicago, and in the aftermath of the Lou Thesz-Edouard Carpentier scandal, Jones pulled his membership in the NWA. He recognized Carpentier, then strongman Paul Anderson, of Toccoa, Georgia, as titleholder in the 1958–59 period. In the 1960s, they used a strand of the WWA championship, brought into the territory by Fred Blassie, and held by Eddie Graham and Tarzan Tyler. Atlanta's application into the Alliance was accepted at the 1962 convention, and Thesz reestablished the NWA title with six appearances in five months, even going over the final WWA champ Tyler on June 7, 1963.

Jones and McIntyre sold a majority stake in the A.B.C. Booking Office to Ray Gunkel in 1958, and upon his retirement from the ring, McIntyre became Atlanta's promoter of record in April 1962. Leslie Wolfe replaced McIntyre as the "front" promoter for Atlanta in May 1964, when Don sold out to Buddy Fuller (Edward Welch). Wolfe, a veteran promoter, carried Atlanta through July, when Jones took the wheel. Respected for his wrestling smarts, Jones had several stints as NWA first and second vice president in the 1960s and '70s.

The region was stable until Gunkel's unexpected death on August 1, 1972. His wife Ann gained a senior role in the company, and made suggestions about the future of the promotion. Clashing with Lester Welch, who had previously traded his shares in Florida with his nephew, Fuller, Ann branched off and incorporated Gunkel Enterprises, Inc. on October 24, 1972. Her sanctioning body, All South Wrestling Alliance (ASWA), charmed more than 20 wrestlers from the NWA in Atlanta, leaving Jones and Welch for dead.

Lester and his brother Roy Welch, an NWA collaborator in Tennessee, teamed with Jones to form Mid-South Sports, Inc. in Fulton County on November 22, 1972. The trio would sell percentages of the company to Bill Watts and Jack Brisco, and receive creative help from Watts and Jerry Jarrett. Jones procured talent from surrounding booking offices, specifically from Florida, and Eddie Graham and his son Mike often journeyed to Atlanta. He also hired Gordon Solie, the longtime Florida commentator, to host his Saturday television program. At the August 1973 NWA convention in Las Vegas, Australian promoter Jim Barnett made it clear that he wanted to return to the U.S., and within the next month, he bought out the Welches in Atlanta.

On March 29, 1974, Mid-South Sports, Inc. owners voted to rename the corporation Georgia Championship Wrestling, Inc. The bitter war with Gunkel lasted for two years, finally coming to a close in November. Jones remained the head of the Atlanta promotional scheme, but Barnett ran the day-to-day operations. Their territory got a boost when their Saturday wrestling program on WTCG (later Superstation WTBS) was shared with a large audience via satellite in December 1976. Exceedingly philanthropic, Jones owned the Atlanta Sports Arena and other property in the city, and was one of the richest NWA members in history. He held a wrestling promoter's license for 40 years, retiring in July 1984. Jones passed away on April 17, 1988, at the age of 86.

The Islands of Hawaii were represented in the Alliance by **Alexander Karasick**, named commissioner of Hawaii and the Far East Territories at the November 1949 NWA caucus in St. Louis. Karasick was born in Kharkov, Russia, on June 24, 1890, and was a dancer touring with the Russian ballet when he settled in the United States in 1914. A year later, he met a 17-year-old Hungarian woman named Wilma and married her. Employed at the Judson Iron Works and by the Southern Pacific Railroad, Karasick wrestled as an amateur as a hobby at the Olympic Club in San Francisco, and his family lived in Oakland. To earn extra cash, he used the name "Jim Prokus" and toured as a professional.

Karasick was an amateur for several years, making his debut under his real name as a welterweight grappler around 1920. Using an unorthodox style, Al perplexed opponents in carnival shoots and arena performances. Intelligent and methodical, he rose to the light heavyweight level and claimed a version of the world title. In 1936, he retired from wrestling and moved to Honolulu, obtaining a permit and lease to promote at the Civic Auditorium. With assistance from his daughter Bette and son-in-law Randy, Karasick promoted wrestling shows in Honolulu until May 1961, featuring all of the sport's stars. The islands saw Londos, Thesz, Rikidozan, Primo Carnera, The Sheik, Gene Kiniski, The Sharpes, Joe Savoldi, Leo Nomellini, and Sandor Szabo.

On July 4, 1962, he jumped into politics, running for the Hawaiian State House of Representatives, but placed tenth overall. A party celebrating his 75th birthday saw Governor John Burns present him with a special crest medallion. Karasick died on May 24, 1965, at Queen's Hospital in Honolulu. Hawaiian affiliation with the NWA was continued by Ed Francis, then High Chief Fanene Leifi Pita Maivia, identified by fans as Peter Maivia, the grandfather of The Rock (Tuifea Dwayne Johnson).

Rudy Dusek wasn't the only NWA booker with three brothers involved in wrestling. **Roy Welch** was the oldest of four siblings, followed by Lester, Herbert, and Jack, and unlike the Duseks, the Welch family had children and other legit-imate family also absorbed with wrestling, spanning more than six decades. The Welch Empire enlarged to the point where family members were part-owners of four different Alliance territories. Roy controlled the Mid-South Booking Office from offices in Nashville and Dyersburg, and his allegiance to the NWA began in November 1949. Born on December 19, 1902, in Sallisaw, Oklahoma, Roy Edward was the first son of Ed and Birdie Sumpter Welch. Before he was 30, he was married with children, and was a working as farmer in Graham.

Roy was trained in the fundamentals by his father, a former wrestler himself, and went to Texas, where he added to his repertoire under the guidance of Cal Farley and Dutch Mantell. By 1937, he was claiming a version of the much-dis-puted light heavyweight title, and invested his time and money into introducing a trained bear to wrestle in matches against opponents.

Roy was the handler for "Miss Ginger," a 350-pound "monster," a task that later went to Pat Malone. Welch's brothers, Herb, Jack, and Lester, all turned pro under the tutelage of their father and older brother, and when Roy planted roots in Tennessee booking wrestlers in several states, each benefited greatly.

Welch partnered with an enterprising businessman from Birmingham named Nick Gulas (1914–1991), a protégé of ex-wrestler and promoter Chris Jordan. Gulas, who traveled to Nashville with $600 in his pocket and reportedly grossed over $5,000 a week at his height, became the "Music City's" matchmaker. Running per-haps 40 towns, six nights per week, 52 weeks a year, the Welch-Gulas combine ruled a region known as the "gasoline circuit," sending more than 100 wrestlers to dozens of promoters in parts of Tennessee, Mississippi, Kentucky, Alabama, Arkansas, Florida, Missouri, Indiana, and Virginia. Among their better drawing arenas were those in Nashville, Birmingham, Memphis, Chattanooga, Evansville, Louisville, and Knoxville.

It was necessary for Welch's ownership stake in many cities to stay hidden during the years he wrestled, to prevent charges of conflict of interest. In July 1955, his agency established television in Nashville on WSIX-TV. His son Edward wrestled as "Buddy Fuller," and Edward's boys, Ronald and Robert, were also grapplers. Roy's sister Bonnie married Virgil Hatfield and had three sons, Albert Lee, Donald, and Luther Eugene, dubbed, in the wrestling world, Lee, Don, and Bobby Fields, respectively.

But serving terms as NWA first vice president in the 1960s, Welch and Gulas were invaluable members of the Alliance, and were heavily protected with inside con-nections at various state athletic commissions. That protection, coupled with their political ties to Tennessee Senator Carey Estes Kefauver (1903–1963), sustained them through thick and thin. Kefauver, an amateur grappler in his youth, enjoyed the dramatics of pro wrestling, and was occasionally seen at events at the Capitol Arena in Washington D.C.

From 1957 to '63, as the ink on the NWA's consent decree was drying and associates were scrambling to better hide their illegal tactics, Kefauver was the chairman of the U.S. Senate Judiciary Subcommittee on Antitrust and Monopoly. The FBI was still getting complaints, and their investigation remained active, but the government did not lay charges. Kefauver had been looking into the monopolies of professional boxing during those prime years, and the NWA escaped an open-ended disaster. The Welch-Gulas clan believed they had something to do with the redirection of heat from the Alliance, and they were probably right.

Outside of wrestling, Roy owned a large and flourishing dairy farm in Gibson County, Tennessee, and a champion canine, a boxer named "Dickey Dock." Roy became ill and retired from promotions two years shy of his 50th anniversary in wrestling. He died on September 27, 1977, at Trenton Memorial Hospital in Trenton, Tennessee, at the age of 75. In 1981, subsequent to the retirement of Gulas, Edward Welch promoted the Sports Arena in Nashville with NWA affiliation.

As shocking as it might sound, the old "Cowboy" once received a shot at the National Wrestling Alliance world heavyweight title. No, it wasn't a bout at the Fort Homer Hesterly Armory with Brisco or Kiniski, it happened in 1944, when the NWA was still a localized promotion in Iowa. On February 16, 1944, **Cowboy Luttrall** wrestled Alliance titleholder Ray Steele, in Des Moines. Of course, Luttrall was defeated in straight falls. No one said he was championship material as a grappler, but he was a top-notch promoter. He put Florida on the wrestling map, and was the NWA's first delegate in the Sunshine State in 1950.

Clarence Preston Luttrall was born on March 27, 1906, the third of five sons, in Jack County, Texas. The family relocated to Loraine when Clarence was a young man, and farming was a natural step for all of the children as they grew older. One always quick to fight, he was lured into wrestling by southeastern Texas promoter Arthur Mondt and was soon competing regularly in carnivals. Clarence took the moniker Cowboy Luttrall, a name that would stick forever. In July 1940, he gained national news attention by engaging Jack Dempsey in an infamous and embarrassing boxer vs. wrestler contest in Atlanta. Luttrall was knocked out in the second round, suffered a broken nose, was carried from the ring. Dempsey, on the other hand, admitted to being out of shape and "training on cigars."

As a promoter, Luttrall got his feet wet in Chattanooga and Tampa in the 1940s, but it was his second stab at Tampa in 1949 that started a run that lasted through

1970. He brought a stability to Florida wrestling that set the tone for most of the next half century, and it was on his shoulders that the Florida wrestling empire was built. From Tampa to Orlando, southward to Key West, and even to the Bahamas, Puerto Rico, and Cuba, the Cowboy built a reputable circuit for wrestlers that was the envy of the country.

A familiar grappler from Chattanooga named Eddie Gossett first appeared in Florida in 1952. The Luttrall-Gossett bond strengthened as years passed, and the latter became a big-time star under the guise of "Eddie Graham." Graham, notorious for his work as a heel, took over as lead babyface for Luttrall in Florida in the early 1960s. On February 1, 1954, Luttrall promoted his inaugural "Gasparilla Spectacular" at the Armory, headlined by Baron Michele Leone and Mr. Moto. The annual show was a highlight of Luttrall's promotions, and would see the NWA title switch from Gene Kiniski to Dory Funk Jr. in February 1969.

With Herb Freeman and Graham as matchmakers, Luttrall owned wrestling in Florida. The Cowboy set up weekly wrestling from the WFLA-TV studios, later held at the Sportatorium, and tape was cycled to cities throughout the state. Booking was done from the office of Deep South Sports, Inc., and the television show hosted by Gordon Solie was billed as *Championship Wrestling from Florida*. Luttrall sold his percentage of the company to Graham in September 1970 and he died on March 11, 1980, at the age of 73.

The NWA had a hard-nosed roughian in its midst named **Mike London**. London did not weigh more than 180 pounds — and was likely closer to 165 — but was as tough as they came. An old-school shooter and known for his customary beard, Mike built his athleticism on a family farm in Dudley Township, South Dakota. He was the second child born to a war veteran Ross and homemaker Iva Anshutz, and given the name Harold when he was born on July 29, 1909.

In the 1930s, the family moved to San Joaquin County, California, settling in Lodi. Harold, under his lifelong moniker "Mike London," boxed and wrestled, and officially began his professional career. By 1933, he was making the rounds as a promising middleweight and usually competed for promoters who only featured lighter grapplers.

From time to time, London wrestled in athletic shows in shoot matches against locals for money, and while in Chicago in 1934, took on all comers at the World's Fair. He toured the United States extensively, building a reputation as a heel, and in March 1937, he earned a 60-day suspension in San Francisco after punching out the referee, and brawling with police officers. In 1939, he settled in Albuquerque.

London opened up a booking office in Albuquerque by the late 1940s and then bought El Paso from John McIntosh. In January 1950, he assumed booking rights in Denver, briefly ran Cheyenne, and with his expanded booking circuit, earned himself a place in the Alliance. London and Fred Kohler teamed to incorporate Rocky Mountain Sports Enterprises out of Denver, and television stars Verne Gagne, Pat O'Connor and Reggie Lisowski awakened the audience to topflight wrestling.

Mike retained the services of a legit wrestling hooker Ben "Doc" Sherman (1908–1981). Sherman, born Benjamin Franklin Sherman Jr. in Fairbanks, Alaska, won the 1929 AAU title at 160 pounds representing a Portland athletic club, and turned pro shortly thereafter. Wrestling internationally, he was feared on the mat in a career that lasted more than 25 years. The promotion of wrestling at the Civic Auditorium in Albuquerque continued into the late 1970s, with London's popular live television program on Sunday mornings. On August 26, 1989, London died at the age of 80.

London's colleague in El Paso in the 1950s was **Frank "Sam" Menacker**, born on May 13, 1914, in New York City, the first son of Russian parents, Abraham and Minnie Menacker. Menacker attended George Washington High School and was a baseball star, making it as far as the Class-A division for the New York Yankees at catcher. Around 1936, he was lured into pro wrestling by promoters looking to capitalize on his Jewish heritage, and Menacker competed throughout the country. Menacker was in army from 1941 to 1946, achieving the rank of major.

A booking office with London was organized in El Paso and the two were partners until a serious grudge ousted Menacker in 1955. Friends with "Gorgeous" George Wagner and Johnny Doyle, Menacker trailed the latter to Australia, where he performed as a television commentator during the 1960s. Menacker and Doyle shared a hobby of flying planes, and relished the Australian lifestyle. Once married to women's champion June Byers, Sam was a member of the Screen Actors Guild and acted in a handful of films. He was an announcer for Dick the Bruiser in Indianapolis, and bought a home in Auburn, Illinois, promoting sporadically as late as the 1980s. On January 7, 1994, Menacker passed away at the age of 79, leaving his wife Sandra and three daughters.

The *New York Times* reported that a newcomer by the name of "Rudy Dosek" was making his local debut on January 1, 1929 at the St. Nicholas Arena. Dosek, was none other than **Rudolph Dusek**, a Farmer Burns–trained grappler and the patriarch of the famous Dusek clan. Rudy encouraged his three brothers to follow him into wrestling, and their antics entertained audiences from coast to coast.

Hason was the Dusek brothers' true birth name. Rudy was the fourth son born to Bohemian parents, Anton and Maria Hason on January 25, 1901, in Omaha, Nebraska, and was followed by Walter, Emil, Lillian, Ernest, and Joe. By the age of 18, Rudolph was a machinist on the railroad with brother Walter, helping to support his parents. After studying under Burns, Rudy embraced the name "Dusek," and joined the Ed "Strangler" Lewis combine as a light heavyweight. In New York, he aligned himself with masterful promoter Jack Curley and Toots Mondt, a twosome who were transforming the entire territory into gold by 1930.

Dusek had a profitable series of matches with Jim Londos that included a bout in Washington on August 12, 1931, that drew an estimated 15,000 fans to Griffith Stadium. The Omaha grappler united with Londos and the Johnstons against Curley and Mondt in 1932. They staged programs at the Broadway Arena in Brooklyn on Mondays, and St. Nichols Arena in Manhattan on Wednesday nights, but Rudy was pushed out by Londos in a double-cross late in the summer of 1933. For $20,000, he bought into the Curley troupe, and saw his investment squandered. In November 1933, the "Trust" was assembled and was favorable to all key wrestling promoters, with one exception, Rudy's arch-enemy, Jack Pfefer.

For more than 20 years, Rudy maintained offices at 1650 Broadway in Manhattan, and booked wrestlers to shows from Connecticut to Pennsylvania. When Curley died in 1937, it was the Dusek-Johnston faction that seized the city's wrestling scene. Rudy was involved in the final Garden show on March 30, 1938, and when they restarted the heartbeat of the Eighth Avenue arena on February 22, 1949, with brother Ernie as a headliner. The National Wrestling Alliance opened their doors to secondary associates in Chicago and New York City in 1951, and the membership committee accepted Leonard Schwartz and Dusek.

The curtain closed on the Duseks in New York City right around the time Joe was taking the reigns from the late Max Clayton in Omaha in 1957. But the end of Rudy's booking office didn't come as a result of a preplanned retirement, but at the whim of a new configuration run by Toots Mondt and Vincent McMahon. The rise of Capitol Wrestling eliminated many promoters, among them, Dusek and Edward Contos of Baltimore. Eleven months after Contos's death in March 1959, his family filed a $300,000 civil suit against Capitol, alleging antitrust violations. Rudy was a little more willing to step aside.

Dan Parker, the kayfabe breaker for the *New York Daily Mirror*, wrote about Dusek in his October 5, 1957, column: "Does the Department of Justice know that, although the wrestling promoters signed a code of conduct after entering a 'no defense' plea in the Antitrust suit brought against them by the government, they are up to their old monopolistic tricks again, with Toots Mondt and his accomplices freezing Rudy Dusek out of all the arenas where he used to operate and refusing to let him use their wrestlers, in violation of the agreement filed with the U.S. Government?"

Rudy and his wife Edna had four daughters, and surprisingly, none of the four Duseks had sons. He passed away on October 27, 1971, at the age of 70.

Bill Lewis was the NWA's Richmond booking affiliate from 1951 to 1961. Born James Arthur Whitfield on May 28, 1898 and reared in Rocky Mount, North Carolina, Lewis was a carnival wrestler before being trained by Farmer Burns in Omaha. During the 1920s, and after the death of his father, he toiled on a tobacco farm, and competed at fairs and in circus tents under the alias "Captain Bluebeard." Ed Lewis reportedly gave him the name "Bill Lewis," and by 1927, he was promoting wrestling in Greensboro. Lewis, a portly gentleman, was very outspoken, and received much admiration for developing Richmond into a premier wrestling town. He promoted until his death on March 31, 1961.

Down the coast from Lewis's promotion was the territory of **James Allen Crockett Sr.**, booker to dozens of cities in the mid-atlantic states from his headquarters in Charlotte. James was born on June 2, 1908, in Bristol, Virginia, the fifth child of Charles Samuel and Josie Berry Crockett. The studious son of a railroad conductor, Jim broke into the business in 1934, promoting the Armory in Charlotte. With a talent-sharing deal through Bill Lewis that stretched up to the New York syndicates, Crockett and an old pal from Bristol, Pete Moore, invaded Tampa in 1935. Their goals to rid the south of Jim Downing (1878–1960) was achieved, and with the collaboration of Rudy Miller booking in Florida, they increased the market share for their outfit, Southeastern Co.

Accepted into the NWA in 1951, Crockett was an advocate of tag-team wrestling, and was very protective of his wrestlers in the face of possible double-crosses. A large man, Jim was well liked by his staff and peers, and was named second vice president of the Alliance in August 1963. He earned a fortune in wrestling promotions and his union with Lewis, the Murnicks, and other neighbors sheltered the regional monopolies from any real competition.

He died on April 1, 1973, leaving Jim Crockett Promotions to his wife Elizabeth, children James, David, Jackie, and Frances, and son-in-law John Ringley. Jim Junior took the controls of the corporation, and was the Alliance's second vice president in 1976. In August 1980, he became NWA president, and his aggressive approach expanded Crockett Promotions throughout the United States. The promotion was sold to Turner Broadcasting in November 1988 for a substantial sum of money, and closed the book on a family company active for more than 50 years.

The booker of the NWA world light heavyweight champion from 1953 to '58 was Nealon Walter Hager, better known as **Tex Hager**. Nealon was born on January 26, 1915, the son of Walter and Catherine Hager, and raised in Lane County, Oregon. He attended Eugene High School and wrestled for the University of Oregon before making his pro debut in the mid-1930s. Weighing 170 pounds and billed as being from El Paso, Tex also competed as a professional rodeo star in Wyoming and Oregon. By the late 1940s, he was promoting Tri-State Sports out of Boise, with cards in 20 cities across four states.

Hager focused on lightweight competitors, was inducted into the NWA in 1951, and moved his home base from Boise to Spokane in 1955. By the early 1960s, his career in wrestling began to wind down, and he went into hotel management for the Carson City Nugget. Hager hired upstarts Wayne Newton and his brother to play the casino's lounge. He was later involved in hotels in Reno and Eugene. Hager died on May 25, 1989, at the Washoe Medical Center in Reno.

There were few individuals who could honestly bad mouth **Donald Owen**. Even his bitter promotional rivals had a tough time whining about his business sense without paying him at least one compliment. It was universal amongst wrestlers that the Pacific Northwest, albeit a distance from other NWA territories, was a superior circuit because of Owen's reliable payoffs. Born on March 16, 1912, in Pendleton, Oregon, Don was the second child of Herbert and Bertha Owen, and grew up in Union and Lane Counties. He attended the University of Oregon, and joined his father in sports promotions in Eugene in the mid-1930s.

Don and his brother Elton ran the family company following the death of their father in February 1942, and balanced their operations with the endeavors of Ted Thye, Virgil Hamlin, Bob Murray, Hat Freeman, Jerry Meeker, and Tex Hager. The Owens relied on talent from the Western Athletic Club in Portland, then opened up their own offices, and were granted membership in the Alliance in September 1951. Don Owen Sports, Inc. maintained an association with the NWA until 1992, giving Don the distinction of having had the longest tenure in Alliance history. He died at 90 on August 1, 2002.

Born in Phoenix, of Mexican decent, on February 6, 1915, **Ignacio "Pedro" Martinez** wrestled prior to becoming a promoter in Rochester around 1948. In January 1952, he bought the illustrious Manhattan Booking Agency in New York City. Martinez's eagerness to be in New York faded when the financial gamble didn't pay the dividends he expected, and he sold 75 percent of the corporation. He dropped the final 25 to Toots Mondt, but was stiffed out of almost $20,000.

The previously sturdy partnership between Pedro and booker Ed Don George of Buffalo soured, and the latter used his firm dominance over upstate New York to lock Martinez out. Martinez ran opposition to George in Rochester with outlaw talent from Canada, and with Ray Arcel, revived pro boxing in the area. By late August 1955, George's towns were faltering, and he decided to sell the Upstate Athletic Club to Martinez for $100,000. The deal included an Alliance membership and wrestling licenses to promote in more than 15 cities. Pedro established studio wrestling on WBEN-TV and started the famous annual *Parade of Champions* program that drew tens of thousands of fans.

The 1956 consent decree contributed to the decline of the NWA, and Martinez found the advantages of being tied to the group vanishing. He was a member through the first part of the 1960s, and had strong working arrangements with Frank Tunney in Toronto. Martinez sold the Buffalo Wrestling Club to Johnny Powers for $50,000 in 1968, but maintained a financial interest. Powers, who launched the Erie Wrestling Club, hired former St. Louis booker Bobby Bruns as his matchmaker and debuted in April 1968 with NWA support.

Buffalo didn't recover under Powers and Bruns. Martinez formed the National Wrestling Federation with Powers and Wallace Dunk as president in 1971. Using Bulldog Brower, the Mongols, Waldo Von Erich, Dominic DeNucci, Crusher Verdu, and Powers, the NWF riveted fans in Buffalo and Rochester. Additional shows were held in Cleveland, Akron, and in Pennsylvania. In 1975, Pedro was a special advisor to Eddie Einhorn's International Wrestling Association, a new promotion with national implications.

Martinez became one of the most successful wrestling promoters in history. Having learned the ropes inside and out, he provided a plethora of wisdom to any venture. He was an expert at publicity, and was smartly connected to people in the radio and newspaper industry. The strong-minded family man was charitable, thoughtful, and protective of the business. Occupied in wrestling for more than 40 years, Pedro retired to Fort Lauderdale with his wife Mary in 1977. His daughter Ethel married wrestler Ilio DiPaolo, and son Ronald became a wrestler and announcer. Martinez passed away on February 4, 1998, at 82 years of age.

A booking office in Mexico City governed by **Salvador Lutteroth Gonzalez** since September 1933 was accepted into the National Wrestling Alliance fold in 1952. Known as "Salvador Lutteroth," he was born on March 21, 1897, in Colotlan, Jalisco, and served in the military during the Mexican Revolution. Educated on the finer points of professional wrestling in El Paso, Lutteroth created a promotion in Mexico (Empresa Mexica de la Lucha Libra) and sought talent from American promoters.

EMLL was a member of the NWA from 1952 to 1986, and Lutteroth controlled the Alliance world light heavyweight, middleweight and welterweight titles. Muchnick and Thesz, together, made a handful of trips to Mexico, and Lutteroth, with his son Salvador Junior, hosted NWA conventions in August 1960 (Acapulco) and August 1971 (Mexico City).

Lutteroth Sr. was a frequent second and third NWA vice president in the 1950s, and was an innovative businessman. He promoted boxing and wrestling for four decades, and died in 1987.

Lutteroth Jr. commissioned the manufacture of the famous "domed" belt used by the NWA heavyweight champion from 1973–1986 in Mexico, and was the organization's first vice president in 1974. EMLL morphed into "CMLL" (Consejo Mundial de Lucha Libre), and is still in existence today.

Cal Eaton was in good standing with the National Wrestling Alliance from 1954 to '56, and represented Los Angeles. He was born Alvah "Cal" Eaton on June 26, 1908, to Edwin and Alzoa Emily Eaton, and raised in Los Angeles. After obtaining his degree from Southwestern Law School and acting as a member of the California State Athletic Commission, Cal was hired to work as part of a promotional team for the Olympic Auditorium by owner Frank Garbutt and manager Aileen Goldstein LeBell in the summer of 1942. The draw for boxing at the Olympic at the time was mediocre at best, and this unique group turned things around within months. On the wrestling side, Fabiani booked matches until 1944, and Walter Miller had a short stretch as promoter at the Olympic prior to Eaton taking over completely.

Eaton married Aileen LeBell in 1947, adding her children, Mike and Gene, to his son Robert from a previous marriage. In December 1948, Robert wed Marilyn Knight, the 21-year-old daughter of then Lt. Governor Goodwin Knight. Cal joined wrestling bookers "Musty" Musgrave and Doyle, and boxing matchmaker Babe McCoy, to solidify his position as southern California's lead promoter. The emergence of ring idols Gorgeous George, Primo Carnera and Baron Leone improved several-thousand-a-night houses at the Olympic to the magic number of 10,400, a sellout, and gates that made the Eatons and the matchmakers rich.

Cal and Aileen were friends with many powerful people in the newspaper business and on the board that dictated the rules and regulations of sport, the California Athletic Commission. These connections, before and after Knight was elected Governor in 1953, provided the Eatons with unchallenged authority. Instead of the athletic commission supervising their promotional outfit, the Eatons were thought to have overseen the commission itself, and assisting in the hiring and firing of state licensed officials.

The increase in television sales and relevance of pro wrestling on the tube brought on a new era of profit distribution, contractual disputes, and promotional wars. In February 1950, when a coup erupted, the Eatons were faced with a possible walkout. Wrestlers were angry about the dispersment of television money, to the point where they didn't want their matches shown on TV. Realizing that they would be out in the cold if a strike occurred, the Eatons needed insurance.

Cal invested in the booking office, John J. Doyle Enterprises, an equal share with Doyle and Mike Hirsch, to guard his interests, listing his son Robert on all documents. The maneuvering circumvented California law that prohibited licensed promoters from also working as booking agents, but Eaton considered it a way to ensure that the top wrestlers would always been seen at the Olympic. It also gave the Eatons a share of the astronomical booking fees generated by the agency.

Statute 974 of the California Boxing and Wrestling Code stated that no promoter could be linked to a syndicate of any kind. The NWA was certainly seen as a monopoly, and those on the outside of the tight-knit combine complained to the California Athletic Commission, and later the Department of Justice. While the commission ignored the conspiracy theories, the Antitrust Division used the grievances to start their own investigation.

In the meantime, the television empire widened tremendously. The southern California wrestling audience grew and culminated in a record-shattering gate of $103,277.75 for a Thesz-Baron Leone bout on May 22, 1952. The 1953 season started off spectacularly when Doyle, Eaton, KECA (channel 7 in Los Angeles), and the ABC network signed a contract to broadcast live footage from the Olympic. The multi-million-dollar deal sent footage of the Wednesday night wrestling shows to 11 western states and Mexico. Within weeks of the landmark contract, a rift among the principals began to appear.

Crowds diminished, and Cal became convinced the new TV arrangement was doing more harm than good. Doyle moved his office from the Olympic to the Legion Stadium in March 1953, indicative the quarrel over television profits had drawn a line in the sand between the NWA bookers (Doyle and Nichols) and Eaton. Cal had previously believed that his percentage in the booking office shielded him from a potential revolt, but soon realized it was the affiliation to the NWA that had preserved the key talent. Without that connection, he had no name wrestlers to use.

A further declaration of war came when Hugh Nichols acquired a temporary permit to switch his San Diego wrestling shows from Tuesday to Wednesday evenings. The move allowed Doyle and Nichols to substitute the KECA feed from the Olympic to San Diego, cutting Eaton out altogether. Eaton was furious, and also knew the San Diego broadcast was damaging the attendance at his live programs at the Auditorium.

Two options were available to rectify the crisis, and Eaton tried both. First, he contacted Sam Muchnick in an effort to obtain membership in the NWA himself. Since admittance was only granted at the annual conventions, and there were already a pair of NWA bookers in Los Angeles, odds of success were slim. The second option was to sign on with another NWA booker for wrestlers, and Eaton discussed that possibility with Muchnick and Fred Kohler. He also worked briefly with Doc Sarpolis in August.

On August 19, Nichols and Doyle supplied Cal with competitors normally seen at the Olympic: Red Berry, Gino Garibaldi, Billy Varga, Warren Bockwinkel, Ted Christy, and young stars Larry Hamilton and John Tolos. The following week, with the Eaton-Alliance arrangement finished, Cal held what was regarded to be a second-rate show with mostly independent wrestlers. Dizzy Davis and Benito Gardini headlined, with Pfefer regular Sheik Lawrence battling Pedro Godoy in the semifinal.

Cut off from the wrestlers he needed to draw at the Olympic, Eaton felt the wrath of Alliance. At the September NWA meeting in Chicago, Eaton accepted the Alliance proposal of 45 percent of Olympic receipts going to Doyle and Nichols, plus ten percent of his television revenue, thus ending the wrestling war. On September 9, days after the pact, Cal's second-stringers did their best to entice customers, but drew a dismal 2,800 fans. The Eatons griped that the parameters of the Chicago treaty were already being broken, and the best wrestlers were not being provided.

Meanwhile, Nichols and Doyle were relentless, bringing in the rematch of all rematches, Thesz vs. Leone. On September 22, round two attracted an estimated 5,000 to the Legion Stadium, and a gate of $23,000. Of course, Thesz was victorious, as were Doyle and Nichols. Eaton was still watching big-time wrestling from the sidelines.

Eaton closed the Olympic due to the talent difficulties from September 24 to October 13, and in that span, reservations for Muchnick to fly in and mediate were made. A new agreement was signed, and Eaton took on the task of rebuilding his Olympic fan base. He scheduled Olympic programs for consecutive days to spark a little interest, and received an opportune booking for Thesz against The Great Bolo (Al Lovelock). The first show, McShain vs. Lord Carlton in the main event, drew 1,800 on November 11, and the next night, Thesz and Bolo brought in 7,200. Admission to Eaton's November 18 show was free to all fans.

The dispute in Los Angeles seemed settled, but the truth was, things were far from normal. The sour relationship between Eaton and Doyle eventually saw the latter sell his stock and bow out of the NWA entirely. John J. Doyle Enterprises was replaced with the "California Wrestling Office" as the area's chief booking agency, and, in September 1954, Eaton was given membership into the NWA. Fending off indictments and lawsuits, Cal braced himself for the challenges to come.

A California State Assembly subcommittee initiated an investigation into wrestling and boxing in October 1955 after reading about the plight of Frank Pasquale (Frank Depasquale, 1906–1992) in the press. Breaking new ground in the meetings was none other than Doyle, a man fully prepared to talk outside the rules of kayfabe and blow the whistle. There was no love lost, and much of what was said about Eaton was less than flattering. There were accusations that Eaton was illegally acting as both a promoter and a booker, which violated the California Code. Doyle also stated that he wasn't able to book his wrestlers to promoters because of the Eaton monopoly. Finally, there was an allegation that Eaton had an influence over the athletic commission, using that clout to control the employment of officials.

The testimony of Dr. John Fahey corroborated Doyle's statements, and wrestling, in general, was hurt by the comments of two rogue referees who explained how matches were prearranged. Eaton defended his reputation vehemently, but the damage was done. Another examination delved into the actions of Olympic's matchmaker Harry Rudolph "Babe" McCoy (1901–1962). McCoy disclosed earning as much as $100,000 in five years through the booking of Antonino Rocca and Primo Carnera with Toots Mondt, and faced down charges that he was involved in fight-fixing. He denied getting any illegal profits from bouts as an unlicensed manager. Boxer Watson Jones accused McCoy and Aileen Eaton of slicing huge chunks from his pay, using the word "robbed" when describing what happened to him.

Furthermore, Eaton and McCoy confessed to knowing notorious underworld figure Frankie Carbo (Paul Carbo, 1904–1976), one time hitman for Murder, Inc. now turned boxing maestro. Striving to save his tainted name, Eaton filed a $300,000 lawsuit against James Cox, the attorney heading the Governor's inquiry, alleging that Cox had made malicious comments. Soon thereafter, he settled pending lawsuits out of court with Pasquale and Valley Athletic Club, Inc. for a combined $25,000. At the close of the inquiry, Eaton and McCoy were among 25 people facing possible suspension, and the committee recommended that both men have their licenses revoked.

On December 24, 1956, McCoy was banned for life, and four days later, the chief enforcement officer for the California Athletic Commission, David Luce, charged Eaton with six rule violations, and suggested that he be suspended. Luce specifically mentioned the skim off the Thesz-Leone bout in May 1952, and Eaton's role in the California Wrestling Office with Hirsch and Nichols as being infractions. The California Athletic Commission renewed Eaton's license, but more complaints came to light. The athletic commission, in May 1957, found Cal guilty of a half dozen boxing violations and put him on two years probation.

The proceeds for wrestling shows fluctuated from 1954 to 1957. In 1958, Eaton and his stepson Mike LeBell, who had taken a majority stake on the wrestling side of things, created the North American Wrestling Alliance, a new sanctioning body for their enterprises in southern California. Not having paid his dues since 1955 nor officially resigned, Eaton was theoretically still attached to the NWA, though excluded from active rosters. It was commonly believed that the Justice Department's antitrust investigation was the reason behind his sudden lack of interest in the union. Surprisingly, in November 1957, he spent capital publicizing Dick Hutton as the new NWA champion, when he wasn't in a position to receive a booking because of his murky status in the combine.

The NAWA ensured that Eaton's territory would always have an available provincial "world" champion, and initially drew criticism from Muchnick for going forward on its own. However, the consent decree made the formation of collaborative promotions in various sections of the country possible. The NAWA, like the AWA in Minneapolis beginning in 1960, or the WWWF in the Northeast starting in 1963, was a cooperative of promoters who, in no way stood as enemies of the National Wrestling Alliance. Yet the new organizations gave the appearance of competition in the marketplace. In an act of solidarity, Eaton sent his matchmaker Jules Strongbow (John Ralph Bilbo) to NWA galas, and talent agreements remained in place.

In late 1959, the popular Edouard Carpentier was declared heavyweight champion by the NAWA, after a vote by its officers. By 1961, the promotion had morphed into the Worldwide Wrestling Alliance (WWA). Thesz, Fred Blassie, the Destroyer, Rikidozan, Don Leo Jonathan, and Bearcat Wright were some of the grapplers featured by the WWA at the Olympic.

Eaton passed away on January 10, 1966, at the age of 57. For a quarter of a century he had been a prominent figure in California sports. He'd hobnobbed with community leaders, judges, the district attorney, chief of police, and, as a member of the Wilshire Country Club, rubbed shoulders with the local elite.

On August 18, 1968, Mike LeBell rejoined the NWA and served as a vice president in the 1970s. He had a close relationship with Vince McMahon and helped with the coordination for the Muhammad Ali–Antonio Inoki mixed match in

1976. The ties to Capitol Wrestling continued through the early 1980s, and in 1983, Mike pulled out of the NWA when Vince Jr. bought into his promotion to corner the market for his WWF stars. Aileen Eaton died on November 7, 1987, and was the first woman inducted into the International Boxing Hall of Fame in 2002.

Peter and Elizabeth Sarpolis, Polish-Russian immigrants, had six boys between 1886 and 1897 in Wanamie, a township of Newport, Pennsylvania. Their final child was named **Karl Sarpolis**, born on August 31, 1897. Initially a coal miner, Peter explored business ventures in the area, becoming the proprietor of a hotel and saloon. His children labored in the mines as teenagers, and shared the same passion for music that he had. Karl played several instruments, and during his enrollment at the University of Chicago, he earned cash performing in a band. He also played football for coach Amos Alonzo Stagg.

After service in the war, Karl completed his courses at Chicago, then attended medical school at Rush College. In 1926, he earned a medical degree from Loyola, becoming the second member of the Sarpolis family to become a doctor, following his brother John. Lured into wrestling by Jack Pfefer, who recommended that he play up his Lithuanian family background, Sarpolis turned professional late in 1926. Among the highlights of his career as a wrestler was his July 12, 1932, match in San Francisco against Jim Londos, which reportedly drew 10,000 fans to the Auditorium. In 1933, he claimed the undisputed championship of Lithuania, winning a tournament for the synthetic title in Cleveland. He made Houston his wrestling home, and on February 3, 1936, married Vivian Proctor in Sigel's wrestling office. Wrestler Ellis Bashara was his best man.

Karl married a second time, to Lucille Gertrude Owen, and had a daughter named Betty Jane "Janie" on July 23, 1944. In the 1930s and '40s, he was pivotal in the booking of Dallas for Ed McLemore, and provided sound guidance for Sigel's operations in Houston. He refereed on the circuit, and filled in for injured wrestlers or those that missed bookings. Nicknamed "Doc," Sarpolis purchased one-third of the Texas Wrestling Agency with Sigel and Burke, booking grapplers into Dallas, San Antonio, and other key cities in Texas. In April 1953, he sold his stake in Houston, and jumped to McLemore's anti-NWA outfit.

In 1955, Sarpolis and Dory Funk Sr. (Southwestern States Enterprises) bought out Dory Detton in Amarillo for a reported $75,000. As a territory, West Texas set a new benchmark for ingenuity with the Funk family as its centerpiece. All the superstars toured through, and Dory Sr. went to great lengths not to burn cities out. He understood that he couldn't always be the victorious hero, and was willing to step off the throne and bow out when necessary. Amarillo transformed from a city known for featuring junior heavyweights to one offering diverse action from grapplers of all shapes and sizes. Creative and bloody matches were the norm at the Sports Arena.

Advertising Funk as a potential replacement for Pat O'Connor as NWA champion, Sarpolis bit his tongue when the decision to go with Capitol Wrestling's attraction Buddy Rogers was made. The controversial move to the Nature Boy signalled another kink in the armor of the NWA, and Sarpolis and Funk were now prepared to fight the system. Rogers had burnt bridges across West Texas and didn't wrestle once in Amarillo through the first nine months of his reign. It was finally decided that he wasn't wanted at all. Amarillo, instead, went with Gene Kiniski as champion in March 1962.

Sarpolis kept paying membership dues, despite being disenfranchised, and remained a hugely important associate, as made clear in August 1962, when he was elected to head the NWA. Nevertheless, he was still the first sitting president to recognize a champion other than the official titleholder. Two months after Thesz stripped Buddy of the belt in Toronto, Kiniski was defeated by Dory Funk Jr., on March 28, 1963, in Amarillo. The West Texas branch of the NWA was still not satisfied with the heavyweight title lineage, placing the significance of Dory Jr.'s championship above that of Thesz. At the August 1963 convention in St. Louis, members labored to iron out the problems in an attempt to find common ground, and the Amarillo delegates agreed to follow the agenda.

A rift between Dory Sr., Sarpolis, and Thesz was rumored, but the latter's appearances in Amarillo in 1963 ended any speculation. The NWA title regained prominence in Amarillo, and Funk's influence in the Alliance grew mightily. In the 1960s, Sarpolis and Funk had agreements with Muchnick, Verne Gagne, Bob Geigel, and Jim Barnett. They used Stanley Blackburn as their commissioner, Shelton Key as ring announcer, and taped wrestling on Saturday afternoons from the studios of KVII (channel 7).

Doc Sarpolis was connected to all parts of the political spectrum in Amarillo, and devoted much of his time and energy to charity. He gave money to the Boys Ranch and promoted until he died of a heart attack after a small boating accident on May 28, 1967. He was 69 years of age. Karl's slice of the business was sold by his family to Funk's sons Dory Jr. and Terry.

San Francisco returned to the NWA in August 1968, with Roy P. Shropshire, a bright and candid new member. Shropshire had wrestled as **Roy Shire**, and in a career that lasted more than 30 years, engaged in thousands of matches, ripped crowd favorites as part of a heel tag team with a gimmicked brother, fought boxer

Archie Moore, built one of the nation's top promotions, and even tried to coax Wilt Chamberlain into wrestling. Shire was colorful and crafty, and was aware that the Bay Area had been controlled by two old school promoters when he arrived. The inability of Ad Santel and Joe Malcewicz to seize the opportunities that television offered was capitalized on by Shire and his financial backers beginning in October 1960.

Born in 1921, Shire went to Hammond High School in Indiana and was in the military during World War II. He claimed Northwestern University as his alma mater, and that he'd won an AAU wrestling championship, but both were just wrestling lore. Roy teamed with Ray Stevens (Carl Stevens), who used the name Ray Shire, as the Shire Brothers, and held a version of the world tag title in 1959–60. With matchmaker Johnny Doyle at his side, he broke into San Francisco; together, they invested $25,000 in the city to start up under the auspices of the Pacific Coast Athletic Corporation. Malcewicz and Santel adamantly protested the issuing of a license to Shire, but to prove there wasn't a monopoly, the California Athletic Commission agreed to permit Roy to hold shows at the Cow Palace, with TV from Oakland's KTVU studios.

Malcewicz and Santel, even with help from the NWA, couldn't fend off Shire's advance and went bust. The independent squad debuted on March 4, 1961, with an array of wrestlers from across the country. Antonino Rocca, Don Leo Jonathan, Bob Ellis, Verne Gagne, Angelo Savoldi, Bruno Sammartino, and Stevens drew more than 16,000 fans to the Palace and started a run that grossed Shire $175,000 in his first year.

Shire was brought into the Alliance in 1968, but was never impressed with the outfit overall. He did manage to serve as a vice president in the early 1970s. A controversial situation arose in June 1973, when Uptown Arena promoter Johnny Miller, of Modesto, requested an investigation by the California Athletic Commission into the booking practices of Shire, and his "gangsteristic" activities. In a letter to Shire printed in the June 20, 1973, *Modesto Bee*, Miller claimed the San Francisco booker had "threatened . . . on several occasions" to ruin their towns unless they did exactly as they were told.

Miller also claimed former women's champion Mildred Burke had told him that Shire "threatened to kill her for arranging an all-girl wrestling card in Las Vegas," and that Shire was the "dreaded boss of wrestling in northern California, not the California State Athletic Commission." Despite the accusations, Roy worked to resolve his differences with Miller, and resumed booking Modesto in August. Their feud flared up again briefly in April 1978 after five of eight grapplers booked by Shire for Miller failed to appear at their events.

In his 20 years in San Francisco, Shire was known as a creative matchmaker who generated a fortune. He closed his doors in 1981, and two years later, broke kayfabe to eager reporters with an ugly spin on grappling. He made derogatory comments about Baron Leone, Buddy Rogers, and fellow promoters that showed an intense resentment. Shire passed away on September 24, 1992, in Sebastopol at the age of 70.

Jim Barnett became a member of the National Wrestling Alliance in August 1969, a surprising fact considering that he had already been promoting professional wrestling for twenty years. The road from motivated student to powerful wrestling leader took him from Oklahoma City to the most expensive hotels in New York, Chicago, and Atlanta. He worked with many Alliance bookers, and always seemed wiser than his years. Learning from the ground up, Barnett stockpiled information, and used his intelligence to make the systems for trading talent, promoting matches, and making money in wrestling, better.

By the time Jim was accepted as a card-carrying member of the NWA, he had earned a high degree of respect from his peers. On the other hand, there were individuals who believed Barnett had entered wrestling with a silver spoon in his mouth, and had never faced any real hardships. Was it jealousy? Possibly. During the early 1960s, Barnett roamed freely from territory to territory, investing money and juggling his interests. He manufactured an empire that included a percentage ownership or talent sharing deals in up to 15 cities between 1958 and 1964, with ties to dozens more. He set records in Indianapolis and Detroit, and rebuilt Denver and New Orleans.

The animosity towards Barnett wasn't helped when he tried to create a national cartel in the 1960s. It didn't change when he was presiding over Australia, or Georgia and Florida later on. It especially didn't stop when he was on the staff of World Championship Wrestling or the World Wrestling Federation. For more than 40 years, his influence was felt in the world of wrestling, whether as a merger assistant on a weekly wrestling program, or an alleged "godfather" for the entire industry. To different people, he meant different things.

Barnett did break into wrestling at a time and place that was about to boom in every way a wrestling promotion could. In fact, he joined Fred Kohler when wrestling on television was just becoming a viable business in itself. Born on June 9, 1924, in Oklahoma City, James Edward Barnett was the son of Isaac Cleveland and Sara Barnett. He attended Classen High School, graduating in 1942, and was employed at the Jack Lincoln Shops at 2927 Paseo. Idolizing Eugene O'Neill, Barnett enrolled in the University of Chicago on October 2, 1945, hoping to study theater. Even after his graduation with a Ph.B. on December 19, 1947, he worked as the manager for the school's newspaper, the *Maroon*, and became acquainted with the hysteria of the local professional wrestling scene.

Chicago promoter Kohler hired Barnett as a deputy editor for his program, *Wrestling As You Like It*, in 1949, and Jim learned from the famous publicist Dick Axman. Axman made a significant impression on Barnett, and the two collaborated on a 64-page magazine entitled *Wrestling Stars*, published in 1953. As Chicago's television franchise expanded, the daily duties of the intelligent young man evolved from the publicity department to agent when Kohler needed someone he could trust to conduct matters on the road. With the new title came a huge pay increase, and a new level of responsibility and respect.

Traveling with wrestlers Verne Gagne, Pat O'Connor, Sonny Myers, and Hans Schmidt, Barnett got a percentage of booking fees for each grappler, up to 30 percent of their income, and the amount was hefty. In 1953, from the contract of Myers alone, Jimmy garnered $2,250. Lucrative arrangements were made that supplied promoters with Chicago wrestlers from arena shows for flat rates, and Barnett was constantly acting as a go-between for Kohler's enterprises.

The political sway of Kohler, and ultimately the respect earned by Barnett, gave Jim the distinct honor of being awarded a wrestling manager's license by the Illinois Athletic Commission on November 16, 1955, the first such license issued in the organization's 29-year history. Barnett acquired a permit in conjunction with his three-year contract with Dick the Bruiser. Barnett and Kohler bought Indianapolis for $15,000 from Billy Thom, investing in Indiana Wrestling, Inc., a corporation administered by Dick Patton. They started television on WTTV from the Armory, sponsored by Champagne Velvet Beer, on November 1, 1956.

Maintaining ties with Chicago, Barnett organized his own booking office at the Claypool Hotel in Indianapolis, and slowly began to branch out into surrounding cities. In November 1958, he came to terms with the Cincinnati Gardens that would see his grapplers featured beginning on January 23, 1959, with wrestling from the WCPO-TV studios on Saturdays. In his initial year, an estimated 100,000 fans were lured to the Gardens.

Barnett banded together with veteran booker Johnny Doyle to found the Barnett-Doyle Corporation out of the Penobscot Building in Detroit on March 31, 1959. Their debut in early April had an attendance of 16,226 at the Olympic. Their Detroit ventures produced big profits — $134,809 in their first four shows, drawing 55,228. Using their television outlets in Windsor, Indianapolis, and Cincinnati to further their cause, Barnett and Doyle made remarkable headway very swiftly. The bond with Kohler concluded in January 1960, cutting the latter off from Barnett's grapplers.

While Doyle was out west planting flags in Denver and Los Angeles, Barnett devised a way to get the attention of Alliance affiliates. He put money into Lexington, Milwaukee, Hammond, Atlanta, Birmingham, New Orleans, Evansville, and Kansas City. He committed assets to a war with Al Haft in Columbus, though it was unknown to him at the time that Haft was one of the people who'd supported his entry into the NWA only months before. That endorsement was likely gone by the summer of 1962.

The havoc created nationally by Barnett and Doyle alarmed many promoters, and Jim's rift with Kohler was significant. In August 1961, Kohler was elected to the NWA presidency, ironically, at the same time Barnett and Doyle were applying for membership in the Alliance. Their applications were submitted on August 31, and Muchnick corresponded at length with Lee Loevinger, Assistant Attorney General of the Department of Justice Antitrust Division, concerning their status. Muchnick considered them eligible, and polled the others for feedback. Sigel, Crockett, Luttrall, Sarpolis, Haft, Gulas/Welch, McGuirk, Owen, Tunney, and Muchnick, ten of the 17 associates, were in favor.

But Kohler held the power, and felt Muchnick had overstepped his bounds by polling the membership. He leisurely selected a membership committee, stacked with his friends, and essentially, enemies of Barnett and Doyle. Of the seven promoters on the board, Fred was partners with four (Mondt, McMahon, Light, London), while the other three (Owen, Crockett, Sigel) supported the pair's approval. Kohler, Mondt, McMahon, and Light were in cahoots against Barnett and Doyle in Detroit, promoting the Olympia Stadium.

Muchnick, the executive secretary of the NWA, sent out a special bulletin dated September 8, 1961, stating, "[Barnett] informed this office that he has had several calls from members, some of them on the membership committee, and they told him they thought he would make a good member of the NWA, and they were for him. In fact, one member advised him that the committee was not against him . . . they were merely mad at the executive secretary because he took too much authority in admitting him to membership before having a vote of the entire Alliance."

Whether or not it was spiteful manipulation on Kohler's part, or simply an adverse reaction to Muchnick's tactics, the applications remained in limbo. Barnett's positive momentum propelled him into transactions behind the scenes with Muchnick, Tunney, Gulas, Welch, Jones, McIntyre, and Crockett. In a letter to Muchnick on August 30, 1961, "Cowboy" Luttrall said he "cannot understand why the National Wrestling Alliance should refuse a man like him[Barnett] membership in our organization," and threatened to resign if the coalition didn't admit him.

Despite the support, their membership was never approved. But they did sock away enough cash to take over Australia. Once their plans were implemented, and "World Championship Wrestling" opened up in October 1964, a system was devised that gave each man about six months vacation a year. A man with a taste for luxury, Jim lived in the finest apartments, enjoyed expensive fixtures and artwork, and was rarely reluctant to seek out his next personal triumph. The Australian outback provided peaceful living, without promotional battles or disruptions to his lifestyle.

Talent from America was imported regularly, and the combo promoted the International Wrestling Alliance, with a version of a heavyweight and tag title present in the country at all times. Wisely, they connected with foremost businessmen and political groups, and had weekly programs across the National Television Network, TCN-9 in Sydney, and GTV-9 in Melbourne.

They created a circuit offering wrestling somewhere every day of the week, and Barnett enforced a policy of dress that differed greatly from anything in the United States. Wrestlers were required to behave with etiquette, and the new rules added credibility to the sport. Operating in conjunction with the owners of Stadiums Ltd. (Richard Lean), a promotional group that owned many Australian sports facilities, including Sydney Stadium and Festival Hall in Melbourne, Barnett and Doyle built a kingdom from scratch.

Featuring Mark Lewin, Killer Kowalski, Dominic DeNucci, Spiros Arion, Roy Heffernan, Professor Toru Tanaka, Skull Murphy, Mario Milano, Buddy Austin, Killer Karl Kox, King Curtis Iaukea, the Funks, and the Briscos, Barnett gave Australian fans nine years of exceptional wrestling under his promotional banner. In August 1969, his membership application into the National Wrestling Alliance was approved unanimously, and two months later, he suffered the loss of Doyle, his promotional partner of ten years, of cancer.

Muchnick appointed Barnett the NWA's executive secretary in August 1972. In September 1973, Barnett paid $268,000 cash, buying out Roy and Lester Welch, for 38 percent of Mid-South Sports, Inc., the corporation behind the Atlanta booking office. The investment also earned him 20 percent of Championship Wrestling from Florida, Inc. of Tampa. Barnett sold Australia to Tony Kolonie, but kept ties to the promotion he fostered.

Mid-South Sports' chairman of the board and chief executive officer, Barnett oversaw a meeting on March 29, 1974, that officially changed the name of the corporation to Georgia Championship Wrestling, Inc. He stood as the commander-in-chief in his company's war with Ann Gunkel. In August 1975, Jim took on the task of booking the NWA world heavyweight champion. He would arrange the schedules for Brisco, Funk, Race, Rhodes, Rich, and Flair from 1975 to

1983, making him one of the most important people in the syndicate. Besides his responsibilities in the NWA, Atlanta, and Tampa, Barnett was the president and director of the Southeastern Wrestling Corporation out of Knoxville.

The shareholders of Georgia Championship Wrestling voted him out as chairman in December 1982, and at the August 1983 convention, he resigned from the NWA. Employed by Titan Sports, a corporation run by Vincent K. McMahon, Barnett was an advisor as the World Wrestling Federation began their national takeover. Before cable television lifted territorial boundaries, no promoter had ever made such an impact in more regions, coast to coast, than Jim Barnett. Barnett had many failures along the way, but McMahon was wise to look to him for advice. He knew the influence of television and how to barter with station managers about program availability. Vince Sr. called him "an outstanding promoter, probably the best in the country" in 1980. From 1983 to '87, including three WrestleManias and a slowly rising annual profit, the WWF relied on Barnett.

After becoming a free agent, Barnett was hired by Jim Crockett, and aided in the negotiations between the latter's company and Turner Broadcasting in 1988 that spawned World Championship Wrestling. He was a consultant for WCW and WWE, at different points, until his death on September 17, 2004, at the age of 80.

Barnett rubbed shoulders with the wealthy decision-makers of the world, and through his campaign donations, mingled with governors and presidents. He rented his Lexington penthouse for a dollar a month to Kentucky Senator Marlow Cook in the early 1970s, and socialized with representatives from all levels of government. Intrigued by the arts, Jim was on the board of the Georgia Opera Company, the Atlanta Symphony, and Atlanta Ballet, and was a member of the Georgia Council of the Arts and Humanities. In 1980, he was on the National Council on the Arts for five months, after being nominated by President Jimmy Carter.

Possessing a cultured personality and a keen business mind, Barnett always carried himself with dignity. He lived extravagantly and enjoyed life to the fullest. In many settings, from the Kentucky Derby to NWA confabs, he was regarded as a celebrity, and his counsel was heeded by those who admired his accomplishments. Barnett affected more than 30 years of Alliance history, and when the membership decided to construct a Hall of Fame in 2005, Jim was in the inaugural class.

Eddie Graham's membership in the NWA succeeded Cowboy Luttrall, a prominent associate in Tampa since 1950. Although he contributed to the booking of Florida for most of the decade prior, Graham officially took the helm from Luttrall on September 2, 1970, when the Cowboy retired because of illness, and sold Deep South Sports, Inc., in which both were partners, outright to Graham.

Of the wrestlers to become promoters and members of the Alliance in the 1960s, including Adkisson, Farhat, Shire, Boesch, and Geigel, none were more rough around the edges than Edward Gossett. Eddie, born on January 15, 1930, to Jess and Velma Louise Gossett in Dayton, Tennessee, was educated in the industries of rural America, and finally on the streets of Chattanooga, where his family relocated. Eddie joined his father and uncle as house painters, doing hard, physical labor, and despite being born blind in one eye, he prospered in all avenues of life.

It was at the Chattanooga YMCA that Eddie began fighting and wrestling formally. He wore the mark of an unruly ruffian, always prepared to mix it up. Conventional styles were taught in the gym, and he learned the basics of catch wrestling from local tutors. The inspired grappler met Clarence Luttrall, a preeminent heel, and was tutored in the different ways of obtaining heat in matches. The Cowboy trained his protégé in all aspects of performance. In late 1948, Eddie made his pro debut with a turkey as payment, and slowly his stock rose. With Luttrall in his corner, Gossett branched out to towns managed by Gulas and Welch, and was featured in Memphis and Knoxville. At 205 pounds, he was among the most promising junior heavyweights.

Gossett married at 20 to Lucille, and after a short spell in the army, he renewed his pursuit of wrestling. His parents, by 1952, had moved to the Tampa area, and Eddie made regular trips to Florida. Luttrall also set up shop in Tampa, designing a booking office that controlled wrestling across most of the peninsula, and enrolled in the NWA. In 1956, Gossett adopted the persona "Rip Rogers" in Western Texas, and as a blond heel, reminded many of Buddy Rogers, though Rip was far tougher and more brutish than Buddy. The techniques perfected in Texas came in handy when he made the transition to "Eddie Graham," "brother" of Dr. Jerry Graham, in 1958.

The Grahams set a new standard as a dastardly duo, and were a draw in the Northeast for Capitol Wrestling. Vince McMahon gave Antonino Rocca and Miguel Perez the ideal antihero tandem, and the Grahams became instant superstars. During the holiday season of 1958 and early '59, the Grahams were in Florida, and over the next several years, Eddie bounced back and forth between Capitol and appearances in what was becoming his home terrain. Graham became a favorite in Florida, brawling with the Great Malenko, Johnny Valentine, and the Von Brauners. He won an abundance of championships, from a claim to the WWA world title in Atlanta to the Southern and Florida titles.

In preparation for a match in the dressing room of the Armory in Tampa on October 8, 1968, Graham was severely injured when a 75-pound steel window crashed down onto his head. He suffered torn retinas in both eyes, and needed more than 300 stitches. Graham would undergo surgery in Houston to repair his eyes, and needed more than a year to recover.

Graham, the promoter, was as creative as they came. Feuds were stylishly molded and quality angles and gimmicks were used that solidified Florida as a place of wrestling excellence. Even before taking over Tampa, Graham sat on the NWA council. In the 1970s, he was a regular on the board of directors, and had the confidence of Sam Muchnick that he too looked out for the entire organization, and not just for the interests of his own promotion. He was elected to replace Jack Adkisson as NWA president in August 1976 at the conference at Lake Tahoe.

Weeks before he was named president, Graham incorporated National Wrestling Alliance, Inc., and NWA, Inc., out of a Tampa office, with the plans to transfer the trademarks out of the non-profit company in Iowa. Those plans were stymied by a conflict in the United States Patent and Trademark Office (USPTO) regarding a similar pending request by the National Wrestling Federation. Seven months after his reelection at the 1977 meeting, Graham resigned due to health problems.

Eddie gave endlessly to charity, and with Luttrall and Ed Blackburn, his humanitarianism aided in getting the Florida Sheriff's Boys Ranch off the ground in 1957. He later assisted in the establishment of the Girls Villa, and donated to schools and colleges. Florida Senator Richard Stone honored Eddie for his civic philanthropy. He teamed with John Smith, owner of Brewmaster Steakhouse Restaurants, to purchase the Orlando Sports Stadium for $400,000, and from 1972 to 1980, he owned the Tallahassee Sports Stadium with lawyer Thomas Smith and Lester Welch.

Graham retired from wrestling in 1980. He trained his son Mike, Steve Keirn, Paul Orndorff, Hulk Hogan, Bob Roop, Terry Taylor, and Bob Orton Jr., and was respected internationally for his ability to scout talent. Although wrestling's popularity in Florida wavered, and there was an overall decline in the capacity of NWA members to ward off the incursions of Vince McMahon, Graham was gifted enough to revitalize the region. Unfortunately, a deep depression brought on by financial concerns preoccupied his mind, and on January 21, 1985, the 55-year-old wrestling legend shot himself in the right temple with a .38 caliber revolver.

Robert Frederick Geigel was elected NWA president at six annual conventions. An amateur champion in college, a survivor of combat in war, and a regular main-event wrestler, Geigel was a spokesman for harmony among the members of the Alliance. Spearheading many consequential decisions between 1978 and 1987, he offered a veteran point of view at meetings, and occasionally clashed with Jim Crockett Jr.

Son of Fred and Leota Hackman Geigel, Bob was born on October 1, 1924, in

Algona, Iowa. He shined on the mat and on the football field in high school, and after graduation in 1942, went into the navy. His stint with the Seabees lasted four years, two of them in the Pacific. In 1946, he was admitted to the University of Iowa, where he was awarded four letters in football at right tackle for coach Eddie Anderson. Geigel achieved three letters in wrestling from 1947 to 1949 under the tutelage of Mike Howard, and was an all-American in 1948. That year, he came in third in the NCAA wrestling tournament in the 191-pound division, after Verne Gagne and Charles Gottfried. At the 1949 AAU National Tournament in Cedar Rapids, Bob lost a referee's decision to Gagne and placed second. He graduated from college with a degree in physical education in 1950.

Recruited into pro wrestling by Alphonse Bisignano, Geigel debuted in 1950 in Florida. He used his amateur background to bolster his credibility going into new areas. A star in the central states for Pinkie George and on the circuit of Orville Brown, Bob found a niche as a heel, earning his stripes from fans as a hated grappler. He settled in Amarillo, learned from Dory Funk and Doc Sarpolis, and participated in many outstanding feuds. He held the Southwest junior, NWA world junior, North American, central states, and AWA world tag titles.

Geigel had notable ring battles with former tag partner "Bulldog" Bob Brown, Pat O'Connor, and Sonny Myers, and switched to promoting with the formation of Heart of America Sports Attractions, Inc. on November 26, 1963. He joined Karras, O'Connor, and George Simpson to manage the new corporation, which aspired to take over the old Alliance territories of George in Iowa and Brown of Kansas City.

Mimicking the savvy promotional methods used by Muchnick in St. Louis, the quartet in Kansas City realized the potential of their market. Geigel replaced Simpson in the late 1960s as promoter for the famed Memorial Hall, and bought into St. Louis when Muchnick retired in January 1982. At that time, Bob was in his third run as NWA president.

The old school membership may not have seen it coming, but the advances of cable television simplified hostile takeovers. The older, experienced NWA associates in the twilight of their careers failed to pass their organizations on to bright, combat-ready promoters who could ward off the expansion of Vince McMahon. Geigel's central states was on its last legs by 1985, and the NWA's downslide was on automatic pilot.

The St. Louis Wrestling Club lost in its war against the WWF in 1986, and Crockett seized the city. It was obvious that Crockett had a chance to compete with McMahon, and Geigel made a deal, giving over his territory. In exchange, he'd stay active on Crockett's national television programs, and receive a percentage of money from shows in Kansas City. Geigel took a role as figurehead president on Crockett's TV shows, and was in a couple of high-profile angles, including being attacked by Magnum T.A. with a bat in May 1986.

The Kansas City deal contained a clause that said if Crockett didn't to live up to certain obligations, Geigel would return to promote, and that's what happened. During the summer of 1986, Geigel was elected to his final term as NWA president, and incorporated NWA All Star Wrestling, Inc. in October. He withdrew from the Alliance late in 1987 and launched the World Wrestling Alliance, a doomed sanctioning body that recognized Mike George as world champion. A sharing agreement with Shohei Baba's All-Japan led to the "International Bash" on February 2, 1989, at the Memorial Hall. The make-or-break show drew less than 500 fans, with wrestlers such as the Funk Brothers, British Bulldogs, Tiger Mask, Rock and Roll Express, Jumbo Tsuruta, Stan Hansen, Terry Gordy, and Genichiro Tenryu appearing.

Geigel left wrestling promotions and worked as a security guard at Kansas City's Woodlands Race Track. An energetic businessman, Geigel was admired for his leadership and for being fair to wrestlers. He was a legitimate tough guy, and, at 6′1″, 250 pounds, could handle himself if tested in or out of the ring. Protective of its many secrets, he reveled in all facets of professional wrestling. He was connected up and down the civic ladder in Kansas City, and was a significant charitable donor. In August 2002, he was enshrined in the Tragos/Thesz Wrestling Hall of Fame at the International Wrestling Institute and Museum in Newton, Iowa.

The Gulf Coast territory was operated by **Lee Fields** (Albert Lee Hatfield) of Mobile from 1959 to 1978. A nephew of NWA booker Roy Welch of the famous Welch Brothers, Lee wrestled through the 1950s with his siblings Bobby and Don. In December 1959, he bought the territory from Roy's son Buddy Fuller, and received talent for numerous arenas from the Welch-Gulas Mid-South booking office. Lee obtained his own membership in the Alliance in 1969, and sustained his promotion through 1978, when he sold out to Ron Fuller. He passed away on June 4, 2000, at the age of 69.

The National Wrestling Alliance had dozens of other esteemed members. Several months prior to the 1950 convention, **David Reynolds** (1913–1998) of Orem, Utah, booker to Salt Lake City and pieces of Colorado and Wyoming, was accepted into the organization. His membership lasted about a decade. **Dory Detton** (1912–1991) paid his dues from 1951 to '55, when he sold West Texas to Karl Sarpolis and Dory Funk. **Joseph Gunther** (1912–1996) of Birmingham was welcomed into the NWA in September 1950, and, like Detton, used a majority of lighter-weight grapplers on his shows in New Orleans and Baton Rouge. He dropped from the rolls in the years after the government forced the consent decree. **Clifford Cleo Maupin** (1898–1967), a man who wanted to take credit for assigning George Wagner the "Gorgeous" gimmick, controlled the Toledo booking office from September 1951 through the early 1960s.

Seattle's **Robert Murray** entered the Alliance in September 1952, but sold out to "Whipper" Billy Watson in 1955. **Stewart Edward Hart** (1915–2003) replaced Larry Tillman in 1952 as the NWA booker in Calgary, and was one of the longest serving associates. Aside from a few interruptions, Hart was involved with the Alliance until selling his company to Vince McMahon in September 1983. **Edward George Farhat** (The Sheik) (1926–2003) became a member of the NWA in the mid-1960s and had an official booking office in Detroit, serving Michigan and parts of Ohio and Ontario until 1980.

CHAPTER SEVENTEEN

NWA WORLD HEAVYWEIGHT CHAMPIONS

(1975–Present)

The celebrated mat technician, **Jack Brisco** was a two-time NWA champion. Remarkably agile in the ring, he combined athleticism and skill, and went from the amateur championship circle to the professional. Born Fred Joe Brisco on September 21, 1941, in his father's hometown of Seminole, Oklahoma, "Jack" was the third child of Floyd George and Iona I. Brisco. During the last year of World War II, Floyd, son of white and Indian parents, served in the U.S. army, and five years later, abandoned his wife and six children for the West Coast. Floyd later married second wife Elinor Ann and lived until August 27, 1977.

Iona Brisco migrated with her four youngest to Blackwell in the northern part of the state in the 1950s. Fred earned the moniker "Jack" from his grandfather (on his father's side) while chasing jackrabbits, a pastime that helped his coordination. At Blackwell High School, he won three Oklahoma State wrestling titles between 1958 and 1960, the last one at 195 pounds, for coach Chuck Hetrick. Brisco took a position on the Oklahoma State wrestling squad led by Myron Roderick, a champion wrestler who was only a few years older than Jack. On March 27, 1965, Jack trumped his second-place finish at Ithaca the year before with a Division I NCAA title at 191 pounds at the University of Wyoming.

Attracted by professional wrestling, Brisco was trained by Leroy McGuirk, who had worked his magic on Dick Hutton and Danny Hodge. On June 5, 1965, Brisco made his debut in Oklahoma City at WKY Studios, defeating Roger Barnes (Ronnie Garvin). In trips outside of Oklahoma, Jack, known as "Tiger Brisco," was recognized for his wrestling prowess, but relegated to preliminaries. Some promoters stubbornly refused to sell him on his amateur credentials.

Brisco won the esteem of Jack Adkisson and Paul Boesch in 1967, and embraced his first push outside of the tri-state area. He went to Japan and Australia, then, in the summer of 1968, debuted in Florida. The relocation to Eddie Graham's territory was successful, and Brisco, after three years in the pro ranks, found increased popularity in the Sunshine State. Brisco was booked into a match with the Southern champion Missouri Mauler (Larry Hamilton) at Tampa's biggest annual show, the Gasparilla event, on February 11, 1969. Jack won the championship, but the switch was voided when it was realized that the Mauler never had a clear claim to lose. The February 11 program in Tampa was the night Dory Jr. won the NWA title from Kiniski.

Brisco beat Mauler again on July 8, 1969, at the Armory in Tampa, this time oficially capturing the Southern title. Later in the year, he flew to All Japan and the Southern title was stripped. On February 10, 1970, at Brisco's second Gasparilla event appearance in Tampa, he beat Mr. Saito for the Florida title. With matches in several territories against Funk for the NWA title, Brisco impressed influential Alliance members and wrestling fans. There was little question who Funk's greatest adversary was on the mat, and it wasn't unusual for the two competitors to wrestle 60 minutes in hotly contested draws. Brisco's home base shifted from Tulsa to Tampa, and it was now Graham who was pondering the future of the heavyweight star.

Thirty months into Dory Funk's reign, the members of the NWA board were forced to pick a successor, and the two top nominees were Brisco and Harley Race. Dory Funk Sr. and Bob Geigel were in favor of the latter choice, and Nick Gulas and Graham were for Jack. With votes in from Muchnick, Mike LeBell, and Shohei Baba, a decision was rendered, and Brisco got the nod. The Houston territory was given the match, marked on the calendar for early March 1973. Brisco traveled extensively, preparing the circuit and getting his name fresh in the minds of fans. Unfortunately, it was all for naught. Dory Jr. was injured on his father's ranch, and the Houston match was cancelled. The NWA board still wanted the title on Brisco, but the title switch was delayed, and the lineage later changed, to include an intermediate champion, Race.

NWA officials prepared a new championship belt for the Brisco-Race contest on July 20, 1973, at the Coliseum in Houston, replacing the old strap used by every champion back to Pat O'Connor. In a pre-match ceremony, Race gave his tattered strap to NWA president Muchnick and received the $10,000 belt, which was produced in Mexico and weighed ten pounds. His ownership of the valued prize wouldn't last long. The champion won the initial fall in 12 minutes, but Brisco tied it up with a submission victory. In honor of his idol, Brisco used a "Thesz press" to pin Race in the third fall, seizing the NWA Title. Jack followed Hutton as only the second man in history to win both NCAA and NWA titles.

Upholding the honor of the National Wrestling Alliance heavyweight title was foremost in the mind of Brisco. He understood what the crown meant and how it should be protected, by performance or by shooting. Race, the Funks, Wahoo McDaniel, Johnny Valentine, Bill Watts, Thesz, and Kiniski were among his toughest opponents. But it was another figure outside of the United States who broke the reign of Brisco into halves, and it was done for money, pure and simple.

The Japanese wrestling scene was a war zone, with fans torn between Shohei Baba's All Japan and Antonio Inoki's New Japan. Brisco had made a name for himself in Asia in 1967 for All Japan, and Baba looked forward to the titleholder's visits. Baba was also ready to negotiate with the champion — outside the walls of an NWA convention — about a cash trade for the world's championship. Baba wasn't greedy, he just wanted it for a week or so, and was willing to pay top dollar. Eagerly listening to the propositions, Jack knew a figure could be reached that made such a deal worth it. When $25,000 was decided upon, a date was fixed for the December 1974 tour.

Baba was champion for seven days from December 2 to December 9, 1974, and the exposure did wonders for his career. Brisco, however, was strapped for cash, literally, and upon his arrival in the U.S., resumed the schedule Muchnick had planned for him. At the August 1975 convention in New Orleans, a vote took place on Jack's replacement, after he indicated that he had had enough. Jack Adkisson broke a 3–3 tie, making Terry Funk the next titleholder. On December 10, 1975, Brisco did the job at the Convention Center in Miami Beach, losing the strap in front of 5,164 fans at a show promoted by Chris Dundee. His $25,000 bond was returned.

From December 1975 until his retirement in February 1985, Brisco remained one of wrestling's best grapplers. He was also a smart entrepreneur, forming Brisco Brothers Body Shop, Inc. at 4315 N. Hubert in Tampa, in April 1974 with wrestling sibling Floyd "Jerry" Brisco. The Briscos, by the late 1970s, owned 30 percent of the Georgia territory, and with Paul Jones and Jerry Oates, sold GCW to Titan Sports in April 1984. Jack ended his career with the WWF. In 2005, he was inducted into the Professional Wrestling Hall of Fame in Amsterdam, New York.

Giant Baba was a mammoth man and his imposing size made him a colorful character inside the wrestling ring. Outside, he was a kind gentleman, respected by his peers and known for his astute business sense. Shohei Baba was born on January 23, 1938, in Sanjo Niigata, Japan, the fourth child of Kazuo and Mitsu Baba. When he was five years old, his oldest brother was killed in World War II. Shohei stood more than 6'9'' by the age of 17, almost two feet taller than his parents. In 1953, he attended Niigata Prefectural Sanjo Industry High School, where he enjoyed swimming and baseball. Two years later, he was courted by the Yomiuri Giants for his dominant pitching skill, and won numerous awards in his five years of professional ball.

With a 60-inch chest, a size 18 boot, and a 20-inch neck, Shoehi was forced to retire from baseball after an arm injury, and was convinced to try wrestling by Rikidozan in April 1960. Rikidozan's Japan Wrestling Association had begun promoting programs in Japan in July 1953, but it was on September 30, 1960, with the pro debuts of Baba and Kanji Inoki, that the future of the sport in Asia was assured. Little did anyone know at the time that Baba and Inoki would dominate the culture of wrestling in Japan for the next 40 years. On September 30, Baba made his debut with a win over Yonetaro Tanaka in 5:15 in Tokyo.

In July 1961, Shohei arrived in the United States with the intent of furthering his wrestling knowledge. Accompanied by his "agent" Fred Atkins, Baba debuted in San Diego on August 25, 1961, and over the next three years, headlined at the Olympic Auditorium, International Amphitheater, Maple Leaf Gardens, and Madison Square Garden. He faced world champions Fred Blassie (WWA), Buddy Rogers (NWA), and Bruno Sammartino (WWWF). The wrestler returned to his home country a hero at 27 years of age. Rikidozan died from stab wounds in 1963, and together, Baba and Inoki replaced him as Asia's preeminent grapplers.

The JWA was affiliated to the NWA, and many gaijin wrestlers made the voyage to Asia to perform. On November 24, 1965, Baba beat Dick the Bruiser to claim the JWA international title. He held the belt three times between 1965 and 1970, trading the championship with Bobo Brazil and Gene Kiniski. The Japanese wrestling culture found a system of tournaments to be very appealing, and the annual "World League" event regularly brought international names to the country. Baba shined in the tournament, winning from 1966 to 1968 and from 1970 to 1972, with victories over Wilbur Snyder, the Destroyer, Killer Kowalski, Don Leo Jonathan, Abdullah the Butcher, and Gorilla Monsoon. Unhappy with his place in the pecking order behind Baba, Antonio Inoki broke free from the JWA in 1971 and created New Japan Pro Wrestling.

The same politics that compelled Inoki to go elsewhere were taking their toll on Shohei, and on September 2, 1972, he left the promotion to pursue his own ventures. With Yoshihiro and Mitsuo Momota, the sons of Rikidozan, as investors, Baba devised his own company, All Japan Pro Wrestling. They arranged television, wrestlers from the United States were imported, and AJPW debuted on October 21, 1972, in Tokyo. In the main event, Baba teamed with Thunder Sugiyama against heels Bruno Sammartino and Terry Funk, and were defeated in the third fall by countout. Ten months later, All Japan enrolled in the Alliance, a move Inoki hadn't yet made.

The head-to-head rivalry offered a vast collection of wrestlers from a multitude of countries. Baba and Inoki already had a long history, and it was only fitting that they'd be striving against each other for the top spot in the market for over 25 years as wrestler-promoters. Baba's decision to enter the Alliance, at that point in time, showed a wisdom that eclipsed his counterpart, and made it possible to book appearances by the NWA champion. He also wanted to make a bid for the belt itself, with a financial proposal that was previously unheard of. A new precedent was set when Jack Brisco sold the title to Baba for $25,000 in December 1974, making Shohei the first Japanese wrestler to wear the championship. His reign was only a week long, but the ramifications lasted a lifetime.

In that same manner, Baba won the NWA belt on two other occasions from Harley Race, holding the strap from October 31 to November 7, 1979, and from September 4 to September 10, 1980. Of all the six title switches in Japan, none were held in Tokyo. All Japan thrived with its Alliance favoritism, even after Inoki became a member himself in 1975. Baba's connections to Muchnick, Barnett, Adkisson, Gagne, and the Funks was a significant weapon in the promotional war, and he served on the Alliance board of directors. Inoki, however, joined a clique of his own that included promoters Vince McMahon, Mike LeBell, Frank Tunney, Francisco Flores, and Stu Hart. The importation of athletes from North and Central America played a key role in the success of wrestling in Japan.

Strategic planning and creative booking with desirable newcomers helped Inoki's organization eventually gain the advantage in the ongoing conflict. All Japan maintained an even course despite the losses, and benefited from Baba's leadership. Like

Rikidozan, Shohei demonstrated his eye for talent, scouting Olympian Tomomi "Jumbo" Tsuruta (1951–2000), who went on to an illustrious career himself. Other notables Baba trained were Mitsuharu Misawa and Toshiaki Kawada. Baba was a four-time PWF champion, a twelve-time JWA/AJPW international tag champ with Tsuruta, Inoki, Seiji Sakaguchi, and Michiaki Yoshimura. He also won the Champion Carnival tournament seven times between 1973 and 1982.

Giant Baba died on January 31, 1999, in Tokyo. All Japan went forward under Baba's wife Motoko Kawai Baba, whom he married in 1971, and new president Misawa. A strain in the relationship between Motoko and Misawa ended with Misawa breaking from All Japan to assemble Pro Wrestling NOAH, taking a substantial amount of AJPW's workers. Most believed that the disastrous situation would bring death to the promotion, but Motoko was determined. She hired Keiji Mutoh and Satoshi Kojima from New Japan and saw a rejuvenated interest. In September 2002, Mutoh took over from her as AJPW president. The promotion created by the peaceful and quiet gentleman who was Shohei Baba continues today.

Terry Funk is known by younger fans as a "hardcore icon" for his dedication to the extreme styles of professional wrestling. He holds a doctorate in ring psychology, can brawl with guys 40 years his junior, and can just about guarantee an entertaining match. The older crowd who watched Terry Dee — born on June 30, 1944, the second wrestling son of Dory Funk Sr. and Dorothy Matlock Funk — evolve from a doughty battler to a worldwide superstar relished his everlasting devotion to the sport he loved. Terry gave his soul to wrestling, and earned respect that will never diminish, even as he competes in matches at the age of 62. His ability to always live up to expectations has established a benchmark that can only be admired.

An athlete through high school, at Cisco Junior College and at West Texas, Terry fit into the wrestling community perfectly. He was coached by his father, and trained extensively with his brother Dory and other legends at the family's makeshift gym. Terry was an intense brawler who mixed science with fisticuffs. From his December 1965 debut, he overcame his limitations and furthered his own cause as a potential world champion by impressing audiences and promoters across the world.

A confirmed warrior, Funk was considered as a possible replacement for NWA titleholder Jack Brisco in 1975. The Alliance was going through many changes, the most noteworthy was being Sam Muchnick stepping down as president, and Jim Barnett taking over booking the champion. Terry was given the deciding vote and stepped into an angle where he substituted for his brother Dory in a match against

Brisco on December 10, 1975, at the Miami Beach Convention Center. The match concluded with the coveted strap being taken from the ring by the lively wrestler from Amarillo.

At 240 pounds, Funk was in good shape and carefully walked the unpainted line between face and heel. He understood the complexities of being champion, and how imperative it was to sell for local guys in the various territories. Funk made a title change seem like a possibility every night, bolstering his value, and showing his own humility. During a run of 424 days, Terry showed all the traits of a champion, and carried his exuberance into international territories. His NWA world title reign ended on February 6, 1977, in Toronto, losing the belt to Harley Race.

The Funk Brothers were longtime celebrities in Japan, and even engaged each other to a draw in 1981. Terry has remained loyal to wrestling and is unable to get the bug out of his system, even though he's participated in numerous retirement matches. His feuds with Ric Flair and Dusty Rhodes remain keenly in the minds of his supporters, and as he moves towards another year of wrestling, his fans are reminded of his allegiance to the squared circle.

The charismatic **Dusty Rhodes** was a performer who could enliven crowds with his entertaining style, and streaked to the top of the wrestling world in the 1970s. In a way, he was the opposite of Thesz, O'Connor, and Brisco as far as wrestling legitimacy was concerned, but he did have a real knack for relating to fans. Rhodes, although standing over 6′2′′, was eye level with the audience, and his uncanny popularity was not limited to Florida or Texas, but applied nationwide.

Virgil Riley Runnels was born on October 12, 1945, the first son of Virgil Raleigh and Katherine Maxine Sanders Runnels. The Runnels family lived on the east side of Austin, where Virgil Sr. was employed as a plumbing contractor. In 1949 and 1951, two additional children were born into the family, Larry and Constance. As a child, Virgil was influenced by his tough father and understanding mother, and played baseball, football, and wrestled within the neighborhood.

The development of Virgil's gimmick for wrestling began unknowingly when he performed as a member of the Johnston High School drama club. The teenager took to acting, and found that he was not only naturally talented, but that he was partial to being in front of a crowd. Runnels, known as "Dusty" to his family and friends, balanced drama with football, and after graduation in 1963, attended Sul Ross College on a baseball scholarship. He later transferred to West Texas State University in Canyon (1966–67), and became associated with the Funks, Hoyt Richard "Dick" Murdock and Frank Goodish.

With the college football experience under his belt, Dusty played semipro ball for the Hartford Charter Oaks later in 1967. Following a tip to try his hand at pro wrestling, Dusty registered for a camp being run by Tony Santos in Boston, and made his debut under the name "Dusty Runnels." Substantial paydays were reserved for the veterans of the circuit, and Dusty left the territory broke. Motivated to try again, Dusty subscribed to the teachings of Joe Blanchard in San Antonio, and returned to the mat in early 1968 on the Southwestern circuit.

Dusty married Sandra Kay Harris and only hours after the birth of his first child, Dustin Patrick, on April 11, 1969, suffered the loss of his father to emphysema. By that time, he was known in many different territories as "Dusty Rhodes," one-half of the heel tandem Texas Outlaws with Murdock. In 1970, after touring the Central States, Texas, Detroit, and Toronto, the duo debuted in Florida and held the district team championship.

The appearances in Florida as a heel broke ground that he would travel extensively as a fan favorite. The angle that turned Dusty into a face occurred with Gary Hart and Pak Song in Tampa in May 1974, and was, without question, the turning point of his career. Using the gimmick of the "American Dream," Dusty embraced a growing fan base throughout the entire territory from Key West to Tallahassee. His appeal spread, and the magnetism that had captivated fans in the Southeast was soon spreading to the entire wrestling culture.

Rhodes was easily in contention for most popular wrestler every year from 1975 to 1985, and brought exceptionally diverse techniques to the mat. His colorful demeanor was the ultimate counter to leading heels, especially NWA champions Terry Funk and Harley Race. On September 26, 1977, Dusty debuted at Madison Square Garden against WWWF champion Billy Graham, and won by countout before 22,000 fans. A month later, their rematch drew more than 26,000 to the Garden. Rhodes traveled from territory to territory, highlighted as an elite attraction much like the NWA champion or Andre the Giant.

For his robust size, Dusty was surprisingly swift and conditioned. When Tampa booker Eddie Graham lobbied for Rhodes to become NWA champion, there was opposition. The championship had always been geared towards a certain image, and Dusty failed to meet some of the preconceived requirements. These antiquated notions were toppled by Graham's influence, and Rhodes beat Race in Tampa for the NWA belt on August 21, 1979. He lost the title in a rematch five days later at the Sports Stadium in Orlando, but the switch boasted Dusty's commercial value and gave a tremedous spike to the territory.

Rhodes's second reign lasted 88 days between the run of Race and the first championship victory of "Nature Boy" Ric Flair. Rhodes won the belt on June 21, 1981, at Atlanta's Omni, and lost it to Flair in Kansas City on September 17. All across the country, he continued to sell tickets, defining his legend. His ring psychology and business-oriented mind procured booker roles in Florida for Graham and in the Mid-Atlantic territory for Jim Crockett. The majority of power in the Alliance was solidly in the pocket of Crockett's enterprises, and Jim relied heavily on Dusty's prowess, particularly from 1984 to 1987.

Wrestling's smart fanbase criticized Rhodes as a booker, especially the scripting of high profile main-event matches that were becoming more predictable, and less effective. On an important date of the 1986 Great American Bash tour, July 26 at the Greensboro Coliseum, Rhodes captured his third and final NWA title in a cage match. At the Kiel in St. Louis, he was pinned by Flair while locked in a figure-four, and lost the championship on August 9. In 1989, after playing an essential role in the success of Crockett, and laying the foundations for what would become World Championship Wrestling, Dusty returned to Florida, where he became involved with a promising independent promotion, Florida Championship Wrestling.

Dusty's FCW, sanctioned by the Professional Wrestling Federation, was packed with name grapplers, and had the television commentary of Gordon Solie, but it failed in its bid to revive the territory. In need of a job, Rhodes went to the head of the WWF, Vince McMahon. Rhodes had been a draw in the Northeast a decade earlier for Vince McMahon Sr., but his employment with the WWF was not sold on his past achievements. McMahon saw another concept for the "American Dream," and the new gimmick was one that might have ended the career of the average wrestler.

Wearing polka dots and conveying a common man image, Rhodes built a steady base of fans in the WWF and feuded with Ted DiBiase, Big Bossman, and Randy Savage. His 20-month stay in the WWF ended in January 1991, when both he and his son Dustin left for WCW. Dusty was a commentator, booker, wrestler, and member of the NWO at various times in the 1990s. In 1995, he was inducted into the WCW Hall of Fame, and was given the privilege of inducting Solie. Turnbuckle Championship Wrestling was launched in 1998, and Rhodes held indie shows in Georgia, Florida, Alabama, and Tennessee from 2000 to 2002.

He partnered with Dustin to beat Flair and Jeff Jarrett on March 18, 2001, and completed a cycle of having participated in Crockett's initial pay per view, Starrcade 1987, and WCW's concluding event, Greed. On January 8, 2003, Rhodes appeared for NWA TNA in Nashville and was reunited with the Road Warriors. He appeared a week later and did an angle with Nikita Koloff. From November 2004 until June 2005, Dusty appeared on TNA telecasts as the governing "power" who had the authority to script matches. He gave advice to the creative team and participated in televised angles. In 2005, he also released his autobiography, *Dusty* —

Reflections of an American Dream, cowritten by Howard Brody.

Remembered for his unique mannerisms and comedic catchphrases, Dusty held numerous championships during his time in wrestling. He excelled as an entertainer and put his body on the line to sell a match. Looking at him, you'd think he was always outgunned, but the underdog became a national hero, turning casual fans into regular customers. Dusty was the guy you could have a beer with, and if you needed someone around to drop a bionic elbow, or "tell it like it is, if you will," he was the man to go to.

In 1974, an 18-year-old high school football player from Hendersonville, Tennessee, named Thomas Richardson made his wrestling debut. Adopting the name **Tommy Rich**, he was schooled in the mat profession by Tojo Yamamoto, Jerry Jarrett, and Dick Steinborn. Rich, having grown up watching wrestling, was an eager student, and developed his skills on the booking circuit out of Memphis and Nashville. His popularity spread and outrageous kayfabe magazines profited from his marketability, just as promoters in the Southeast did. He appealed to various sections of the wrestling public, and earned esteem as a draw at the box office.

Nicknamed "Wildfire," Rich was willing to go all the way to sell a match, and his fame, with the proper publicity, soon stretched across the country. He was regarded as one of the most outstanding talents under the age of 25. His backer in the Peach State was Jim Barnett, and consistent with the modern era of leadership in the Alliance, Barnett pulled the strings for a flip of the world title in his home territory. The maneuver would help twofold, building the credentials of his chief babyface while sparking gates in the entire territory. Fans would believe that if the belt could switch in Augusta and Gainesville, it could happen anywhere. Rich was going to be added to the list of NWA heavyweight champions.

As Barnett and NWA president Jim Crockett observed from the crowd, Rich dethroned Race for the NWA title on April 27, 1981, at the Augusta Civic Center, unexpectedly pinning the champ with a Thesz Press in 27:22. Rich was 24 years of age, making him, at the time, the youngest National Wrestling Alliance champion since Sonny Myers held the regional version of the title in 1947. Four days later in Gainesville, Rich lost a rematch to Race, and his run concluded.

If you ignore Shane Douglas's momentary recognition in 1994, Rich owns the second shortest title reign in history, after Race and Flair's South Pacific exchange in 1984. It was a distinction that he would forever carry, underlined in any biography, and emphasized by every fiery commentator. Rich was often a titleholder, capturing the Georgia State, National, and Southern (Memphis) titles on three occasions each, and the USWA title four times.

Remembered for his Georgia war with Buzz Sawyer, and his membership in the York Foundation and FBI, Rich still wrestles sporadically, continuing a career now lasting more than 30 years. He has gained the admiration of fans for his willingness to sign autographs, and there is a universal appreciation for what he has given to wrestling. Rich now lives south of Atlanta and enjoys time with his wife and three daughters.

The collection of "Whooos" that accompany each and every chest chop, from major arenas to makeshift indie cards in school gyms, today stand as a reminder of the "Nature Boy" **Ric Flair**. Not that he'll soon be forgotten, as the 57-year-old Flair is commonly seen on WWE programming. During the 1980s, Flair was more associated with the NWA, as a whole, than any other single individual. In total, he won the Alliance world title ten times between 1981 and 1993. Flair was a dynamic wrestler whose matches usually stole the show, and left fans anticipating his next visit. The character he created, a styling and preening champion who was always in the company of a bevy of beauties, was the paradigm for wrestling cockiness.

In March 1949, a baby born on February 25 in Memphis was adopted by Detroit couple Richard Reid (1918–2000) and Kathleen Virginia Kinsmiller Fliehr (1918–2003) and renamed Richard Morgan Fliehr. The boy was the only child of the well-educated Fliehrs, his father a physician and his mother a journalist, and Richard grew up in the suburbs of Minneapolis. At the Wayland Academy in Wisconsin, Richard played football and wrestled, and enrolled at the University of Minnesota. More interested in the nightlife than school, the hefty offensive lineman ditched college, made friends with Olympian Ken Patera, and was introduced to the man who symbolized pro wrestling excellence in Minnesota, Verne Gagne.

A trained athlete, Fliehr was convinced he could survive the high intensity wrestling school of Gagne, and joined a group of five prospective pro grapplers in Wayzata. The grueling instruction, taught by Gagne and Billy Robinson, cracked the spirit of the once-confident Fliehr, but after deliberating on the quickest way to the exit, he found the heart to graduate.

As "Ric Flair," weighing upwards of 260 pounds, Fliehr made his professional debut in Rice Lake, Wisconsin, on December 10, 1972, and wrestled to a ten-minute draw with George Gadaski. He fit easily into a preliminary role, and lost a good percentage of his matches. Learning how to "work," Flair committed to the craft, dropped weight, and the beginnings of his potential started to show. In the summer of 1973, he toured Japan with International Wrestling Enterprises, and, on a tip from Wahoo McDaniel, left the AWA for the Mid-Atlantic territory in May 1974. Claiming roots in Minnesota, Flair was booked as a "relative" of the Anderson Brothers, and hopped into the heavy rotation created by matchmaker George Scott for the Crockett Family.

The platform for development in the Mid-Atlantic states made it possible for Flair to find a routine that put him over. Scott, who was a lifelong friend of the original "Nature Boy" Buddy Rogers, helped Ric mature, and Flair drew comparisons to all of history's notable blond heels: Fred Blassie, Ray Stevens, and, of course, Rogers. By 1975, he was already on the road to greater triumphs, but a fateful flight from Charlotte to Wilmington on a Cessna almost ended his dream. On October 4, 1975, Flair, Bob Bruggers, David Crockett, Tim Woods, and Johnny Valentine were on their way to an outdoor program when their plane ran out of fuel and crashed short of the airport. The 26-year-old Flair suffered a broken back in the accident, and doctors told him he'd never wrestle again.

Ignoring the prognosis, Ric returned in late January 1976, and gave himself time to adjust to the physical demands. A bloody series with McDaniel made the rounds, and Flair was crawling to the top of the promotion on his own merits. He was a perennial champion, in singles and as part of a tag team, and was reportedly earning $100,000 a year by the end of the decade. His matches with Dusty Rhodes, Paul Jones, Bobo Brazil, Jimmy Snuka, Blackjack Mulligan, and Ricky Steamboat were praised, and his name was brought up at the annual NWA conventions as a possible candidate for the world heavyweight title. A hurdle was passed when the Nature Boy went into St. Louis in January 1978 and impressed Sam Muchnick. There was little question that the board of directors were going to carefully watch his progression. Timing was an issue, and with Race and Rhodes getting spells as NWA champion in the late 1970s and into the early '80s, it seemed an ideal time for Crockett to make the case for Flair. The NWA approved a title reign, but the question of whether or not he could meets the demands placed on the champ remained.

On September 17, 1981, after posting a $25,000 bond, Flair beat Dusty Rhodes to capture the NWA world title in Kansas City, with Lou Thesz acting as the referee. Adding his name to the historic list of Alliance champions, Ric surpassed all expectations. He reached all strategic cities of the NWA circuit from Tokyo to St. Louis, and from Nova Scotia to San Juan. During a time in which there was a consolidation of booking offices and a growing national war over territories, Flair held the heavyweight title with a conscientiousness that gave the wavering organization credibility.

Flair's styled performance left him with few equals in the industry. He matched well with fan favorites, but walked a line against heels that made him successful in towns from coast to coast. Employing a measure of psychology, he developed a well-known routine that usually had him acting as the typical bad guy. He'd thumb the eye, beg off, and blade after a tough-looking bump. Flair would sell the corner flip and the essential running across the apron, then be caught on the top turnbuckle. And then there was his "dead to the world," face-first drop to the canvas.

On June 10, 1983, Flair was defeated for the NWA championship by Harley Race in St. Louis, but regained the belt at Starrcade on November 24. Following the sudden death of the gifted David Von Erich, Flair lost the title to David's brother Kerry on May 6, 1984, at Texas Stadium outside Dallas. Several weeks later, he won a two-of-three-fall rematch in Yokosuka City, Japan, and commenced his fourth title run.

By 1986, Crockett was one of only a handful of NWA members still afloat, and was expanding his operations to many cities once considered off limits due to territorial lines, including promotions in St. Louis, Chicago, Los Angeles, Boston, Detroit, East Rutherford (near New York City), Houston, and Philadelphia. The control of Crockett over the Alliance gave him power over where the belt went, and who the interim champions would be when his star didn't have the crown. His booker Rhodes, Ronnie Garvin, and the always competent Steamboat, were all given the title between 1986 and 1989.

The purchase of Crockett's corporate interests by Turner Broadcasting in late 1988 gave the new promotion, known as World Championship Wrestling, a road into the mainstream that, as time went by, found itself increasingly lambasted by smart marks. Flair, to most, was the glue holding the organization together, but WCW's infamous booking patterns left it firmly behind the WWF in terms of national acclaim. Talent in WCW wasn't a problem, and in 1989, Flair was proving his worth in matches with Steamboat and Terry Funk. A slowly building feud with Sting climaxed with the latter capturing the NWA title on July 7, 1990, but Ric regained the championship in January 1991.

WCW's approach to wrestling was light years away from what the Crocketts were doing in the Mid-Atlantic states, and a thousand RoboCops couldn't have made their pay-per-view buy rates any better. In July 1991, after a number of dreadful angles, Flair clashed with WCW executive vice president Jim Herd, and was subsequently fired from the company. Taking his official Alliance backing, gold belt, and reputation, Flair jumped to the WWF. The NWA was left with no choice but to strip him of the title in September.

Flair's WWF tenure featured a long-awaited feud with Hulk Hogan, beginning on October 22, 1991, in Dayton. Ric outlasted the Royal Rumble field, wrestling more than 60 minutes, and won the vacant WWF title on January 19, 1992. Ironically, Flair became the second man in history to have held both the NWA and wwwf/wwf championships, the first being Buddy Rogers, the principal inspiration for his image. Flair traded the belt with Randy Savage on April 5 and September 1, 1992, prior to losing the strap to "Hitman" Bret Hart in Saskatoon on October 12. On January 18, 1993, at a *Monday Night Raw* taping at the Manhattan Center, Ric lost a "loser-leaves wwf" match, and fulfilled contractual obligations through mid-February 1993, including a trek to Europe.

Flair returned to the still-struggling wcw and grabbed his tenth NWA title on July 18, 1993, with a win over Barry Windham. Before the end of the year, he'd also won the wcw title. Wanting to change the direction of the promotion once again, executives signed Hulk Hogan in 1994, and had Flair lose the wcw title to him in Orlando on July 17. wcw's booking around Hogan and veteran wrestlers Jim Duggan, Honky Tonk Man, and Ed Leslie ignored the promise of their younger wrestlers, a fact that the wwf capitalized on, and Flair was buried in the mix. The ever-changing environment, which fostered the development of the Monday night cable television wars, saw Ric move from headliner to role player, and in 1996, a torn rotator cuff put him on the shelf for more than six months.

Feeling generally unappreciated and functioning as a lower echelon wrestler, Flair's contract with wcw expired in February 1998 without resolution. He anticipated resolving his differences with Eric Bischoff and signing a deal, but after rejecting a booking for a show in Tallahassee to encourage his son Reid in an amateur wrestling tournament, Ric was fired. Both sides then filed lawsuits. For months, Flair sat on the sidelines, his pride hurt, watching wcw squander its ratings advantage. The wrestling audience called for Flair's reemergence. An agreement led to an emotional night in Greenville on September 14, 1998. While Flair was always celebrated by his fans, his distinguished career was repeatedly damaged by infamous angles that did nothing but further sink the promotion. His willingness to commit his all to the organization was obvious, especially when angles included his sons and wife Beth.

By March 2001, when wcw was sold, Flair had won the wcw title eight times. Fittingly, Ric and Sting wrestled on the final edition of *Nitro* on March 26, 2001, and Flair gave his opponent the match by submission. With the wwf dominating all major professional wrestling in the United States, Flair took a job with Vince McMahon and debuted on November 19, 2001, in Charlotte. He served as company "owner" and ally of Triple H, Randy Orton, and David Batista. Flair grappled often and was willing to put anyone over. The quality of his matches, even at more than 50 years of age, was leaving an impression with a new era of wrestling enthusiasts.

The jet-flying, limo-riding Nature Boy continues to strut around wwe rings, and his promos reel them in as they've always done. A ten-time NWA champion, an eight-time wcw champion, and a two-time wwf champion, Flair is one of the most accomplished and respected wrestlers in history. His autobiography *Ric Flair: To Be The Man,* published in 2004, is a must-read for all wrestling fans.

Jack Adkisson introduced his sons David, Kevin, and **Kerry Gene Adkisson** to fellow members during the August 1979 convention at the Sahara in Las Vegas. The athletes were touted by their father, and under the "Von Erich" alias, were symbols of babyface wrestling in Texas. On an agenda devised by their father, the clan spent time in St. Louis, where the cautious eye of Sam Muchnick was nurturing the growth of future champions. The third-youngest Adkisson, Kerry, born on February 3, 1960, in upstate New York, debuted as a teenager in May 1978, and was also a talented discus thrower at the University of Houston.

But the wrestling mat at the Sportatorium and the screams of fans was much more of a lure than collegiate or Olympic success. Kerry joined his brothers and father in lifting the banner of World Class wrestling to the height of popularity with creative angles and inspired action. His athleticism translated well to the ring, and in addition to his achievements in Dallas, he gained national publicity in 1983 when he won the Missouri title from Harley Race in St. Louis. David, who was 18 months older, was on a fast track in the Alliance with experience in Florida, time served as a heel, and a crucial tour of All Japan in February 1984. His father's political maneuvering did what was necessary to get the 6'4'' athlete considered for a run with the NWA title. On February 10, 1984, before wrestling a single match in that country, David died in a Tokyo hotel room at the age of 25.

The wrestling world was pinned by the stunning loss. In a show of support to the Adkissons, the NWA Board agreed to give the belt to Kerry, and on May 6, 1984, at Texas Stadium in Irving, an estimated 40,000 fans saw Von Erich emerge as the champion in a highly emotional event. Kerry beat Ric Flair in 25:42 for the title in tribute to his brother. His 18-day stint as titleholder included a cruise through Florida, and end in Yokosuka City, Japan on May 24, 1984, with a three-fall loss to Flair.

Kerry was almost killed in a motorcycle accident on June 4, 1986, on US 373 in Argyle, Texas. The severity of the wreck forced doctors to amputate part of his lower right leg and foot. It was a fact that went unknown to the wrestling world and to the people who watched him grapple (with a prothesis). In 1990, he held the wwf intercontinental title and wrestled for the Global Wrestling Federation at the Sportatorium until his suicide on February 18, 1993, at the age of 33.

The Adkisson family were faced with unprecedented pain and suffering in the midst of their very public wrestling lives. Fritz, Kevin, David, Kerry, Mike, and

Chris Von Erich each gave their hearts to professional wrestling, and the fans of Texas were always elated to see the famed family on the bill. They were bigger than life itself, and their legacy will be remembered by the people who treasured their enthusiasm for wrestling.

From Quebec, the third Canadian-born NWA champion was "Hands of Stone" **Ronnie Garvin**. Born Roger Barnes on March 30, 1945, into a poor but loving family, Ron spent his early years in the Eastern Quebec town of Gaspé, and later was a teenager in the city of his birth, Montreal. He primarily played hockey as a kid, but gave amateur boxing a shot before wrestling at a nearby religious athletic center. Taught by wrestler Pat Girard, Garvin made his debut at 17 years of age and made his initial trip outside of his hometown to the territory of Tony Santos of Boston, who was known for giving wrestling hopefuls a shot. Making less than $70 a week and speaking little English, Ronnie was unimpressed with the first chapter of his American experience. Fortunately, Leroy McGuirk in Tulsa offered something more.

The stocky Garvin bounced from territory to territory, finding employment with Morris Sigel, the Fields Brothers, Eddie Graham, Larry Kasaboski, and Jim Crockett. He had success in a gimmicked brother tandem with a friend from Montreal, Terry Garvin (Terry Joyal), and their colorful antics propelled them to regional championships in the 1960s and '70s. Known as a hard-hitting, serious-minded journeyman, Garvin was 42 years old when he was pushed by promoter Jim Crockett Jr. and booker Dusty Rhodes. His fateful match with Ric Flair occurred in Detroit, during the expansion of Crockett's enterprises outside of the Mid-Atlantic, on September 25, 1987. Garvin won a cage match and the NWA title with a sunset flip from the top rope at the Joe Louis Arena in 33:17.

Bringing his ring savvy and toughness to the NWA belt, Garvin was champion until November 26, 1987, losing a rematch to Flair at Starrcade in Chicago. The 62-day reign lacked a profound, signature moment, but rewarded a ring veteran for his decades of warfare with an honor that could never be forgotten. Garvin worked for the WWF for two years, where he admittedly didn't fit in, and then went into a self-imposed retirement. He saved his money from his time in wrestling and had invested in several Charlotte-area businesses, including a used car sales operation, and flies planes as a hobby.

The lightning-fast **Ricky Steamboat** was a throwback NWA champion, a popular grappler with science and smarts. He could match hold for hold, brawl, fly from the turnbuckles, and carry the championship belt with dignity. Following the purchase of Crockett's wrestling empire by the Turner group, and in the midst of a heated war with the World Wrestling Federation, Steamboat was given the top spot. His feud with Ric Flair highlighted wrestling on TBS in 1989, and their matches are still talked about today.

Steamboat was born Richard Henry Blood Jr. on February 28, 1953, the son of Richard Henry Sr. and Takako Blood. Attending Boca Ciega High in Gulfport, Florida, he lettered in football and wrestling. In the backfield for the Bogies, Blood scored eight touchdowns as a senior and has awarded an All-City honorable mention. As a wrestler, he had a record of 49 wins and nine losses over three years and was named most valuable player at the Seminole Classic, 1st All-District and 1st All-Conference. For the 1970–71 school year, Boca Ciega students named Blood outstanding athlete of the year, and he reportedly went to the Florida State wrestling championships two years in a row.

A twist of fate and a desire to pursue athletics led Blood to enroll at Verne Gagne's wrestling camp. Influenced by Championship Wrestling from Florida as a teenager, he had limited knowledge of what it meant to be a pro wrestler, but was dedicated to following through on what he started. Blood acquired the basic skillset from Gagne and Khosrow Vaziri and took to the road after his debut on February 15, 1976, versus Scott Irwin.

Using the name "Dick Blood," Ricky competed in preliminaries with other graduates of the camp and battled numerous old pros who helped him progress. From there, he traveled to his home state of Florida, where he was renamed Ricky Steamboat by CWF honcho Eddie Graham. Tagged the "nephew" of wrestler Sammy Steamboat (Sam Mokuahi), a gimmick that seemed to help the up-and-comer, Rick's ability to perform spoke for itself, without excessive hyperbole. He paid his dues, and spent plenty of time at the bottom of the card.

A tour of Georgia led to a gig into the Mid-Atlantic region, where he would attain his first pro mat accomplishments for Jim Crockett. In total, he held area versions of the U.S. title three times and world tag-team title on six occasions. Steamboat was introduced to his ultimate foe, "Nature Boy" Ric Flair, and their matches never disappointed.

The Mid-Atlantic excursion made Steamboat a nationally recognizable superstar. Featured in magazines and on shows of the ever-developing Crockett promotions, he established himself as a hot ticket, capable of holding down his half of a main event in any city. He announced an abrupt, self-imposed retirement in early 1984, but it lasted only a few months. When he went to the WWF, it was clear that the organization wasn't going to build their plans around him. After all, he was second fiddle to Hulk Hogan. Steamboat did hold the distinction of having wrestled at both the first Starrcade and at the initial WrestleMania.

It was Ricky's WrestleMania III classic against Randy Savage that catapulted him into wrestling lore, and their dramatic match was considered the high point of the program. With a number of near falls, the two culminated a well-written storyline with Steamboat winning with a small package and capturing the Intercontinental title. That was the best it was going to get for Steamboat in the WWF, and two months later, he lost the championship to the Honky Tonk Man (Wayne Farris). He was gone from the WWF by the end of the year.

Steamboat was hired by World Championship Wrestling in 1989, and a feud with heel champion Flair was quickly scripted. In the throes of a head-to-head war with the WWF, Steamboat provided a perfect foil for WCW's ace heel. On February 20, 1989, at the Chi-Town Rumble pay-per-view from the UIC Pavilion in Chicago, Steamboat beat Flair in 23:06 and won the NWA title.

WCW held "Rajin' Cajin," Clash of the Champions VI on the same day as the WWF's WrestleMania, and ten past and future NWA champions were on hand, including the Funk Brothers, Kiniski, O'Connor, Rogers, and Thesz. Steamboat defended his championship against Flair in a rare best-of-three-falls match with his wife and son looking on. Steamboat won the second and third falls to retain his title in what was regarded as a classic bout. Ricky lost the title to Flair on May 7, 1989 at the Music City Showdown pay-per-view in Nashville, and the feud closed when Flair turned face to wrestle Terry Funk. Steamboat's reign totaled 76 days.

The WWF gave him a job and a Dragon gimmick that saw him breathing fire prior to matches. The exhibition was more remarkable than his push, and Ricky bailed for WCW by the end of 1991. He was a headliner for most of the three years that followed, and won numerous titles. In the spring of 1994, he resumed his feud with Flair, and briefly held the WCW championship. A serious back injury forced him into retirement several months later.

Since 1994, Steamboat has made occasional appearances, including acting as a guest referee. He was the third man for the NWA-TNA Gauntlet finale between Ken Shamrock and Malice for the vacant NWA title on June 19, 2002, in Huntsville, and bouts for Ring of Honor. In Cornelius, North Carolina, he owned the Lake Norman Health Club and other businesses, and supported his son's interests in race car driving. In December 2004, he was given a three-week tryout for a road agent position, then was hired by WWE. He was a natural athlete and brought a heightened level of performance to the squared circle. Determined, confident, and proficient, Ricky was respected by wrestling fans for his abilities, and his talent would have made him a star in any generation.

The traditional and conservative NWA board of directors would have had a hard time voting for Steven L. Borden as heavyweight champion. It wouldn't have been based on any lack of charisma, popularity, or a drab execution in the ring, but the seven-member panel would have been stuck on his layer of face paint and his gimmick, known to the world as **Sting**. Borden used the character to define his wrestling career, and, under the leadership of Jim Crockett Jr., and later for Jim Herd in World Championship Wrestling, he successfully climbed the championship ladder to grab the most desired title in professional grappling.

On March 20, 1959, Borden was born in Omaha, but raised in Northern Los Angeles County, California. He went to William S. Hart High School in Newhall in the Santa Clarita Valley, and excelled as a forward on the school's basketball team from 1975 to 1977. Not a wrestling fan of any kind growing up, Steve went to the College of the Canyons for several years, balancing his academics with a social life, and work as a bartender or bouncer. By the mid-1980s, he had invested in a local gymnasium, where he met manager Rick Bassman. Bassman was composing a unique clique of athletic weightlifters, known as Power Team USA, hoping to get a break in the world of professional wrestling, and offered Borden a place on the squad.

Impressed with the spectacle of wrestling, Borden attended an eight-week training camp led by Red Bastien in 1985, and made his debut shortly thereafter. With James Hellwig, another member of the Power Team, Borden traveled to Memphis for Jerry Jarrett's CWA. He used the alias "Flash," while Hellwig was known as "Justice" in a team known as the Freedom Fighters. Traveling southward to Bill Watts's UWF, Steve and his tag partner formed the Blade Runners, and the wearing of face paint for both rookies became an everyday custom. Borden gained increased attention in 1986 when he took the name "Sting" and began learning from the intelligent and experienced Eddie Gilbert.

Gilbert mentored Borden in the UWF, and Steve developed his ring personality as a member of Hyatt and Hot Stuff, Inc., a heel group. The two grapplers feuded viciously with the Fantastics (Bobby Fulton and Tommy Rogers), and held the UWF tag title on two occasions. In 1987, Borden held the championship again with Rick Steiner. In the end, Watts sold the UWF to Crockett Promotions, which, at the time, was the leading front for the NWA. The combination of the UWF and Crockett's organization gave their wrestlers wide national exposure, and Sting was rapidly making headway as a fan favorite.

Sting entered the championship picture when Crockett gave him a match with NWA champion Ric Flair on March 27, 1988, at the initial Clash of the Champions broadcast on TBS, in direct competition with the WWF's WrestleMania pay-per-view. The ultimate underdog, Sting had the crowd in his corner as he matched up with the dirtiest player in the game, and the celebrated match went more than 35 minutes to a draw. The bout made him a star, gave kayfabe writers a new figure to exploit, and wrestling fans hoped that he would vanquish the Nature Boy in the not so distant future. The politics of wcw placed Borden lower on the list of heavyweight contenders, and Sting was lost behind Lex Luger, Ricky Steamboat, and Terry Funk in 1989.

The spiky-blond-haired athlete with the famous "Stinger" splash returned to the spotlight in late 1989, when he won the Iron Man competition at the annual Starrcade with 40 points and a pinfall victory over Flair. The booking was finally in Borden's favor, and it was to culminate in his getting the NWA title at WrestleWar on February 25, 1990. But at the close of a dramatic Clash of the Champions on February 6, Sting ruptured his left patella, an injury that forced him to miss more than four months. The angle was put on hold until July 7, 1990, in Baltimore at the Great American Bash. In 16:06, Sting pinned the champion and won the NWA world title.

The forces driving wcw were faltering, and Sting was caught in the middle of the promotion's attempts to make it more mainstream — geared toward children rather than their loyal fanbase. Dreary matchmaking locked him into a long winded feud with the mysterious Black Scorpion, and turned his championship reign cold. A change would be made after the first of the year, and on January 11, 1991, at a house show at the Meadowlands outside New York City, Sting lost the belt to Flair — capping his reign at 188 days.

Borden was at or near the helm of wcw through 1994, when the signing of Hulk Hogan began to erode his longtime position as lead face. The decision to bring Hogan aboard was all business, and although Sting continued part of the backbone of wcw, his importance was reduced. Eventually, in 1996, he altered his ring guise from the blond beach image to a dark, brooding persona, one who walked a line between fan favorite and heel. The new Sting carried a bat, rappelled in from the rafters, and delivered a Scorpion Death Drop. Fans responded, buying his merchandise, and cheering his sly behavior. A feud with Hollywood Hogan in 1997 energized the promotion, but failed to meet expectations.

The abundance of big money superstars in wcw precluded a sustained run at the top for Sting, and the unstable management was steering the promotion towards disaster. Borden, who had been with wcw through thick and thin, could not make up for the mediocre performances of his colleagues with his own motivation. Born again into Christianity, he found a new inspiration for his life, and began to distance himself from wrestling. He fulfilled obligations until the sale of wcw assets to World Wrestling Federation Entertainment, Inc. in March 2001, and was inactive until making his debut for the World Wrestling All Stars promotion in December 2002.

Borden dabbled in acting, made appearances for TNA — where he captured his second NWA title on October 22, 2006 — and has used his public image and notoriety to spread his religious beliefs. He is known for his charity work, and even if he were to never step into the ring again, his time as a wrestling hero will be remembered by the "Little Stingers" who followed him every step of the way.

In 1991 and 1992, during the talent sharing agreement among the NWA board of directors, WCW, and New Japan Pro Wrestling, three Japanese grapplers added their names alongside Shohei "Giant" Baba's as Asian-born NWA world heavyweight champions. **Tatsumi Fujinami**, a wrestler leading NJPW to new financial heights, won a controversial match over Ric Flair on March 21, 1991, before more than 64,000 fans at the Tokyo Dome. American wrestling fans saw Flair, who was recognized as titleholder by both WCW and the NWA, retain his crown. Officially, however, the Alliance title switched hands and was reported in Japan. Fujinami won the championship, but the gold belt emblematic of the title was transported home by Flair. The angle sparked a rematch at a pay-per-view in St. Petersburg on May 19, but little else. Flair beat Fujinami and regained the NWA title.

Months after the Alliance stripped Flair of the championship in July 1991, NWA president Jim Herd and his counterpart in NJPW, Seiji Sakaguchi, organized a tournament to resurrect the championship. Twenty-eight-year-old **Masahiro Chono**, on August 12, 1992, in Tokyo's famous Sumo Hall, beat Rick Rude (Richard Erwin Rood, 1958–1999) in the finals to win the vacant title. At the annual Tokyo Dome show on January 4, 1993, **Keiji Mutoh** won the belt, adding the strap to the IWGP title he was already holding. The title change occurred in front of an estimated 63,000 fans, and the sometimes Great Muta won the belt his mentor Hiro Matsuda had chased more than two decades earlier.

Barry Clinton Windham was a top contender to NWA champion Flair during the 1980s, but never got the opportunity to wear the belt. On February 21, 1993, the second-generation wrestler beat Mutoh at the Asheville Civic Center and took the NWA title. While, understandably, he lost a few steps due to knee problems, Windham was still a proficient mat technician, and brought a sense of history to the championship. The feud of Barry and Flair was reignited by booker Bill Watts, setting up their match at Beach Blast in Biloxi on July 18, 1993. That night, Flair won the title for the tenth time. Windham was champion for 147 days.

The Shane Douglas and Eastern Championship Wrestling debacle in August 1994 damaged the standing of the NWA heavyweight title, and its value, when it was thrown to the mat as if it was a piece of trash. Hoping to beat the odds and rebuild on the longstanding history of the Alliance, Dennis Coralluzzo staged a second tournament to crown a champion. On November 19, 1994, Christopher B. Candito, known to wrestling fans as **Chris Candido**, beat Tracey Smothers in the finals at the National Guard Armory in Cherry Hill, New Jersey, and captured the vacant NWA title, represented by the old style (1973–1986) globe belt.

Candido was blond, had worked as an arrogant heel, and at 22 was the youngest, and shortest (5′8′′), NWA champion in history. He had a strong build of 225 pounds, and was well liked by his peers. The veteran indie star was a graduate of Red Bank Catholic High School and wrestled professionally since he was a teenager. He was world champion until February 24, 1995, losing the strap to Dan Severn in Erlanger, Kentucky, after signing a contract with the WWF. On April 28, 2005, Candido passed away after complications from surgery. He was survived by his wife and wrestling manager, Tamara "Tammy" Sytch. At 33 years, one month, and 7 days, Chris was the second youngest NWA champion to pass away, after Kerry Von Erich, who died at 33 years and 15 days.

In the mold of legendary amateurs Dick Hutton and Jack Brisco, **Daniel Severn**, nicknamed the "Beast," took the world title at a bleak moment in Alliance history. Desperately in need of credibility, Coralluzzo and the members of the NWA looked to Severn, a respected shooter. Son of Marvin and Barbara Severn, Dan was born on June 9, 1958, and with his three athletic brothers, rose to fame at McCloy High School in Montrose, Michigan. Dan began wrestling at age 11 and won a string of AAU championships. At Arizona State University from 1977 to 1981, he won 127 matches and had a winning percentage of .917.

During the 1980s, he was a leading amateur grappler, placing second in the Olympic trials at 220 pounds behind Lou Banach in May 1984, and winning gold at the National Sports Festival in August 1985. As a member of the U.S. team, Severn traveled the globe and, in July 1986, participated in the Goodwill Games at Moscow. He turned professional in the 1990s, and won the NWA world title from Candido on February 24, 1995 at Peel's Palace in Erlanger. On April 7, he won the Ultimate Fighting Championship V, and wore both championship belts draped on his shoulders. In 1998, Severn was featured on WWF programming and the NWA received the publicity it was looking for.

Severn wore the belt for 1,479 days, the third-longest reign in NWA title history.

When he became champion there were only seven promoters affiliated with the Alliance, and at the time he lost the strap, there were at least 18, with the collective expanding. He toured the world with the NWA title, defending the championship in Singapore, Canada and Japan, giving the title a boost in esteem. He lost the belt to Naoya Ogawa on March 14, 1999, in Yokohama. The man who held the second-longest NWA championship reign, Dory Funk Jr. (Lou Thesz was first), acted as the referee.

On March 9, 2002, Severn won the belt for a second time over Shinya Hashimoto at the Korakuen Hall in Tokyo. The NWA board of directors stripped him of the title because he was unable to wrestle at the initial NWA-TNA pay-per-view on June 19. In August 2002, he was given the Frank Gotch Award from the Professional Wrestling Hall of Fame at the International Wrestling Institute and Museum in Newton, Iowa.

Following Severn's lengthy stretch from 1995 to 1999, NWA champions have included Naoya Ogawa, Gary Steele (first British-born NWA champion), Michael Rapada, Terry Michael Brunk (Sabu), Steven Corino, Shinya Hashimoto, Kenneth Wayne Shamrock, Ronald Killings (the first African American to hold the NWA title), Jeffrey Jarrett, Allen Jones (A.J. Styles), Scott Levy (Raven), Terrance Gerin (Rhino), and Jason Reso (Christian Cage). Since 2002, the NWA belt has been controlled, in part, by NWA-TNA , and licensed by the Alliance Board of Directors in a long-term contract that will keep the NWA name in the news.

CHAPTER EIGHTEEN

NWA HISTORY

(1975–Present)

Over the course of the past 30 years, the National Wrestling Alliance has become a shell of its former self. Collective agreements amongst promoters have fallen apart for the sole benefit of a particular company, and the changing wrestling environment has made the market uneven. The most ingenious minds have found ways to survive, while the old system of kayfabe and protecting what was known as professional wrestling has morphed into what today is commonly known as "sports entertainment."

There wasn't a specific incident that could be seen as the turning point in the history of the NWA, rather there were a series of small decisions that altered the path. In some interpretations, Sam Muchnick's stepping down as NWA president in

1975 was the beginning of the end. Admired by the Alliance faithful, Muchnick had all the qualities of a fine politician, and his ideas were usually for the betterment of the whole membership.

The NWA, in August 1975, included a number of intelligent businessmen. There were promoters recognized for their honest payoffs, good bookers, and guys looking to make their next buck in any way possible. But did the annual convention in New Orleans have someone who could match Muchnick's integrity and sense of duty? The members voted unanimously, putting their trust behind Jack Adkisson, known to fans as Fritz Von Erich.

There was yet another pivotal election in 1975. Having reached his threshold, heavyweight champion Jack Brisco was ready to give up the championship, and the two logical candidates to inherit the throne were Harley Race and Terry Funk. The balloting to name Adkisson president proceeded smoothly, but the board was deadlocked at three apiece in finding Brisco's successor. Adkisson cast the deciding vote in favor of Funk.

Jim Barnett replaced Muchnick as the heavyweight titleholder's booker, and his office at 310 Chester Street in Atlanta became the official NWA headquarters. Much to the satisfaction of members, he was not given, however, the same wage Sam had earned. Barnett had the incentive to pencil-in extra dates for the champion throughout the Southeast because he owned a percentage of several territories. Realistically, he too had something to gain from the labor of the NWA king.

The NWA increased its standing in Asia in 1975 when New Japan Pro Wrestling, operated by Antonio Inoki, was accepted for membership. Inoki's induction added a second Alliance booker to Japan, although at the time, inferior to Shohei Baba's All Japan. In terms of NWA spotlight in the Far East, all eyes were on Baba's promotion, and the clear favoritism leaning his way was the result of years of political maneuvering. Japan had plenty of room for two wrestling agencies fighting for the hearts of fans, and an array of gimmicks were tossed into the ring, including the 1976 Inoki vs. Muhammad Ali mixed contest in Tokyo. While Baba would have three reigns as NWA champion, Inoki measured up with credible distinctions and popular feuds that kept New Japan competitive.

Adkisson, who wasn't bogged down with the booking of Brisco or Funk, had to meet the demands of the presidency and worry about his own territory. He also was the father of a few teenage sons who were considering going pro. They did, and became, in the eyes of some, the future of the sport. Adkisson was respected for what he accomplished in Dallas, but he couldn't maintain the principals of the Alliance in the mold of Muchnick. It was a near-impossible task. Promoters were moving in to seize the moment during a volatile period, using friendships and political connections to push their agendas. Again, the rampant self-interest of individuals in the fraternity was becoming more and more apparent.

A sly eleventh-hour substitute for his brother Dory, Terry Funk stepped through the ropes on the historic night of December 10, 1975, and challenged Brisco for the NWA title in Miami Beach. The unsuspecting audience watched Funk go over and capture the belt. Terry brought something different than his sibling, Dory Funk Jr., but he was just as competent. He wrestled as a technical heel, habitually dragging bouts into brawls, and was a match for all his contenders, from Dusty Rhodes to Mr. Wrestling II. Crowd tension was constantly high with Terry wearing the strap, and his opponents always looked like they had a chance to be champions.

The referee of the match that gave Funk his championship in December 1975 was the same man who'd sued the National Wrestling Alliance for antitrust violations 20 years earlier — Sonny Myers. Similar complaints were being heard in many forms during the mid-to-late 1970s, and there was an ever-growing list of plaintiffs bemoaning the practices of the NWA.

Muchnick was content, maybe relieved, in writing his August 9, 1975, letter to Assistant Attorney General Thomas Kauper of the Department of Justice Antitrust Division in Washington D.C., stating: "In keeping with my custom of keeping your department informed of activities of the National Wrestling Alliance, am sending you the names of the new officers, as I have stepped out as the president after serving many years." He offered the names and addresses of Adkisson, Barnett, and second vice president Mike LeBell.

Lingering allegations of continuing antitrust abuse were a major cause for concern. People were coming forward to tell their stories, and the NWA's reputation was at a low. Ex-wrestler Jim Wilson was one of the more motivated whistleblowers, and he pursued his action against the NWA to a settlement. The money spent legally defending the organization was mind-boggling, but the remaining promoters believed in the cooperative, and felt their only way to survive was to stick together.

The August 1976 convention at Lake Tahoe saw Eddie Graham rise to the presidency. LeBell, the NWA's representative in Los Angeles, and fresh off a role in the infamous Inoki-Ali match in June, was elevated to first vice president. Barnett stayed on as secretary-treasurer and booker of Funk, until his mandatory title loss to Harley Race. Reports came in from the chairmen of the membership, TV, finance, and grievance committees, and updated members on the status of the heavyweight, junior heavyweight, and light heavyweight divisions.

Race defeated Funk on February 6, 1977 and grabbed his second NWA title. The globetrotter assumed the scheduled dates for the champion that Barnett arranged, including an important visit to Houston for a man known for his fairness, Paul

Boesch. Boesch, who had acquired the Houston office in early 1967, was a key Alliance promoter, and unlike his predecessor Morris Sigel, didn't run a booking office. He relied on a number of outlets for talent, specifically Adkisson in Dallas, and went to great lengths to prepare his biggest card in years on Sunday, May 29, 1977, at the Summit. In addition to a Race-Funk rematch, the extravaganza featured AWA world champion Nick Bockwinkel, WWWF champion Billy Graham, and women's champion Fabulous Moolah. Boesch invested a bundle of money with television and radio commercials, and a large throng was projected.

The matinee went on without the arrival of Race, and Bockwinkel proved to be an iron man, wrestling 20 minutes with Jose Lothario, and then an hour with Funk. Race had thought it was a night program, and his no-show infuriated Boesch. The dispute was resolved when Harley took responsibility for his mistake, and in October, participated in Boesch's 45th anniversary program along with Bockwinkel. As an affiliate of the NWA, and after selling ten percent of the Gulf Athletic Club to Bockwinkel, Boesch was able to book two of the top heavyweight champions regularly.

Wrestling in Tennessee became a disaster zone in the aftermath of Jerry Jarrett's declaration of independence from Nick Gulas on February 14, 1977. The 34-year-old capitalist saw the errors of his employers and chose a course of his own. Gulas, associated with the Alliance since 1949, had only a short time earlier crushed the dreams of the UWA. By the late '70s, the illness of his partner Roy Welch robbed the business of its counterbalance. Jarrett's defection was devastating, and in his efforts to start a new promotion in Memphis, he snatched the bulk of Gulas's talent. Following Welch's death in September 1977, Roy's son Edward (Buddy Fuller) quickly joined Jarrett and helped create the Jarrett-Welch Wrestling Co.

The animosity cooled, enough for Jarrett and Welch to register with the NWA in 1978. Jarrett created the Continental Wrestling Association, which, after a decay in relations between the promoter and the NWA, sanctioned a "world" champion from 1979 to '81. The uneasy ties to the NWA would continue into the mid-1980s, but Jarrett relied primarily on his agreements with Verne Gagne's AWA. Gulas sold out to Welch in 1980 and subsequently retired.

A high point for fans in the late 1970s was the obvious interaction between the NWA, WWWF and the AWA. The peaceful movement of wrestlers across promotional lines was better in 1977 than at any point in years. Promoters were reaping the benefits, and a mix of heavyweight champions on the same bill was soon commonplace. The joint promotion of Race and Graham in St. Louis, Houston, and St. Petersburg offered a unique, engrossing spectacle.

Title versus title matches were on the horizon, and on January 25, 1978, a mob of 12,000 braved wet weather at Miami's Orange Bowl to see Graham and Race battle. Their one-hour deadlock, in what was branded the "Superbowl of Wrestling," was an instant classic, and promoters hoped the high-profile attractions would lure many more thousands.

Three nights after Superstar Graham was dethroned by Bob Backlund in New York City on February 20, 1978, the WWWF champion was in Jacksonville in what was supposed to be a rematch versus Race. The finish was identical. Backlund engaged Race three additional times over the next two years in unification matches, and wrestled Bockwinkel in Toronto on March 25, 1979. When the champions of the AWA, NWA, and WWWF met in the ring, it resonated throughout wrestling, and a once seemingly taboo idea was now being used by savvy entrepreneurs to generate interest.

Eddie Graham vacated the presidency of the Alliance in April 1978 because of ill health, and vice president Bob Geigel filled the vacancy. A partner in the Kansas City office, Geigel had been a backer of Harley Race as titleholder, and opposed a sudden change at the heavyweight level. Several months later, Bob was formally elected to the office and Harley's term was solidified for at least another year. Appreciative of his long stretch as champ, and for the support he'd received, Race thanked the NWA fellowship on August 3, 1979, during the initial day of the convention in Las Vegas.

Graham wasn't present at the conference, but his intentions were clear. Co-owner Duke Keomuka and Eddie's son Mike urged members to heed their boss's advice, and reward Dusty Rhodes with the NWA title. The Alliance board of directors, consisting of Geigel, Adkisson, Barnett, LeBell, Jim Crockett, Dory Funk Jr., Vincent J. McMahon, Don Owen, and Fred Ward, agreed, and seconded his motion with a priceless gift.

Dusty threw Race for the belt at the Armory in Tampa on August 21, 1979. No one outside the chieftains of the CWF wanted a prolonged tenure, especially Funk and Shohei Baba, who expected the NWA champion for four tours of All Japan in a 16-month span. Those visits by Race resulted in two title exchanges with Baba. Dusty, obligated to New Japan, lost a rematch to Harley on August 26 in Orlando at the Sports Stadium. Still the five-day stint boosted Dusty's reputation.

Barnett pulled the champion's number on April 27, 1981, when Tommy Rich beat Race for the strap. The switch was an obvious gesture from the board of directors to Barnett for his five years as the champ's booker, and for his eight years as secretary.

The act of giving the heavyweight title to a member as token of goodwill to help an individual territory was symptomatic of an illness spreading within the Alliance. There was no precedent for such action. Previous title changes were made with the notion that the reigning champions would benefit both the promotion or the driving force behind the titleholder, *and* the entire NWA.

In the cases of Rhodes, Baba, and Rich, the title switches helped individual members, and though the title runs of the trio were short, it marked a significant change in philosophy from an era in which the NWA supported a democratic doctrine to a time where political favors were granted for the right price.

Race recaptured the NWA belt for the sixth time on May 1, 1981, in Gainesville. Fifty-one days later, on June 21 in Atlanta, Rhodes conquered Harley for his second NWA belt. Known as a guy who appealed to blue-collar fans, Dusty held the championship until September 17, 1981, when he lost to Ric Flair in 23:54 in Kansas City, with Lou Thesz as the guest referee.

An examination of the heavyweight champions and the locations of title swaps between 1979 and 1983 paints a perfect picture of the hierarchy of the NWA. Race was a decorated champion with encouragement from Geigel in Kansas City. Rhodes was popular nationally, but lived and breathed for the Florida office. Flair was the premier young star for Crockett. Rich and the Georgia spots assisted Barnett. Baba was also pleased with the way things had transpired.

Nightmares became reality for Boesch in Houston in April 1981, when Race missed a second scheduled title defense, this time versus Wahoo McDaniel at the Sam Houston Coliseum. Boesch was once again obliged to explain the mysterious absence of the main-event star to his frustrated fans, but he acted quickly, naming McDaniel champion via forfeit. Instead of accepting an apology, this time Boesch focused his attention on AWA champion Bockwinkel, and severed ties with the NWA. Houston had been associated with the NWA since 1949. McDaniel was defeated by Bockwinkel in a unification match on August 14, 1981.

Leroy McGuirk and Bill Watts were very successful together in the promotion of Oklahoma, Arkansas, Mississippi, and Louisiana. A decade before their Superdome triumph drew an estimated 31,000 fans and a gate of $140,000 on July 22, 1978, McGuirk submitted the only vote in favor of passing the NWA world title to Watts. Since his pro debut in 1962, the Cowboy distinguished himself as a preeminent grappler wherever he traveled, and had a catalog of regional achievements. Watts was capable of running neck-and-neck, on any given night, with Verne Gagne, Bruno Sammartino, or Gene Kiniski, and was a master of ring performance. As a matchmaker, he was invaluable to McGuirk, but a dispute splintered their empire in August 1979.

On September 11, 1979, Watts incorporated Mid-South Sports, Inc. in New Orleans and opted not to apply for NWA membership. The Mid-South Wrestling Association booking office grew in size and advanced the careers of Ted DiBiase,

Junkyard Dog, Paul Orndorff, and the Freebirds. Watts added agreements with Boesch, Barnett, Graham, Adkisson, and McMahon that helped his territory become one of the country's most noteworthy.

McGuirk, in contrast, experimented with everything under the sun in efforts to keep afloat. Even bringing in clever booker George Scott failed to regenerate the territory. When Watts filed corporate documents for his Mid-South promotion in Tulsa on February 23, 1981, Leroy knew that war loomed. On August 21, seven of his wrestlers went on strike, claiming that they hadn't been paid for their work a week before, and McGuirk turned to Amarillo for talent. In 1982, Leroy closed up shop forever, selling the remnants of his office to Watts.

Some wrestling promoters were finding it easier to toil as an independent entity than remain attached to the odd-shaped structure of the NWA. Others were folding up completely. Casualties included Roy Shire in San Francisco, Mike London's weekly shows at the Auditorium in Albuquerque, and the once-heated West Texas scene. Detroit was another city that fell by the wayside, and promoters tried to resurrect the promotion with the standard shenanigans. While the Alliance was in decline, there were perceptive people thinking of ways to exploit the weakened national syndicate. Survival would be the name of the game.

The NWA's traditional leaders, Muchnick and Frank Tunney, by the summer of 1983, were no longer the sounding board for grievances or monitoring the organization's progress. Toronto, in fact, became a WWF satellite later that year. Crockett and Geigel were the NWA's current directors. The former, initially elected president at the 1980 convention in Reno, was awarded his second term in August 1981, and was succeeded by Geigel at the confab in Puerto Rico in 1982. Geigel, by that time, was the managing partner in Kansas City and St. Louis.

Two of the more profitable outfits in the NWA were Jim Crockett Promotions, Inc., and Georgia Championship Wrestling. GCW, partly owned by Barnett, Paul Jones, and Ole Anderson, had increased its audience considerably with their weekend programs on cable network Superstation WTBS, based in Atlanta. With Anderson laying down the script as chief booker, GCW advanced on turf in Michigan, Ohio, and West Virginia. This move marked the first time in many years that an Alliance member had expanded beyond their sphere and planted a flag in a different state.

The implications of cable television was a contentious topic, and members intensely debated ways to combat the medium's growth. Several years earlier, in 1979, Mike LeBell warned promoters at the annual convention that they would "have to learn to live with the appearances of outside shows on cable in the various towns in which they promoted," according to the meeting minutes. Barnett added a blunt statement: "Cable cannot be stopped."

Like GCW, there was another man who was intent on integrating the use of cable television to secure exposure in other territories. Vincent Kennedy McMahon incorporated Titan Sports, Inc. on February 21, 1980. Two years later, he purchased the Capitol Wrestling Corporation, the firm behind the World Wrestling Federation. From New Japan to the UWA in Mexico, the WWF's tentacles were connected to all points of the wrestling map, and McMahon was driven to expand. What concerned NWA members the most was that any previously set and respected boundaries meant very little to him.

McMahon bought into the southern California office governed by LeBell, opening the door to live exhibitions in Los Angeles and San Diego with WWF talent. In an attempt to gain control of the Pacific Northwest, Vince offered to buy out Don Owen, but was repelled. It was evident that McMahon was encroaching on the once-sacred territories of the NWA. Barnett, who was booking NWA champions Flair and Race in 1983, had worked with McMahon Sr. in the past, and had a reason to trek to Allentown for a WWF TV taping to discuss their plans for the future.

Barnett, still fuming about being expelled as GCW President, sold out of Atlanta, conspired with the WWF to damage the promotion's scheme in Ohio. It was proof positive that there was some sort of pact between the McMahons and Barnett, but no one knew the extent of it. At the convention in August 1983, both McMahon and Barnett left the NWA, tearing a hole in the institution. Barnett's leadership was key to keeping the Alliance stable. With him now giving his knowledge to the enemy, the NWA was in danger of losing more ground.

The controversial takeover continued. Titan next acquired Calgary from Stu Hart, signifying the end of the line for another ranking NWA member. McMahon looked to fight GCW in Ohio, and was even examining the possibilities of a complete acquisition of the Georgia company. Barnett acted as a conduit between Titan and shareholders Jim Oates, Frances Jones, and the Briscos. McMahon grabbed a majority stake in Atlanta beginning on April 9, 1984, and three months later, "Black Saturday" occurred when the WWF's product commandeered GCW 's timeslot on WTBS, the real prize of the investment.

Multimillionaire Ted Turner, owner of WTBS, was aware of the revenue brought in by wrestling, and felt there was a perfect harmony between his station and GCW. He was irritated that McMahon was using his outlet to transmit out-of-state wrestling that had absolutely no regional feel. He wanted what the grappling fans were used to seeing, and distributed a timeslot to Ralph Freed, Fred Ward, and Ole Anderson, and to Watts's Mid-South promotion. Watts's Sunday show, hosted by

Jim Ross, became the most-watched wrestling broadcast on the station.

Jim Crockett, from inside the Alliance, was also looking at potential territorial takeovers, but his maneuvering was seen as a lot less aggressive than McMahon's. Watching the wrestling scene from his Charlotte office, he sought to purchase open markets or those fading promotions with "for sale" signs on them. Wrestling's scope was diminishing, one domain at a time, and more than a dozen companies allied with the NWA in 1979 were bust by 1983.

Crockett's strategies were varied. On November 24, 1983, he promoted the inaugural Starrcade in Greensboro with closed-circuit footage sent to parts of the southeastern U.S., the Caribbean, and New Zealand. In the main event, Flair regained the world title from Race in a cage match before a sellout crowd of 15,447. With Rhodes helping on the creative side, Crockett was having astonishing success, unparalleled for an NWA member. The promotion had the capacity and wrestlers to run every day of the week in a set town, plus spot shows. As promoters crumbled around him, his enterprises thrived, and a protracted war with Titan was inevitable.

Bockwinkel was still headlining as AWA champion in Minnesota, and it was suspected that budding fan favorite Terrence Gene Bollea, known in the ring as Hulk Hogan, was going to soon grab the title. Hogan had been featured in the 1982 film *Rocky III*, and had momentum in his favor. The idea was teased in several controversial bouts with Bockwinkel, but the switch never materialized. More or a risk-taker than Gagne, McMahon saw the promise of Hogan, and tempted him to New York. His departure was a crushing blow to the AWA.

At a St. Louis television taping on December 27, 1983, Hogan returned to the WWF. He wasn't paired with a loud-mouthed manager, nor was he trying to mimic "Thunderlips," his movie character. Hogan was an extraordinary hero, and on January 23, 1984, he defeated The Iron Sheik (Khosrow Vaziri) in 5:40 for the WWF title at Madison Square Garden. Hulk was barely established on TV when he was given the belt, but McMahon was confident his newcomer would lead the promotion to the next level. Important additional hirings were Paul Orndroff, Roddy Piper, Gene Okerlund, Barry Windham, Mike Rotundo, Junkyard Dog, and Sergeant Slaughter.

In 1982, Larry Matysik severed his bonds to the St. Louis office and formed a group independent of the NWA. Getting wrestlers from the ICW (Poffo), SCW, (Blanchard) and later the WWF, Matysik debuted in opposition to the NWA office on June 18, 1983. Race sold out in early 1986 and made his debut for the WWF, which was operating at the Kiel more than ten times a year, in May. A combination of Crockett, central states and AWA wrestlers worked the city until November 1985, when McMahon took over.

Pro Wrestling USA was the product of an early 1984 meeting at the O'Hare Hilton in Chicago. Chicago White Sox co-owner Edward Einhorn, who was known for his television wisdom and had promoted the short-lived IWA in 1975, was a key ingredient at the conference. Others participating in the roundtable discussion were Jerry Jarrett, Gagne, Crockett, Watts, Graham, Geigel, Ole Anderson, and Gary Juster. It was the largest assembly of promoters outside an NWA conventions in years, and had been called to try to determine a way to stop the barnstorming of Titan Sports. Pleas to McMahon's father had fallen on deaf ears, and the WWF was gaining steam, much to the fury of attending promoters.

Fans were thrilled with the prospects of the coalition, but insiders were left asking themselves how long the egomaniacs could go at it together before they fizzled out? McMahon, while he had his own problems, surrounded himself with people he could rely on. The promoters in Pro Wrestling USA were paranoid, and essentially, vulnerable, left to wondering whether the next theatre of war would be in their backyard.

Einhorn and his cohorts had television on channel 11 (WPIX) in New York City, and hyped a Meadowlands show on February 24, 1985. That night, the kingpins of both the NWA, Flair, and the AWA, Rick Martel, defended their championships, and an estimated 18,000 fans paid in excess of $150,000 to see the rare spectacle. The Pro Wrestling USA consortium sank shortly thereafter, weighed down by self-interest.

The sons of Jack Adkisson — David, Kevin, Kerry, and Mike — were wrestlers by 1983, and the World Class territory flourished based on their popularity. Dallas saw a multitude of great title matches and hot feuds. But the one thing Dallas hadn't seen was a homegrown world heavyweight champion. Adkisson, like Dory Funk Sr., had lobbied for recognition of his sons from the minute they were introduced at the 1979 convention. David's shocking death in February 1984 gave the NWA reason to endorse a term by a member of the Adkisson family as world champion.

On May 6, 1984, Kerry ("Von Erich") beat Flair at Texas Stadium, but the Nature Boy won back the strap in Yokosuka City 18 days later. Flair was representing the remaining bookers of the NWA, but abided by the directives issued by Crockett. Crockett released him for dates in all affiliated jurisdictions, and Flair shined with a distinctly different style from that of WWF champion Hogan.

Before Von Erich captured the title, Flair and Race exchanged the belt in New Zealand and Singapore over a two-day period in March 1984 (March 21 and March 23). Their actions further proved that the title could be manipulated. The booking of Flair in disqualification or countout losses demeaned the championship, and would never have been approved during Muchnick's tenure. Angles that included random interferences in title matches became the norm, and wrestling fans grew weary of main event finishes without a clear-cut pinfall. The system that had protected wrestling's credibility was repealed by the whims of bookers devising dramatized performances better left to actors. Soon, the cartoon antics of Titan Sports were angering anyone familiar with the more randomly colorful and scientific aspects of pro wrestling.

A wave of publicity was crashing around the WWF as a consequence of Captain Lou Albano's portrayal of Cyndi Lauper's father in the video for "Girls Just Want to Have Fun." The video was a staple on MTV, a cable channel geared towards a valuable demographic. Wanting to milk it for everything it was worth, McMahon pushed ahead with the "Rock and Wrestling Connection," which produced two MTV specials earning record ratings for the channel. WWF wrestling was becoming mainstream, and the trend was growing.

Championship Wrestling from Florida was in trouble after years of supplying some of the country's best grappling, and in the midst of a depression, Eddie Graham committed suicide on January 21, 1985. Seven months later, the WWF toured the state with Hogan on top, and sold out in Miami and Tampa. In San Francisco, McMahon obtained television on KTZO (channel 20) and outdrew the AWA at the Cow Palace with cards from the Coliseum Arena.

Ole Anderson ran in opposition to the WWF in Atlanta until McMahon abandoned the city and dumped the Saturday WTBS timeslot off to Crockett for a purported $1 million during the first quarter of 1985. Titan faced immense financial risk in their haste to take over the wrestling landscape, and all of McMahon's eggs were in one basket with WrestleMania at the Garden in New York on March 31, 1985.

Crockett's Starrcade had laid down the gauntlet, but McMahon was going to trump it. He arranged 200 closed-circuit television locations, celebrity cameos, and invested about $900,000. The event captivated the wrestling world, and with his business out on a limb, McMahon fought negative press to bring WrestleMania to the public. The Garden was packed to the rafters, and even some of his closed-circuit houses had double the typical attendance of his competitors. McMahon's gamble paid off and WrestleMania's festivities are still an annual highlight for aficionados today.

The NWA lost mainstay Jack Adkisson, a member since 1967, when he withdrew World Class from the syndicate on February 18, 1986. His American title evolved into a "world" championship, and, besides jousting with the WWF in Dallas, he attempted to spread to other states. All Japan added its name to the exodus, separating from the NWA after an affiliation of 13 years.

Rights to Florida were sold to the Crocketts in February 1987 by the Graham family, Duke Keomuka, and Hiro Matsuda. On May 1, 1987, Crockett acquired Bill Watts's Mid-South Sports, Inc. (Universal Wrestling Federation). Crockett Promotions, easily the grandest NWA booking office in years, now had agencies in Atlanta, Dallas, and Tampa. With an average of 21 events a week staged by Crockett into countless former Alliance strongholds, his company appeared sturdy enough to battle the WWF.

By 1987, there were fewer than ten active territories bound to the NWA. Most casual fans were unaware that part of the Alliance's power during its glory days was its overall geographical control and the ability of a member to create shows from a regional bureau. A single company trying to stabilize an entire country, where there once were practically 40 individual offices, was a daunting and unrealistic task. Crockett didn't own the National Wrestling Alliance, but had all remaining authority, and dictated where the cherished championship went. Many fans believed that the NWA was an actual promotion administered by Crockett rather than what it really was, a collaborative union of promoters.

The most fundamental components of the NWA were vanishing during the consolidation, almost, in fact, serving McMahon's interests. The disappearance of sectional bookers and configured circuits stretching to towns large and small, under the auspices of the Alliance, left chunks of territories without big-time wrestling. Basically, the organization was minus its unique local presence.

Forty-two percent of the television audience got WTBS and their three wrestling telecasts, and the station claimed a viewership of over 1.5 million people every Saturday night. They also had syndicated shows that were available in 62 markets on 88 stations before the purchase of Mid-South Sports, which gave them an extra 98 stations (eventually more than 220 outlets). With 105 wrestlers on the payroll, Crockett envisioned producing 1,000 shows annually, and planned to move his headquarters to Dallas.

Turner made the environment for Crockett suitable for advancement in all areas of production at WTBS. Crockett followed McMahon into the next frontier of pay-per-view, presenting Starrcade from Chicago on Thanksgiving, November 26, 1987. Not to be outdone, McMahon scheduled the inaugural Survivor Series that same night, using his veteran status as a promoter of pay-per-views to fight the ambitions of Crockett. Starrcade, beginning at 5:00 p.m. (EST), wasn't even offered by most cable systems because of McMahon's established position.

The Survivor Series at the Richfield Coliseum in Ohio, earned a seven share of the pay-per-view audience, and Starrcade achieved a little more than a three. The WWF had superior television production, colorful characters, kid-friendly antics, and imaginative advertising, giving them a distinct edge over their adversaries.

Diehard wrestling fans were attracted to the NWA for Flair, Ricky Steamboat, the Road Warriors, Barry Windham, Sting, and a style that was deemed more old school. The routines of WWF stars and the general theatrics steered many devotees to Crockett's promotion, and the criticism by smart marks was just beginning. That fact didn't matter, as a greater percentage of the money being spent on wrestling was by families who were stimulated by the "Hulking" up of Hogan, the mischief of the Honky Tonk Man, and the animal acts of Koko B. Ware and Jake "The Snake" Roberts.

Hostilities between Crockett and McMahon generated two more head-to-head shows. The first occurred on January 24, 1988, with the NWA staging a pay-per-view at the Nassau Coliseum and the WWF holding their "Royal Rumble," broadcast live on the USA Network. On March 27, 1988, in opposition with the WWF's WrestleMania from Atlantic City, Crockett debuted Clash of the Champions on WTBS. The cable spectacular got good ratings with classic matches, but the web being spun by Crockett was unmanageable, and significant cuts in staff were necessary. More than 30 wrestlers were let go, with other layoffs anticipated. Several months after the Clash, representatives of the wrestling corporation were negotiating with the Turner Broadcasting System, and the sale of Crockett Promotions was imminent.

Rumors of the Crockett-Turner negotiations circulated in newspapers, but there were early denials. The talks went on for seven months, and Jim Crockett was quoted as saying, "We're real close to a deal," in the September 27, 1988, edition of the *Charlotte Observer*. In preparations to handle the transfer of resources, the Universal Wrestling Corporation was incorporated on October 11, 1988, by Turner Broadcasting and the Crockett family. The sale was made official on November 2, and Turner obtained all active assets from the Charlotte company for a reported $9 million. David and Jackie Crockett got positions with the new federation, and Jim was retained as a consultant and advisor with a five-year no-compete clause in the contract.

The original concept of the Alliance had been reduced to the mindset of a lone outfit, and beginning in November 1988, was a part of the TBS conglomerate. Employing a label included in the sale, Turner and his officers named their brand World Championship Wrestling, and preserved the front that they stood united with the legacy of Alliance. The NWA gave WCW credibility, and it wasn't until late 1990 that the letters "NWA" were totally phased out of telecasts.

On December 16, 1990, Starrcade was held at the illustrious Kiel Auditorium, where the Alliance championship had changed hands five times (the most for a single location), and featured a special Pat O'Connor Memorial Tag Team

Tournament, a guest refereeing spot for Dick the Bruiser, and promos by Sam Muchnick. The show celebrated decades of wrestling in St. Louis, and the institution Muchnick had broken his back protecting, the National Wrestling Alliance. When the program was over, wcw commentators hadn't mentioned the nwa once, instead craftily inserting the letters and logo of wcw.

Gary Juster, a versed promoter and key player in the expansion of Crockett's empire, was wcw's liaison in the nwa. A member of the Alliance since 1984, Juster had presented shows in Baltimore, Detroit, and other cities for the coalition, and learned a great deal from his mentor, Jim Barnett. He facilitated communication, which was argumentative at times, between the last remaining members and wcw. While wcw was the nwa's most important affiliate, there was a promoter involved with the Alliance in 1991 that is frequently overlooked given his accomplishments in wrestling. Don Owen survived the demise of his colleagues during the 1980s, and brushed off the idea of selling to Titan.

Wrestling in the Pacific Northwest ran hot and cold under Owen's leadership, and his booking office sparked many notable careers. Fans counted on weekly television on kptv, and events at the Armory or Sports Center in Portland, and wrestlers could expect a fair shake from the thoughtful tycoon during their tour of the territory. When Owen tumbled in May 1992, the nwa lost the last of the old guard.

Four years of Crockett at helm of the nwa came to an end in 1991 with the election of wcw's executive vice president in charge of wrestling operations, James Herd. Herd, born on August 13, 1932, formerly acted as the general manager of kplr-tv, a vice president of the St. Louis Blues, and executive vice president of Middleton Enterprises, Inc., owners of the 68 Pizza Hut restaurants in the St. Louis area. In gatherings of the 1-2-3 Club, Herd hobnobbed with sports luminaries, and was a personal friend of Sam Muchnick. After the Turner-Crockett transaction was finalized, Herd signed on and moved to Atlanta.

With the awa defunct, wcw and the wwf were acknowledged as the "Big Two." wcw was making one-fifth of the annual profits of its counterpart, and Herd knew that adjustments needed to be made to alter their direction. Those consisted of everything from television production, pay-per-view strategies, gimmick development, target audience, and overall philosophy. To make the promotion more marketable to families, the style of wrestling had to be reformed, and that was going to further aggravate a lot of people. Not only had the nwa as a whole seemingly shrunk into a solitary promotion, but that company was now looking to the wwf for ideas.

Herd wanted to reach children and teenagers, and concluded that newly fashioned lines of trademarked toys, video games, and advertising would be the way to get the job done. He asked Turner if they could use famous monikers from the expansive TBS movie vault for wrestling characters, and when Oz (Kevin Nash) debuted in St. Petersburg at SuperBrawl on May 19, 1991, Jack Pfefer, the legendary gimmick master, turned over in his grave.

Changing the image of WCW was similar to moving an elephant, and it would have taken Herd forever to turn the promotion around with the plan he was using. Other ideas from his often stormy regime were the Ding Dongs, a RoboCop angle, the Black Scorpion, trying to coax Minnesota Twins slugger Kent Hrbek into the sport, and authorizing the use of sophisticated entrances that integrated fireworks and pyrotechnics.

On March 21, 1991, in Tokyo, Tatsumi Fujinami, the IWGP world champion for NWA member Seiji Sakaguchi, Antonio Inoki and New Japan Pro Wrestling, beat Ric Flair in a controversial match at the Tokyo Dome. During the match, referee Bill Alfonso was knocked out, and Fujinami scored a pinfall with alternate official Masao Hattori counting the three. Fujinami won the match and was given the NWA title in name only. Flair kept possession of the famed gold belt, emblematic of the NWA championship since February 1986, because, ironically, it was owned by WCW. In a rematch at SuperBrawl in St. Petersburg, Flair prevailed over Fujinami for his ninth NWA title, a record-breaking feat.

In what was cited as a disagreement over creative differences, Flair was fired by WCW and Herd on July 1, 1991, leaving WCW without a heavyweight champion going into their Great American Bash pay-per-view. The Alliance still recognized Flair, and although Ric expected his $25,000 belt deposit back upon termination, the money was misplaced somewhere between the treasury office of Barnett and the bank accounts of Crockett Promotions and Turner Broadcasting.

The gold strap was featured on WWF television in August, followed by Flair's reemergence. On September 8, the Alliance had no choice but to strip Ric of the championship, and a check was received by the Nature Boy postmarked from Atlanta at some point later on. Herd resigned from WCW on January 8, 1992. He rejoined his associate George Middleton in the growth of the Archview Riverboat Casino, and produced *Know It Alls*, a television game show.

New Japan's Sakaguchi was elected to lead the NWA in 1992 and it was decided that the selection of an NWA champion was a priority. A tournament was held in Japan in August 1992, ending with Masahiro Chono conquering Rick Rude for the gold belt, which, by that time, had been returned to WCW by Flair. IWGP champion Keiji Mutoh defeated Chono for the NWA title on January 4, 1993, before 63,500 fans, the largest crowd ever to see the belt change hands, at the Tokyo Dome.

Barry Windham finally got the NWA belt at SuperBrawl on February 21, 1993, and was champion until July 18, 1993, when Flair won his tenth title. The NWA embraced the national publicity, and the prospects of getting a wrestler of repute from either WCW or New Japan to an independent arena was incredibly alluring. The syndicate added Philadelphia's Tod Gordon and Dennis Coralluzzo of South Jersey to its rolls in 1992 and '93.

Coralluzzo was the dean of NWA Championship Wrestling America, promoting at the Woodbury Armory. He first entered the trade in the mid-1980s as an employee of Larry Sharpe's Monster Factory wrestling school outside Philadelphia. Known for his weakness for iced teas, Coralluzzo shared wrestlers with many indie promotions, including Gordon, whose Eastern Championship Wrestling had attracted attention with Sabu, Terry Funk, and Shane Douglas.

The WCW-NWA accord tread shaky ground when Eric Bischoff, a newcomer to the ever-shuffling WCW management, wanted Rude to win the NWA title on September 19, 1993 at Fall Brawl. The Alliance Board of Directors was unhappy with the lack of support their members were getting from Atlanta, and refused to sanction the switch. A compromise couldn't be reached, and with Juster's membership expiring on September 1, the two entities went their own ways. Flair was subsequently stripped of recognition by the NWA.

On September 13, 1993, Charles E. Lyons of the Charlotte firm Sellers, Hinshaw, Ayers, Dortch & Lyons, P.A., on behalf of the National Wrestling Alliance, filed suit in U.S. District Court, Western District of North Carolina against World Championship Wrestling Inc. *(National Wrestling Alliance v. World Championship Wrestling 3:93-cv-00304).* The NWA charged trademark infringement and supplied signed affidavits from Crockett, Coralluzzo, and attorney Robert K. Trobich seeking to restrain WCW from exploiting their designation on their Fall Brawl telecast.

WCW, in turn, furnished a 1992 contract reportedly endorsed by NWA president Sakaguchi and WCW executive vice president Bill Watts that had transferred full rights to the gold championship belt to the latter organization. U.S. District Judge Richard Voorhees examined the evidence and ruled the contract legitimate, permitting the Flair-Rude contest to go ahead as planned, with the victor walking off with the famed strap. However, WCW was prevented from "making any explicit affirmative representations within the actual telecast of the match, as defined or within any future promotions of the match within defendants reasonable control, to the effect that the match is sponsored or sanctioned by the plaintiff."

A $25,000 security deposit being held by the Alliance was returned to WCW, and the case was voluntarily dismissed on September 16. Three nights later in Houston,

Rude pinned Flair for the gold belt, a championship that evolved into the "international world heavyweight" title, and wcw upheld its word by not mentioning the letters "nwa" during the Fall Brawl event. The Alliance lost its most visible member, but affiliates went forward. Rather than voting for a president at the 1993 convention, a three-man committee was formed of Coralluzzo, Crockett and Steve Rickard.

Crockett launched the short-lived World Wrestling Network, and held a television taping at the Manhattan Center in New York City on February 28, 1994. He traded grapplers with Paul Heyman and Gordon with the hopes that interest would be kindled, but there was a lackluster response. The bonds between Coralluzzo and friends Jerry Lawler and Jim Cornette, promoters of the uswa and smw respectively, helped their respective aspirations. Lawler and Cornette also had relations with the wwf.

Coralluzzo and Gordon's ecw worked to rejuvenate the Alliance with a world title tournament on August 27, 1994 at the renowned ecw Arena in South Philadelphia. The eight-man tournament was won by Shane Douglas with everyone observing the script. After the match, Douglas grabbed the house microphone, and from the ring, denounced the nwa. He proceeded to throw the belt (a duplicate of the 1973–86 version) to the mat, and declare himself champion of Extreme Championship Wrestling. Coralluzzo thought the mad rant was just furthering the angle, but quickly realized the Alliance was being double-crossed. The nwa was embarrassed to its core.

The betrayal was harsh, but Coralluzzo wouldn't surrender. He was determined to breathe air back into the National Wrestling Alliance with an esteemed titleholder. Dennis went to a man he could trust, Cornette, and staged a second tournament with help from Smoky Mountain Wrestling. On November 19, 1994, at Cherry Hill's National Guard Armory in New Jersey, Chris Candido beat Tracey Smothers in a ten-wrestler tournament for the vacant title. Candido took his belt home.

In the aftermath of the wwn fiasco, Crockett started an nwa franchise in Dallas. By the end of 1994, the Alliance had six members. One of the newest territories in the fold was Florida, run by Howard Brody, a relative novice to wrestling promotions. Brody was born on June 10, 1960, in Brooklyn, and educated at the University of Florida. On October 27, 1989, he incorporated Ladies Major League Wrestling, Inc. with several investors, and promoted the ill-fated Wild Women of Wrestling. He went into business with Hiro Matsuda and revived the Tampa office (Major League Wrestling), receiving admittance into the nwa in 1994.

Crockett failed to pay his dues and was evicted from the Alliance in January

1995. Brody replaced him on the committee directing the future of the NWA, and was elected president in 1996. The combination of Brody, Coralluzzo, and Trobich shifted the three registered trademarks of the NWA from Iowa to a business established in Trobich's hometown, Charlotte, effectively plugging a lifeline into the federation and safeguarding the brand name. Pro Wrestling Organization, LLC was incorporated on January 28, 1998, and would serve as the company behind the Alliance until it was administratively dissolved in April 2005.

The NWA gained ground when world-class amateur wrestler Dan Severn accepted a role as heavyweight titleholder, going over Candido at Peel's Palace, an arena in Erlanger, Kentucky on February 24, 1995. On April 7, Severn was anointed champion of the Ultimate Fighting Championship competition, and wore his NWA belt proudly to the octagon. Severn's credibility as a freestyle and Greco-Roman wrestler gave the Alliance a reputable champion along the lines of Hutton and Brisco, and although the handful of Alliance members were rarely holding shows, Dan turned heads. People were talking about the NWA.

In May 1995, Crockett's promotion in Dallas suspended operations. Reelected president of the NWA seven times, Jim left wrestling for good. He managed the White Mountain Creamery at Sniper Plaza in Dallas, a celebrated ice cream shop, and ran a successful auto dealership. Today, Crockett sells real estate in the Dallas area with his wife Myra Kay Boyle, and has three children, James Allen III, Austin, and Chandler. A family business was alluded to on his official website, www.jim-crockett.com, but promoting pro wrestling, a trade the Crockett family had been involved in for 60 years, was not mentioned.

Severn carried the championship proudly for 1,479 days, the third-longest world title reign in Alliance history. Efforts by the WWF to create a buzz in their war with WCW spawned a provocative treaty with the NWA, mediated by Jim Cornette. During a WWF television taping for *Raw* on December 30, 1997, in New Haven, NWA president Brody and vice president Coralluzzo were in attendance to award the North American title to the winner of a match between Barry Windham and Jeff Jarrett. Getting assistance from Cornette's tennis racket, Jarrett won the match and the title. The NWA incursion into the WWF included appearances by Severn, who was booked into angles with Owen Hart and Ken Shamrock; the Rock and Roll Express, an updated edition of the Midnight Express; and referee Tommy Young.

The combination of TV exposure, a convincing champion, and resolute leadership invigorated the NWA in 1998. The year before, the Alliance had added only one territory, Dallas-Fort Worth, with the admission of Ken Taylor, but with the NWA name publicized on WWF TV, indie promoters from across the country were ready to enroll. Thirteen new promoters enlisted before the end of the year, among them Bill Behrens and Antonio Inoki. The annual convention was held in conjunction with the 50th anniversary celebration of the NWA in Cherry Hill, New Jersey, October 23–25, 1998, and fans mingled with Lou Thesz, Dory Funk Jr., Killer Kowalski, Harley Race, and Danny Hodge.

The NWA board of directors increased from five to seven people, led by president Brody, vice president Behrens, Rickard, Coralluzzo, Victor Quinones, and newcomers Victoria Van Ellen and Ernie Todd. Recognizing that they had to play up their extraordinary tradition, the crew contributed to the formation of a central website, and carefully plotted ways to prolong the expansion. The shadow cast by the "Big Two" remained impressive, but the Alliance was out of the gutter and making progress.

In 1999, the NWA expanded to 24 members worldwide. Severn dropped the title to Inoki's UFO star and Olympic silver medallist (Judo) Naoya Ogawa on March 14, 1999, at the Yokohama Arena. Ogawa beat Severn by submission in 7:56 with Dory Funk Jr. acting as the referee. Andre Baker's NWA-UK Hammerlock was catapulted into the headlines when Gary Steele triumphed in a three-way bout over Ogawa and Brian Anthony for the NWA title at the 51st annual event in Charlotte on September 25, 1999. A week later at a high school in Thomaston, Connecticut, Ogawa regained the belt on a show presented by NWA New England (Ellen Magliaro).

The political structure in 2000 mirrored that of 1950 in some ways, with the larger, more-profitable territories having the most influence. Of course, there were dues-paying members in 2000 that were not running any shows at all, so any operations were a plus. The roster had additions and withdrawals, most notably Coralluzzo's exit in December 1999, and the NWA title passed through the hands of Mike Rapada, Sabu, and Steve Corino. Security concerns after the terrorist attacks of September 11, 2001, and the continued fear of anthrax attacks trimmed plans for the 53rd anniversary show on October 13. Brody moved the show from the legendary Fort Homer Hesterly Armory in Tampa to the Florida Wrestleplex in St. Petersburg, with a capacity of only 300.

Brody also discussed things with Zero-One owner Shinya Hashimoto of Japan, who, three days before the card, decided that it wasn't safe to make the journey. He was persuaded to change his mind, and on October 13, Shinya defeated Corino for the NWA title. At the convention, Brody left the presidency, capping his fifth term, and was replaced by James Miller.

In the months that followed, Brody left the NWA, frustrated with the organization's management and inspired to start a new venture. He worked with Dusty Rhodes's Turnbuckle Championship Wrestling, and helped the American Dream pen his autobiography. Steve Rickard, who teamed with Brody and Coralluzzo to keep the Alliance alive during the 1990s, also left, going into semi-retirement. On July 30, 2001, Coralluzzo died at the age of 48.

NWA president Miller and the board of directors allowed J Sports & Entertainment, Inc. to use the trademarked name "National Wrestling Alliance" for their promotion, Total Nonstop Action. NWA-TNA, WWW.NWATNA.com, was announced by chief executive officer Jerry Jarrett on May 9, 2002, after a deal with IN DEMAND, LLC, was made to promote weekly pay-per-view events on Wednesday nights. In a press release, Jarrett said, "We're thrilled to be using the NWA name for our program. The National Wrestling Alliance has a long and prestigious history, and was at one time the dominant name in the professional wrestling industry. We believe it's important for our company to be affiliated with a name that fans will recognize and we believe the NWA name is a familiar one to most fans of professional wrestling."

Miller said, "This is a win-win for everybody involved. I'm very excited about the prospects of working with J Sports & Entertainment to make NWA: Total Nonstop Action a tremendous success. The pay-per-view broadcasts will expose the NWA to fans in a way that hasn't been possible before, and the opportunities for our member organizations will be better than ever."

Using TNA as an outlet to spread the gospel of the Alliance, the board approved the use of the NWA world heavyweight and the NWA world tag team titles. Dan Severn, in the midst of his second spell as NWA world champion, was stripped of the belt on May 29, 2002 because he wasn't able to participate in TNA's initial pay-per-view in Huntsville because of a prior commitment. On June 19, 2002, TNA debuted with Rick Steamboat, Harley Race, Dory Funk Jr., Bob Armstrong, and Jackie Fargo in attendance as guests. In the main event, Ken Shamrock pinned Malice after a belly-to-belly suplex in the finals of a 20-man gauntlet battle royal, and captured the vacant NWA title.

TNA was a mix of old-style wrestling, inventive angles, and celebrity interaction, and offered fans an alternative to WWE. The NWA benefited from the rapport with the Jarretts, and promoters received occasional visits by the heavyweight champion. The X-Division was conceived, and offered a remarkable venue for some of the most innovative performers in the business. Although the class was generally thought of as being for high-flying non-heavyweights, TNA has booked the division for grapplers of all sizes, and fans have witnessed stunning displays of athleticism. Many formerly unknown wrestlers were presented to the masses for the first time, and TNA demonstrated that not every wrestler had to be 6'5'' to generate heat.

In late October 2002, Panda Energy International, Inc., a leading environmentally friendly energy company based in Dallas, bought a three-fourths stake in NWA-TNA, and with J Sports & Entertainment, fashioned TNA Entertainment, LLC, a corporation holding 60-plus wrestling-related trademarks. The daughter of Panda Energy owners Robert and Janice Carter, Dixie, became the president of TNA. Coordinating with the Jarretts, bookers were hired, and novel tactics were pondered.

In what could be viewed as one entity needing the other more, TNA altered their promotion name from NWA-TNA to just TNA, and their website to www.tnawrestling.com. Meetings between the management of TNA Entertainment and the NWA board of directors passionately discussed their relationship and whether common ground could be reached.

With the legacy of the Alliance behind it, TNA had a degree of credibility officials wanted to maintain, but it was more important to the often-wavering promoters of the NWA to keep their brand in the public's eye. So much so that the board agreed to a ten-year accord that gave TNA licensing rights to the trademarks, and complete control of the NWA world heavyweight and tag team titles. TNA would ordain titleholders and dispense dates on their champion to Alliance promoters when available.

In 2005, TNA Entertainment continued to charge forward with syndication on Fox Sports and, in July, signed off on a pact with cable network Spike-TV for a one-hour telecast.

Robert Trobich resigned as legal council for the NWA in November 2004, but rejoined the Alliance at the 2005 convention in Nashville. Designated "executive director," Trobich took over a job handled by the NWA president, and labored with the board of directors to shape the union. With the intentions of helping the NWA of 2005 become more functional by applying a corporate imprint and modernizing to fit the times, the board of directors dropped the officer positions and its once crucial bylaws in favor of an "operating agreement."

For 57 years, the NWA had lived and breathed by its written bylaws. Sam Muchnick spent years etching the foundations of the Alliance in stone, adding, amending, and dissolving the rules all members complied with. The controversial regulations had affected the livelihoods of promoters and wrestlers, and drawn the attention of the U.S. Department of Justice. The elimination of their bylaws set a new precedent that the board of directors hope will better fit the marketplace and ensure the Alliance's future.

ACKNOWLEDGMENTS

In preparing this book, I came into contact with many gracious individuals — from New Zealand to small-town Missouri. Along the way, the assistance I received allowed me to better understand professional wrestling and the deep history of the National Wrestling Alliance. For their part in this project, I would like to thank the following people and institutions:

Penny Banner, Joan Benner, the Broward County Main Library (Fort Lauderdale, Florida), Jane Byrnes and both the Byrnes and Riley Families, the Chicago Historical Society, Frank Cody, Amy Coleman (Hocken Collections; University of Otago, Dunedin, New Zealand), Phil Conger (Bethany Republican-Clipper, Bethany, Missouri), the Denver Main Public Library, Victoria Doyle, Tom Ellis, Dory Funk Jr., Bob Geigel, Celeste Haines, the Harrison County Genealogical Society (Bethany, Missouri), Dave Levin and family, Wayne Lewis, Richard Longson, Eve Manoogian, Lucy Marsden (Massey University, New Zealand), the Missouri State Historical Society (Columbia, Missouri), Sid Munn, Mary Soumas Nelson, Erin O'Connor Diven and Robyn O'Connor Walker, Russell Owen, Kevin Pesek, Margaret Posehn, Timothy Rives (National Archives; Central Plain Region), Fred Romanski (National Archives; College Park), John Rohde and the Rohde Family, Sue Pearson (Waterloo Public Library, Waterloo, Iowa), Mrs. Dorothy Sauder, Russ L. Smith, Dick Steinborn, Amy Surak (Manhattan College Archives), Lou Thesz, Bill and Nick Tragos, Maurice and Paul Vachon, and Geneva Wiskemann.

The exceptional researchers I've worked with over the years:

Steve Yohe, J. Michael Kenyon, Don Luce, Ross Schneider, George Lentz, Jim Melby, Tom Burke, Fred Hornby, and Daniel Chernau.

And a very special thanks to:

Michael Holmes and everyone at ECW Press, Jim Cypher, Holly Gilzenberg, Susan Kohler Ehr and Betty Kohler Hopkinson, Dorothy Mondt Baldwin, Richard Baumann and Billy E. Sandow, Paul George, Tasha Lang, Richard Muchnick, Kathy Muchnick Schneider, Michael S. Karbo, Richard Brown, Gail Palmer, Al Ney, Peggy A. Ford (Research Coordinator, Division of Museums, Greeley, Colorado), George Rugg (curator, Pfefer Collection, University of Notre Dame), and, of course, Amy Miller of the Broward County Library System, whose ability to obtain resources from all corners of the world made this book possible.

The Hornbakers — Tim, Barbara and Melissa, Virginia Hall, Jodi Babaganov, and John and Christine Hopkins.

For more nformation on the history of professional wrestling, questions, or comments, go to www.legacyofwrestling.com

ABOUT THE PHOTOS

Page 1
Wrestling magnate Paul Bowser of Boston (right) created many international superstars including ex-pro football star Gus Sonnenberg (left).

Page 13
Orville Brown (left), one of the NWA founders and first world champion, presents the Central States title to Lenny Montana, known to movie-buffs as mob enforcer Luca Brasi (*The Godfather*), in 1953.

Page 30
A youthful Lou Thesz wears the new National Wrestling Association heavyweight belt in 1939.

Page 46
Possessing great leadership qualities, Sam Muchnick helped the NWA endure and evolve into a worldwide conglomerate with almost unheralded power.

Page 61
Ed "Strangler" Lewis, in his army garb during World War I, reviews a document held by his vociferous manager Billy Sandow (at left).

Page 77
From the streets of Chicago, Fred Kohler rose up to dominate the Windy City's wrestling landscape and ultimately run a multi-million dollar empire.

Page 94
Toots Mondt (left) of Greeley, Colorado matches grips with his younger brother Frank while their nephews look on, circa 1930.

Page 109
The famed journeyman Michele Leone before he adopted the "Baron" gimmick in 1949.

Page 120
Congressman Melvin Price was a Washington powerbroker and also Sam Muchnick's best friend. He may have helped the NWA survive the Government's wrath in 1956.

Page 143
Longtime fan favorite Sonny Myers proudly displays his newly won Texas Heavyweight Title.

Page 160
From left to right: NWA founder Pinkie George, his son Paul, former boxing great Jack Dempsey, and Pinkie's brother Andy.

Page 174
The heads of Capitol Wrestling gather with their wives to celebrate another year of remarkable success Left (front to back) — Alda Mondt, Vincent J. McMahon, Juanita McMahon; Right (front to back) — Lillian Gilzenberg, Willie Gilzenberg, Toots Mondt.

Page 196
New Zealander Pat O'Connor wore the prized NWA strap from 1959 to 1961, and returned a sense of unity to the crumbling organization.

Page 220
Amateur and professional wrestling great Verne Gagne was a class act and perennial champion.

Page 250
Promoter Jack Pfefer (middle) was as shrewd as they came, and here presided over a contract signing between Sandor Szabo (left) and Dick Shikat (right) as a New York sports editor looks on, circa 1931.

Page 272
Taking a moment away from their rigorous negotiations, the delegates of the 1961 NWA convention in Toronto gather for a photo.

Page 323
Ten-time NWA World Champion "Nature Boy" Ric Flair struts to the ring under police protection.

Page 346
TNA standout Samoa Joe displays his awesome power and is regarded as a budding superstar heading toward legendary status.

PHOTO CREDITS

PHOTO SECTION

Toots Mondt; William Muldoon, Jack Curley, Jim McMillian, Jim Londos and others; Tom Packs, The Stechers, Jim Londos, Joe Coffey; Jim Londos; John Pesek; The Duseks; Al Haft; Billy Wolfe; Mildred Burke; Sam Muchnick and Ray Steele; Bill Longson; Buddy Rogers and Tom Packs; Roy Dunn; Ede Virag; Ed McLemore and Lillian Ellison; Ed "Strangler" Lewis and Lou Thesz; "Baron" Michele Leone; Buddy Rogers, Eddie Graham, Cowboy Luttrall: Pfefer Collection, Department of Special Collections, University of Notre Dame.

Edouard Carpentier; Wilbur Snyder; Gene Kiniski; Fritz Von Erich; Roy Graham and Jack O'Brien; Verne Gagne; Estes Kefauver and Antonino Rocca: from the collection of Tim Hornbaker.

Billy Sandow (wrestling pose); Ed "Strangler" Lewis and Billy Sandow: courtesy Billy E. Sandow.

Toots and Ralph Mondt: courtesy Dorothy Mondt Baldwin.

Chicago Wrestlers (Kohler): courtesy The Kohler Family.

Vincent McMahon, Bruno Sammartino, Willie Gilzenberg; The Gilzenbergs, Tunneys, Marellas: courtesy Holly Gilzenberg.

NOTE: All photos from the Pfefer Collection are reproduced from an original held by Department of Special Collections of the University Libraries of Notre Dame.